AFRICAN SEMINARS: SCHOLARSHIP FROM THE INTERNATIONAL AFRICAN INSTITUTE

Volume 3

PATRONS AND POWER

PATRONS AND POWER
Creating a Political Community in Metropolitan Lagos

SANDRA T. BARNES

Routledge
Taylor & Francis Group
LONDON AND NEW YORK

First published in 1986 by Manchester University Press for the International African Institute

This edition first published in 2019
by Routledge
2 Park Square, Milton Park, Abingdon, Oxon OX14 4RN

and by Routledge
711 Third Avenue, New York, NY 10017

Routledge is an imprint of the Taylor & Francis Group, an informa business

British Library Cataloguing in Publication Data
A catalogue record for this book is available from the British Library

ISBN: 978-1-138-33510-3 (Set)
ISBN: 978-0-429-44366-4 (Set) (ebk)
ISBN: 978-0-367-00121-6 (Volume 3) (hbk)
ISBN: 978-0-367-00128-5 (Volume 3) (pbk)
ISBN: 978-0-429-44443-2 (Volume 3) (ebk)

Publisher's Note
The publisher has gone to great lengths to ensure the quality of this reprint but points out that some imperfections in the original copies may be apparent.

Disclaimer
The publisher has made every effort to trace copyright holders and would welcome correspondence from those they have been unable to trace.

PATRONS AND POWER
CREATING A POLITICAL COMMUNITY
IN METROPOLITAN LAGOS

Sandra T. Barnes

MANCHESTER UNIVERSITY PRESS
for the INTERNATIONAL AFRICAN INSTITUTE, London

Published by
Manchester University Press, Oxford Road, Manchester, M13 9PL, UK

British Library cataloguing in publication data
Barnes, Sandra T.
  Patrons and power: creating a political community in metropolitan
  Lagos.—(International African library; v. 1)
  1. Urbanization—Nigeria—Lagos—History 2. Lagos (Nigeria)—Social
  conditions I. Title   II. Series
  307.7'6'096691   HN831.L3

  ISBN 0–7190–1944–3 *cased only*

Typeset in Linotron Plantin
by Northern Phototypesetting Co., Bolton
Printed in Great Britain
at the Alden Press, Oxford

CONTENTS

Lists of maps, tables and figures   viii
Preface   ix

1 **Introduction**

The distribution of power in contemporary Africa   2
Patterns of political activity   4
The client paradigm   7
The setting   11
Plan of the book   15

2 **The making of Mushin**

The eve of colonial takeover: 1850–61   19
Early colonial administration: 1861–1927   23
Administrative neglect   29
Unofficial authorities: the village *Baalẹ* and the *Baba Isalẹ*   31
Late colonial administration: 1927–55   36
First steps toward unifying Mushin villages   39
Unofficial authorities: the emergence of settler leaders   43

3 **Land and housing as sources of power**

Competition for urban land   47
The legal background to competition for urban land   50
The economics of land and housing   55
   The case of Timothy Abiola   56
   The case of I. A. Adeyemi   57
The social benefits of owning urban property   61
   The descent group   61
   The nuclear and extended families   65
   The community   66
The status of owners   67

4 **The residential basis of leadership**

Neighbourhood interaction   71
Patterns of neighbourhood support   75
Bases of neighbourhood power   76
Leadership roles   78
   Dimensions of the dispute-settler role   85
   Dimensions of the patron and middleman roles   88

Leadership skills   93
Converting non-political resources into political capital   95

5 The chieftaincy system

The birth of a chieftaincy system   98
Chieftaincy politics in the party era   103
Chieftaincy politics under the military government   105
The structure and function of the chieftancy system   109
The problems of urban chiefs   120
The contemporary meaning of chieftaincy   122

6 The consolidation of leadership

Community leadership: the institutional route to the top   126
    Local government   128
    Political parties   130
The pyramiding of power   135
The role of the public in political processes   143
The emergence of a political machine   145
Responses to the contraction of power   147
Explanations for survival   153

7 The role of factions in the struggle for power

The local response to military rule   157
The political importance of markets   159
Factionalism in markets   163
    Market conflict: episode one   163
    Market conflict: episode two   167
    Market conflict: episode three   171
    Market conflict: episode four   177
Factionalism in Mushin   180

8 The institutionalisation of power

Title-giving and title-receiving in the mobilisation of support   184
    Chieftaincy conflict: episode one   186
Public legitimation of unofficial authority   192
    Chieftaincy conflict: episode two   192
Shifting alliances   194
Bureaucratic legitimation of unofficial authority   196

9 Conclusions

Political problems of urban settlers   202

Particular and universal aspects of clientelism   204
Political advantages of individually-contracted ties   205
Political advantages of instrumental and moral ties   207
Political advantages of reciprocity   210
The organising powers in client relationships   213
  Organising diversity   213
  Centralising power   215
The perpetuation of power   216

Epilogue   220

Appendix: Methods of research   223
Notes   227
Bibliography   243
Index   252

MAPS, TABLES AND FIGURES

Maps

1	Metropolitan Lagos c.1975	12
2	Lagos region, 1865	24
3	Villages connected to the early history of Mushin	28
4	Adeyemi's neighbourhood: partial neighbourhood network	80

Tables

1	Population growth: Mushin area compared to municipal Lagos, 1871–1952	27
2	Occupations of residents in the Mushin area, 1881–1963	41
3	Educational attainments of owners and tenants	60
4	Occupations of owners and tenants	60
5	Households of owners and tenants	65
6	Urban experience of owners and tenants	66
7	Association memberships of owners and tenants	66
8	Ethnic group heterogeneity in Mushin houses	71
9	Languages spoken by housemates in Mushin	72
10	Neighbourhood business index	74
11	Cases handled by I. A. Adeyemi: a ten-week sample	82
12	Mushin chieftaincy divisions: succession rules and title-holders, 1975	112
13	Mushin district councillors, elected 1955	129
14	Action Group party organisation compared to Western Region Government organisation, 1955–65	136
15	a) Political influence and affiliations of 21 Mushin leaders	138

Figures

1	Typical block-type house in Mushin	59
2	The effect of property purchase on descent group structure	63
3	Patron–client ties among 21 Mushin leaders	140

PREFACE

One of the most dramatic changes in our century has been the urbanisation of the world's population. Accompanying this unprecedented demographic change has been a social change: the need for people to adapt themselves to new jobs, new friends, new ways of living together. It was the desire to discover people's strategies for creating new lives that led me to Lagos and served as the guiding theme of my early research. Initially I concentrated on people's first adaptations. How did they find jobs, shelter, spouses, and friends? How did they reconstruct kinship relationships? What voluntary ties did they establish? Only at the end of my first research period did I turn to the end point in constructing new lives – a point which consisted of constructing new 'citizenship' and with it a permanent commitment to a new place.

The beginning step in producing this book, then, was the realisation that one of the critical elements in adapting permanently to a new urban residence meant establishing rights to participate in local political affairs. The next step lay in capturing that process. Here I chose to concentrate on the pragmatic aspects of urban politics. How did people meet their material needs and goals? How did their desires draw them into the community? Where did the lines lead? And, most importantly, what were the ramifications? The third step was methodological, and here it was necessary to choose among many ways of acquiring data. I relied on the extended case study method, and added to it extensive interviews, and biographical, quantitative, and historical data.

Mushin caught my attention because of its frontier-like quality – a recent suburb with a reputation for disorder – and my anthropological predilection for investigating those domains where order is least expected. My attention was more than rewarded when it became clear that Mushin offered an arresting example of grassroots political activity, dominated neither by indigenous interests nor the national ruling elite. It was a community constructed by people of diverse backgrounds. In creating a community, residents were guided by the past, and their various cultural heritages; by the present, and a host of examples of contemporary political institutions and processes which were colonial legacies or post-colonial creations; and by their own opportunistic instincts and abilities to put together and even invent new combinations.

Research in Mushin was carried out in 1971 and 1972 and for three months in 1975. During this time I was a Research Associate of the Institute of African Studies, University of Ibadan, and I am grateful to the members of this body for the privilege of working with them and under their sponsorship. I also appreciate having been allowed to use many archives and files, including those of the Mushin Town Council, the National Archives in Ibadan, and the Public Records Office in London. Research was financed by the National Institute of Mental Health, a faculty grant from the University of Pennsylvania, and a grant from the Social Science Research Council, to all of which I am indebted.

Many people have taken a hand in offering the assistance, hospitality, advice, and friendship that are necessary parts of carrying out a project of this kind. In Lagos, Dr Babatunde Agiri deserves a special vote of thanks for befriending me in every way, from introducing me to officials to reading and offering criticism of an early draft of the manuscript. Dr Agiri's family also befriended me, and I am particularly appreciative of their kindness and generosity over the years. I benefited from the wisdom of other scholars resident in Lagos, including Professor Margaret Peil, Dr

Carol Scotton, Dr James Scotton, Dr Pauline Baker, Dr Deirdre LaPin, Mrs Jane Grant and Mr Neville Grant.

I am indebted to a large number of people in Mushin, its Town Council, and the Lagos State Government who were unfailingly considerate and giving of their time, knowledge, and counsel. In particular, among those who assisted me, and without whose expertise this study would not have been possible, I wish to mention Mr Timothy Adeniyi, Chief G. A. Akanro, Chief J. S. Odetola, Chief Otunba Oyebola, Mrs V. E. Tytler, the late Alhaji Y. A. B. Ajimobi, Chief J. S. Jinadu, Chief I. A. Ogunwa, and Court President J. O. Tade.

Professor Aidan Southall is responsible for an unending supply of encouragement over the years. He contributed to my training in anthropology and has remained a source of inspiration and unflagging help. Professor Herbert Lewis made a signifi-cant contribution to my thinking while I was in the field. Although their contri-butions are more indirect, three historians have supported my work at important stages: Professor Philip Curtin, Professor Steven Feierman, and Professor Jan Vansina.

Many people have read and offered valuable criticism of this book. Professor J. D. Y. Peel and Professor Abner Cohen contributed in large measure to its improvement, although they are not responsible for advice I did not heed. Aside from reading this book in whole or in part, my colleagues Professor Igor Kopytoff and Professor Arjun Appadurai deserve special thanks for intellectual sustenance and unstinting support. I am grateful to the members of the Social Anthropology Seminar of the University of Pennsylvania's Anthropology Department for devoting a session to commenting on Chapter 8. Professor Paula Ben-Amos gave Chapter 2 the benefit of her observant eye. Professor Arnold Strickon and Professor Sidney Greenfield commented on Chapter 4, and provided me with an opportunity to present it at the Annual Meeting of the Society for Economic Anthropology. Finally, I thank Ms Nina Schuster for reading and commenting on the entire manuscript.

An earlier draft was read by Professor Mark Ross, Dr Joel Judkowitz, and Professor Jennie Keith, and I am indebted to them for thoughtful and perceptive comments. Professor Nancy Farriss patiently listened to and offered cogent advice at nearly every stage in producing this book; in addition, her encouragement and friendship are highly valued.

I would also like to thank my assistants: Messrs D. A. Ajayi, Akintunde Ayando-kun, Fatayi Balogun, Charles Ezenduka and Lekan Ojelade who helped in col-lecting quantitative data in Mushin. Mr Carl Beetz ably drew all of the maps and diagrams save Map 4 which was drawn by Ms Helen Schenck.

I am deeply grateful to my children, Roby and Stephen. Not only did they share one of their precious years with me in Mushin, but they also helped in many ways toward making this book possible. Most of all I wish to thank my husband, Greg; he, too, shared a year with me in Mushin, and throughout subsequent research and writing of this book gave unending encouragement, gentle advice, and patience. No family could be more generous with their support and I dedicate this book to them.

S. T. B.

CHAPTER ONE

INTRODUCTION

This is a book about power – getting it, wielding it, and perpetuating it. The general wisdom concerning these processes was laid down by Machiavelli, who inaugurated modern political scholarship with his penetrating insights concerning the importance of skill in securing and then keeping political power; by Marx, who insisted that power could not be retained unless it was firmly anchored in a material base; and by Weber, who showed us that power had to be institutionalised to be perpetuated. Each of these political thinkers established principles which thereafter dominated political scholarship with little change.

Yet the patterns of political power – the ways in which some people control others and control rewards – always change. The organisation and distribution of power are continually reshaped to the extent that, while scholars seldom find exceptions to the general principles, the various patterns which the quest for power take are never exhausted. In fact, they unfold in unending kaleidoscopic fashion. As each new pattern is revealed, we expand our understanding of the ways in which some people become politically dominant and others become subordinate. The unprecedented proliferation of new nations during the second half of this century provides an embarrassment of riches in this respect.

My goal here is to explain one of these new patterns. I wish to bring attention to the people of an African city who began at the bottom of their society's structure of power, acquired resources, and developed political skills. In the process they gained sufficient stature to wield power over others below them, and to gain access to institutions of the state above them.

THE DISTRIBUTION OF POWER IN CONTEMPORARY AFRICA

In sub-Saharan Africa, the creation of new states by European rulers transformed the ways in which political power was distributed. At one end of the spectrum, a literate ruling elite – a foreign elite operating from newly introduced bureaucratic institutions – was superimposed over indigenous populations. Independence did not change this new element in the pattern of stratification. Nor did it change the basic determinants of ruling-elite status: education, relative wealth, and the holding of high office in state institutions.[1] When European powers departed, a highly educated, Western-oriented African ruling elite succeeded to their governmental posts. This was particularly striking in Nigeria, where this study took place, and where 87 per cent of the college-educated population was employed by government, mainly in senior service positions, following independence.[2] At the opposite end of the spectrum, there was the African public. In contrast to elite leaders, the general public was decidedly less educated, and therefore less exposed to Western ideas, and less economically rewarded than the rulers. Furthermore African societies did not boast a large middle class which, in the West, tended to blur the distinctions between the upper and lower strata. Africa's relatively small middle class consisted of people who achieved a modicum of wealth, education, or prestige in a community, for example merchants, clerks, school-teachers, or clergymen, and who often occupied local-level political offices. While the middle class provided a thin bridge spanning the gulf between the overwhelmingly large mass-public and the very small elite, it enjoyed considerably less visibility and scholarly attention than the other two extremes.

Colonial rule and the creation of new nations also changed political boundaries. For the most part, small polities were brought together into large states. Some had been old antagonists, others had experienced little contact, but whatever their prior relationships, the new amalgamations engendered antagonisms, as various small groups tried to gain supremacy over one another. The success of stronger groups over weaker ones meant that power became distributed along another axis – that of ethnicity. The dynamics of ethnic group competition had the dual effect of inhibiting the forces of integration and of generating cleavages for which there were few social bridges.

Additionally, the creation of new nations transformed the way in which economic power was distributed. Before the colonial period, wealth, as reflected by the standard of living, was fairly equally distributed. This pattern was altered when colonial powers placed the control of economic resources in the hands of the colonial state and, in so doing, reversed the Marxist proposition that control of political institutions derived from control of the major economic resources. Europeans built empires in response to economic motivations: desires for trading profits, raw materials, and cheap labour. Therefore, they placed the control of overseas resources in their governmental outposts where they could be efficiently extracted and exported. After independence was granted, the new governments perpetuated this concentration of economic power in the governmental sector. Officials who held high offices thus controlled their countries' economies, while people who did not hold governmental positions automatically had less access to state-held resources and state-allocated wealth in the form of high salaries, pensions, and fringe benefits. All in all, the concentration of economic and governmental power in the hands of the same small elite stratum only reinforced the boundaries between the relatively privileged and the relatively deprived.[3]

Nowhere were political, economic, and ethnic group cleavages more striking than in the cities. The coming together of elites and masses in Africa's new states was largely an urban phenomenon. National leaders lived and worked primarily in capital cities and other major urban centres where state institutions were located. Large numbers of workers from diverse backgrounds were attracted to these same places in search of economic opportunities and the freedom of urban living.

Yet the very nature of urban development contributed to the gulf between the ordinary citizens and the officials of the state. The two most prominent features in this respect were the rapidity and the volume of population growth. Before the colonial period, a few cities were found scattered along Africa's East Coast, in the Western Sahara, and along the Guinea Coast, especially in present-day Nigeria. At the turn of the century, Africa was the least urbanised continent, with a city population of only one per cent. The newly entrenched foreign powers stimulated the development of new cities, especially following the world wars, so that soon after independence, the urban population had jumped to more than 28 per cent. Two dramatic examples tell the tale. The population of Kinshasa, capital of Zaire, increased tenfold – from 208,000 to 2,049,000 – in the twenty-five-year period between 1950 and 1975. The population of metropolitan Lagos did the same between 1952, when it was estimated to have 346,137, and 1977, when it reached 3.5 million people. And this was only a beginning, for both cities are expected to exceed nine million by the year 2,000.[4]

Growth rates of this magnitude presented problems which were insurmountable. Urban institutions were unable to keep pace with mushrooming populations. Industrial, manufacturing, and other large-scale sources of employment failed to grow at rates which could absorb the large numbers of migrants who sought wage employment. This led to high unemployment rates, large sectors of informally or partially employed workers, and extreme poverty and hardship. Similarly, governmental institutions failed to keep up with the forces of urbanisation. They were hampered by a lack of funds, trained personnel, and organisational elasticity, leaving them unable to respond to most residents' needs for basic services and protection. They were additionally hampered by an inability to disseminate adequate information about official operations and the ways in which services could be secured.

The average person in the cities of new nations, as one observer aptly summed it up, lived in 'an environment of scarcity'.[5] The most basic urban resources – things taken for granted in the wealthy nations such as shelter, jobs, and education, or even simple amenities such as licences, water supplies, and public transportation – were scarce resources in the burgeoning cities of the less advantaged world. The few resources which were available, and the limited services public officials were able to perform, went first to those people who were in the most favoured position to secure them – the ruling elites and those close to them. Needless to say, imbalances such as these contributed to the average resident's feelings of helplessness and estrangement from official institutions.[6]

PATTERNS OF POLITICAL ACTIVITY

Given the gulf between the general public and the official world, the ability of ordinary citizens to participate in, or influence, government affairs was a matter of serious question.[7] One school of thought held that the capacity of the people at the bottom to influence political processes at the top declined as independent regimes in Africa moved from relatively inclusive to relatively exclusive forms of government. The ordinary citizen had not engaged in much formal political activity under multi-party systems. When military or other regimes removed formal outlets, such as voting, party membership, or certain interest groups, the participation of the common people became even more restricted. Studies which promulgated a departicipation point of view tended to begin at the top of the national political system, to dwell on patterns of government at their widest and most powerful extent, and to concentrate their attentions on corporate, institutionalised, and stable groups.[8] There was little place in these inquiries for the public, largely because in *formal* governmental terms there were, in fact, fewer and fewer places where its presence was strongly imprinted.

On the other side, was a school which documented high levels of *informal* political activity on the part of the non-elite. Such studies examined political action at the bottom of the system and tended to concentrate on small towns, the urban grassroots, or relatively homogeneous enclaves.[9] One of the most significant contributions of these studies was to hammer home the message that informal relationships and activities had meaningful political content. In this vein, Cohen carefully documented a variety of informal strategies that (minority) ethnic groups employed in order to retain or compete for power.[10] In the old Yoruba city of Ibadan, Hausa traders who lived together in the Sabo Quarter embedded their political activities in an extended network of patron–client relationships and ritual activities. Despite being veiled in an ostensibly non-political guise, these ties enabled the Hausa to rally together and collectively to protect their economically powerful position in the city. The major underlying premise was that shared culture was the key to success. The Hausa, and others like them, were successful in their political efforts because they reinforced them with common values, common goals, and common moral imperatives, all of which grew out of, or nurtured feelings of, common identity. Cohen's work, and a number of related studies tended to restrict their analyses to relatively contained contexts, as was their intention. But as a consequence, they rarely demonstrated how connections were made across the boundaries of the various segments of the political system.

Still another school focused attention on informal political relationships, but in this case it did so with an eye to examining their ability to transcend the boundaries of class or ethnic group. The goal here was to uncover linking mechanisms. The initial questions asked by this school shifted from the way political functions were carried out by institutions or groups on behalf of people to the way people themselves attempted to fulfil their political needs and goals. The starting point for analysis thus became personal relationships, especially patron–client ties in the broad sense, and the solidarities created from them: networks, cliques, or factions. Once the first layer of informal political relationships was examined, larger and more formal bodies – interest groups, parties, or administrative agencies – were brought into the analysis. At its broadest, this method enabled one to determine, step-by-step, how and by what mechanisms one field of political action became connected to another.

The linking approach in anthropology came of age when research moved from homogeneous to complex societies. At this point, anthropologists were obliged to expand the basic units of analysis from relationships based on status to those based on contract. An important contribution came from Latin America, where patron–client ties (which by definition were voluntary and not ascriptive) were found to be important ways of establishing extra-familial and extra-community relationships.[11] A later contribution was action theory, an approach which began with individuals and which, then, added to the mix a particular concern for the values and effects of personal transactions.[12] The two approaches shared common ground in that they treated politics as a process – the dynamic process of *acquiring* power – and not the static system of *exercising* it. Hence they were able to move away from concentrating on people who already had power to those who sought it. This shift in focus led to the conclusion that through informal, personal relationships, and the kinds of transactions and inter-dependencies associated with them, some people reached beyond the confi-nes of 'we' and linked themselves into the world of 'they' for politically significant reasons and with politically significant results.

A substantial addition to the linking approach came from political scientists who took the client paradigm – the combined patron–client and action theory approaches – and applied it to large-scale political systems in Africa, Latin America, the Mediterranean, and Southeast Asia.[13] Adoption of the client paradigm grew out of a recognition that old analytic frame-works were not adequately explaining contemporary political systems then under observation.

On the one hand, there was dissatisfaction with the class concept as a primary tool for explaining political action. When viewed from the bottom up, political linkages tended to be more vertical than horizontal. Further-more, in Africa classes rarely functioned as vehicles for mobilising people, but rather as categories for classifying them.[14] True enough, elites were conscious of themselves as a group and acted to protect their privileged position. But ruling elites were torn by internal factional struggles which forced leaders to cultivate relationships with those below them in order to gain support in their power struggles with one another. With regard to the lower class, the usual vehicles for organising protest across ethnic group lines, especially unions, were too small and fragmented to be effective. Indeed, by the early 1970s the entire wage-earning, working-class popu-lation of a country such as Nigeria totalled only 3.2 per cent.[15] For this and other reasons, people at the bottom were limited in their potential to act as a class, reaching outward to one another, and therefore they were forced to reach upward in order to be politically effective.

On the other hand, there was dissatisfaction with the concept of ethnicity in isolation, and for good reason.[16] As a heuristic device, ethnicity seemed appropriate for explaining societal conflict, the preservation of boundaries, and the basis for group action, but not for explaining cooperation between, or the penetration of, these boundaries. To be sure, many urbanites related to the new cosmopolitan milieu through 'a screen of ethnicity'.[17] But many did not.

Something else was needed. Barrows went so far as to suggest that 'in the African context, a politics based on *utility* (instrumentality, expedience, goal seeking, value maximization) provided a more serviceable research paradigm than a politics based on *identity* (likeness, compatibility; for instance, religion, traditionality, class, ideology, ethnicity).'[18] While Barrows went too far in rejecting identity as an organising principle, he was correct in identifying utility as an important and, I would add, comple-mentary force in organising political action. There were any number of instrumentally-based linking relationships: patron–client, host–guest, merchant–customer, citizen–non-citizen, boss–worker. Each implied a superordinate–subordinate relationship and, hence, could be subsumed within one all-embracing concept. The choice of clientelism as that concept rested on its ability to serve as a broad paradigm for the instrumental aspects of political life and, especially, for nascent leader–follower relationships.

While clientelism and ethnicity were different ways of organising political relationships they did complement one another. For example, one of the basic principles of social organisation among the ethnically homogeneous Creole of Sierra Leone was clientelism; in the Zongo enclave of Kumasi, clientelism was one of the most common forms of cooperation; and in Kinshasa and Dakar ethnic group and client relations were both strikingly significant aspects of political life.[19] These two forms of social organisation also overlapped. Lemarchand drew attention to the very important point that clientelism in contemporary Africa was a prime ingredient in developing pan-ethnic identities, since (as in the Hausa case) the process of incorporating individuals into an ethnic group could be accomplished through patron–client relationships. Similarly, client ties could be used to redefine ethnic identity. The Bobo of Mali, for instance, adopted the ethnic identity and even some of the behaviours of their Mopti patrons as part of the process of settling in to new urban roles.[20]

THE CLIENT PARADIGM

The client paradigm thus provides a powerful tool for examining and explaining one style of political interaction. But there is no single type of situation to which it is applied. Rather, the client paradigm is put to use by scholars in several ways. It is used, for one thing, to explain the way low-status actors participate in large-scale political processes. The East African leader Tom Mboya captured the essence of this phenomenon with his observation that clientelism mushroomed as a dominant style of expressing political concerns in Nairobi after people who had always been assured of a voice of influence in traditional political systems found that, in cities, there were only limited opportunities for doing so. Hence they turned to people in high positions who they felt would listen to their needs and opinions and, in the best of all possible worlds, act upon them.[21] The client paradigm, to cite a second example, is used to account for the prevalence and the efficacy of informal power in structures such as parties, bureaucracies, or governing bodies. The typical pattern consists of prominent figures – office holders or notables – participating in state bodies with, and because they have the support of, large networks of client-followers. Their power is based on the fact that they command significant numbers of people whom they can mobilise for various forms of action – voting, influencing, disrupting, and so on. The benefit is that patron-leaders are able to promote their own and their clients' interests over and above the collective interests of the institutions involved.[22] Accordingly, clientelism is seen as a way of competing for public resources either individually or collectively. A third use is to show how clientelism offers ways for low-status actors to improve their social and economic positions by acquiring clients of their own or by acting as clients to high-status patrons.[23] Finally, the paradigm is used to describe the linking roles played by significant urban actors who tie groups together by participating in and performing services for several of them. In so doing, of course, they are seen as societal integrators.[24]

One common denominator in each of these applications is that all of the relationships stretch across social boundaries in some way. At the minimum, they link two people who are not of the same social status. At the maximum, they link two groups, say a minority ethnic association to a mainstream political community.

Another common denominator is the reliance on the patron–client concept and general agreement as to what it means. Throughout this study I rely on these two common denominators and on the following operating definition: patron–client relationships are *reciprocal*, but they are *unequal* in that the status of the patron is higher than that of the client and, further, the things exchanged are not of the same order. As indicated, an important property of these ties is that they are *contractual*, not ascriptive, *informal*, and not jural. Feelings of closeness between the two parties arise from the fact that the ties are *personal*, and that over time they involve a wide variety of *multiple* exchanges between the same people – all of which heightens their potential to endure over long periods of time with increasing levels of indebtedness and obligation.[25]

The middleman also plays a meaningful role in clientelism. In making this claim, I take issue with some observers who feel that the role of the middleman or broker (I use the terms interchangeably) cannot be likened to that of the patron.[26] It is useful to distinguish between the two roles analytically, but it is often impossible to separate them practically. Both patron and middleman roles are usually performed by the same people, for the same clients, to the same ends. Those who feel that the middleman–client relationship must be fully separated from the patron–client paradigm argue that (a) a patron controls the resources he distributes directly while the middleman controls them indirectly; (b) the middleman stands between his client and the client's ultimate goal and therefore is not involved in two-person, but in three-person exchanges; and (c) the status of the middleman is not necessarily higher than that of the client, since it is the direct control of resources which ultimately determines the relative status of the parties involved. My own view is that the middleman does have resources – connections, information, and expertise – and therefore does control the thing that is exchanged. The control of these resources, furthermore, elevates the status of the middleman so that for purposes of the exchange the client's status is, indeed, lower than that of the benefactor. Finally, the client–middleman transaction is not a single three-person, but two, separate, two-person transactions. The client who needs a taxi licence is indebted to the middleman who gets it through his bureaucratic connection; the client must repay the middleman for the help he has received. Meantime, the middleman is a client to the bureaucrat for the purposes of the licence transaction and must repay his bureaucratic connection for helping his client. There are, then, two analytically separate transactions, two favours done, and two sets of obligations incurred. It is precisely at this point that the middleman's importance is revealed. For he is a key figure in helping us to visualise how it is that two-person client relationships are expanded into many-person client networks.

Client exchanges do not simply tie two people together. Each exchange has social ramifications. Middlemen are automatically involved in two transactions which have linked three people into the same chain. By the same token patrons are not solely involved with clients; in hierarchical societies they, too, must have patrons. Clientelism is a many-tiered phenomenon. The coming together of a series of patron – or middleman–client exchanges forms a network. An extensive network of people bound together by reciprocal obligations may stretch across large segments, or the whole, of a society so that it forms a system.

Mauss's enduring contribution to our understanding of social processes has been to show that a 'gift' is not freely given.[27] It creates an obligation that must be repaid, and in turn establishes counter obligations. Gifts and counter gifts, debts and credits, lead to a flow of interactions which have a marked beginning, but rarely a discernible ending. This flow of exchanges extends through time and through social space. Like the gift, patron–client exchanges bring members of a society into chains of transactions which endure beyond the life of any single encounter. They link people together, creating mutual dependencies – the need for followers balanced against the need for an ongoing stream of gifts, favours, or protection. For Mauss, exchanges were a form of social glue. And it is for this reason that they are significant components of political systems.

There is no disagreement over the universality of clientelism nor its ability to draw people together through their exchanges into long-lasting and politically significant relationships. There is, however, some argument over the conditions under which patron–client relationships are prominent in a political system, as opposed to being one style of conducting political business among many. In short, why is clientelism a dominant system in some societies and not others?

The Weberian view is that client-dominated political systems are a transitional stage in the development of governments from patrimonial (kin-organised) to bureaucratic (impersonally organised).[28] Hence, they are prominent in societies which must straddle traditional and modern forms of government. This in-between position is based on the rationale that clientelism combines the freedom and detachment of contractual relationships with the kind of personal interaction which arouses feelings of loyalty and moral obligation. For this reason it has been aptly described as 'the privatisation of public affairs'.[29] The drawback in this exercise in typology is that it fails to delve deeply into the external influences which play on modern governmental systems, on their structure, or on their orientations and functions. Therefore, it is an unsatisfactory explanation for the prominence of clientelism as it appears in contemporary urban settings.

An alternative approach is to see clientelism as a response to structural constraints. Gellner suggests that patron–client relationships proliferate when societies are incompletely centralised, that is, when there are structural cleavages between segments which are not filled by official institutions.[30] Incomplete centralisation often is the correlate of scarcity, poverty and insecurity – when benefits of the state are not distributed to all segments of a society according to official rules or when communications channels between segments are blocked.

A third approach is to see clientelism as a pragmatic response to a certain type of political orientation. Scott has drawn attention to the fact that political processes in many new nations have been misunderstood because, unlike the West, where a major process is influencing legislation through interest groups or electioneering, the dominant process in many new nations is one in which people try to influence the system after – not before – legislation is passed, when the distribution of resources and services has begun.[31] In these systems, usually found in association with incomplete centralisation, the common political denominator for all citizens is the *allocation* process. Responses to this orientation, however, differ. The general public concentrates most of its political energy on competing for publicly held resources whereas the elite concentrates its attention on securing and distributing them. Competition for resources, almost all of which are controlled by government in the new nations, is enhanced by virtue of the fact that, in the absence of other political outlets, the public also must compete for the attentions of the people who can help them fulfil their goals. Needless to say, the allocation process lends itself to a clientelistic style of conducting political affairs.

It was precisely this attention to the allocation process, and the incomplete centralisation of urban government, which drew my attention to clientelism as it was practised in Mushin, a suburb of metropolitan Lagos. I was struck by the insecurity in peoples' lives, their preoccupations with acquiring the basics of urban life – jobs, housing, schooling, loans – and their belief that to get them they must have personal help. 'What kind of help?' was the key question. Through this inquiry, I learned of the importance of 'godfathers' (patrons) and of having 'long legs' (many connections). The fact that clientelism permeated the system of competition for urban resources was readily apparent.[32] So, too, was the fact that ethnicity often played a strong role in that same exercise. What was not so apparent was that clientelism, like ethnicity, was used toward other ends.

The public were seekers. Political aspirants were givers, who used patron and middleman roles in their quest for authority. Leaders who had large numbers of client followers were able to legitimate their political actions and, consequently, to influence community affairs because they had these followers. For people who did not hold official positions in government, the politics of clientelism was thus an effective vehicle for generating attention and moving upward in the political hierarchy.

THE SETTING

Lagos was Nigeria's premier city for the period covered by this study, 1861–1975. It was the capital of the Colony and then the nation, and therefore it housed the bulk of the nation's governmental institutions and the cream of the ruling elite. In 1967, it also became a state capital and played host to the bureaucratic establishment of Lagos State. In economic terms, Lagos was the most diversified city in the nation. By 1975, more than 55 per cent of Nigeria's industrial establishments were located in the metropolitan area and they, in turn, contributed 70 per cent of the national gross industrial output. Lagos was the focal point of international trade: three-quarters of the total import and export trade, excluding petroleum, went through its ports. The headquarters of the nation's largest commercial establishments, its major banks and the only stock exchange were also located in the city.[33]

Given its advantages, Lagos became the nation's largest urban area (see Map 1). In order to govern its vast 1975 population of 3.5 million,[34] the metropolitan area had been divided into four administrative districts. Mushin, the largest with a population of 1.5 million, was administered by the Mushin Town Council; municipal Lagos (i.e. Lagos City) the actual home of the ancient city-state of Lagos, with a population of 1.2 million, was administered by the Lagos City Council; and the other two suburbs of Ajegunle and Ikeja, inhabited by a total of 0.8 million people, were run by the Awori–Ajeromi and Ikeja District Councils, respectively. Each of the councils was run independently of the other, although all four were supervised as separate entities by the Ministry of Local Government and

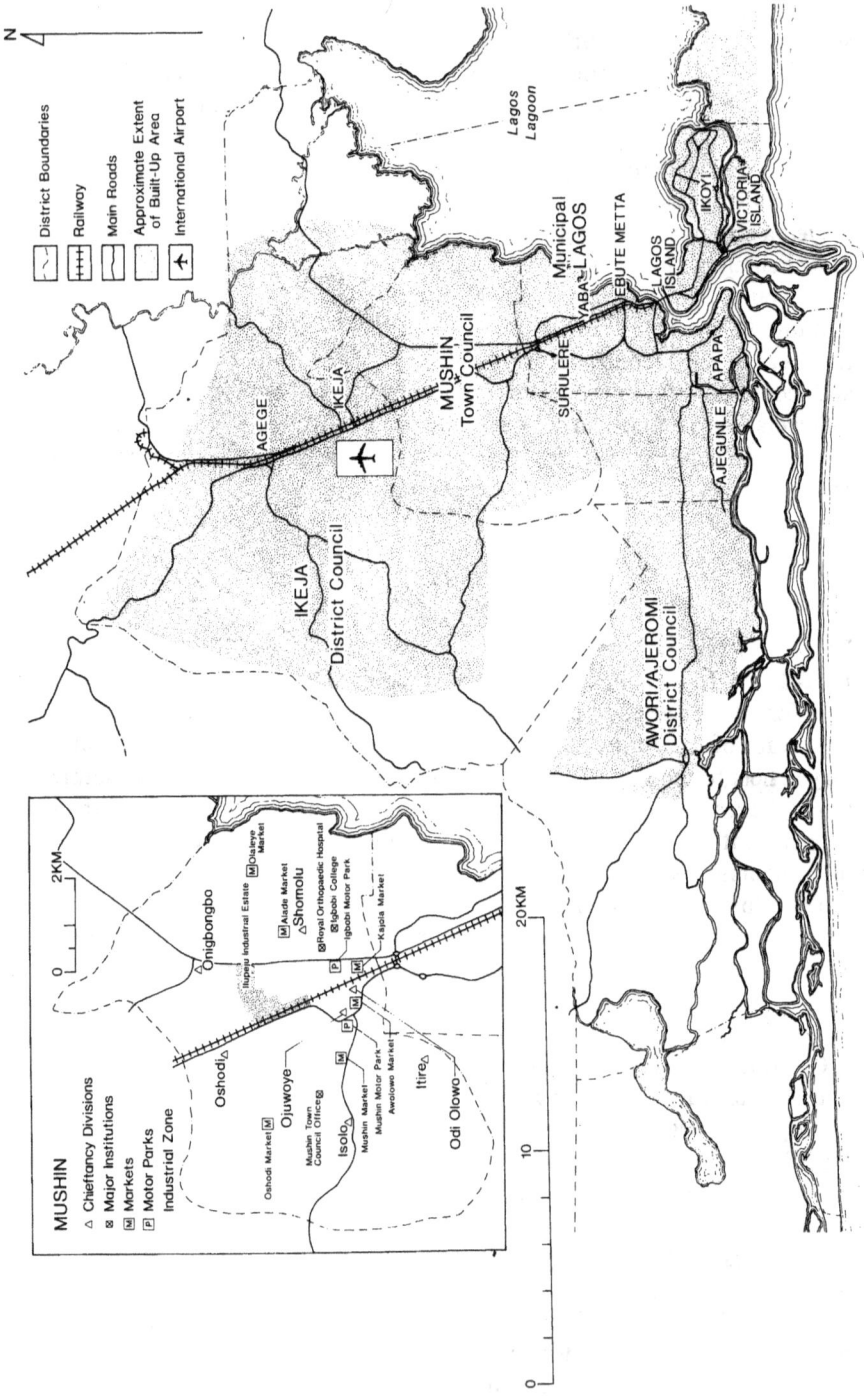

Map 1 *Metropolitan Lagos, c. 1975*

MUSHIN

△ Chieftancy Divisions
Ⓜ Major Institutions
Ⓜ Markets
Ⓟ Motor Parks
    Industrial Zone

Oshodi△

Ojuwoye

Isolo△

Itire△

Odi Olowo

Oshodi Market Ⓜ

Mushin Town Council Offices Ⓜ

Mushin Market

Mushin Motor Park

Awoliowo Market

Onigbongbo

Ilupeju Industrial Estate

Oshodi Market Ⓜ Olaiye Market

Asade Market Ⓜ Shomolu

△ Royal Orthopaedic Hospital

Ⓜ Igbobi College
Igbobi Motor Park

Kajola Market

0   2KM

District Boundaries
Railway
Main Roads
Approximate Extent of Built-Up Area
✈ International Airport

AGEGE

IKEJA

IKEJA District Council

MUSHIN Town Council

AWORI/AJEROMI District Council

SURULERE

YABA

EBUTE METTA

Municipal LAGOS

LAGOS ISLAND

IKOYI

VICTORIA ISLAND

APAPA

AJEGUNLE

Lagos Lagoon

Bight of Benin

0   10   20KM

Chieftaincy Affairs of Lagos State. In turn, Lagos State was one of nineteen states in the Federation.

The drawing card for Lagos was its economic opportunities. Altogether they created outlets for a heavy concentration of Nigeria's most talented and highly educated citizens. The highest earning rate, for both professionals and skilled workers, was found in Lagos, although this was neutralised by the fact that it also had the nation's highest cost of living. Furthermore, it had the highest concentration of wage-employed workers in the nation.[35] But there was a built-in paradox in the situation.

Lagos's superior economic and occupational advantages were quite unevenly distributed. Opportunities for work did not expand in sufficient quantity to absorb the vast numbers of incoming migrants who hoped to partake of them. Hence there was a high unemployment rate reaching 17 to 20 per cent of the labour force in the early 1970s.[36] More indicative of the situation was the fact that at least 50 per cent of the working population was classified as informally employed – some, mainly women, by choice and many others by necessity.[37] Among other things they engaged in interim endeavours such as hawking goods on the streets, performing minor *ad hoc* services, or engaging in day labour. The insecurity in the employment market was intensified by the fact that residents did not have immediate recourse to agriculture in order to supplement earnings in bad times, nor did they have the immediate back-up of the kin group, as they did in their homeplaces. Work was basically an individual endeavour, and this was a prime difference between life in a contemporary urban place and a traditional one.

There also was a sharp division between the elite and the ordinary public both in numbers and income. High ranking managers, civil servants, and professionals constituted about 6 per cent of the metropolitan area population. In the early 1970s, their annual earnings, which could be thirty times greater than a small business worker's wages, ranged from ₦1,700 to ₦10,550.[38] Middle level clerks, who made up 11.5 per cent of the population, earned between ₦700 and ₦1,050 if they worked for relatively large organisations. The vast majority, then, was a work force which included traders, craftsmen, labourers, or transporters and made up 82.5 per cent of the working population. A full-time industrial worker earned between ₦100 and ₦300 per annum; at that period the national per capita income was ₦200.[39]

There was a striking division in the living arrangements of these urbanites. And this is where Mushin entered the picture. The national elite did not live in Mushin. Rather, the nation's ruling class lived almost exclusively in luxury housing located in separate estates or 'reservations', as they had been designated by the British, located mainly in municipal Lagos or suburban Ikeja. The one luxury estate in Mushin's borders, Ilupeju, was actually under the control of Lagos State and thus it was removed from its administrative and political life. The separation of the elite from the general public was in every other respect an anomaly.

For the ordinary people, residence was a social melting pot. The metropolitan area housed one of the more heterogeneous concentrations of people in the nation. Houses and neighbourhoods reflected this heterogeneity with one exception: Northern Nigerians, mainly Hausa, often lived in fairly homogeneous enclaves, at least in the first generation. Otherwise the many linguistic and cultural groups represented in Lagos were spread throughout the metropolitan area. Yoruba-speaking peoples – themselves highly differentiated – dominated the population (roughly 70 per cent) demographically, culturally, and politically.

The term *Yoruba* was a colonial creation applied to some ten million people of southwestern Nigeria (and some from the Republic of Benin) who shared the same general language, some traditions of common origin, and similar symbols and customs surrounding political and mystical authority. The Yoruba-speaking peoples were divided into many sub-groups which represented more than ten dialects – more or less mutually intelligible – and many pre-colonial political boundaries. Most Yoruba still associated themselves with earlier political identities, e.g. Egba, Ijebu, Oyo, Ondo, and so on, which were once attached to kingdoms and city-states, or to dialect groups, e.g. Awori. These divisions had left their mark. One manifestation was an intense conflict over rights of indigenous and migrant sub-groups in Mushin to participate and hold offices in local political bodies. The point is that, in national terms, Yoruba peoples were sometimes united, but in local or regional terms they were often deeply divided to the extent that sub-groups or coalitions of sub-groups acted as separate ethnic groups.

As for the rest of the Lagos population, there were heavy concentrations of Igbo-speaking peoples (15 per cent), Edo (Bini), Hausa, Efik, Ijaw, Nupe, Urhobo, Igbira, Ibibio, Isoko, Tiv, and a significant number of non-Nigerians from other African and European countries.[40]

Mushin was the home of the low-income, low-status residents of the metropolitan area. It housed a lower percentage of professionals, executives, and clerks, and a higher percentage of informally employed traders and artisans than did the city.[41] Its designation as a suburb reversed the stereotypic picture of affluence, homogeneity, and spaciousness that is ordinarily associated with the term. Indeed, it was, along with Ajegunle, the least physically developed area with the least desirable, most crowded living conditions.[42] Houses often lacked water, electricity, or indoor sanitary and cooking facilities. The residents were neglected by government, which failed to supply such basic services as roads or water taps, adequate facilities such as medical clinics, schools, or courts, and even police protection.

The lack of development was due in part to Mushin's lack of resources.

There were no large bureaucratic and business offices located in Mushin. Only 14 per cent of the industrial plant of greater Lagos had been situated in this suburban district by 1975.[43] Its one advantage was a vast quantity of housing, designed primarily to accommodate both owners and large numbers of their tenants. Taxes from housing, in fact, provided the major source of locally generated revenue for the administrative budget. Still, this revenue did not compare with that available in municipal Lagos. The greater disparity between city and suburban living was summed up by the differences in per capita expenditures made by the local governments in 1975, which were as great as fifteen times higher in municipal Lagos than in Mushin.[44]

The most significant division between Mushin and the city proper was political. As in any metropolitan area, the boundaries between suburbs and city were infinitely porous with respect to economic and social relationships. But this was not true in governmental affairs. The existence of four separate administrative units each with its own budget, staff, and area of jurisdiction meant that there were four separate political arenas, each with its own leadership, agenda, and carefully guarded boundaries. In local political affairs, there was little overlap among the four districts.

As in any large urban setting, only a small percentage of the population was politically active in local community affairs. In Mushin this active segment consisted of the indigenous people of the area, the Awori Yoruba, and migrant settlers of diverse backgrounds, but primarily from Yoruba-speaking sub-groups. Starting in 1955, leaders from these two segments of the community were involved in activities of Mushin's three main authority structures: a traditional chieftaincy system, political parties (when they existed), and the Mushin District (later Town) Council. In these endeavours they were supported by extensive client networks. Historically, however, things had been different.

PLAN OF THE BOOK

The colonial history of Mushin, recounted in Chapter 2, was one in which residents had to find solutions to their own political needs from the earliest times. Mushin was not a political community when it was brought into Lagos Colony in 1861. Rather, it was a collection of many small villages and neighbourhoods where formal government was virtually absent. Therefore, connections to the foreign rulers were made primarily through a series of patrons and middlemen.

For nearly a century, Mushin was without its own administration. When a District Council was finally established in 1955, however, the process began of bringing Mushin's many separate parts together. Again, it was a task that was left largely to the residents themselves. Their attempts to provide their own leadership in the new district are the subjects of the next two chapters. The material base on which political aspirants built positions of power is the subject of Chapter 3, and the leadership skills they acquired in order to attract a following are explored in Chapter 4. The point I develop is that, once again, the means used by Mushin's leadership to move ahead was largely through clientelism.

Up to this point, the study is essentially concerned with *historical change* in the patterns of power. Thereafter the emphasis shifts to *processes* associated with the organisation of power.

Mushin's leaders organised their political relations in three ways. The first, discussed in Chapter 5, was a chieftaincy system. It was designed along traditional lines primarily in order to legitimate the political endeavours of active citizens who were otherwise unable to secure power and legitimacy through official means. The second way of organising political relations, examined in Chapter 6, was through official institutions: parties and local government. In each case leaders brought to these institutions extended networks of client-followers who enhanced their ability to wield influence. Their major accomplishment was to solidify these relatively amorphous support networks into a political machine. The third way of organising political relationships was through factions. Client networks were as amenable to factional political battles as they were to partisan campaigns. Thus, in Chapter 7, we see the solidity of local politicians in the partisan era give way to a relatively fragmented, competitive phase under the military – but a phase in which leaders still relied on their same sources of clientelistic support.

The process of institutionalising and, therefore, perpetuating political power is the subject of Chapter 8. Institutionalisation was accomplished when many of the informal authority figures who had provided local leadership during the first twenty years of Mushin's existence were legally recognised as chiefs by the bureaucracy. I point out that in a contemporary urban situation, institutionalisation was a two-sided process. It required support on one side from the public, without which there could be no support from the other side – the ruling elite. The leaders of Mushin were thus obliged to find a way to appeal to the ordinary people who had no power, and wished to get it, and the high officials who had power, but wished to husband it. Essentially it was the middleman role of Mushin's leaders and their ability to address critical needs on both sides, which brought official rewards.

In concluding, Chapter 9 examines the relationship between clientelism and the quest for power. In Mushin, as in many other urban areas, client relationships are essential ingredients in developing and exercising authority. Hence this chapter discusses those elements – both universal and contextual – which make client relationships powerful tools in political struggles and which allow those who wield them to influence political processes.

Throughout this study, my concern is less with telling the actual story of one group's political success than it is with the processes involved in their achieving it. Hence the book lays stress on the kinds of social relationships, institutions, and strategies which enabled politically motivated people to acquire power and organise an authority system, in preference to the actual personalities and events which took place. As in most studies of this nature, I have used fictitious names (marked by an asterisk the first time they are used) in order to protect those persons who played active political roles, and to disguise certain events (relating to personal case histories) and places (primarily markets) where events took place. Otherwise names of historical figures and well-known officials or places and widely-publicised events have not been changed.

CHAPTER TWO

THE MAKING OF MUSHIN

Our knowledge of Mushin dates back to the mid-nineteenth century when the British were about to bring the Lagos area into the Empire. Initially its settlements were not joined together in higher levels of political organisation. Instead the small villages that dotted the rural landscape arching around the island-bound city-state of Lagos were politically autonomous with respect to one another. Yet these settlements grew in response to opportunities accompanying urbanisation of the area and, in so doing, grew in their need for institutions which would draw them together.

The process of unifying Mushin's settlements took nearly a century to accomplish. Much of the responsibility for their inability to unite can be traced to the policies of the British rulers who acquired the area as part of Lagos Colony in 1861. Government officials were preoccupied with an ongoing series of administrative reorganisations, the desire to establish trade links to the hinterland, and the need to pacify and acquire more territory in order to do so. Consequently, Mushin's settlements were deplorably neglected and the people who lived in them met their political needs with solutions of their own devising. They relied on an authority system which pre-dated colonial rule and which remained active throughout the colonial era. Order was maintained by village headmen and elders' councils. Contact with the British was made via patron–client and middleman–client relationships.

Clientelism played a strong role in the history of Mushin. The nature of the client relationships varied from one period to another, but they were greatly influenced by two forces: the consistently remote role played by the central government in Mushin-area affairs and the slow process of drawing the settlements of Mushin into a unified political community.

The history of Mushin falls into three periods. The first period was from 1850 to 1861 – the eve of colonial takeover. In this period the villages of

Mushin were drawn into a number of mutually reinforcing relationships with Lagos City which later helped them adjust to the colonial regime. The second was from 1861 to 1927 – the rural period. During this time the villages of Mushin were administered jointly with the City of Lagos. Paradoxically, the Mushin area was overlooked by officials who gave greater attention to the city than was given at that time to many English towns. During these first two periods, Lagos City chiefs served as patrons and middlemen to Mushin-area villages in a relatively institutionalised form of patronage. The third period was from 1927 to 1955 – the onset of urbanisation – when migrant settlers began to dominate the area. Villagers broke away from their Lagos patron-chiefs and turned instead to up-and-coming settler leaders who assumed the patron–middleman roles in a more flexible and individually-oriented client system than the one which preceded it. These newcomers brought new notions of the way their political lives should be ordered, and as a result of their efforts, the settlements of Mushin began to unite.

THE EVE OF COLONIAL TAKEOVER: 1850–61

The ancient site of Lagos was known to Europeans as early as the sixteenth century because of its favoured coastal position on the Bight of Benin.[1] It is believed to have been settled by Awori Yoruba seeking to escape the hostile advances of Ijebu and Egbado warriors. It survived an invasion and conquest by the King of Benin, but was relatively unimportant as a coastal port until the 1790s when local entrepreneurs became heavily involved in the slave trade. For more than fifty years there was a flourishing slave market in the city's harbours and an increasing involvement with European merchants, until the British concluded that their economic interests could be secured, and slave-trading curtailed, if Lagos were brought under its influence. In 1851 the British bombarded and then occupied Lagos, routing its king and enthroning a successor who they believed would support their anti-slavery movement. British merchants were taking up residence in Lagos in order to expand their legitimate trade in palm oil, ivory, and indigenously made cloth, and a consul was installed to protect those interests.

The Lagos of 1850 was a small city-state. Its political system consisted of an *ọba* (king) who presided over an elaborate hierarchy of chiefs. They represented most of the groups and interests of the population, and were divided into four chiefly lines: administrative, landowning, warrior, and medical/spiritual. Lagos was surrounded by an unknown number of villages, including those of the Mushin area. The people of these outlying villages and the city were brought together by a number of close ties and mutually advantageous interactions.

The indigenous peoples of the oldest villages and the city shared a common origin myth.[2] Ọlọfin[3] was the founder of Lagos, and like other founders of Yoruba-speaking communities, was legitimated in the eyes of the Yoruba world by having a genealogical pedigree that was traced to Oduduwa, the legendary ancestor of all Yoruba. According to oral traditions, at least five centuries ago, Ọlọfin and has many sons left Isheri, a town twelve miles north of Lagos, following a succession dispute with his brother. They were of the Aworl Yoruba-speaking sub-group who lived at the southernmost extremity of Yorubaland.[4] Ọlọfin settled on Lagos Island, where he allocated land to some of his sons, whose descendants became known as *Idejo* (landowning) chiefs. Other sons of Ọlọfin, who were allocated no land on the Island of Lagos, moved to the nearby mainland where they established small settlements of their own and thereafter were considered *ọmọ ibilẹ*, sons of the soil. The original landowners were not dislodged from their holdings despite a long period of subordination to Benin which otherwise had a strong influence on the local political system, language, and oral traditions. People claiming to be descendants of the original settlers remained in the heart of the traditional Isale Eko quarter of Lagos Island and in such outlying villages as Iro, Ado, Irenpa, Otta, Ojo, Ogudu, Isolo, Itire, and Ojuwoye,[5] many of which can still be identified because their irregular house placement patterns interrupt the more grid-like patterns that emerged later.

The nearby settlements and the city also shared economic ties. Produce grown on mainland farms was essential to the city-dwelling population. Some Lagos merchants established farm settlements run by slaves, domestic servants, and paid labourers, whose descendants were absorbed, in some cases, into their masters' families only to become heirs to what eventually would be valuable suburban property. The main cash crops coming from the settlements in this period were kola nut and palm products. Later products included cocoa, cassava, corn, raffia, and firewood.[6] Valuable raw materials also were available in outlying areas. Otta, and its environs to the north of Mushin, was an iron-mining and smelting centre.[7] By the nineteenth century most of the metal was shipped northward – imported metal having replaced indigenous supplies in coastal areas – but its earlier importance to Lagos had no doubt helped to buttress the links between the two areas.

The marketing system brought outlying areas and the city into constant contact. Markets in the district provided bulking and distribution centres for the foodstuffs and other products required by Lagosians. By the same token, Lagos' markets funnelled valuable imported items to their outlying counterparts. A strategically placed market, and the one that would give a vast suburb its name, was Mushin, place of the *iṣin* (akee apple) tree.

Mushin market was attended by people of Lagos and many surrounding areas, and in the nineteenth century it was known as the hub from which a network of roads fanned out to Otta, Abeokuta, Isolo, Itire, Agege, Muroko, Onigbongbo, and Ogba. Other markets were at Oshodi, Ayobo, Agege, Alagbado, and Ogudu.[8] The markets were fed, in part, by trading camps that dotted the city's perimeter and served as stations between the city and points farther north. Slaves, and later, ivory, kola, and palm produce were the major commodities intended for export that passed through these camps. In return, guns, ammunition, rum, cloth, sugar, and metals were imported and then sent via the markets and trade camps to the north. At Igbobi ('the kola grove'), traders from the Shabe Yoruba kingdom established a permanent camp where they stored valuable loads of ivory before sending them on to the city. Nearby at Alase (a settlement named after a well-known resident who sifted maize flour there),[9] the famous Abeokutan trader, Madam Efunroye Tinubu, set up a trading camp and farm under her retainer, Ali Tinubu.

Links between adjacent settlements and Lagos City also rested on military ties. Rural settlements provided a line of defence for Lagosians against slave raiders from the north and places of refuge for townsmen when they were attacked from the sea. When the British bombarded Lagos in 1851 many of Lagos' inhabitants sought sanctuary in the surrounding villages.[10] Conversely, the city provided a refuge for villagers when warfare and slave-raiding from the north, during the first half of the nineteenth century, nearly decimated the area.[11] The last vestiges of walled fortifications are to be found immediately north of the city boundaries at Odi Olowo, variously translated as 'the hill of the rich woman' or 'the fence of the ruler', in the southernmost division of today's Mushin. Oral traditions recall the legacy of Shongbo, a childless but wealthy woman, who directed her many slaves to dig a trench-fort stretching from Ijebu country in the northeast to the west beyond the city.[12] During wartime or slave raids, people from miles around sought safety in the trench beneath the protective wall. Some of the Lagos warriors stationed at Odi Olowo were rewarded with gifts of land that a century later were turned into urban house plots by their heirs.

The most enduring bonds between villages and the city were patron–client ties. The patrons, or *Baba Isalẹ* (father in the courtyard/quarter) were either ranking chiefs or well-placed notables in Lagos City. There were two types of *Baba Isalẹ*–village relationships. The strongest was when a Lagos chief served as overlord of a village whose inhabitants paid tribute to the chieftaincy ruling house and submitted to its authority. In this case, Lagos chiefs spoke of *owning* a village and the relationship might be passed down from one generation to the next. There appear to have been few of these overlord type relationships with Mushin villages to the north of Lagos Island; instead, they seem to have existed mainly in coastal villages to the east and west of Lagos Island. Research in this aspect of the *Baba Isalę*–village relationships is, however, incomplete.

The other type of *Baba Isalę*–village relationship was a loose bond in which Lagos chiefs acted as middleman on behalf of a client village, *representing* that community's political interests to the *ǫba* at court and its economic interests in the city's market places. They also acted as patrons, dispensing specialised knowledge and favours, and as dispute settlers hearing cases when a village *Baalę* (headman) and his council of elders could not resolve an issue satisfactorily. In some cases, *Baba Isalę* presided over the ritual installation of a village *Baalę* providing a symbolic stamp of legitimacy to his office and a public affirmation of the *Baba Isalę*'s influence in that place. But this was an act of confirmation, for the *Baba Isalę* did not have rights to select a village *Baalę*. Nor did he have rights to intervene in internal village affairs on his own accord. In return for their various political, economic, and ritual services, *Baba Isalę* were given gifts such as foodstuffs, access to up-country trade routes, preferential treatment in village-controlled markets, or even plots of land. Villages did not, however, pay tribute to their patrons, and this helped to preserve their autonomy. There was keen competition among *Baba Isalę* to acquire client villages. If their relationship was of the second, representational type, villages were able to shift their loyalties from one patron to another, and this added to their ability to maintain internal autonomy.

The villages of the Mushin area thus enjoyed a certain amount of independence. This independence was reinforced by an emphasis on their Awori identity, for the villagers did not assume the Lagosian identity of their *Baba Isalę* benefactors despite their proximity and their traditions of common origin. Awori was, and still is, a kin-based identity in that membership was ascribed according to one's status as a member of a descent group. In the city, social processes relating to urbanisation had led the descendants of the original settlers to subordinate their Awori ancestry to an identity, i.e. Lagosian, that was based on territorial criteria.[13] No doubt the rural orientation of the Awori and the slow growth of their area, as opposed to the more speedy, urban growth of Lagos City, meant that newcomers could be absorbed into Awori kin groups without recourse to identifying themselves according to broader, territorial criteria. It also meant that the Awori could accentuate the social distance between themselves and their Lagosian patrons. This probably was not a conscious process, but it had an important effect. By stressing their Awori identity, indigenous villagers provided a justification for emphasising their separateness from the politically powerful Lagosian *Baba Isalę*. As time passed, this became an increasingly important posture.

The Awori were, nevertheless, at one disadvantage in maintaining their independence since, unlike most of their Yoruba-speaking neighbours, they did not join together under centralised political institutions above the village or village group level. Instead, the independence they did maintain was cultural, and based on their claims of sharing a similar dialect and similar customs, especially those regulating land tenure and religious activity. Awori culture of 1850, however, was no doubt different from Awori culture of today. Awori descent groups were very absorptive during the rural period of Mushin history, slowly incorporating, as kinsmen, peoples of Bini, Nupe, Dahomean, and other Yoruba origins, and this undoubtedly brought new elements and continual change to this group of people, if not to each of their villages.[14]

Our knowledge of the patron–client relationships, which became known as the *Baba Isalẹ* system, comes from colonial documents which record the inner workings after British rule was imposed. Nevertheless we know the *Baba Isalẹ* system was strong when the British came into the picture because the boundaries of the new colony were based partly on the range of its influence. While the cession of these outlying settlements by the *Ọba* of Lagos may have been a violation of some villages' sovereignty, and in the view of a British administrator not in accord with historical evidence, it was not resisted.[15] Villages were not united, and therefore they did not organise a collective response to their new British rulers.

EARLY COLONIAL ADMINISTRATION: 1861–1927

In 1861, the British presence in the Lagos area was concretely formalised with a treaty ceding it to the Queen. The new colony[16] consisted of a large section considered to be 'under British Protection' and four small sections considered to be actual 'British territory' (see Map 2). It contained all of the territory, and more, what eventually would be known as metropolitan Lagos. This included the port and Island of Lagos and the nearby villages that the British presumed to be under the influence of the city's chiefs. Although undefined in the treaty, the protected territory consisted of a wedge of land stretching some five miles north of the lagoon behind Lagos, and slightly beyond Mushin (Munsho), the only place in the colony outside the city that was large enough to be designated a town.[17] The territory immediately surrounding the Island was known officially as the Vicinity of Lagos and the territory beyond it was the Northern District. Villages in these places ranged in size from 50 to 200 inhabitants. Most of the settlements in the Vicinity of Lagos eventually became part of the city proper, while those in the Northern District, including the Mushin area, were incorporated into the suburbs. The rest of the colony consisted of Eastern and Western Districts; with few exceptions they were not incorporated into metropolitan Lagos. Thus defined, the colony retained its original form

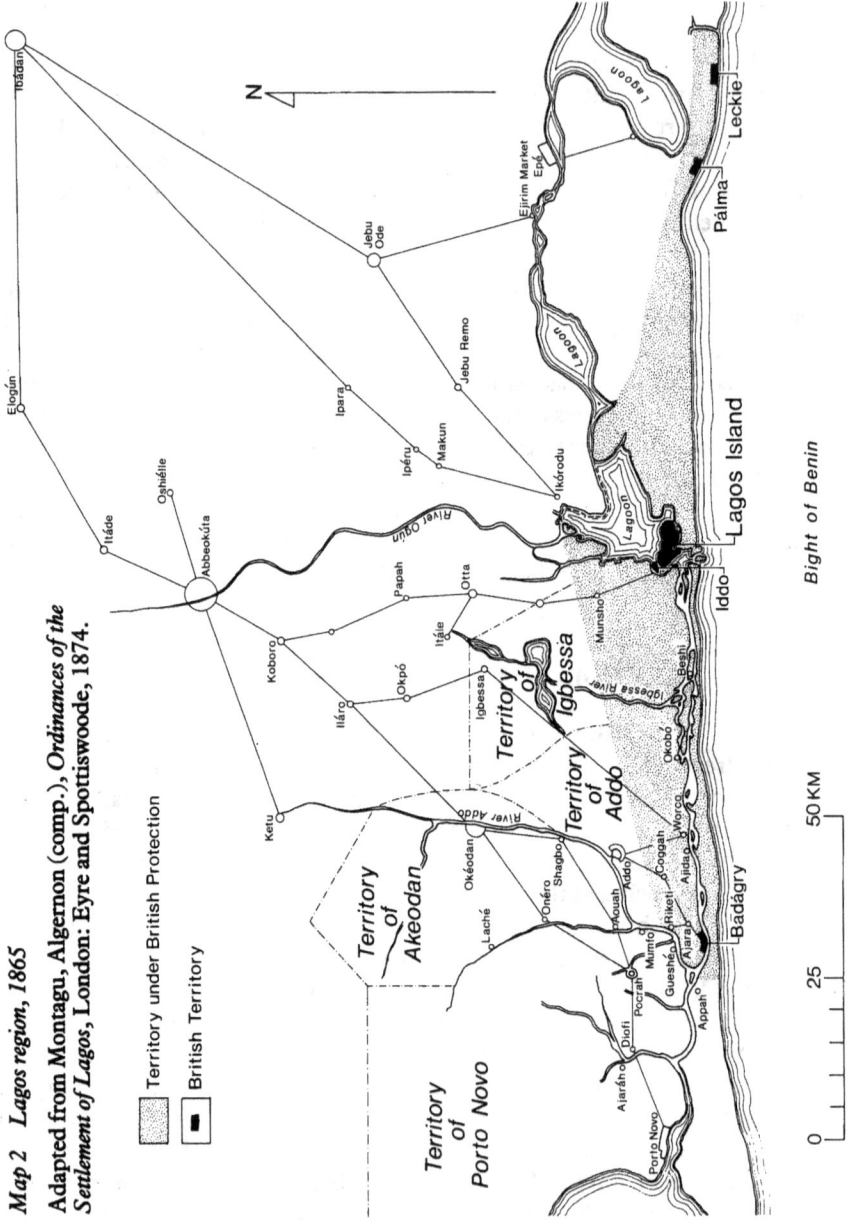

Map 2 *Lagos region, 1865*

Adapted from Montagu, Algernon (comp.), *Ordinances of the Settlement of Lagos*, London: Eyre and Spottiswoode, 1874.

with only a few small extensions.[18]

From the start, the British intended to unite the separate settlements of the colony by establishing a government that operated according to the principles of direct rule.[19] Early administrators felt the colony's 62,000 inhabitants[20] should not be ruled indirectly by traditional authorities for several reasons. First, the chiefs of Lagos initially were distrusted because they were strongly involved in the slave trade. Second, the populations of city and villages were perceived as being too fragmented to be subjected to the authority of just one element. Third, all colony residents were made British subjects by the treaty of cession and as such were entitled to be governed directly under the laws of the Crown.[21] But there was some ambivalence in this position. While the city dwellers were viewed as relatively urbane, the inhabitants of the villages were viewed as the most backward, and least culturally and economically advanced of all Yoruba peoples.[22] Could they be treated similarly? Despite reservations, the response of the new rulers was to introduce a central administrative authority modelled on British lines for the whole colony rather than separate, local authorities for each of its districts. Captain (later Sir) John H. Glover, the first governor, established headquarters on the Island from which he ran the affairs of the new possession with two appointed advice-and-consent-giving bodies, the Executive and Legislative Councils.[23]

The ability of the new rulers to devote their attentions to developing a unified administrative system for all sectors of the populace was compromised from the start by a series of governmental reorganisations.[24] For twenty-five years, the administration abruptly shifted from place to place. No sooner was the foreign administration established, than control of it was shifted out of the colony. A governor-in-chief resident in Freetown, Sierra Leone, was put in charge, and in 1866 Lagos officially became part of the West African Settlements. An Administrator and Legislative Council then tended to local affairs, but the arrangement was short-lived. Within eight years, responsibility for Lagos Colony was transferred to the governor of the Gold Coast Colony residing in Accra who, again, exercised his authority through a deputy resident in Lagos. The deputy was expected to participate in making policy for the colony as a member of a supra-local Executive Council of the Gold Coast and Lagos. Such arrangements made for a cumbersome administration, particularly since all departmental headquarters were removed to Accra, and communications and travel between coastal outposts was difficult and slow. The arrangement was terminated in 1886 after strong protest from Lagos leaders, and the colony received a new charter and a separate administration. The original governmental structure, utilising a resident governor and Legislative and Executive Councils to administer the whole colony, was restored and remained in place for the next three decades.

The British were by this time faced with political turmoil which threatened their trade arrangements with the hinterland.[25] Thus when control of
the colony finally returned to Lagos, new preoccupations compromised the
administrative development of the colony and the unification of villages
outside it. In brief, the independent Yoruba kingdoms to the north of the
colony were engaging in an ongoing series of wars. By the 1880s they
seriously interfered with commerce to and from Lagos and threatened the
economic prosperity of its trading population, both indigenous and foreign.
The British response was to protect territory already held and to uphold the
commercial interests of all subjects by pacifying and acquiring more territory. In this way, Yorubaland was slowly brought under British control.

There had been no real colonial government outside Lagos Colony until
1885, which meant that the next few decades were also spent in establishing
administrative machinery in new territories and not in those already under
control. By 1897, all of the Yoruba territory that would be part of present-
day Nigeria and many non-Yoruba areas were annexed as a protectorate to
the colony. Among the most important were the amalgamation of the
Colony of Lagos with the Protectorate of Southern Nigeria in 1906, and a
final merger of the Colony and Protectorate of Southern Nigeria with the
Protectorate of Northern Nigeria in 1914. There had been an ongoing
stream of governmental reorganisations. But the boundaries of modern
Nigeria were at last in place, and Lagos was designated as the capital.

Meantime, great changes had taken place in the Lagos area. Between
1871 and 1891 the population of the Northern District of Lagos Colony had
increased by more than 75 per cent, far exceeding the 14 per cent growth
rate of the city (see Table 1). This was a portent of things to come. By the
1920s the population of the same area had expanded some 300 per cent,
surpassing the 250 per cent growth rate of the city – despite the fact that the
city's boundaries were enlarged by eighteen square miles in order to annex
some outlying settlements to its north.

The population was becoming increasingly heterogeneous, and therefore
increasingly complex to govern. Cultural heterogeneity in Lagos dated at
least as far back as sixteenth-century contact with Benin, but it accelerated
in the nineteenth century, with freed slaves returning from Sierra Leone,
Cuba, and Brazil; refugees from the war-ravaged Yoruba kingdoms to the
north and from Dahomey; former Tapa (Nupe) and Hausa domestic slaves,
who by 1889 made up more than 50 per cent of the Lagos population; and,
finally, northern military recruits.[26] For many newcomers, the Island was
the first stop in a migration that culminated in the surrounding settlements
up to, but rarely north of, the villages of Onigbongbo and Ogba, at the
northern edge of the colony (see Map 3). For example, Vicente and George,
both freed slaves from Brazil, established villages, the former at Muroko in
today's Shomolu where he became its headman, and the latter at George,

Table 1 Population growth of districts which administered the Mushin area as compared to municipal Lagos, 1871[a]–1952

	1871[b]	1881	1891[c]	1901	1911[d]	1921	1931[e]	1952[f]
District over Mushin Area	12,401	9,563	21,808	?	28,402	49,836	79,076	112,396
Municipal Lagos	28,518	37,452	32,508	41,847	73,788	99,690	126,108	267,407

[a] The first census was taken in Lagos Colony in 1871.
[b] Northern District.
[c] Central District (excluding municipal Lagos).
[d] Lagos District (excluding municipal Lagos).
[e] Ikeja District (as of April, 1932).
[f] No census was taken during the war years.

Note: Each change in a district's name also indicated a minor readjustment was made in the boundaries.

Sources: A. C. Burns, *The Nigeria Handbook*, Lagos: Government Printer, 1919 (2nd edition), p. 138; CO 150/1, 'No. 7. Government Gazette. Settlement of Lagos', 1881, p. 2; CO 151/29, 1891, p. 42; P. Amaury Talbot, *The Peoples of Southern Nigeria*, Vol. IV, London: Oxford University Press, 1926, p. 176; CO 657/34, 'Annual Report on the Colony 1932', Lagos: Government Printer, 1933, p. 12; Nigeria, *Census of Nigeria, 1931*, Vol. III, London: Crown Agents for the Colonies, 1932; Nigeria, *Population Census, Lagos, 1950*, Lagos: Federal Office of Statistics, 1950; Nigeria, *Population Census of the Western Region of Nigeria, 1952*, Lagos: Government Statistician, 1953–4; Nigeria, *Population Census, Lagos, 1963*, Vol. I and II; *Population Census, Western Region, 1963*, Vol. I, II, III, Lagos: Federal Office of Statistics, 1963.

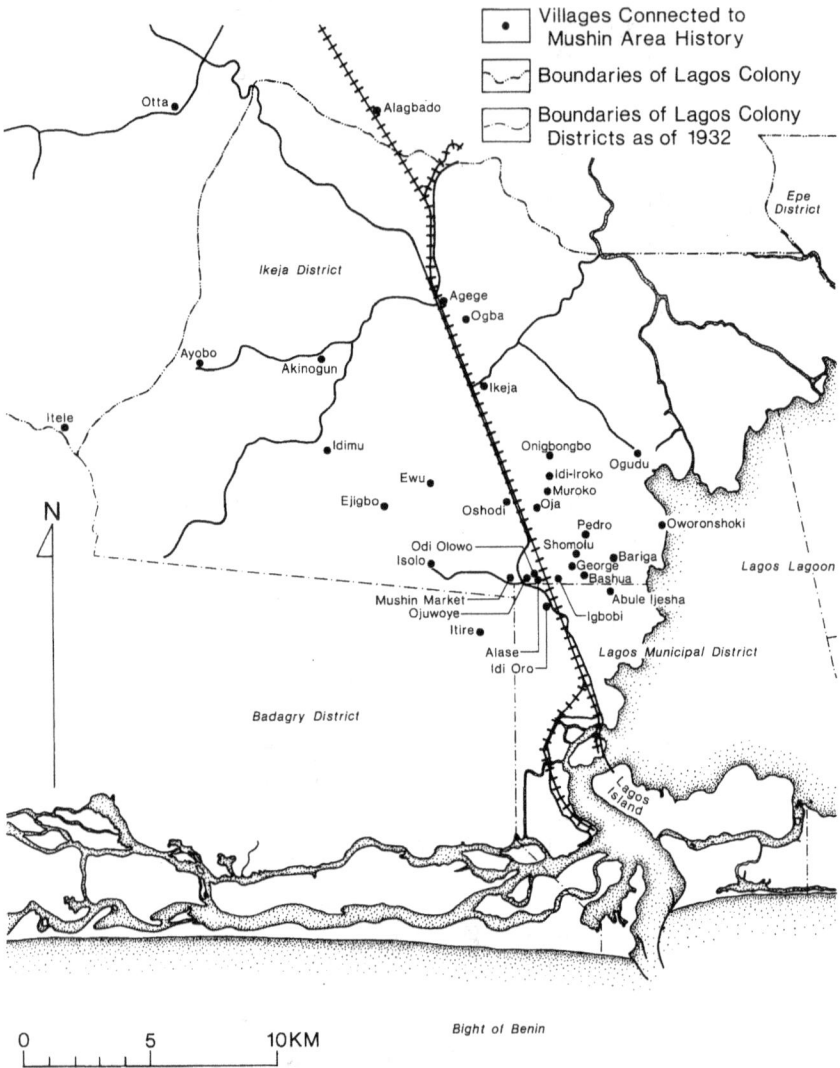

Map 3   Villages connected to the early history of Mushin

named for him. Migrants from many distant places – Benin, Nupe, Hausa,
Igbira, and Bariba – found their way to the outlying settlements, as did a
substantial contingent of Keta fishermen from the Gold Coast and Mende
from Sierra Leone. Large groups of Yoruba-speaking peoples of the former
kingdoms of Ketu and Shabe also founded settlements bearing their names
of origin. The up-country wars brought refugees from Oyo, Ijebu, Ede,
Egba, Ijesha, Ibadan, Ekiti, Ilorin, and Egbado – all Yoruba-speaking.

These were only some of the incoming peoples who were altering the character of the outlying area.[27]

The British response was to bolster the administration of the city but to ignore its immediate environs. Lagos City was given its first, separate administrative agency (a sanitary board) and it was designated a municipality in 1899. Concurrently boundaries between the city and nearby settlements were clarified for the first time.[28] Farther afield, district commissioners were assigned to take up residence in, and oversee local affairs of the Eastern and Western Districts of the colony. As for Lagos District (a new name for the Northern District), administrative responsibility remained on Lagos Island. It was vested in the Supreme Court and a small coterie of court commissioners who lived and worked, not in the area they administered, but in the city. This, like previous arrangements, kept the formal apparatus of government centred in Lagos, and attentions directed away from outlying areas. And so it was, for the first sixty-six years of colonial rule.

ADMINISTRATIVE NEGLECT

Despite their intentions to the contrary, the Lagos-centred administration gave rise to a contradiction concerning the very principle on which the government of Lagos Colony rested: the principle of direct rule. In theory, the new rulers were opposed to the indigenous authority system which, it will be recalled, consisted of *Baalẹ* and elders in outlying settlements and an *ọba* and chiefs in the city. In practice, these traditional authority figures were valuable to the British. The hot, humid, and malarial coast discouraged permanent settlement by expatriates and civil servants who preferred the more favourable environments of, say, eastern and southern Africa. Tours of duty were relatively brief, leave policies liberal, and turnover among colonial civil servants high. At the turn of the century, there were only ninety Europeans in the entire colony's civil service. There was not a single official assigned to the areas outside the city in Lagos District, although a small number of postal workers, doctors, and policemen worked there.[29] The personnel problem was exacerbated during the war years, 1914–18, when civil posts were 'hopelessly undermanned'.[30] In short, the number of foreign officials was never great enough for the British to run the government single-handedly nor to fulfil all of the governmental needs of the public. Although they espoused a policy of direct rule, the foreign administration needed indigenous authority figures to fill the immense governmental gaps they did not fill themselves and did not train local people to fill.

As might be expected, the machinery of government in the municipality and in the outlying settlements was vastly uneven. Lagos City, despite reorganisations and expansionist distractions, was given an advanced administration that had 'more of the apparatus of the modern European state than could have been found in some of the states of Europe at the time'.[31] By contrast, the one formal arrangement in the outlying settlements, and a predictable one, was to protect trade. In 1863, Governor Glover authorised village headmen throughout the colony to keep trade routes open to interior territories in return for stipends of between 12s. 6d. and £2 10s.[32] A further move to protect this vital commerce with the interior was taken a few years later when a handful of military personnel was assigned to oversee the stipendiary headmen.[33] Otherwise inhabitants living in the colony but outside the town were left to themselves.

The settlements in Lagos District suffered the greatest neglect. Since no government officials lived or worked in them, residents had to travel to Lagos Island to seek bureaucratic or legal assistance. The only official body with direct jurisdiction over district residents, the British-styled Supreme Court,[34] was further removed from the people by virtue of its use of unfamiliar procedures and legal principles. In time, commissioners of the court travelled on a circuit to hear cases, and much later the judicial system became attuned to local custom by establishing native courts. This took place in some outlying areas in 1928, but did not occur in the Mushin area until 1944. Likewise, access to law enforcement and protection required trips to the municipality. The small contingent of thirty-one policemen deployed in 1872 for the colony areas outside the city was considerably augmented by 1924 when the colony enjoyed a total force of 715 men. Still, it was not for another fifteen years that Lagos District managed to secure its own force of thirty-two, and this at a time when its population, living in more than 500 settlements, far exceeded that of any other colony district.[35] Even the management of resources – land and produce marketing – received no direct, official supervision. Indigenous landowners took responsibility for regulating land transactions and disputes until well into the 1920s and later. Finally, no efforts were made, as they were in the city, to sample public opinion through indigenous representation on advisory or legislative bodies, although opinions of district headmen were once solicited in 1934.[36]

So extreme was the alienation between the foreign rulers and the people of Lagos District that in the late 1920s and early 1930s officials themselves complained they were completely out of touch with that part of the colony to the extent that the district 'appears to have passed into oblivion'.[37] The Annual Report for Lagos Colony of 1927 stated that the District had never been visited systematically by any administrative officer.[38] The extent of governmental neglect was all the more surprising in view of the developments that were taking place. A railway line, opened in the 1890s, bisected Lagos District giving rise to a thin, dense settlement of urban-oriented people whose residences adjoined the tracks. A few mission-sponsored schools opened, markets handled an increased output of cash crops, and housing construction expanded.[39] The community of Idi-Oro at the northern boundary of the city became heavily populated at the turn of the century, intensifying the needs of its residents for more concentrated administrative attentions. But even the most urban areas were neglected if they lay outside the boundaries of the city proper. All in all, the territory was of little interest to foreign rulers so long as the inhabitants supplied foodstuffs to city markets and refrained from interfering with their lucrative north–south trade. The result was an attitude of 'live and let live' directed towards one part of a colony where, paradoxically, a policy of official involvement was highly elaborated toward the other part.

The fact that governmental standards were applied differently in Lagos City and in adjacent settlements naturally contributed to their developing quite differently. To be sure, they shared a common heritage and had interlocking social ties which drew them together. Yet they were treated differently, reacted differently, and ultimately defined themselves differently. The goal of amalgamating the two areas was not realised. The people of the settlements had separate authority systems, separate leaders, and strong boundaries around separate political domains. This separation profoundly affected the eventual political configuration of metropolitan Lagos to the extent that, even though the city and suburbs were part of a geographically contiguous and in many ways interdependent metropolis, they remained politically divided, each with its own authority system which acted independently.

UNOFFICIAL AUTHORITIES: THE VILLAGE OF *BAALẸ* AND THE *BABA ISALẸ*

Given this governmental vacuum, the people of Mushin's settlements provided their own system of authority. Each village or settlement was presided over by a *Baalẹ*, assisted by a council of elders representing village descent groups or other interests. They operated without official government recognition, but with official knowledge of their political roles and the significance of their activities.

The *Baalẹ* was the paramount authority figure in each settlement. He, or in a few cases she, was chosen either because he was a member of a founding kin group, or was of suitable age and ability, or had other desirable qualities such as relative wealth or charisma. The lack of governmental centralisation meant that each village enjoyed varying degrees of internal political autonomy, even under colonial rule. In most cases the *Baalẹ* was the ultimate source of law and order in his settlement. In actual practice, a

Baalẹ rarely acted alone but consulted with the senior and important members of his village in a council that reached decisions by consensus. In larger or older settlements, the *Baalẹ* and select elders were given chieftaincy titles either by the founding descent group(s) or by the community at large, and title-holders were usually ranked according to their relative seniority. The *Baalẹ* in consultation with his council performed functions that had changed little from the pre-colonial era: managing land, befriending newcomers, taking decisions relating to the welfare of the group, and to the best of their abilities, preventing crime.

Judicial functions were perhaps the most prominent activities of *Baalẹ*, elders, and other unofficial authority figures. It was well known that people of the outlying areas preferred informal arbitration and adjudication to the British-style courts and, to the surprise of colonial officials, usually complied with these decisions. As stated, the *Baba Isalẹ* acted as an appellate judge in difficult cases. They were most frequently sought out when succession disputes arose in a village. In most instances these dispute-settling mechanisms appear to have involved an authority figure who acted as convener and judge. But there were reports of full-scale informal courts that met, decided, and even succeeded in enforcing their decisions.[40] Around 1912, the Agege Planters Union served its more than 200 members in the far north of Lagos District (not an area that would be incorporated into Mushin) by establishing its own dispute settlement and arbitration service.[41]

The villages in the Mushin area differed from one another in their composition and their internal political structure.[42] There were four types. (See Map 3 for locations of historically important villages.) The first, son-of-the-soil, Awori villages such as Isolo, Itire, Ojuwoye, Idimu, or Onigbongbo were either founded by the first people to live in the area, founded as offshoots of the first villages, or founded by former clients who were given (not sold) land, either by the original or offshoot villagers. Most of these villages were established before 1861. In most instances, a *Baalẹ* was selected by village elders from a ruling house, i.e. a founding descent group, and his council consisted of selected descent group heads or title holders. Political ties between ancient villages and their offshoots or former clients were strong in the beginning but were severed in time. Where severance did not occur, the *Baalẹ* of the offshoot or client village eventually was treated as an equal by the parent village in their interactions. In other words, village autonomy was the eventual outcome.

Strangers were often absorbed into the son-of-the-soil villages as kinsmen. The Eyisha descent group, as an illustration, was said to be of Awori descent, but its members also were known to have non-Yoruba (Hausa or Nupe) ancestors and to have served an Itire ruling house as its slaves, domestic servants, or tenant farmers (accounts vary), and to have received from Itire a large gift of land at the southern boundary of Mushin on which they lived and farmed for several generations. Isolo, moreover, was said to have absorbed into its kin groups peoples of Bini and Dahomean origins before 1840–50 and who, by 1930, were known as Awori.[43] The acquisition of land through service, use, or gift, as the Eyisha and other cases that I collected demonstrated, served as a legitimating transaction and a public signal that individuals had a right to assume the identity of their benefactors. The identity could be lost, however, if the rights and duties pertaining to the use of that property and the exercise of appropriate kinship obligations were not actively exercised.

The second type, tenant villages, founded after the colony was established, such as Oshodi, Shomolu, Bashua, Oworonshoki, or Bariga, consisted of people who paid land rent to son-of-the-soil villagers, or other owners, and whose ties to their landlords were perpetuated until they and their heirs gained ownership rights through the use of that property. The first settler ordinarily served as *Baalẹ* and the heads of other incoming descent groups acted as his council. In later generations, the *Baalẹ* tended to come from any resident group and appears to have been chosen on the basis of seniority, skill, or other relevant criteria. Originally tenants were absorbed into son-of-the-soil descent groups; the manner in which later newcomers were absorbed, if they were absorbed, into the settlements of their ruling houses is unclear. Some simply assumed Awori identity without demonstrating how they were incorporated, or even if they were incorporated, into their descent groups or settlements.

The third type, migrant villages, established after 1861, consisted of incoming settlers who purchased land from son-of-the-soil descent groups. They included Pedro, Oja, Idi-Iroko – all of whose residents bought land from Ojuwoye. They chose their own *Baalẹ* on the basis of his being the founder or simply the most able senior person in the settlement. Some migrant villages had councils of non-related people who served according to interest, influence, or other criteria and who functioned, as one informant recalled, rather as a town meeting. Strangers were not absorbed into the descent groups of the villages, since the latter, too, were of settler origins and, more importantly, since they were not in control of sufficient land to allocate it to newcomers and thus establish long-term reciprocal ties. But strangers were accepted as citizens of the migrant settlements initially if they participated in civic affairs and later if they were property owners. Hence incoming strangers were no longer establishing permanent ties through incorporation into an indigenous (Awori) kin group but by assuming a territorial (settler) identity.

A fourth type, absentee-owner villages, were founded by wealthy Lagosians or other non-resident owners who sometimes purchased (after colonisation) or sometimes received their property as gifts (both before and after colonisation) from son-of-the-soil descent groups. One such village was Akinogun. In these places, residents were sometimes paid labourers, and the owner, or heirs of the owner, were considered their heads *in absentia*. In a few cases (rarely in the actual Mushin area), absentee-owner villages, such as Alagbado, were the property of people from Otta, a northern Awori town, or were inhabited by their tenants, both of whom maintained dual residence in the village and in Otta. Authority relationships were, therefore, Otta-oriented.

Internal authority appears to have been stronger in son-of-the-soil and tenant villages than in migrant and absentee-owner settlements. Few of the villages, however, displayed an interest in joining together, unless they were offshoot villages. The villages of the Mushin area were thus self-suffi- cient and self-contained in most every respect but their contact with the outside.

To reach the unfamiliar world of the foreign government, Mushin's villagers looked to the *Baba Isalẹ* of Lagos, just as they had looked to them to represent their concerns to the *ọba* and his council before the arrival of the British. The city's chiefs were the answer to the peoples' needs for repre- sentatives who would, as one scholar put it, act as buffers between them- selves and foreign administrators, present the demands of the masses to the government, and in turn transmit and translate the policies of a structurally remote ruling class to the ordinary citizen.[44]

The *Baba Isalẹ* were useful to villages because under the new regime they often served as unofficial advisors to government figures. Although their political functions as chiefs had been truncated, they retained important ritual duties and devoted considerable energy to serving as arbiters and dispute settlers. Indeed, the *ọba* was specifically allowed to carry out a judicial role under the treaty of cession.[45] Their real value, however, was in their ability to wield influence. Chief Taiwo Olowo counselled both the *ọba* and the governor, and the latter sometimes commissioned him to settle political problems with hinterland peoples. Similarly, Chief Oshodi Tapa was a personal friend and trusted advisor of Governor Glover who consulted him before implementing new public projects.[46] Later, a Native Advisory Board of Lagos' principal chiefs, lesser ward chiefs, and other influentials was constituted to provide a communications channel between the people and government. The Board existed for twelve years. On several occasions it gave approval to the selection of chiefs, *Baalẹs*, or lesser title-holders in Lagos City and nearby villages including Ojuwoye and Isolo in the Mushin area. The approval was a formality since the chiefs stated they did 'not know how [internal] affairs are managed' in the villages.[47] A larger, Central Native Council succeeded the Native Advisory Board. This proximity of the Lagos chiefs to the British via these two advisory boards only enhanced their ability to serve effectively as *Baba Isalẹ*.

The *Baba Isalẹ* system was strong in the areas where colonial government was weak. One of these was the village which controlled Mushin Market. Ojuwoye Village, named for the founding descent group and not the market, was in the early colonial years under the patronage of the *Ẹlẹtu Odibo*, a kingmaker and head of the most senior class of chiefs – the *Akarigbere* (administrative) class – and often characterised as prime minister to the *Ọba* of Lagos. The *Ẹlẹtu* was, in turn, represented at Ojuwoye by a domestic servant, Ifadu Alashe, who lived in the village and was duly allocated farmland as a customary tenant to an Ojuwoye descent group. Ifadu acted as spokesman for the village to outsiders and as a priest of Ifa, the divination deity. In recognition of his services, Ifadu was awarded a minor ritual title by Ojuwoye ruling house leaders. In 1884, when a missionary passed through the then heavily forested area near Ojuwoye, Ifadu received him on behalf of the estimated 100 villagers in his role as spokesman, and, because he also bore a title, was believed to be its headman, which he was not.[48] Although we may never be certain, perhaps the influence of the *Ẹlẹtu* together with the importance of Mushin Market made Ojuwoye one of the few settlements to have a policeman stationed in its precincts in the nineteenth century.[49]

Baba Isalẹ represented many other important Lagos District settlements.[50] These were not permanent relationships. Changes or vacancies in the power structure of Lagos resulted in, or perhaps precipitated, shifts from one notable to another or from one titled chief to his successor. A case in point was Akessan, a village west of Ejigbo which, between 1830 and 1930, was represented by five *Baba Isalẹ*: Chiefs Opeluwa, Ọbanikoro and Oluwa, all title-holders from separate Lagos chieftaincy families, and Taiwo Olowo and Herbert Macaulay, neither of whom held Lagos titles but both of whom were outstanding city politicians with close ties to the British.

In the nineteenth century, the *Ẹlẹtu Odibo* served the sister villages of Ojuwoye, Itire, and Isolo, all three of whose core descent groups claimed descent from a common ancestor. Farther north, the village of Ejigbo was also a client to the *Ẹlẹtu* as, possibly, was the settlement of Itele (Etele), where Ifadu Alashe's 'sister', Odu-Oya, held the chiefly title of *Ẹlẹmọ* of Itele. Elsewhere the ruling Kosoko descent group acted as collective patron to Ewu, another Awori settlement. Oshodi was linked to the Oshodi Tapa chieftaincy line, founded by Ọba Kosoko's famous general, Oshodi Tapa, a Nupe (Tapa) slave who became one of Lagos' influential leaders and chiefs. Several settlements in Shomolu – a large tract founded by a hunter and Ifa priest named Shomolu which later formed the eastern wedge of Mushin – were believed to have been clients to Bashua, a Lagos war chief. Other settlements in Shomolu, such as Abule Ijesha and Igbobi were founded by people who received land gifts from an Itire descent group and therefore joined their benefactors as clients to *Ẹlẹtu Odibo*. Taiwo Olowo, who helped many newcomers secure land, became an important *Baba Isalẹ* in the area between 1870 and 1900, and for a time appears to have replaced the *Ẹlẹtu Odibo* and other chiefs in many villages. Later, Chief Obanikoro was thought to play the *Baba Isalẹ* role in much of the Mushin area.

The legitimacy accorded to the *Baba Isalẹ*, the *Baalẹ* and the elders by the public, in their unofficial system of authority, gave them power in the official system. Indeed, their support, emanating from below, was a resource that could be used in the colonial peoples' struggle for political influence with a foreign regime. In the eyes of the general public, indigenous authorities were, through historical precedent and present circumstance, legitimated as political actors. They demonstrated this by, for example, complying with the judicial decisions of chiefs and headmen even when such decisions could not be backed by the legal force of the state. In fulfilling the many obligations of office, *Baalẹ* and *Baba Isalẹ* acquired a constituency of followers who accorded them the prestige, the rights, and the privileges attached to that status. The authority of the *Baalẹ* and *Baba Isalẹ* was a potent force in colonial society that foreign rulers could not ignore – despite their official stance to the contrary. From the perspective of the British, customary authority figures were allowed to exercise political roles because of the strength of support accorded them by the people, because of the ramifications of this strength in terms of controlling the public, and because of the very real need of government for their services and cooperation.

LATE COLONIAL ADMINISTRATION: 1927–1955

In 1927, Lagos District was administratively separated from municipal Lagos. This separation opened a new chapter in the political development of the metropolitan area and a new way of organising client relationships. British officials shifted the centre of authority for the adjacent settlement away from Lagos City and established local government headquarters first at Agege, and later eleven miles north at Ikeja. In 1932 the district encompassing the Mushin area was renamed Ikeja District. It consisted of two towns and 832 villages.[51] The decision to set up a separate administration for the outlying settlements had been delayed by African representatives of the Lagos Legislative Council. They opposed it as a 'retrograde step' which, because of its provision to include headmen and chiefs in some governmental tasks, would be 'an infringement of the rights of British subjects'. Others felt it weakened the bureaucratic hegemony of municipal Lagos. Still others opposed it because they were reluctant to see the important client villages of Lagos' *Baba Isalẹ* develop their own direct ties to government.[52]

Yet the growing power of the *Baba Isalę* alarmed foreign officials. Factional struggles in the city were increasingly fuelled by the contest for outside clients.[53] Chieftaincy politics was one of the only participatory outlets open to city residents, aside from using higher education, to move into politically influential occupations, such as the law or bureaucratic posts. It was, as a result, a highly competitive and active arena. The larger the following of a Lagos chief, the greater was his potential power in battling for supremacy in traditional politics and subsequently in influencing government. *Baba Isalę* had gone so far as to pose, wrongfully, as the owners or overlords of certain villages.[54] Others, paradoxically, had gained enough control to obstruct rather than facilitate relations between villagers and government. Client villages, not unaware of their importance to the patron-chiefs, as indicated, shifted their loyalties from one to another when it was advantageous to do so. To the benefit of some and the detriment of others, the *Baba Isalę* flourished in an environment which gave them a strong hand in manipulating the political activities of a sizable number of people. Consequently, in an effort to curtail them, colonial authorities found it desirable to separate the administration of Lagos City and the outlying settlements.

Unrest was another of the compelling reasons for separating the two areas. Outside the city there were rising incidents of outright lawlessness in the form of gangs, armed and violent thefts, and counterfeiting.[55] Still another problem was mutual distrust, suspicion, and hostility among villages. Both conditions were interpreted by one element in the administration as a failure of unofficial authorities to regulate social interaction. The number of migrant villages was steadily increasing. They were more loosely organised than son-of-the-soil villages, and less bound together by the rights and obligations of kinship. The influx of many new residents to the outlying areas expanded the scale of interactions that could be managed by the particularistic, village form of political organisation. Therefore, some administrators – not all – felt that more powerful and generalised mechanisms for maintaining order, which would reside in the bureaucratic and legal institutions of the state, were needed.

The prime rationale behind the separation of the two areas was economic.[56] The tax potential of outlying villages had never been tapped, and thus to facilitate tax collection a new outlying office was opened. Here was an increasingly attractive source of revenue that could augment the colony's budget and pay for administrative expansion.

The *Baba Isalę* system began to wither when the new district office was put in place. A survey of 200 village *Baalę* in 1934 indicated that most of them wished to have no further contact with Lagos chiefs and their *Baba Isalę*.[57] For the population at large, there was no longer a pressing need for contact with officials in the city. A district officer mandated to establish contact with each village now resided in the area. But tradition died slowly.

Both Ojuwoye and Isolo villagers took disputes to the *Ęlętu Obido* as late as 1934, and participated in his ceremonies.[58] Even in the 1970s, the legacy of the *Baba Isalę* was not forgotten. The reigning *Ęlętu Obido* – successor to Ojuwoye's former *Baba Isalę* – was called to an inquiry of the Chieftaincy Committee of the Mushin Town Council in 1974 to explain why he had capped (ritually installed) William Ladega as Chief *Alashe* of Ojuwoye, a village title, it will be recalled, which was held by Ladega's ancestor, Ifadu Alashe. The *Ęlętu Odibo* testified that in capping Ladega he rightfully exercised the customary role of a *Baba Isalę*. But the Mushin chiefs ruled against him, stating that he had exceeded the bounds of local custom by both choosing and capping a title-holder. The two were separate acts. In their view the rights to choose the title-holder properly resided within the jurisdiction of Ojuwoye, whereas capping, an act of ratification, could be performed by an outside authority.[59] At no time did Mushin's chiefs question the *Ęlętu*'s right to claim *Baba Isalę* status in relation to Ojuwoye. What they did question, however, was his right to exercise authority in matters which were within the internal jurisdiction of a client village.

The need for unofficial authority in Mushin-area villages did not diminish with the decline of the *Baba Isalę* system or the rise of a new officialdom in the district. Once again government relied on a form of administration that was direct, in law, but indirect, in practice. Despite the fact that his superiors had cast aside a proposal that a modified, official form of indirect rule be adopted, a district officer reported that to carry out his official duties he was forced to rely on the influence and functioning of village *Baalę*. 'It is palpably impossible,' he wrote, 'for one European officer and 15 police constables to control 63,000 primitive people without the assistance of their elders', whom he credited – in opposition to prevailing opinion – with being 'remarkably successful' in their efforts to maintain law and order.[60] I. F. W. Schofield, a Supreme Court Commissioner and first resident officer in the district, also needed village headmen in order to oversee a newly-instituted system of taxation that, paradoxically, relied on an indirect form of collection. *Baalę* received a 10 per cent commission on all tax collected from male residents – of whom there were 12,583 in 1928-9 – who were taxed at a rate of 1 per cent on incomes of £15 and above.[61] Schofield and an assistant also sought the advice of headmen and village leaders on local custom in order to preside effectively over their increasingly heavy load of court cases, which had escalated from 129 civil and criminal cases heard during his first year to 1,350 cases only two years later.[62]

The most important task still facing government was to unite the many separate settlements of the district. Up to this time there had been no natural higher units of indigenous government and few if any cooperative alliances. The *Baba Isalę* system, its benefits notwithstanding, fostered petty jealousies and a competitive atmosphere among local leaders. 'No village,' wrote one investigator, 'has any interest in or solicitude for the welfare of its neighbors.'[63] Up to this time, each village could contact colonial officials separately through middlemen, which meant that there was no advantage in villages banding together. Indeed, villages saw one another as rivals. The initial step in unifying the area, then, was to make sure the *Baba Isalẹ* system was unnecessary. In a spate of activity, the District Officer made contact with each village and attempted to establish himself as the central figure in the flow of information to and from government. Additionally, an advisory council of representatives was convened to meet with the District Officer, a Native Treasury was established to stimulate communal projects, and efforts were made to make tax collection a community concern.[64]

Progress in establishing a viable local government was none the less slow and painstaking. In 1928, Schofield spent only sixteen of his 305 duty days touring the villages of the district to establish direct contact. No doubt some of the torpor stemmed from the still prevalent attitude among officials that the district was one of the least developed areas of Nigeria. Inhabitants, who were in some contexts viewed as too advanced to be subjected to indirect rule, were in others seen as illiterate peasants and fishermen who were even unable to enjoy the benefits of 'tribal and clan' cohesion.[65]

A sample of public opinion pointed to other problems. The people of Ikeja District were divided in their desire to have a local government that made use of traditional authorities such as the *Baalẹ* and elders, and one that was modern and urban, and relied on a heterogeneous mix of public participants in officially designated bodies.[66]

FIRST STEPS TOWARD UNIFYING MUSHIN VILLAGES

Out of this dilemma the first step toward unity was taken by the residents. An emerging group of public-spirited, migrant leaders banded together and formed seven Village Group Councils.[67] These leaders sought to blend the traditional and modern elements of local government by cooperating with the *Baalẹ* and acting as representatives of the village authority figures. For the first time, a communal forum emerged where ties were forged among and between villages and nascent urban neighbourhoods, and where mutual concerns could be shared. The Councils were unofficial, and had no funds to support their activities. Their village representatives met fortnightly to discuss local affairs, settle disputes (even though they had no powers of enforcement), and debate problems – the paucity of schools, courts, and other administrative services and amenities – they wished to bring to the attention of the district officer. One prime source of discontent was the lack of roads, another the lack of protection.[68] In the near absence of law

enforcement officers, residents were increasingly subjected to a high incidence of crime, particularly theft. A gang of thirty-six was brought to trial
after terrorising the area, but its apprehension was more the exception than
the rule, since some residents had been driven from their homes for inform-
ing police of the whereabouts of criminals.[69] Consequently, a regulation
introducing mandatory dog licensing was a hotly contested issue, and one
that was abandoned after local representatives pleaded before the district
officer that their dogs were replacing the police protection they so desper-
ately needed. Still later, residents united to set up night patrols using
themselves and hired guards.[70]

After an initial flurry of interest, the Village Group Councils lapsed into
inaction. The Second World War directed many members' attentions to
war-time activities. Certainly it directed administrative attentions away
from all but the most pressing problems, and Ikeja lost its district officer
and other staff in 1939.[71] Concurrently, incomes declined due to a dip in the
price of palm products,[72] tax revenue was too low to promote development,
and an inequitable system of taxation further demoralised residents from
whom it was increasingly difficult to collect. The area suffered from the lack
of an overall plan for administration and development, and from a lack of
legislation that would allow administrators to deal effectively with the
unique problems of the district.

The war, none the less, brought major changes to the area. Above all,
urbanising processes accelerated. The Ikeja District population mushroomed thanks to military installations and an air station which was situated
within its boundaries. Accompanying the war was a boom in real estate
speculation and construction, so that increasingly large parts of the area
were densely settled. Indeed at the close of the war, officials began to refer to
the area as a suburb, and to some of its sectors as truly cosmopolitan.[73]

The strongest indicator of the area's shift from rural to urban was its
occupational structure (see Table 2). Agricultural pursuits – farming,
fishing, and hunting – declined markedly while commercial and other
occupational endeavours increased. In 1881, 78 per cent of the men and
women in the district that encompassed Mushin (census reports did not
separate the sexes) were engaged primarily in agricultural pursuits. When
the outlying areas were finally separated from the municipality in 1927, but
before urbanisation began, it was ascertained that 55 per cent of the men
were agriculturalists. By 1963, slightly beyond the time period discussed in
this chapter – but a strong indicator of what had taken place – only 14 per
cent of the men of the area were still engaging in agricultural occupations.

Another indicator was an acute problem with maintaining law and order.
Crime rates doubled from 1946 to 1947, yet the government increased the
Ikeja District police force only to thirty-eight despite the recognition that
such a force was woefully inadequate. Officials felt the area attracted many

Table 2   Occupations of residents in districts which administered the Mushin area, reflecting changes from rural to urban orientations, 1881–1963

	1881[a]		1927[b]		1963[c]	
	N	%	N	%	N	%
Agriculture, fishing and hunting	8,634	78	6,918	55	22,455	14
Commerce (trade)	500	4	246	2	18,720	12
All other[d]	1,992	18	5,419	43	120,392	74
Total	11,126	100	12,583	100	161,567	100

[a] Occupations of males and females in the vicinity of Lagos and Northern District. The census does not separate men and women.
[b] Occupations of male taxpayers (whose incomes exceeded £15) in Ikeja District.
[c] Occupations of males in Ikeja Division.
[d] Includes: craftsmen, labourers, service workers (e.g. transporters), clerks, technicians, and managers.

Sources: CO 150/1, 'No. 7. Government Gazette. Settlement of Lagos, 1881', p. 2; CO 657/22, 'Annual Report on the Colony for the Year 1928', Sessional Paper No. 20 of 1929, Lagos: Government Printer, 1929, Appendix III; Nigeria, *Population Census, Western Region, 1963*, Vol. II, Lagos: Federal Office of Statistics, 1963, p. 158.

undesirable elements, but they took no concrete measures to discourage their presence.[74] Indeed, they were strangely disturbed by the continuing popularity of unofficial courts or dispute settlement mechanisms, the public's most easily available means of dealing with conflict. These courts were operated by *Baalẹ* who ran them with 'all the trappings of a duly constituted court with records and uniformed messengers and salaried scribes', and who enjoyed sufficient support to impose fines effectively. Although officials felt their activities were not 'very wicked', they did appear 'to offer enough competition' to the official system that they should be replaced with properly supervised Native Courts.[75]

On the heels of the war came administrative reform. In 1944 a Native Authority and the first Native Court were established at Ikeja, relying on the participation of 'men of standing' in the area who represented various walks of life. The customary court paid a small fee to the district leaders who served as its president and associates in rotations of one to six months duty.[76] A few years later, the Ikeja Town Planning Authority, run by the district officer and by local representatives, was established, and soon a United Native Authority School opened its doors.[77]

Attempts by local people to unite resumed after the war. The Village Group Councils were rejuvenated and grew from seven to fifteen councils now serving the whole of the district. The most active Councils represented the most urbanised populations: Onigbongbo Village Group Council (containing much of the area known today as Shomolu and Bariga and their settlements of George, Apata, Bashua, Bright, Pedro, Adaranijo, Apelehin, Oworonshoki, Obanikoro, Bajulaiye, and Akoka) and the Isolo Village Group Council (consisting of Ojuwoye, Itire, Isolo, and Odi Olowo).[78] The next move was the formation of five higher-level Federal Group Councils. This meant that there were three levels in the authority system: at the lowest were villages and settlements wherein landowners or elders formed councils (later associations) under the leadership of a *Baalẹ*; in the middle were fifteen Village Group Councils made up of representatives from the villages and neighbourhoods; and at the top were five Federal Group Councils made up of representatives from the Village Group Councils. Although still not united at the top, this three-tiered hierarchy of representatives further encouraged the interchange of ideas and cooperation among settlements and their residents.

The process of unifying the outlying area was accelerated by a major event on the national political scene: the independence movement. As the capital of Nigeria, Lagos City was a focal point for nationalist activism. But because political affairs were largely dominated by an entrenched and highly educated elite consisting mainly of prominent Lagosians and other Nigerians, the public outside the municipality was relatively uninvolved to this point. Older residents of Mushin remembered that they had little political interest beyond their immediate surroundings until 1951 when a 'ladder election',[79] designed to ready the population for self-government, was held.[80]

Preparations for self-government brought about more administrative reorganisations which created a further wedge between the city and the adjacent areas. Briefly, the newly instituted Macpherson Constitution placed the whole of Lagos Colony under the Western Region, one of the three regional governments created by that document. The colony had been governed separately from the rest of Nigeria since 1861, and integration with the Western Region to its north was bitterly fought on the grounds that the status of the capital would be compromised if it were placed under another, larger authority. For three years this reorganisation was contested. As a result, in 1954, a second Lyttleton Constitution, was drafted to rectify the problems of the earlier document. It restored separate status to Lagos City, and placed it under the direct jurisdiction of the federal government in a separate administrative unit known as the Federal Territory of Lagos. Surprisingly, Ikeja, and of course its Mushin component, was not rejoined to the municipality. It remained under the jurisdiction of the Western Region. This shifted the administrative focus of Mushin residents to the Western Region capital of Ibadan, some 100 miles to the north.

These reorganisations led to even greater administrative neglect of the Mushin area. Despite the fact that this section of Ikeja District was one of the most heavily populated districts in the Western Region, Mushin was treated as a fiscal stepchild. Budgetary allocations did not recognise growth, let alone keep pace with it. Development funding was withheld, and few spoils seeped down to the area. The justification for Mushin's neglect was that it might be severed from the Western Region at any time and rejoined to municipal Lagos.[81] An exception was the Ikeja District Council area which, because it was north of Mushin and therefore closer to the Western Region, was favoured in 1960 with the development of a large industrial estate and slightly higher revenue allocations for running its administrative council. Mushin, however, was considered by regional politicians to be a poor investment. Moreover local leadership was not yet strong enough to exert the kind of pressure necessary to secure the finances and the adminis-trative personnel which were needed.

Preparations for self-government did bring one large benefit to Mushin. It brought party politics to the area and this, more than any prior stimulus, kindled the interest of residents in local affairs. Some formed small, short-lived local parties. Others, encouraged by the attentions of politicians and their inclusion in activities of regional parties, banded together and used party connections in order to petition the Western Region government to create a new administrative body for Ikeja's most urbanised sector.[82] Many of these people were local leaders who had earlier met in Village Group Councils. Once again public initiative was responsible for meeting local needs, and in 1955 the Mushin District Council was created.[83]

UNOFFICIAL AUTHORITIES: THE EMERGENCE OF SETTLER LEADERS

After 1927, new authority figures slowly emerged in the Mushin area. They were settlers who now performed the roles of middleman and patron. Reminiscent of the *Baba Isalę* system, settler leaders in the Mushin area began to represent people to the official world beyond the village and the emerging urban neighbourhood. Quite unlike the *Baba Isalę*, they did not belong to ruling house chieftaincy families and they did not hold chiefly titles. One of the most significant things about them was that they came from within Mushin's settlements and not from outside them. Another was that they made representations not only between their settlements and higher authorities, but also between one settlement and another. In contrast to the *Baba Isalę* system, the ties between settler middlemen/patrons and their clients appeared to be oriented toward individuals and their needs and not centred on villages as groups. There also was an increase in the scale of client relationships. The ties were more numerous – a plethora of interme-diaries, according to one administrator[84] – less persistent, less formal, and less monopolistic than the ones with *Baba Isalę* had been.

The emphasis on settler leadership, rather than indigenous leadership, was the result of many factors. It stemmed partly from the stimulus of urbanisation and the influx of migrants and partly from a lack of vision on the part of local Awori. Settlers tended to be better educated, or to ally themselves with better educated leaders, than the Awori, and this led Mushin's indigenous *Baalę*, particularly those of the relatively ancient Awori son-of-the-soil villages, to take a background role at a critical time. Their choice was encouraged by their physical isolation from the main thrust of urban expansion. An Awori *Baalę*, for instance, did not live in the Odi Olowo sector of Mushin, one of the earliest to become urban, because this sector was sold in its entirety to newcomers as houseplots.[85] Their choice also stemmed from the reluctance of many of them to serve on emerging councils and to come into contact with their village rivals. Not realising that the contacts and knowledge gained in the Village Group Councils, the Native Court, or the Native Authority would enhance their positions, Awori took few leadership roles outside their own settlements in the critical years when a unified polity was developing. 'They were in their villages without opening their eyes', as one settler recalled. 'It was we who introduced new ideas. We took the first steps to ensure that we would no longer be considered villagers, but city dwellers.' Even a district officer warned Awori headmen that their reticence to serve on the Councils was diminishing their influence and strengthening that of the newcomers.

Settlers were part of an increasingly large number of migrant outsiders. They were a majority, whereas Awori were now a minority. Some settlers came from older tenant or migrant villages, but the bulk were newcomers. They took the settler identity in order to indicate that they wished to be considered relatively permanent residents. Settlers demonstrated their permanence by purchasing or leasing for long terms small houseplots and building houses on them.[86] Acquiring property was a critical element in the incorporation process (as the next chapter indicates). Ordinary migrants who did not acquire property did not take the settler label, but kept their home identities to indicate their impermanence. Similar criteria were used in municipal Lagos as a way of extending the rights of citizenship to an incoming, heterogeneous population who could no longer be incorporated through the kinship system, but who could be incorporated through territorially-defined criteria. In the city, settlers slowly assumed the identity of Lagosian by demonstrating that they held property and therefore were permanent residents, and by demonstrating that the primary locus of their political participation had been transferred to the city.

Newcomers to the Mushin area used the term 'settler' and not a place name to identify their status, for several reasons. As indicated, Awori was a kin-based identity which was acquired at birth or through the slow incorporation of people into an Awori descent group or village. Once the population growth rate exceeded the capacity of kin groups to absorb new-comers, the problem of incorporation took on new dimensions. The logical shift, as in the Lagos case, was to assume a territorial identity. But unlike Lagos City, there was no single community large enough or united enough to provide a point of orientation for the emergence of a broad, common residential focus. The one potential point of orientation was the district, but boundaries were redrawn, reduced, and renamed at fairly regular inter-vals, e.g. the Northern District, Colony (Central) District, Lagos District, Ikeja District, and, finally, Mushin District. Furthermore the mass arrival of migrant settlers was too recent for the full processes of incorporation to take place, even if there was a named, communal focus. Migrants to the city acquired a Lagosian identity only after several generations passed. Most settlers in Mushin were first-generation migrants, and for them and their children the process of becoming permanent residents, who had primary loyalties to a new place, had only begun. Still in all, settlers were a territo-rially-defined category of people with vested interests in that territory.

The historically significant role of settlers in Mushin was as a political force. Settlers were the new intermediaries. They were the prime movers behind the development of the Village Group Councils. They were the figures who attracted the attention of administrators after the war and who were appointed to government councils and the Native Court. Settlers even served as *Baalę* of new settlements and neighbourhoods. They and their incoming neighbours were oriented toward an urban way of life and they desired the material conditions of city living as an accompaniment to that life. Settlers stepped forward at a time when indigenous people stepped back, and they began to search for ways to establish cooperative rela-tionships which would lead them out of the isolation and neglect Mushin had experienced for nearly a century.

The activities of the new settler authority figures had the effect of slowly bringing local people into communication with one another and of estab-lishing common bonds and goals to guide their interactions. A significant part of their role as middlemen was to begin weaving together the disparate parts of Mushin District and to begin closing the structural gaps between them. It was a slow process, and one that did not begin until prime movers resident in the area found it in their interests to amalgamate rather than divide the settlements.

The century between the 1850s and 1950s in the Mushin area was marked by two overriding political facts. The central government, whether it was the pre-colonial city-state of Lagos or the British colonial administra-tion, was remote to the actual running of village affairs. The settlements, moreover, were slow to develop cooperative relationships and structures

among themselves. The stage was thus set for the proliferation of intermediaries to represent each village to higher authorities, and even to neighbouring villages, communicating their mutual needs and concerns to one
another. The ultimate beneficiaries were the patrons and middlemen – first
the *Baba Isalẹ* of Lagos City and then the settler leaders of Mushin – who, in
gaining the support and loyalties of large numbers of residents, gained
political influence and prominence for themselves.

All in all, there were strong traditions of clientelism and strong incentives
for its continuation when Mushin came into its own as an administrative
district and active residents began to form a political community within its
boundaries.

CHAPTER THREE

LAND AND HOUSING
AS SOURCES OF POWER

Mushin had a single resource which was controlled by the general public and not by the state. This was urban real estate. Land and housing were investments leading to political, economic, and even social returns, and therefore throughout the metropolitan area and beyond, the ownership of urban property was highly valued. Nothing, wrote a Yoruba legal expert, attracted as much respect as owning a house; it was a necessary requirement for any claim of eminence or affluence in a community.[1] Yet the process of acquiring real estate was fraught with difficulties. In Lagos Colony, the political battle waged over property made it an all-consuming issue for more than a century.[2] Certainly it was the most sought-after resource in the Mushin area beginning in the 1940s and, as such, its acquisition engendered intense rivalries on the one hand, but gave rise to strong loyalties on the other, enmeshing individuals in the kinds of social relationships that were necessary for the building up of community groups. The people who were successful in securing property were a heterogeneous group but they were similar in one critical respect. Ownership set them apart from tenants to the extent that they occupied a privileged position in the urban social hierarchy.

COMPETITION FOR URBAN LAND

Desirable as it was, there were a number of obstacles facing the would-be owners of real estate. The first was to secure land in the form of a houseplot, and the second was to build a house on that site. Buying land presented the greatest obstacles, and we examine them at the outset. Building a house offered the greatest benefits, and an examination of this process and its rewards follows.

Houseplots were cheaper and more plentiful in Mushin than they were in the city, where demographic pressures and inflating land prices progressively contracted the land market, especially for low-income buyers. In the adjacent districts, however, land traffic was 'uncontrolled', as one investigator put it.[3] Furthermore, not all owners or indigenous landowning descent groups were interested in selling their property, nor were all properties attractive to urbanites. Town planning and administration were almost absent, amenities were limited, and roads and paths often did not exist. Compounding these problems was a lack of communications. Plots were usually advertised by word of mouth – although a real estate agency operated in the southern part of Mushin in the 1920s[4] – so that potential buyers needed to have well-developed information networks to learn of available houseplots. Equally important was their need to know how to negotiate for property and whom to trust in the unfamiliar urban real estate market. In land matters and related issues, the knowledge of the general public was sorely deficient and thus many people fell prey to sharp practices. These and other obstacles nurtured a psychological climate of scarcity.

The sense of scarcity was one of the elements that fuelled the intense competition among those trying to acquire land. Throughout the area's development, real estate transactions led to conflict among potential buyers and to fraud and duplicity among sellers and those purporting to assist both. In the early part of this century, land cases made up three-fourths of all civil suits.[5] By mid century, a special land officer was posted to Ikeja District to deal with the mass of litigation and land-management problems that continued to plague the area.[6] More than 3,000 metropolitan-area land disputes had been taken to the high courts from the earliest days of the colony to 1961.[7] And during a twelve-month period between 1971 and 1972, I found ninety-five stories in local newspapers dealing with land and house problems, including one in which a woman claimed to have been drugged by people who attempted illegally to gain title to her property.[8]

Conflict over Mushin land took many forms. Sellers were forced to guard against deceitful estate agents, imposters who sold their plots illegally, or land thieves who tried surreptitiously to build houses on empty land.[9] They were faced, according to court records, with people who presented forged documents to registration authorities and attempted to institute court cases on the basis of falsified evidence. One of the initial problems was with Lagos lawyers, among whose more notorious acts was the preparation of quasi-legal documents to benefit their buyer-clients and their failure to inform client-sellers they were permanently alienating their land. Surveyors also misrepresented boundaries. And descent group members misrepresented one another.

Buyers had their own kinds of problems. One of the more common was that a transaction was not valid unless all segments of descent groups agreed to a particular sale. From the earliest days members of landowning descent groups were willing to sell property for cash benefits, but owing to their size they often faced organisational problems in so doing. With hundreds of members divided into several segments, descent groups were known to sell, wittingly or unwittingly, the same plot to more than one buyer. It was well known, furthermore, that there had been numerous cases of clandestine sales or mortgages of family-owned land to which leading members were not privy.[10] Buyers sometimes found that key members of a segment of a descent group were not consulted about a purchase, and they were forced to abandon the plot or, if possible, satisfy the new claimant(s) with additional payments.[11] Buyers also found that several descent groups might claim to own the same parcel of land, and consequently make duplicate or invalid sales. But not all property was sold by descent groups. Large parts of Mushin land had moved into the hands of secondary owners who purchased it for speculative purposes or for farming or who were given land as a gift. Consequently another problem was that there had been sales and resales, allocations and reallocations, and these multiple dealings tended to confuse land transactions and to introduce further ambiguities into the question of ownership.[12] Still another problem for buyers came during the period between the time an initial monetary transaction occurred (usually a down payment on a plot) and the time house construction began. Months or years could elapse before a buyer was solvent enough following a land purchase to begin building a house. During the time land was vacant, competitors still attempted to occupy it, usually by making higher counter offers to the seller than the original purchaser paid. Under such inducements sellers were known to nullify earlier sales for more lucrative arrangements.

Needless to say, the acquisition of land and the subsequent protection of that land was a major undertaking for settlers. The story told by one Mushin resident, quite typical in its complexity, exemplified the kinds of problems that arose when an individual decided to purchase real estate. It is as follows:

A building is a security in life, and before I left my job I wanted to purchase land in Mushin. O— sold me a plot near the main road, but what he sold me was really government land. When this was discovered, I got my money back. In about 1948 I bought a second plot near the same road, paying £90, but again I learned it was government land. The second time I could not get my money back and my loss depressed me. A friend heard of my troubles, and brought me to this place. He had bought a plot of land where I now live for £60 and he sold it to me for £70.

A year later, when I was living fifty miles away I heard there was trouble concerning the land. I went to my boss and reported I was ruined. He asked two colleagues to investigate the matter, but they could not help. My friends in the neighbourhood advised that I should forcibly assert possession of the land by putting up a six-room building. I saw to the completion of the building by 1952 and then resigned my job.

But the matter did not end there. In 1970 I had to pay an additional £200 to the family which originally sold the land to the friend who then sold it to me. The problem was that the original purchase had been negotiated with only one segment of the family. The father had many wives, and only one set of children collaborated in selling the land. Other children of the same man were too young to be included in the original decision to sell. When they grew older and learned of the sale, they hired a lawyer and went to those who purchased, but from whom they had not profited, demanding further payment. The court ordered me to pay another £200, and then the court gave me a duly registered conveyance. This was twenty-two years after my original purchase. A neighbour of mine could not pay the extra money; he was ejected from the property and lost the house he had erected on it.

As this account indicates, Nigerian law protected the property seller. The burden of proof for establishing authenticity of ownership was on the buyer. Repurchasing property was one way of authenticating an original transaction and re-establishing ownership rights. But at base, the buyer was left to contend with various forms of duplicity at his own risk.

For both buyers and sellers land problems touched off disputes, many of which were brought to court. Legal action in the colony's Supreme Court, which had jursidiction during the critical years when Mushin was being transformed from rural to urban, introduced its own set of problems. One of them was legal fees and court costs. Frequently litigants paid their lawyers' fees by giving them land, and thereby lost property in the process. One indigenous descent group lost all of its land to the lawyer who represented it in five almost identical cases before the Supreme Court. Litigants also financed cases with the backing of private people and groups who supplied funds for court proceedings in return for a share of the proceeds. Once again their share often consisted of part of the disputed property. Wealthy traders and even political parties in Lagos were known to have profited substantially from land problems in the vicinity of Mushin by financing court cases or influencing their outcome.[13] But financing a court case was only the beginning. Another problem was that, once in court, land cases had to be steered through a legal maze which had developed in response to the colonial presence and to the population pressures associated with urban growth – both of which made land an extremely scarce resource.

THE LEGAL BACKGROUND TO COMPETITION FOR URBAN LAND

The background necessary to understand the legal complexities surrounding land transactions has been presented at length by a number of writers.[14] Nevertheless any understanding of the problems facing both land buyers and sellers must come from some knowledge of customary land law and the effects of a Western legal system on that law.

During the critical years of Mushin's development as an urban place, the legal system was undergoing a profound transformation. A customary land tenure system – based mainly on local Awori principles – was coming into contact with British law and with land tenure principles brought to the area by other immigrant peoples whose systems all varied. Again, their lack of knowledge severely hampered the buyers and sellers of property. The burden of understanding the legal system fell on residents who were forced, if they were to secure property at all, to know and to reconcile, if necessary, the contradictions and confusions that arose when two or more legal systems were being fused together. Buyers and sellers involved in land sales for the first time were required to negotiate in what may have been unfamiliar terms, and to undertake impersonal transactions whereas they previously had been conditioned to rely on face-to-face dealings with people who could be held accountable for their actions. For obvious reasons, people who were highly educated or who had recourse to experienced legal counsel had fewer problems with impersonal land transactions than the general buyer. The bulk of the public, most of whom were illiterate or only minimally educated, had less access to expertise and therefore took greater risks in both buying and selling, mainly because they did so in a customary idiom which, ultimately, had less power.

Customary law was grounded in pre-colonial principles, but it was an ever-evolving system subject to the influences of Western legal notions, just as introduced Western principles were constantly evolving in order to accommodate what were thought to be local customary notions. The eventual outcome was Nigerian law, a system which was general to the country in some respects but attuned to local and regional variations in others. In the 1940s and 1950s, the time period when houseplot sales began to accelerate in the Mushin area, customary and Western legal systems were not as well integrated, nor were they as well understood (on both sides), as they would become after independence. Hence the customary legal system lacked strength at a critical time and in a critical domain because it relied on personal relationships and oral negotiations in an environment in which individuals could evade responsibility for their actions or alter evidence, and because the land tenure system was shifting from the jurisdiction of traditional institutions to the bureaucracy.

The basic concept in customary land law was expressed by the introduced term *family property*. *Family* referred to the corporate descent group, or lineage, i.e. the *idile* or *ẹbi*, into which every member of society was born; The term *idile* was used by most Yoruba migrants in Lagos to refer to the descent group. Elsewhere *ẹbi* also was used to denote the descent group, but depending on context, *ẹbi* additionally referred to nuclear or extended family groups. *Idile* members traced their descent from a common ancestor, although membership also resulted from absorption or adoption. Members shared a common identity, history, and estate – land, houses, or political offices – all of which gave the group permanence. The *idile* existed, then, above and beyond the lives of individual members. Among Awori and some other Yoruba groups surrounding metropolitan Lagos, membership was traced cognatically through both females and males.[15]

Thus, *family property* referred to land and houses recognised to exist in perpetuity for all members of a descent group and their descendants (consanguine and putative). Family property consisted of *rights* to use and manage land and housing, in contrast to Western concepts of *ownership* (such as freehold ownership) or *holdings* (such as lease). In its purest sense, family property was communally held; no single family member was permanently associated with family property or a part of it. However, in the Colony District the family head sometimes assigned usufructuary rights to specific plots of land to a single family member whose ultimate rights to the land remained in the family, in theory, but over time sometimes resulted in a *de facto* partitioning of that land.[16] This was one of the ways in which descent groups segmented permanently and new ones came into being.

The sale or lease of family property brought complications to the local land tenure system. Before intensive contact with Western merchants and colonial administrators, and before the widespread conversion to a cash economy, land and houses were seldom sold in outlying areas. Indeed, there were no recollections of sales before 1861 in the Mushin area. Land was abundant and its transfer consisted of gifts or 'temporary' use-rights conveyed by means of verbal agreements. Some empty land, moreover, was simply claimed by newcomers and they were not challenged. After 1861, and a sudden growth in population, foreign administrators and merchants, returning slaves, and immigrants from the hinterland wished to secure land in the colony and they exerted pressure on land-owning families to sell it. Such sales became a prime source of wealth for some indigenous families. In Mushin sales were common after 1861, but it was not until about 1940 that more than 50 per cent of the land had been transferred out of indigenous descent-group hands and into settler hands. By contrast, in the city, where land was sold before 1861, more than 50 per cent of the land had been sold by 1910.[17]

Sales to foreigners brought legal problems. As disputes arose, foreign owners demanded that they be protected from litigation under customary law which was unfamiliar to them. Since British law was considered to apply in the colony it was used, beginning in 1874, in interpreting and adjudicating land cases. English land law at that time was, in the eyes of a legal expert who had devoted a lifetime to mastering its inconsistencies, a 'disgrace',[18] and as a result the application of English principles in property cases was inconsistent.

The year 1908 marked a high point in attempts by jurists to enforce English land law in the colony. The high court ruled that family property was a 'dying institution' and a 'relic of the past', and refused to apply customary principles to a case despite the presiding judge's recognition that customary law was more appropriate to it. In the following year the decision was overturned when four senior (Lagos) chiefs testified that the people preferred to litigate under customary land tenure principles to such an extent that they were, as we have seen, resorting to informal adjudication outside the formal court system. English law, they argued, had met with apathy on the part of the colony's residents. With that, British jurists abandoned their efforts to nullify customary land law and began to provide a context in which both systems could be utilised.[19]

The intermingling of British and customary land tenure principles was incomplete in many respects. In the courts a tendency emerged for either one system, English, or the other, customary, to be emphasised, and for legal counsel to insist that cases be pleaded under one system or the other. Even then an administrator assigned to investigate land practices found that his compatriots automatically heard cases under English law unless 'manifest injustice would result'.[20]

The legal concept which was accepted in both systems from the outset was the concept of *freehold* ownership. Under this system an individual purchaser was legally recognised as having sole freehold title for life. The concept of freehold ownership by virtue of purchase was readily accepted in the Mushin area because it allowed for easier resale (by speculators) and conveyancing of property, to say nothing of the possibility of amassing personal wealth. Furthermore it did not do violence to customary law as it evolved in the Colony District. Prior to colonial rule – and during its early days – it was the practice to allocate vacant land to an incoming stranger who then exercised principal rights to that land which were 'barely distinguishable from absolute ownership'.[21] Under the customary system, however, the newcomer remained beholden to his benefactor in some way. On the one extreme, his descendants might be absorbed into the grantor's family; on the other, the ties might be forgotten within one to two generations. Freehold ownership, through purchase, altered the customary system after 1861 by automatically severing the ties between buyer and seller.

Another blending of customary and English law which met with little or no resistance involved inheritance practices. After a freehold purchaser's death, ownership rights tended to be passed down in a customary idiom. Judges held that the land and housing of a freehold owner automatically should pass to all of his or her heirs under customary principles and should not be held individually under a freehold title.[22] It was possible under the introduced legal system for a freehold owner to opt out of the domain of customary law and into the domain of English law. To do so, a freehold owner was required to prepare either a written document, such as a will, which would allow him or her to designate an heir or heirs, or articles of incorporation, which stipulated that freehold property be transferred to, and then held by, a corporate body (not necessarily a descent group). Wills and corporate arrangements were more the exception than the rule. Therefore, contrary to the predictions of turn-of-the-century jurists, most freehold real estate devolved in the second generation to the domain of family property.

The blending of the customary and English land tenure systems was difficult to achieve when it came to the introduction of written documents of conveyance, such as titles and deeds. Under customary law, land transfers had been carried out publicly, verbally, and with the use of witnesses. In keeping with the past, initial land sales by Mushin's descent groups often were informal, with verbal agreements or rudimentary receipts serving to verify those transactions. But due to the large number of sales and the wide cross-section of participants, such verbal agreements were forgotten and witnesses moved away. From a bureaucratic point of view, written conveyancing documents and registration were encouraged because they offered at least one piece of evidence when disputes occurred. Under the introduced system, written conveyances tended to isolate and detach family members from their rights by singling out only certain of them to confirm a transaction. Furthermore they carried an assumption of the total transference of property rights to the buyer, and despite the acceptance of freehold ownership the notion of total transfer was inimical to many people.[23] For many years, therefore, written conveyances were unpopular. Many buyers and sellers lacked knowledge of the way to secure and use documents. Even when they did use them, the documents were, as indicated, frequently lost, forged, or improperly executed. As for land registration, people feared among other things that official knowledge of their holdings might somehow put them in jeopardy, and most of the land was still unregistered by 1957.[24] This unevenness in conveyancing practices during the prime years of land sales in Mushin meant that even if there were documents, or registrations were properly carried out, it was impossible to offer proof of a sure title because claims by previous owners, competitors, or others were still apt to emerge at any time.

In the end, the only safe land transaction was the thoroughly investigated one, although this was almost impossible to achieve. As one Mushin owner, a schoolteacher, put it:

Invariably buying land leads to litigation. It is only by gambling that you will know it is a good piece of land. You may have to make a thorough investigation; even then you may win or you may lose; it is just a game of chance. Now I think that on three occasions the parcels of land that I bought had to be let go because I did not want to go to court. I failed on three occasions and lost money, but two other times I was successful. Many suffer. But everyone is willing to take the chance.

All things considered, under whatever legal principles land was conveyed from seller to buyer, it was a high-risk investment.

Changes in the conveyancing system began to be felt in the 1960s, when written documents gained in use and popularity, and especially when the courts themselves issued conveyances after their rulings. Court-ordered conveyances appeared to have been honoured in many cases, and this built confidence in their validity. Court rulings, moreover, slowly began to favour buyers who were in possession of land for a reasonable length of time (not specifically defined), who built housing on it (provided they were not squatters), and who paid at least some segments of the relevant descent group in good faith.[25] Finally the equivalent of a statute of limitations was introduced, but the time limit did not begin to expire until a person first learned that he had been excluded from a property transaction. Be that as it may, these safeguards still offered incomplete protection to would-be purchasers, and land disputes continued in the 1970s to be major issues in Mushin.

THE ECONOMICS OF LAND AND HOUSING

Financing was the next obstacle that people faced in the process of acquiring urban real estate. The extremes of wealth and poverty clearly determined who would and who would not acquire property. But in the vast middle ground between the two, a number of factors came into play, making it virtually impossible to describe the typical economic factors which led to success in real estate matters. One factor, in this respect, was the type of primary income available to prospective buyers. Contrary to what might be thought, purchasers did not necessarily engage in stable, wage-paying employment in order to amass funds for buying property. A majority of Mushin's property owners, in fact, were self-employed traders or artisans at the time they bought land, although elsewhere, in two sectors of the municipality, the majority of the owners earned regular wages.[26]

The important consideration was the ability of a person to save, borrow, or collect enough money to pay for a houseplot, irrespective of the type of primary income he or she had. The land payment was the critical step because it was the point at which one large sum had to be paid out. After that point, house construction could proceed at the owner's pace. A houseplot could stand vacant until the owner was ready to construct a building, slowly, room-by-room. Houses could be built – usually not always – at very low cost and improved at a later date. Finally, part of a structure, however modest, could be rented out and the proceeds used to finance further construction, a strategy to which we shall return. By concentrating intensively on payment for a houseplot and not concentrating initially on financing the structure which was to be built on it, people of relatively modest means were able to enter the ranks of property owners.

The strategies used by two Mushin settlers in paying for houseplots are instructive in this respect. They are typical in that they show, albeit in different ways, the manner in which people of humble backgrounds and modest accomplishments became the owners of valuable Mushin property.

The case of Timothy Abiola[27]

Timothy Abiola* arrived in Lagos in 1939 as a young man with no education. A distant relative befriended him with food and shelter for the many months it took him to become financially independent. As a start, Abiola apprenticed himself to a barber at night, and during the day he hawked petty merchandise on the city streets. With £2 his relatives gave him when he left home, he purchased two dozen neck-ties from an Indian shopkeeper and sold them in a single day at double the price he paid. With half of the profit, Abiola purchased a second batch of two dozen neck-ties. With the other half, he paid for his subsistence. Continuing in this pattern, Abiola was able, in good times, about once a month, to purchase a 10s. postal savings certificate. During the next seven years Abiola's business tactics changed little, except that he completed his apprenticeship and using his savings opened a small barber shop where he worked at night.

After the war, British imports flooded the increasingly prosperous colony, and Abiola realised that if he were able to trade directly with British manufacturers he could avoid middleman costs. He therefore hired a young schoolboy to slip into the post office and copy down the return addresses on packages sent to the stores where he purchased the goods that he hawked on the streets and now sold in his barber shop. His next step was to hire a letter writer who wrote to London for catalogues and import instructions. With postal savings certificates, Abiola ordered, and paid for in advance, six dozen wide-brimmed felt hats which were of a style that had not yet been seen in the colony. Again he doubled his investment within a few days, and again he sent for another six dozen hats.

The profit from four batches of hats in as many months enabled Abiola at age 27 to amass the capital he needed to buy a houseplot in Mushin.[28] He chose remote farmland, but he knew the area would develop quickly because he heard a north–south highway was to be built near the site. Before he had saved enough money from the sale of merchandise to build a house, his land purchase was contested by members of the selling descent group who claimed they had not been consulted about, nor had they profited from, the sale. Abiola was helped by a neighbouring landlord who was faced with the same claims and who negotiated a settlement for both of them. Like many others, Abiola was required to repurchase the land by paying the neglected descent group members.

Abiola continued to order small amounts of merchandise from England and to sell it at profits which enabled him to build, room-by-room, a concrete structure. Abiola imported concrete directly from England and made the cement blocks for the house himself; young relatives provided labour in return for room and board; and a neighbour served as nightwatchman for a small fee. When ten rooms were finished Abiola let them to tenants. Using savings from rent profits, Abiola then added two storeys to the house. From the time he purchased the land to the time he finished a three-storey building on it, fourteen years had passed.

Rental profits increased dramatically at that point and Abiola quickly amassed enough money from his savings and bank loans to purchase three more houseplots and build large rental houses on them. By 1972, twenty-six years after he first planned to save enough money to buy a houseplot, Abiola's yearly rental earnings exceeded £3,500. This placed him in the same income scale as the nation's high-ranking civil servants, business executives, and professional people.[29]

The business strategies of Abiola demonstrated the way in which people made step-by-step advances toward major economic and career goals. The most important advance for Abiola was the purchase of a houseplot which, like the opening of his barbershop, occurred after he slowly saved profits from the sale of petty merchandise. When he finally reached the stage at which he could rent a few rooms, Abiola used his rental income to do the rest of his financing. At this point his holdings increased substantially. Needless to say, Abiola was a far-seeing person who, through pre-planning, was able to accumulate relatively large sums of money. His vision was focused on the future, and taking risks was part of his strategy for success. He correctly predicted that certain merchandise would appeal to his fellow urbanites. More importantly, he saw that remote farmland would eventually be a desirable location for tenants. In keeping with these qualities, Abiola had a formula which he passed on to those who wished to emulate his success: 'To be big, one must think big, and not be afraid to take big risks.'

The case of I. A. Adeyemi

I. A. Adeyemi* arrived in Lagos in 1925 with six years of primary schooling and a metalsmith apprenticeship behind him. The 21-year-old newcomer spent two weeks with a fellow townsman until he found work as a labourer with a government health agency. Adeyemi spent the next twenty-four years in a rented room trying to establish himself as a private transporter. His initial goal was to break away from the constraints of a job, despite the fact that he had been promoted to laboratory research assistant and earned a regular income with potential retirement benefits. Adeyemi saved for many years to purchase a second-hand lorry with which to haul goods between Lagos and up-country towns. But before he could save money for insurance, the lorry was destroyed in an accident. It took many more years before Adeyemi recovered sufficiently from this financial setback to begin saving money for a second investment. He had married early and family responsibilities consistently took priority over savings.

In 1949 at the age of 45, Adeyemi learned that a houseplot in Mushin near the Lagos City boundary was for sale. This was an unexpected opportunity to make a second investment. Adeyemi borrowed half of his plot payment from an in-law, and took the other half from his meagre savings. During the next two years, Adeyemi built a modest structure of ten rooms using traditional mud blocks and timber supports. From his paychecks he eked out enough to buy bags of cement for flooring (at 1s. 3d. a bag) and corrugated metal roofing sheets (at 18s. a bundle). Adeyemi and a few relatives provided most of the labour, although a few specialised tasks were hired out to laborers at 6d. a day. Unlike many of his neighbours, Adeyemi secured a deed to his land, and his ownership rights were not contested during his lifetime.[30]

When the house was complete, Adeyemi rented half of it to tenants, and he and his wives and children moved into the other half. The rental income provided him with the economic security he needed to resign from his government job. He then turned his attention to earning a living by combining his skills as a landlord, metalworker, and politician. He made no more investments, nor did he improve or enlarge his house. Adeyemi was reluctant to discuss his income as much from embarrassment over its smallness as from a cultural prohibition on revealing this kind of very private information. Adult sons and political clients contributed sporadically to his earnings. This and other evidence indicated that his annual income, by 1972, hardly reached £250 – slightly less than the average yearly wages of an industrial worker in the metropolitan area.[31]

Many owners were helped in buying land, and later in building a house, by supplementary sources of income. The range of sources was quite broad and, as in the case of Adeyemi, included monetary gifts which could come from patrons, friends, parents, spouses, children, or other relatives, or, as in Abiola's case, the earnings from two occupations. Loans came from these same sources or from the coffers of revolving credit associations. Maintaining close and creditworthy relationships with others was, therefore, important to prospective owners.

A strategy in financing a land purchase, used by both Abiola and Adeyemi, was to buy a plot in (initially) a remote location where it was cheaper than it would be in settled, more urbanised locations. Adeyemi paid less than £20 for his regulation size, 50 ft. by 100 ft. houseplot in 1949. The asking price for a similarly situated plot 20 years later was £2,000. Hence, as urbanisation advanced, land prices rose, and latter-day settlers, by necessity, had to be more affluent than earlier settlers. This trend has prevailed in the Mushin area from the nineteenth century to the present. Initially it worked to the advantage of low-income people and it was one of the key factors in making it possible for many of them to secure houseplots.

Financing opportunities for the construction of buildings expanded once land was paid for. Of course there were low-cost options for less affluent owners such as Adeyemi. Many like him built single-storey structures emulating the traditional architecture of rural or old urban places, using their own and their kinsmen's labour. It was possible in the 1960s to pay 3s. to 4s. per square foot, or £9 per room, for mud-brick walls, rough timber supports, and corrugated tin roofing.[32] By contrast, owners like Abiola managed their investments in such a way that they could build multi-storey reinforced concrete buildings. A cement house in the 1960s required between 15s. and 20s. per square foot; a decade later these costs quadrupled. Briefly, it should be noted that the unevenness in the abilities of owners to finance house construction was vividly reflected in the unevenness in housing standards of a single neighbourhood. They varied from very unpretentious traditional styles to more elaborate contemporary styles of dwellings, and from one to three, occasionally four, stories.

Profits from room rents, as indicated, often financed construction. Again in incremental fashion, owners such as Abiola slowly enlarged and improved their properties with rental proceeds. As they improved, rents could be increased. Almost all houses in Mushin were multi-family dwellings, and most were intended for tenants and for owners and their families;[33] an average house had forty-five residents living in thirteen rooms, of which ten to eleven were let out.[34] Whether they were one or multi-storeyed, houses typically took a rectangular form with eight to twelve rooms on each floor opening onto a central, bi-secting corridor (see Figure 1). A few houses were of the compound type with connected rooms surrounding a central courtyard; even fewer properties consisted of one building for the owner surrounded by separate, usually lower grade, out-buildings for tenants.

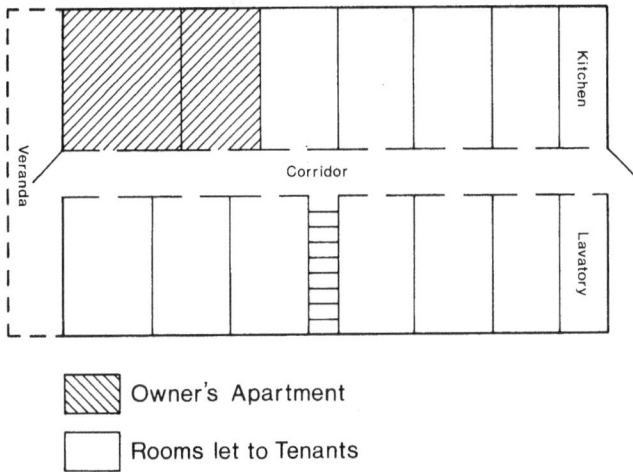

Owner's Apartment

Rooms let to Tenants

Figure 1   Typical block-type house in Mushin

Eight to thirty rooms (on one to three storeys) form a rectangular dwelling that is bisected by a common corridor. Communal facilities such as a veranda, cooking area, and lavatory are at the front and back of each storey. Except for the owner''s apartment, most rooms are let to tenants.

House construction could also be financed with institutional loans from banks, private employers, or government. Yet of the many houseowners I interviewed, none had financed real estate ventures with loans or mortgages from their employers or government.[35] Only Abiola and another landlord acquired bank loans, but they were granted on second land purchases after they no longer had low incomes. Moreover it was necessary to use the first plot as collateral for a loan on the second.

Private moneylenders also were patronised for loans. But, again, they were sought out for second-plot purchases or construction loans since the collateral required for large amounts conventionally had to be a fixed asset such as a piece of land. Moneylenders were able to wield considerable influence over their clientele but they were, as a result, feared and disliked. Their interest rates were exorbitant, and failure to repay loans often resulted in foreclosure.[36]

The difficulties in getting real estate were in a sense what bound Mushin's owners together. Their disadvantage was indicated by their educational levels, which did not compare to those of the national elite. In this respect owners more nearly resembled tenants, the population pool from which they had emerged (see Table 3). Neither landlords nor tenants, in my experience in Mushin, had gone beyond secondary school, but both groups had completed a few years of primary school; in keeping with the overall gap in schooling between men and women, most landladies as well as their female tenants had no formal schooling. Their disadvantage also was indicated by their occupations (see Table 4). They tended toward self-employment and labouring positions rather than the managerial and

Table 3   Educational attainments of owners and tenants (%)
(N=360)

Educational Levels[a]	Owners	Tenants
No education	25	23
Primary (some or all)	47	54
Secondary (some or all)	26	23
No information	2	—
Total	100	100

[a] Male respondents only.

Source: Author's survey, 1972.

Table 4   Occupations of owners and tenants (%)
(N=1,648)

Occupations	Owners[a]	Tenants[b]
Clerical	14.1	24.0
Managerial, professional	3.1	1.0
Unskilled worker	4.7	13.5
Skilled worker	14.1	31.5
Highly skilled worker	6.3	2.0
Trader	34.4	11.6
Merchant	6.0	2.8
Educator, military	—	8.4
Housewife	1.6	1.2
Religious specialist	—	1.0
Prostitute	—	1.3
Other, retired	14.1	1.2
Unknown	1.6	0.7
Total	100	100

[a] N=156.
[b] N=1,492.

Source: Author's census, 1972.

professional positions associated with the nation's elites. Again in this respect, owners were similar to their tenants. Finally, their disadvantage showed up in their inability to secure at the outset institutional or other large-scale sources of financial backing.

All things considered, advantage came after property was acquired, not before. There were marked variations in owners' abilities to capitalise on their investments. Abiola escalated his holdings significantly by investing heavily in a rent-producing building, while Adeyemi built a modest building which he never improved and which netted him, as a result, only a small income and little more. Abiola's skills thus gave him the stature necessary to negotiate and qualify for institutional loans and mortgages; Adeyemi's did not. For every Abiola, it must be stressed, there were many Adeyemis.[37] The majority of the owners remained in the low-income class,[38] and as a consequence of their relative inability to gain in their financial strength as individuals, Mushin was classified as a low-grade residential area.[39] Nevertheless, once owners controlled a resource that placed other members of society in a dependent relationship to them, they moved into a new and privileged position in the community.

THE SOCIAL BENEFITS OF OWNING URBAN PROPERTY

Owners were set apart from tenants in several meaningful ways. They were more socially involved than tenants in their kinship and community relationships, and this brought them a number of benefits. Their social benefits are divided into three categories: descent group, nuclear and extended family, and community.

THE DESCENT GROUP

The purchase of urban real estate was the first step in establishing a corporate kin group in a new place. When an individual purchased property in Mushin as a freehold owner, he or she was considered the founder of a new segment within a larger *idile*, descent group. A purchaser did not cease to be a member of his or her natal descent group(s); rather the purchaser and eventually his or her heirs were a separate land and house-owning unit within the larger group. Membership in the latter did not cease so long as members exercised their rights and obligations. As already stated, while the owner was alive only he or she had legal rights to that real estate but after the purchaser died all direct descendants inherited collective rights to use and manage that property. Direct descendants included children, grandchildren (if the child of the purchaser was deceased), and subsequent descending generations traced through cognatic principles, i.e. through both males and females.[40] Direct inheritors of a purchaser also included junior siblings if a person's natal group was known to practise this form of property inheritance, but as a rule this type of inheritance was often not recognised in the courts. Under the principles of customary law, no descent group members senior in age to the purchaser could inherit rights to use or manage that property; neither could a spouse or in-law inherit it. Therefore inheritance of all individually acquired real estate carved out of a larger descent group a separate property-owning unit consisting of the purchaser and the direct descendants (heirs) of the purchaser. In this way the purchase of urban property insured the perpetuation of a corporate kinship group and the close interaction in managing and using that property on the part of its (eventual) members.

The acquisition of property by outright purchase (not inheritance) created a new corporate land-holding group each time it was purchased. Property in Mushin was rarely sold after a house was constructed. Hence, the creation of a corporate kin group was almost a certainty. Taking a hypothetical case, if a member of each ascending generation of a descent group acquired real estate, the youngest living members would find themselves in the position of belonging to several discrete corporate landholding segments that would be embedded within the larger (maximal) descent group. Figure 2 illustrates this process. D owned property that he himself purchased. He also inherited rights to use real estate acquired by C (his father), by B (his father's father), and by A (his father's father's father). In each case the personnel of the property-holding group of heirs was different. E, who was the son of D's father's brother, shared with D the right to use and manage the property of B (their fathers' father), but not that acquired by C, who was D's own father. Here E was excluded because he was not a direct heir.

It often happened that disputes arose when a house or a small houseplot was held by a large number of people in a single descent group all of whom wanted to use that property. Such pressures could, but need not, pave the way for cleavages between corporate segments of the group. When housing and land were needed, heirs contested intensely in order to assert and defend their own rights to use them and to find reason to deny the rights of others to use them. If they could afford to be on their own, and they wished to avoid friction, members preferred to acquire their own property elsewhere, and to allow their usage rights to real estate, which was held by a large descent group, to lie dormant. Descent group members were well aware that rental income when divided among a large group of heirs could become too insignificant to offer real economic security to anyone. (One descent group, however, banked the accumulated rent from a house and used it as a common loan fund.) This in turn heightened the incentive for individuals to acquire their own property. Nevertheless as population densities in urban areas increased, and as land and housing became more

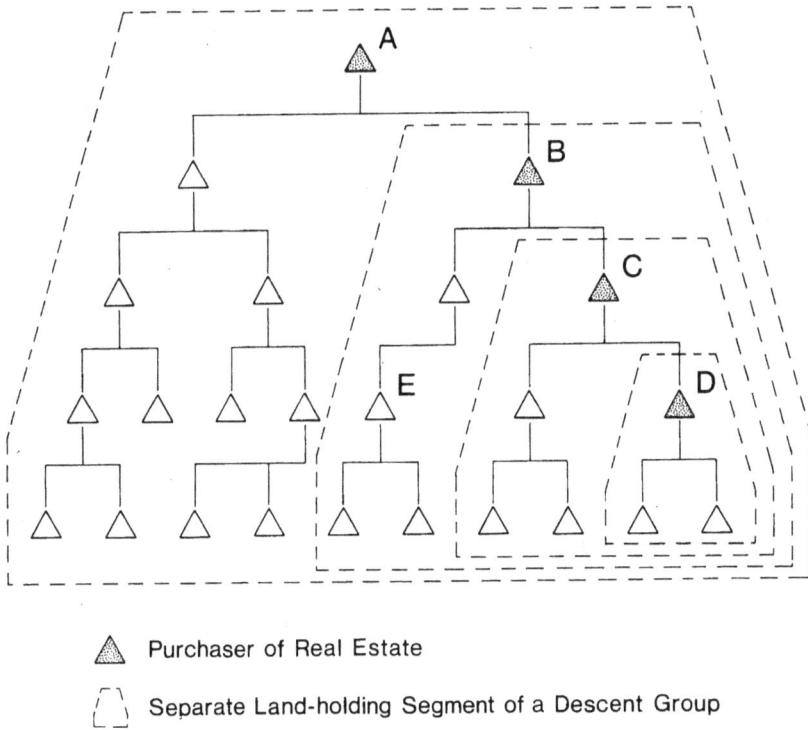

△ (shaded) Purchaser of Real Estate

⌐⌐ Separate Land-holding Segment of a Descent Group

Figure 2   *The effect of property purchase on descent group structure. Each purchase of*
real estate created a new, and separate, segment of a descent group

expensive and more scarce, the pressures to retain and utilise pre-existing property rights intensified.

The purchase of real estate in Mushin by migrants who also had rights to descent-group property in their homeplaces also paved the way for cleavages. First-generation migrants generally retained close ties to their kinsmen at home. Both Abiola and Adeyemi visited their descent group kinsmen frequently. Abiola, in fact, built a house in his hometown on land given by his father's descent group and installed his brother in it as a way of demonstrating his interest in his kinsmen and his hometown. Adeyemi remained close to his roots by attending meetings of both his mother's and father's descent groups. The children of both men, i.e. the second generation, having been socialised in another place, appeared to be less attuned to their parents' home context and therefore were less interested in activating descent group obligations in distant places although the older the children were in age the more they seemed to maintain loose ties as 'an insurance policy', as one put it, 'against future uncertainties'.

The strength or weakness of ties between home descent groups and members residing away from the original homeplace was influenced by three factors: political and economic considerations and the length of time a group's members were involved in metropolitan area life. My inquiries indicated that the more impoverished the home descent group, the less contact there was between Mushin members and home members. Conversely, the more affluent the home descent group – as represented by the holding of large tracts of land, houses, and hereditary chieftaincy titles – the more contact there was between members at home and away. Furthermore, settlers of a group with a long history of involvement in the metropolitan area, such as the Egba, often conducted descent group affairs independently of the home body. Settlers of other groups, particularly the Ijebu, whose history of migration to the metropolitan area was more recent, maintained closer alliances with the home group, despite property purchases in the new place. Hence, those people with the longest history of involvement in the metropolitan area and the least home benefits (titles and land), exhibited the strongest tendency to act independently of the home group. Conversely those people with shorter periods of involvement in the metropolitan area and large property-holdings and prestigious hereditary titles at home had close ties between themselves and other kinsmen in Mushin or metropolitan Lagos and the wider descent group at home.

In Mushin the tendency was for freehold owners and their direct descendants to draw together as a group and, over time, to pay less and less attention to the home descent group. This new closeness was revealed in their preferences for holding descent group meetings, rituals, and ceremonies in Mushin, and in their acceptance of the owner as an elder who had the authority to settle disputes or solve personal problems. By contrast, most tenants depended on descent group elders at home to settle family-related disputes or problems. They also tended to travel to their homeplaces in order to attend meetings or to stage important rituals and ceremonies.[41] The control of a house was a key ingredient. Owners used their properties as visiting centres and as headquarters for descent group activities. Tenants by necessity were more constrained in the use of their tiny rented quarters for such purposes. The dividing line was of course property-rights: owners, and not their tenants, controlled their dwellings and social uses to which they were put.

The important conclusion to be drawn here is that residence in a *new* urban location did not destroy kinship relationships, but, to some extent, it did relocate activities and force members to refocus and even add new functions.

THE NUCLEAR AND EXTENDED FAMILIES

In controlling their own space, owners were able to 'bring others under their umbrella' – thereby fulfilling the ideal associated with nurturing a large number of dependents. Caring for others conferred prestige on owners, allowing them to display publicly the ideal qualities of generosity, hospitality, and responsibility that marked individuals out as exemplary members of society. The ability of owners to care for a large number of dependents in their households was facilitated by the fact that almost all of them lived in two to three rooms whereas only 10 per cent of the tenants occupied more than one room (see Table 5).

Table 5   Households of owners and tenants
(N=360)

	Owners	Tenants
	%	%
Number of rooms occupied (two or more)	90	10
Number of spouses (two or more)	50	4
	(expressed in averages)	
Number of children[a]	4.5	3.5
Number of foster children[a]	2.0	1.6
Total people in household	6.8	4.7

[a] Male respondents only.

Source: Author's survey, 1972.

Landlords had larger nuclear families than tenants did. For example, half of the male owners above the age of 30 had two or more wives living in their Mushin houses,[42] while only 4 per cent of the tenants of the same age had more than one wife living with them.[43] As might be expected, landlords (but not landladies) had more offspring than their tenants.

Both landlords and landladies also had larger extended families under their control. They raised more foster children, hosted more relatives, and sponsored more migrant kinsmen in their first weeks or months in the metropolitan area. On the average, two more members of their extended families lived with owners than with tenants, and, finally, it was common to find three generations residing with owners but only two with tenants.

Owners were not simply the givers of familial support. They had been the recipients of a significantly greater amount of kinship support than tenants, and this appears to have had an effect on their urban fortunes. Owners received more initial help from kinsmen when they arrived in the metropolitan area than the average tenants did (see Table 6). Among those residents who lived twenty years in Mushin, 84 per cent of the owners arrived with kinsmen or townsmen who had preceded them and who helped them settle into life in the new place. By contrast, 60 per cent of the tenants had similar

Table 6   Urban experience of owners and tenants
(N=360)

	Owners	Tenants
	%	%
Presence of preceding kinsmen in Lagos	84	60
Prearranged job plans in Lagos	80	50
	(average)	
Age of arrival in Lagos[a]	17 years	27 years

[a] Male respondents only.

Source: Author's survey, 1972.

assistance. Preceding kinsmen or townsmen arranged jobs, apprentice-ships, or other types of occupational training for those who followed them. Hence 80 per cent of the eventual owners of Mushin arrived with pre-arranged plans, whereas 50 per cent of the non-owners did so. The build-up of kinsmen in a new place steadily strengthened the links in migratory chains, providing the kinds of expertise and social networks which were necessary for, initially, establishing strong footholds in the new environ-ment and, later, making and protecting investments in that place.

THE COMMUNITY

Owners were more involved in community associations than tenants were. This was shown in their very high number of memberships in voluntary associations in the metropolitan area. These included recreational, work-related, friendship, and religious societies[44] (see Table 7). The contrast is notable: 60 per cent of the owners, but only 10 per cent of the tenants, belonged to two or more such groups.

Table 7   Association memberships of owners and tenants (%)
(N=360)

	Owners	Tenants
Number of voluntary association memberships[a]		
None	5	28
One	35	62
Two	37.5	8
Three or more	22.5	2
Total	100	100

[a] Male respondents only.

Source: Author's survey, 1972.

The community involvement of owners was buttressed by the fact that they were more urbanised than tenants. Not only did they have strong pre-existing ties in the area, but they also arrived at a younger age than non-owners – there was a ten-year difference – and thus had more time to expand those ties. By the time they were ready to purchase land, landlords had spent some twenty-five years in the area and had reached an average age of forty-two years. Landladies were even more urbanised because they often were born and raised in the metropolitan area by migrant parents. This did not mean that they inherited their property because most of them did not. But it did mean that they had a head start in gaining a social foothold and in acquiring the networks that were necessary in order to establish themselves permanently. Still, women did not purchase real estate as frequently as men; less than one in six Mushin houses was owned by a woman.

In these social involvements, the differences between owners and tenants were more a matter of degree than of kind. Yet it was by degree that prestige was measured. Thus the more a person was involved in familial affairs, community groups, and social networks, the greater esteem he or she received from friends and neighbours.

THE STATUS OF OWNERS

Owners played a fundamentally different role than tenants in the urban economy. This was a difference in kind and not degree. Put simply, owners controlled and allocated a resource which was basic to the tenants' urban existence. Moreover, they provided a commodity – housing – which stimulated the urban economy. In Mushin, therefore, the possession of real estate enabled owners to assert influence on tenants below and officials above since both relied heavily on private owners to provide shelter in an environment where it was in critically short supply.

Owners were a central link in an economic chain. As much as 40 per cent of an urban worker's pay was used for rent.[45] But not all profits went into the pockets of owners. Some went to property taxes which were, in fact, the single most important sources of local revenue for the Mushin Town Council. It accounted for 43 per cent of the council's budget in 1975–6.[46] Real estate was the basic revenue producer because, it will be recalled, Mushin had no large commercial, educational, or governmental facilities. The few industrial developments in the district were not administered by the council, and provided it no direct revenue. Mushin was therefore a real-estate-oriented community, and this was symbolised by the two crossed door-keys that served as the Mushin Town Council emblem.

The possession of a valuable commodity put owners in a strong position *vis-à-vis* the government. Private builders met most of the area's housing needs. To be sure, government had built housing when it was necessary to house expatriate administrators and other government workers; later it attempted to alleviate acute housing shortages by constructing housing developments or engaging in other building projects. Yet the ratio of private to public housing was at the least 100:1.[47] In addition, the economic vitality of the metropolitan area depended in no small measure on the building industry. Construction provided employment. At least 24,000 workers were directly involved in the area's housing industry;[48] and a host of others supplied short-term labour or engaged in construction-related occupations such as supplying building materials, sub-contracting, or acting as real estate agents, rent collectors, or caretakers.

Ownership of property was itself an important urban occupation. There were more than 35,000 owners in Mushin.[49] For them, real estate was an investment from which all or part of an income could be derived. It also represented a form of savings, a security against unforeseen financial problems, and a pension against retirement. Owners took advantage of the security they got from house-owning to free themselves from what they perceived as the constraints of wage-earning. Like I. A. Adeyemi, many owners left their wage-paying jobs once they acquired rental property and established themselves as self-employed merchants, artisans, or traders, generally dealing in goods or foodstuffs. Among Yoruba, independent self-employed people, *ominira*, were more highly respected than wage earners.[50] They were free to move about, advance themselves, and thereby achieve their utmost potential in life. Those who worked for others were not only reduced in their social position, but also, in their view, they were unable to realise their destinies.

In the urban scheme of values, owners were honoured members of society. Elaborate housewarming ceremonies resembling rites of passage were staged in honour of people after they completed the process of securing land and building a house. Special praise songs were even written for these occasions. One of them celebrated the accomplishments of a new owner as follows:

> This is my house, be it known.
> A chieftaincy-deserving citizen is marked out by his house.
> 'Befitting a man but not easy to build': this is an attributive name
> For a house . . .
> Children shall throng you round, riches with the children,
> And good health, the quintessence of wealth . . .
> We ought to say special prayers for anyone who has built a house.[51]

In marking them out as 'chieftaincy-deserving' citizens, people were placing owners in a privileged position, for chiefs were the custodians of public welfare and, traditionally, the keepers of public order. Thoughout Mushin's history, owners enjoyed an elevated position as we have seen. They were selected to serve as *Baalę* and neighbourhood council members and to serve as middlemen between the settlements and the higher authorities of the state. In the priorities of the community, owners were thereby given high status, tenants low status. As one resident put it: 'Where a man rents he considers himself small.'

In sum, property was a resource from which many forms of power were derived. It afforded economic power, since housing was income producing. It contributed significantly to the urban economy which, as later chapters will show, effectively strengthened the collective position of owners in their dealings with the government. Property gave owners social powers, especially in kinship matters, and served as a permanent estate around which corporate kin groups could develop. The greatest benefit for both settlers and the indigenous sons-of-the-soil was that the ownership of urban property attested to their permanence and hence signified, in a critical manner, their local citizenship. In this way, owners occupied a privileged position in Mushin's status hierarchy. Owners, in fact, constituted the strata out of which local leadership emerged when Mushin began to take shape as an urban political community.

CHAPTER FOUR

THE RESIDENTIAL BASIS
OF LEADERSHIP

Aspiring leaders are, in a manner of speaking, political entrepreneurs. As Bailey has written, they engage in the enterprise of amassing resources and using them, skilfully, to attract followers.[1] In Mushin, a first step in this enterprise as we have seen was acquiring real estate, for it gave people who owned housing an advantage over those who did not. A second step was to capitalise on this inequity, by adding political content to the interactions that grew out of landlord–tenant relationships. The owners who wished to wield power in Mushin typically began a political career by attracting a neighbourhood clientele to whom they acted as patrons, middlemen, and dispute settlers. They dispensed, among other resources, information, contacts, and services that were particularly helpful in meeting the needs of urban life. In return they received support for their political goals.

The neighbourhood was a natural starting point for building a following. Historically in Mushin, settlements had been politically almost self-suffi-cient. Elsewhere in traditional Yoruba towns and cities, the *adugbo* (ward or quarter) was a basic unit of political organisation, and it was represented by its leader(s) in the decision-making councils of the wider community.[2] The political interactions that took place in the neighbourhoods of Mushin were thus a logical continuation of the idea that political life began at home. In the contemporary setting, many of these interactions took the form of clien-telism. Client relationships overlapped with and were reinforced by a high level of social, ritual, and economic interaction among neighbours. So significant was this neighbourhood interaction that it constituted a basis for what may be called the politics of residence.

NEIGHBOURHOOD INTERACTION

The neighbourhoods of Mushin drew people together who would not otherwise associate with one another. Outside of the work place and a few voluntary or religious organisations, residence was one of the only places where people of widely divergent backgrounds were brought together in intense, long-term relationships.[3] A high degree of ethnic group diversity was a critical part of this mix (see Table 8). Only twenty-seven of my 150 census houses were populated solely by Yoruba. As a rule, people of many backgrounds – Yoruba, Igbo, Edo, Kalabari, Urhobo, Nupe, Itsekiri, Idoma, Ijaw, and Efik – were closely involved in day-to-day contact in their houses and neighbourhoods. This diversity stemmed partly from the fact that the majority of the owners, who were Yoruba-speaking,[4] preferred to rent to people of different ethnic groups because it was easier to collect rent from people who were culturally distant.

Table 8   Ethnic group heterogeneity in Mushin houses (as expressed by per cent of Yoruba in houses)
(N=150)

Yoruba in houses %		Houses %
100	live in	18
99–76	live in	15
75–51	live in	21
50–26	live in	21
25– 1	live in	19
0	live in	6
Total	live in	100

Source: Author's census, 1972.

Close interaction was facilitated by the fact that many neighbours, despite their ethnic group differences, shared a common language.[5] Among women, that shared language was usually Yoruba, but among men it was usually English (see Table 9). The tendency for women to use Yoruba as their *lingua franca* reflected the facts that Yoruba were culturally and numerically dominant in the metropolitan area and that most adult women had not been to school – the place where English was generally first acquired. Most of the women who did not speak Yoruba had been in the city only a short time. The tendency for men to use English as their *lingua franca* reflected the fact that the majority had at least a few years of schooling.

Neighbours knew each other well. The closeness of house and neighbourhood interaction was reinforced by the closeness of living. Many household chores were carried out on verandahs, in open courtyards, or even in the central corridors which gave the sole access to rooms. Owing to the hot climate and the need for circulating air, doors were left open and privacy

Table 9   *Languages spoken by housemates in Mushin (%)*
(N=360)

	Yoruba as second lang.		English as second lang.			Igbo as second lang.	
	Good/ Fair	Poor/ None	Good/ Fair	Poor/ None	Pidgin	Good/ Fair	Poor/ None
Igbo							
Males	55.8	44.2	82.5	0.8	16.7	NA	NA
Females	72.3	27.7	61.7	21.3	17.0	NA	NA
Yoruba							
Males	NA	NA	75.2	24.8	—	—	—
Females	NA	NA	39.6	60.4	—	—	—

Source: Author's survey, 1972.

was maintained only with a door curtain. Children moved freely throughout the houses and facilitated communication among and about adults. The amount of knowledge one co-resident had of another, whether through observation or gossip, was extensive. In addition to other things, residents knew the homeplaces, occupations, household composition, and even rough ages, of most of their housemates.

The layout of neighbourhoods, with their close spacing of houses[6] and high population density,[7] drew people out of doors and into one another's company for leisure pursuits. When people returned to their houses after a day's work, neighbourhood streets and shops teemed with activity. Gaming establishments and bars were found on nearly every block, and residents began to fill their empty chairs and benches around 5 o'clock each afternoon. Informal games of ping-pong and draughts, and the weekly lotteries, drew groups together. As the evening passed, music filled the air from the amplifiers of record shops and bars, hawkers called out their wares, food sellers enjoyed their briskest activity of the day, and social visiting reached a peak. This was the time when verandahs were full of relaxing housemates and neighbourhood friends. Men went farther afield to seek out companions, but women preferred to socialise near their houses.

Adult women – four in five – spent most of their time in their neighbourhoods. A few remained inside their houses, but most women engaged in petty trade at small street-side stands in front of or near their houses.[8] The closeness of their trading stalls along the street-sides facilitated contacts between women who worked and conversed in clusters throughout the day; even those who did not trade were drawn into the social lives of those who did. Owners did not tax tenants who traded at the front of their houses; in fact they often provided the tables which were used as trading stands. While they traded, women socialised with one another, minded one another's children, and kept abreast of local gossip. In order to avoid the kind of friction that developed when women traded in similar products and vied with one another for customers, housemates consciously attempted to vary their specialties, as a way of 'keeping a house sweet'.

Fewer adult men – one in five – remained in their neighbourhoods during the working day. And roughly the same proportion worked within one to two miles of their residences.[9] Men who remained near their houses engaged in crafts, ran small trading enterprises, or performed a large number of services. As with the women, their days were interspersed with visits among co-workers, neighbours, and customers. Because most of their shops and stands also opened onto the streets, those workers became easily familiarised with one another's movements.

The very large number of business establishments drew people together and gave them yet another basis for knowing and associating with one another. In one neighbourhood, where commerce was not excessive compared to other areas of the city, there were 1,228 street-side businesses in a space measuring roughly three streets wide and eight streets deep and housing a population of approximately 15,000 people (see Table 10). This number did not include hawkers who solicited business on foot, middlemen who operated supply depots from their rooms, or people who specialised in early morning or late evening trade. At least half of these neighbourhood traders specialised in small quantities of manufactured or consumable commodities that they displayed on small tables or stalls. Others, working in lock-up shops, tended to sell bulkier provisions such as beer and soft drinks, or to specialise in crafts or services. Most day-to-day needs could be met within a short distance of home. Neighbours were therefore their best customers.

Religious life also drew neighbours together. There were nine Christian churches (mainly independent) and mosques in the same neighbourhood of three streets by eight streets.[10] Most residents who were religiously active belonged to an Islamic prayer group or Christian church in their neighbourhoods (55 per cent); and a few were active within a mile of their houses (11 per cent).[11] Religious groups, particularly small Islamic prayer groups and Christian sects, were close-knit and supportive. Members met frequently – once or twice a day – and many friendship sets grew out of these ritual associations.

The most important aspects of residential life were the bonds that developed out of physical closeness and feelings of neighbourliness. These were not the only bonds, or the most salient bonds, that individuals developed. Kinship ties and hometown ties took precedence over allegiances directed toward one's neighbours. Furthermore neighbourhoods were not necessarily the primary sphere of activity for all residents. The activities and allegiances of residents drew them to places, people, and groups throughout the metropolitan area. The degree of involvement in a neighbourhood was generally higher the longer one lived in, or was

Table 10   Neighbourhood business index

Petty traders (open stands)	615	Goldsmiths	6
Beer, soft drinks, provisions		Business offices	6
(lock-up stalls)	118	Dry cleaning/laundry	5
Tailors/seamstresses	69	Painters	5
Prepared food sellers	54	Book sellers	5
Beer parlours/canteens	30	Hostels/brothels	4
Electricians/electrical parts	29	Watch repairers	4
Lotteries/forecasters	26	Record shops	3
Barbers/hair dressers	23	Rediffusion shops	3
Mechanics/welders/blacksmiths	22	Rent collectors/house agents	3
Building materials sellers	17	Plumbers	3
Furniture/home furnishings	14	Bakeries	2
Kerosine depots	13	Tobacconists	2
Carpenters	12	Wood sellers	2
Photo studios	12	Soap makers	2
Schools (private for profit)	12	Wig makers	2
Pepper/food grinders	11	News vendors	2
Auto/scooter parts	9	Handcart rentals	2
Cobblers	9	Engineers	2
Herbalists/private medical		Upholsterers	2
clinics	9	Clothing stores	2
Surveyors/architects/con-		Milk distributor	1
struction contractors	8	Accountant	1
Medicines (patent)	8	Transporter	1
Printers	7	Jeweller	1
Solicitors	7	Shoe store	1
Battery chargers	7	Petrol station	1
Chair/amplifier rentals	7		
Sign maker/spray painters	7	Total	1,228

Source: Author's Neighbourhood business census, 1972.

permanently committed to, an area – but in that case involvements outside the neighbourhood were also more intense.

The point is that in one's neighbourhood, strong bonds *could* develop between people that were not dependent upon the relatively parochial bonds of kinship or homeplace. And it was the expansion of one's range of involvements which was the essential part of developing a cosmopolitan social base. To know many people was to have many sources of support in the inevitable competition for urban resources – jobs, housing, education, loans, and so on. This was as true for those at the bottom, who sought support from those at the top in order to make their way in the urban environment, as it was for those at the top, who sought support from those at the bottom so that they could maximise their urban opportunities.

PATTERNS OF NEIGHBOURHOOD SUPPORT

The urban value system encouraged supportive relationships among neighbours. To use the words of one resident: 'A person has a moral obligation to help his neighbours.' This was demonstrated in several dimensions of neighbourhood life. One of these was in business transactions. Neighbours regularly relied on neighbourhood traders for credit to purchase goods and services, since their low incomes rarely stretched through lean months or business lulls. Credit was not acquired at once. Newcomers initially purchased items on a cash basis. In time, when a trader was 'sure of a customer's face', residence and the type of company she or he kept – a guide to one's character – she was prepared to extend or deny credit. So substantial were credit transactions for some traders that they maintained ledgers, carefully noting each purchase that required repayment. On the other side, a trader was dependent upon her neighbours' knowledge of her and her fair business dealings for the success of her business. For the men and women who worked near their houses, therefore, it was literally profitable to be well known and trusted within the neighbourhood.

A second way in which neighbours were helped by one another was in solving their personal problems. Close living gave rise to a high incidence of conflict. On the basis of his experience as a court judge and owner of several houses, one leader suggested that most of the conflict in a neighbourhood emerged between co-tenants who fought over unpaid loans, the injudicious disciplining of one another's children, or alleged seductions of spouses. Owner–tenant conflict usually arose from failure to pay rent, contentious behaviour, or overcrowding rooms. The resident who required assistance with these and other problems again increased his or her prospects of support by being well known to others. As one neighbourhood leader put it:

The actions of a man cannot be hidden. If you are living in the neighbourhood and you are bad, before you speak your neighbours will know what kind of man or woman you are. If you are good or poor, people of the neighbourhood who watch you will know your condition. If you go to them for help, they will pity you and help you. They may help you settle a quarrel. They may help you get a job. They may give you money. It is not very hard to know a man who is hungry. A man who is hungry and a man who is angry – they are two faces that are the same.

Support, whether it was in business or personal affairs, was given to people who could be held accountable for their actions. It was important to those who extended help (or credit) to know that their clients would reciprocate (or pay back the debt). Hence, relations of support were relations built on trust which grew out of one being known and being involved in face-to-face interactions with others. Personal involvements carried with them moral obligations to perform in expected ways, and those obligations were not easily shirked when people lived, worked, worshipped, and did business together.

People who were in the strongest position to give assistance in the neighbourhood context were owners. As indicated, they occupied positions of high status in comparison with tenants. In their houses, owners were, *ipso facto*, authority figures. It was impossible, for instance, to take my census without first securing the permission of each owner. In owner-absent houses a caretaker, senior tenant, or relative was considered the authority figure, and performed in the owner's stead. In keeping with the traditional role of a landlord as head of a residence, an owner ideally treated his tenants as members of his family, but realistically such treatment was possible only in small houses. Nevertheless, in all houses the status of owner carried with it rights to set house rules, manage conflict, and solve problems. The owner's evaluation of what was or what was not appropriate behaviour extended from the most intimate family matters to matters that affected the neighbourhood itself. Indeed, the authority of owners spilled over into their neighbourhoods. The traditional *Baalẹ* and council arrangement of most settlements in Mushin was an owner-oriented system of authority. Consequently, owners were looked to as a class for help and direction. However, only a few owners were interested in taking on these extra responsibilities.

BASES OF NEIGHBOURHOOD POWER

The basis of power of a neighbourhood leader was, then, the ownership of property, and the high status and authority automatically acquired from occupying an elevated position in the urban social system. This position was buttressed by the very real ability of owners to assert their control over others by evicting unsatisfactory tenants or by persuading other owners that their tenants were undesirable elements in the neighbourhood and should be removed. As indicated, housing was scarce, yet it was vital to the well-being of residents who complied with the dictates of their landlords and landladies in order to keep it. My emphasis on real estate does not negate the fact that sheer wealth and success in entrepreneurial endeavours – especially transporting, contracting, or large-scale merchandising – were significant resources in the political arena for the non-elite.[12] Rather, it reflects the fact that the basic common denominator among political activists in Mushin was property ownership. This was the case whether or not the owners were relatively affluent.

Patronage was another source of a leader's power. Personal wealth, in relative terms, was a valuable asset to anyone who wished to attract a following. Leaders were expected to be generous and to offer hospitality to visitors to the best of their ability. Moreover, they could build up a significant clientele by dispensing loans, giving gifts, or even paying school fees for clients' children – to name only a few ways in which direct patronage manifested itself. Patronage also took the form of resources acquired from higher authorities and passed downwards. The leader who, for example, was responsible for getting government to pave a main street in his neighbourhood or to install a public water tap was credited with securing patronage for his neighbours. This kind of patronage netted him a large number of supporters who were impressed with the leader's abilities to influence higher authorities and who therefore hoped to benefit themselves in some future way.

Connections were another resource. In this domain, less prosperous leaders were eminently able to compete with leaders more prosperous than they. Leaders were only as strong as their contacts. Their reputations rested in large measure on the breadth and importance of the contacts they were able to make on behalf of followers. It was important to develop connections in high places – government, parties, or courts – or with people who had special skills: lawyers and other professionals. Such contacts were useful for acquiring patronage or expertise or for otherwise attending to the many diverse problems that leaders were expected to find a way to solve.

Leaders operated in an environment in which information was yet another scarce resource. Ignorance in the ways of urban systems placed new, transient, or little-educated residents at a strong disadvantage *vis-à-vis* the well-informed. It is hard to convey adequately the dearth of official information that was available to the ordinary resident on ways to solve or meet their problems, and the people's dependence on word-of-mouth transmission for what knowledge they did have. Lagos was a city of 3.5 million residents without anything resembling the *Yellow Pages*, a consumer protection agency, or referral services; instead it had a grapevine, an overburdened press, and leaders who made information their specialty. The paucity of information regarding real estate was, as we have seen, a prime example of this problem. In this realm, ordinary residents were at an extreme disadvantage in knowing how to buy land and how to protect it once they did. The average citizen was perpetually at the mercy of sharp operators, and constantly had to assess the integrity of those who offered advice and the quality of it. Leaders were at an advantage because people sought them out knowing that they had reputations to uphold. Their actions were sufficiently public that sanctions could be applied to them if the information they imparted was deficient or misleading.

Some leaders therefore developed expertise in specific matters, and built reputations around this accomplishment. One area of expertise that many of them cultivated was in the legal–judicial domain. Knowing the law, the courts, and how to redress injustice gave one a strong advantage. Related to this was a leader's own ability to resolve conflict. The public assessed leaders who settled disputes on their wisdom and fairness, their ability to understand and apply accepted norms and standards, and their ability to find ways to satisfy many seemingly conflicting interests. All in all, the effectiveness of leaders was in large measure dependent on their ability to put expertise and knowledge to work.

Finally, great power was derived from the ability to organise people to act collectively. This was done in Mushin in two ways. One was to represent groups in an official capacity. Offices in voluntary associations, religious bodies, occupational groups, or official institutions were valued resources because they gave the occupants the ability to act as legitimate spokesmen for others and to make contacts in higher bodies. Another was to organise people through informal networks. The ability to call upon the public for political purposes, and the rewards which could be derived from so doing, are taken up in subsequent chapters. Here I concentrate on the prior process of acquiring followers.

LEADERSHIP ROLES

The leadership roles which paid the highest dividends in the neighbourhood arena were patron, middleman, and dispute settler.[13] In playing each of these roles, leaders drew on fellow residents' needs for support as a way of obtaining support for themselves. Owners and tenants alike indicated that an essential ingredient in their efforts to cope with city life was the assistance of patrons whom they called 'godfathers' and middlemen, who were described as having 'long legs', ẹsẹ gigun, because of their wide connections.[14] Life without godfathers and long legs, wrote a newspaper columnist in 1972, 'can be and is usually very terrible'. They 'mean the ability to succeed where others have failed . . . a protective jacket'.[15] The dispute-settler role was another essential part of the social fabric because there was a high level of conflict and a low level of official machinery to deal with it. Each of these three roles could be carried out by the same individual, as they almost always were, and with the same client. In practice, it was difficult to separate one role from another.

There were several auxiliary roles that leaders also played. One was the role of initiator. Leaders were initiators both in setting precedents and in giving approval, or direction, to the actions of others. Owners of one neighbourhood I observed would not complain about the lack of refuse collection until a leader initiated action and led a delegation of owners to the town council. It was a short step from initiating action, such as this, to rallying people in support of the other goals the leader might have. Hence neighbourhood leaders, as we shall see (in Chapter 6) were key people in undertaking a second role – that of mobiliser. They mobilised followers in Mushin in order to secure votes and, later, in order to protest about government action. Still another role which Mushin's leaders undertook was that of opinion leader. This role had ramifications in terms of establishing norms, value orientations, and standards of behaviour in the urban setting. It was, to some extent, a socialisation role in that leaders were primary figures – role models – in setting the standards for the development of an ethos, or culture, of metropolitan Lagos.

One of the most active neighbourhood leaders in my experience, I. A. Adeyemi, exercised each of these roles on various occasions. Adeyemi's experiences in acquiring real estate were previously described.[16] When I met Adeyemi he was peaking in his political career. I was introduced to him at the direction of the head of the Mushin Town Council as a person who could assist me in one of the neighbourhoods I had chosen for research purposes. Adeyemi's network of clients and the connections he had made in his own and in adjacent neighbourhoods were remarkable. Aside from the usual participant-type research, my project required a large number of interviews. In a metropolitan area the size of Lagos, where strangers are suspect, and relationships of trust take time and effort to develop, for me alone to find the diverse categories of people I wished to interview would not have been possible. Adeyemi, however, introduced me to 123 people he knew personally and who readily agreed to submit to my questions.[17] These people did not represent all of Adeyemi's primary network; rather, they happened to be some of the people in his network who fitted certain criteria I had established.

The relationships between Adeyemi and the people in his network were developed primarily on the basis of residential familiarity. The residences of these people, all in close proximity to Adeyemi's house, are shown on Map 4. His clients represented a fair cross-section of the population with the exception of the national elite. The overwhelming majority – 85 per cent – were not members of Adeyemi's own Ijebu Yoruba sub-group. Furthermore, most of the people – fifty-five men and twenty-six women, a total of eighty-one – were strictly clients. The others were colleagues from his own and nearby neighbourhood landlords' associations, his former political party, or his local market. These colleagues were in some cases Adeyemi's clients, in others his patrons, and in still others simply acquaintances with whom there had been no previous transactions but merely co-participation in the same groups or events. For the most part, then, this network represented former transactions which had created varying levels of indebtedness between Adeyemi and neighbourhood clients, and on which he was willing to incur a debt with these people because he gained prestige from having been asked by town council officials to assist in my research project, a request he freely publicised.

Adeyemi's reservoir of support was built up over a twenty-year period. In that time, he followed a typical pattern in creating a place for himself in public affairs. He initially attached himself as a client to an important

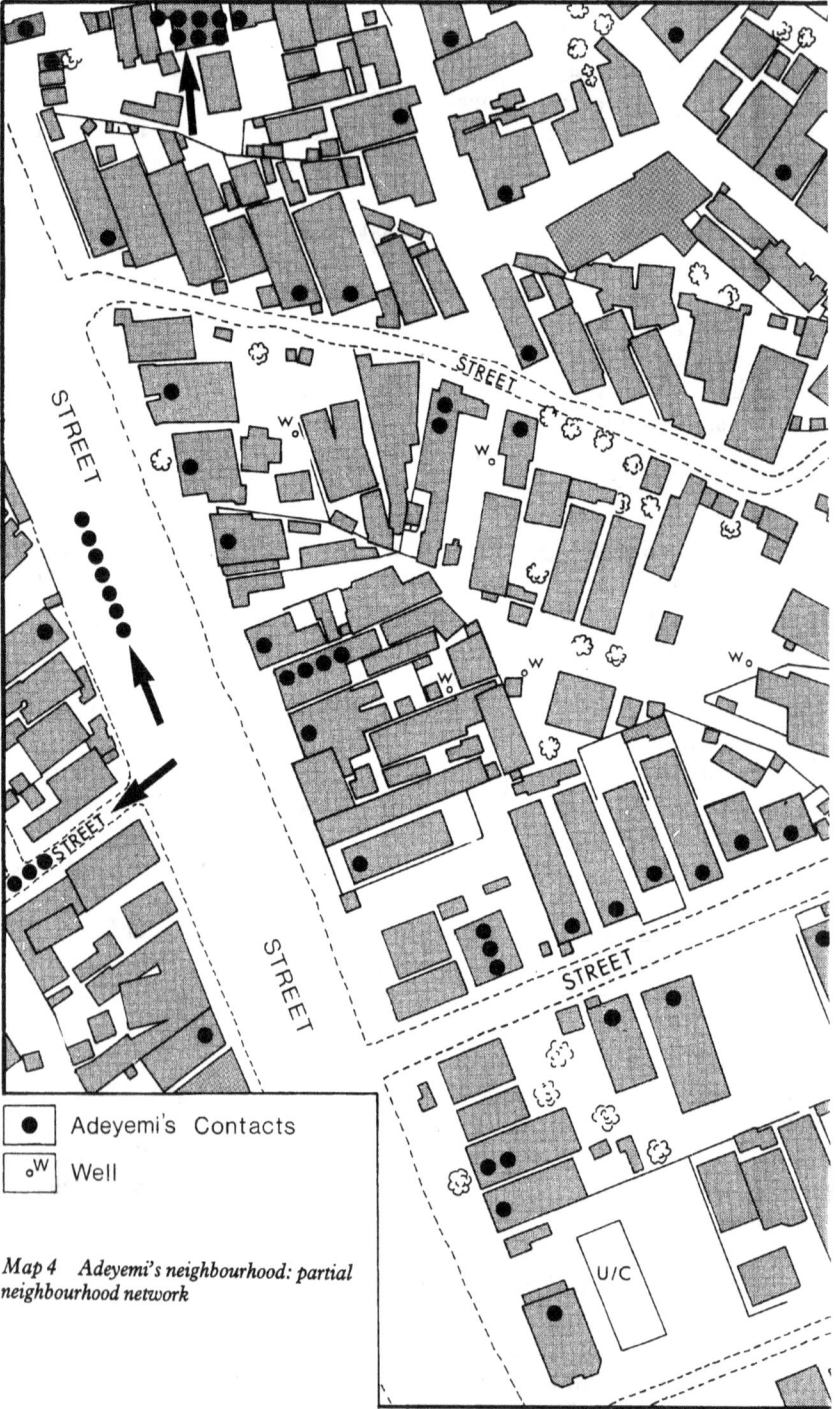

STREET

STREET

STREET

STREET

STREET

W o

W o

W

W o

U/C

● Adeyemi's Contacts

o W Well

Map 4   Adeyemi's neighbourhood: partial
neighbourhood network

person in his neighbourhood – in this case the *Baalẹ* – and performed a number of services for him. He then joined fellow owners on the *Baalẹ*'s council. These steps helped him in two ways. The networks of the *Baalẹ* and the other owners became secondary resources for Adeyemi. This helped him establish a reputation as an active authority figure with good connections in and beyond his neighbourhood. There was a cumulative effect in these tactics. The more people Adeyemi could use as contacts for getting things done, the higher his standing. The higher his standing, the more people he could draw into his sphere of influence. This, then, was the process by which Adeyemi placed himself in a position to attract his own clients.

Still, the exact nature of Adeyemi's transactions with his clients was not entirely clear. What kinds of requests were actually made of a neighbour-hood leader? Who made the requests? How did a leader handle the transactions he engaged in with his clients? To answer these questions, I kept a record of Adeyemi's activities for ten weeks. During this time he was involved in sixty-eight separate transactions with, or on behalf of, clients. They are listed in Table 11. The majority of the requests (74 per cent) came from people who belonged to Yoruba sub-groups or ethnic groups different from his own. Adeyemi was asked most frequently to settle disputes: domestic, neighbourhood, and community-wide disputes. Next in fre-quency were requests for bureaucratic interventions, followed by therapeu-tic services, and then assistance with land and housing problems (many of which took the form of disputes). On a few occasions, Adeyemi was asked to assist clients by 'managing' their neighbourhood reputations, and, most rarely, they asked him for direct patronage.

Table 11   Cases handled by I. A. Adeyemi: a ten-week sample

Domestic disputes		
1	July 5	Neighbour called Adeyemi to settle a marital dispute.[a]
2	9	Adeyemi was called to Ijebu Ode (another city) to settle a father–son dispute.
3	21	Adeyemi returned to Ijebu Ode to continue hearing the father–son dispute.
4	?	Adeyemi was called to admonish four disobedient children of a deceased neighbour whose sister was left as guardian of the children, but of whose estate Adeyemi was made executor.
5	26	Adeyemi was called to settle a neighbour's marital dispute (see narrative, p. 86ff).
6	Aug. 18	Adeyemi was called by Mrs Cole to settle a household dispute (see narrative, p. 89ff).
7	23	Adeyemi was called to reassure the new wife of a neighbour's son that her mother-in-law would not harm her. He advised the new wife to put her faith in the neighbourhood elders who would protect her and support her marriage.
8	Sept. 11	Adeyemi was called to Ijebu Ode to settle a domestic dispute.

Neighbourhood disputes

9	July ?	A neighbouring landlord called Adeyemi to deal with his tenant who owed back rent. Adeyemi asked the tenant's father to remove his son from the premises.
10	?	Adeyemi returned to his landlord–neighbour (no. 9) to deal with the tenant who refused to leave with his father.
11	?	Adeyemi consulted a customary court judge regarding the above rent problem (no. 9). The judge advised the landlord to sue the father.
12	Aug. 4	A neighbouring landlord (no. 9) informed Adeyemi his rent case had been taken to a lawyer whom Adeyemi recommended, and Adeyemi then withdrew from the case.
13	5	Adeyemi was called to hear the grievance of a landlord who was not appointed to a neighbourhood landlords' association committee on which he wanted to serve.
14	8	Adeyemi made two visits to landlords' association officers to solve the above (no. 13) grievance.
15	Sept. 20	Adeyemi was called to Shomolu (part of Mushin) to help a tenant with an eviction dispute. Adeyemi suggested the tenant go to a customary court where he would support her (and where the judge was Adeyemi's in-law).

Wider-community disputes

16	Aug. 8	Adeyemi was summoned to a chieftaincy meeting to help settle a market dispute. The problem involved a factional struggle over control of the market. The matter was not resolved. (See Chapter 7.)
17	16	Adeyemi was summoned to a second chieftaincy meeting to continue settling the market dispute.
18	Sept. 8	Adeyemi was summoned to the Mushin Town Council to give testimony and advice on chieftaincy succession rules.
19	11	Adeyemi was summoned to a chieftaincy meeting to hear again the market dispute.
20	15	Adeyemi was summoned to a chieftaincy meeting to hear a dispute over chiefly succession rules.
21	20	Adeyemi was called to the market to hear a dispute.
22	22	Adeyemi was called back to the market to continue hearing a dispute (no. 21).

Bureaucratic interventions

23	July ?	Adeyemi was asked to help a man secure a taxi licence from the Mushin Town Council.
24	?	Mustapha Adebola* asked Adeyemi to help him get a transfer in the Mushin Town Council (p. 88ff).
25	24	The sanitary inspector met with Adeyemi (p. 89ff). The latter used the occasion to speak on behalf of a neighbour who needed a building permit for a shed.
26	26	The sanitary inspector met Adeyemi to ask for help in investigating a violation.
27	Aug. 4	The sanitary inspector asked Adeyemi to investigate the illegal construction of a shop.
28	5	A neighbour asked Adeyemi to help her secure a lower property tax rating (see p. 88ff). He took no action.

29	16	Adeyemi saw the Mushin Town Council member, and Mustapha Adebola was subsequently transferred.
30	18	Mrs Cole called Adeyemi to secure help with the sanitary inspector over her illegal trading stalls (p. 89ff).
31	23	Adeyemi visited the customary court judge to secure advice regarding Mrs Cole's problem (no. 30) with the sanitary inspector.
32	28	Adeyemi confronted Mrs Cole (no. 30) with an attempt she made to get help from two sources at once. He then told the sanitary inspector to pursue her case in court.
33	Sept. 21	The chief of a neighbouring ward sought out Adeyemi to get help from the Mushin Town Council to solve a flooding problem.
34	21	Adeyemi was asked by a neighbour to help obtain a licence from the Mushin Town Council to sacrifice a cow for a funeral ceremony.

Therapeutic services

35	July 6	Adeyemi was asked to pray for two women with personal problems.
36	27	Adeyemi went to Ijebu Ode for two days to secure medicines for a mentally ill client.
37	30	Adeyemi was called to a nearby neighbourhood to administer medicines to the family of a mentally ill client.
38	Aug. 2	Adeyemi was called to the above family (no. 37) to check on the client.
39	6	Adeyemi went to Ijebu Ode to secure more help for the above (no. 37) family.
40	10	Adeyemi went to Ijebu Ode for medicine for two other clients.
41	11	Adeyemi was summoned by a neighbour who suffered from diabetes and co-tenant problems. She sought curative medicines (p. 91ff).
42	12	Adeyemi was summoned by a policeman to secure medicine for protection with a property problem (i.e. the threat of the loss of his land title).
43	15	Adeyemi was asked by a tailor to cure his headache.
44	17	Adeyemi went to Ijebu Ode for curative soap for the diabetic client (no. 41).
45	19	Adeyemi held a ceremony for the diabetic client (no. 41). The co-tenant made amends.
46	20	Adeyemi went to the family of the mentally ill client to check on its progress (no. 37).
47	21	Adeyemi went to Ijebu Ode for more medicine for the diabetic neighbour (no. 41).
48	25	Adeyemi was asked to pray for an Islamic group which was concerned about its members' problems.
49	Sept. 5	Adeyemi went to Ijebu Ode for more medicine for the family of the mentally ill client (no. 37).
50	12	Adeyemi returned to Ijebu Ode for a different medicine for the first mentally ill man (no. 36).
51	17	Adeyemi went to the latter client (nos. 36 and 50) to check on his progress.

Land and housing problems/disputes

52	July 6	Adeyemi was called to settle a boundary dispute between two neighbours.
53	7	Adeyemi accompanied a friend to court (in Ijebu Ode) for a land case.
54	17	Adeyemi was called to a nearby neighbourhood to settle a dispute between brothers over the management of a house they inherited from their father.
55	24	Adeyemi was called to the house of an Alhaji on a land matter.
56	Aug. 4	Adeyemi was called again to the Alhaji (no. 55) who wanted a small plot of land to lease or buy. Adeyemi searched for a plot.
57	8	Adeyemi was called to help a neighbour who complained that a hotel owner illegally erected a fence on her property.
58	16	Adeyemi was again called to hear the dispute between brothers (no. 54).
59	29	Adeyemi was called to get one brother out of jail, after the dispute (no. 54) became violent.
60	Sept. 2	Adeyemi called on a lawyer friend to seek help for the jailed brother (no. 54).
61	11	Adeyemi went to a neighbouring chief to intervene in the case of the brothers (no. 54).
62	18	Adeyemi returned to Ijebu Ode to attend the court case of his friend involved in the land dispute (no. 53).

Public opinion management

63	Aug. 2	Adeyemi was asked to speak to landlords in a neighbouring ward to clear up a misunderstanding which was impeding the research of the author. He did, and the matter was resolved.
64	4	Adeyemi was asked to speak to the landlords (no. 63) regarding a rumour which interfered, again, with research. He did, and the second problem was resolved.
65	15	Adeyemi was asked by a pools and lottery manager to tell neighbours that the manager was an honest businessman. Adeyemi took no action (p. 94).

Patronage

66	July 27	Adeyemi was asked to arrange an apprenticeship (paid) for a client, and did.
67	29	Adeyemi was asked to house and feed an unemployed man, and did for many months.
68	Sept. 10	Adeyemi gave money to a poor neighbour.

[a] Unless otherwise indicated, Adeyemi took action in response to each client's request.

DIMENSIONS OF THE DISPUTE-SETTLER ROLE

Leaders welcomed the dispute-settler role. In customary terms, elders were expected to resolve disputes. Leaders were willing to exercise this role whether or not the disputes were in their households or their families. It was one thing to carry out an expected role within the confines of a close kin group. It was quite another to attract unrelated clients. Leaders' reputations were enhanced when outsiders came to them. It attested to their legitimacy as authority figures. It broadened their followings, since, in one key respect, settling disputes and intervening with the bureaucracy were similar. Either of them created an indebtedness and this, of course, was the desired goal.

Leaders in Mushin took one of two stances when they agreed to resolve disputes. The one was to act as an *adjudicator*, by hearing the views of parties involved and then deciding how the matter should be resolved. The other was to act as a *mediator* by bringing two sides together and helping them reach solutions and compromises to their problems. Adeyemi chose to act as a mediator in handling the following dispute, for reasons which will be discussed below. This domestic crisis (see case 5 of Table 11) took place in July 1972. It is reconstructed from accounts given to me by Adeyemi.

> A teacher and his first wife, a seamstress, quarrelled over the fact that the husband had taken a second wife. The husband appeared to love his second wife more than the first. Consequently, there was great animosity between the co-wives. The teacher took his two wives to a herbalist to cure them of their jealousy and to restore peace to the household.
>
> The herbalist, however, became infatuated with the seamstress. He asked each wife to come to him for separate treatments. On one occasion he gave the seamstress medicine which would harm her husband. When the teacher learned of this deception, he called on Adeyemi to resolve the problem, which had now got out of hand.
>
> Adeyemi took the husband and his two wives to the house of the herbalist, where he asked each person to state his position in the matter. Following a lengthy hearing, Adeyemi rebuked each one of them for contributing to an intolerable situation. He rebuked the husband for not treating his wives equally. He rebuked the senior wife for allowing her envy to create household discord. He rebuked the junior wife for not respecting and obeying the senior wife as she should. Finally, he rebuked the herbalist for alienating the affections of a woman who had actually been entrusted to his care as a patient. The wives agreed never to return to the herbalist; they and their husband agreed to restore harmony to their household; the herbalist agreed to cease all treatment of the two women.
>
> After the husband and his wives departed, Adeyemi took further action with the herbalist. Adeyemi was familiar with the law regulating indigenous medical practitioners, and he warned the herbalist that he had broken that law by giving the seamstress a treatment which was intended to harm her husband. He warned the herbalist that any further attempts to see or influence the teacher's wife would result in Adeyemi's reporting him to the authorities.

There are several dimensions of the dispute-settler role which were revealed by this case. Adeyemi was performing two tasks simultaneously: dealing with the discord which had arisen within a domestic situation, and acting as a middleman between the domestic group and the herbalist. Each task required a different level of expertise: knowledge of domestic values and customs and of the legal code as it applied to herbal practitioners. Adeyemi's ability to understand 'human nature' and govern his own actions appropriately were revealed in his rebukes to each party – intended to save face for all – which could, none the less, serve as a basis for negotiating an agreement which each party was willing to accept. Additionally, Adeyemi used a powerful sanction – in this case his knowledge of the law – to neutralise the mystical power of the herbalist.

The most meaningful element in the case was that it strikingly displayed the fine line existing between the role of mediator – a judicial role – and that of middleman – an administrative (or allocative) role. The parties who asked for assistance became Adeyemi's clients. Their relationship with him as their dispute settler, like the relationship with the middleman or patron, was a personal, contractual, and informal (not legal) relationship. It also required reciprocity. Here, then, was the basis for a political relationship.

Another meaningful aspect of the dispute-settler role brought out by the case was that the leader needed to display skill in choosing how he would deal with the case and the parties involved. Above all else, a leader such as Adeyemi needed to avoid damaging his reputation when he performed his various functions. In the delicate task of settling disputes, leaders were exposed to a high risk of failure. The risk, as has been pointed out in other contexts,[18] was the loss of prestige that occurred if a decision was defied. Dispute settlers were evaluated on their ability to make wise and balanced judgments – judgments which were in line with social expectations and which could be reinforced by public accord regarding their correctness. No doubt this was why meditation was a safe approach to resolving certain kinds of conflict. Mediation allowed for compromise solutions. A compromise did not involve a loss of face for clients. Similarly, it did not involve a loss of face for the dispute-settler, since a mediator did not hand down a judgment but helped clients to reach their own solutions. Adeyemi was cautious in his approach to domestic quarrels and often relied on compromise in these matters. In community disputes, too, he and other leaders displayed caution and preferred compromise and conciliation to an outright decision.

The other side of the coin was that adjudication – in which there was a clear decision made by the dispute settler – brought greater credit to the leader whose judgments were followed than did a compromise. Because owners had the ability to evict tenants, they were willing to take more risks in adjudicating tenant disputes. Adjudication, it must be said, exposed the dispute settler to greater danger than mediation since the decision could be ignored. And this was no doubt why it seemed to be a secondary method of dealing with disputes among leaders who, after all, had few other formal sanctions at their disposal.

DIMENSIONS OF THE PATRON AND MIDDLEMAN ROLES

Followers in Mushin primarily came from the clientele that leaders amassed through their roles as middlemen and patrons. Both roles involved allocating resources or directing people to the place where they could be obtained. Direct patronage, as will be shown, was quite important at high levels of the political system, where leaders were obliged to use economic power in order to expand and to solidify political control. Indirect patronage, or middlemanship, was more often found at lower levels of the political system. The two roles were combined to a greater degree as one moved up in the system. The middleman in Mushin filled an important niche. At the same time, it was the one role which allowed political aspirants who were not affluent to operate effectively. A leader such as Adeyemi was far more involved in acting as a middleman or dispute settler than as a patron. But like the patron, the middleman automatically had higher status than his clients because both kinds of relationship were perceived by the public, irrespective of any differences in content of transactions, as superior/subordinate interactions.

Much of the power leaders enjoyed derived from the fact that their clientele formed extensive networks of people who were involved with them for long periods of time and who could be mobilised for many kinds of support. The following sequence of events illustrates the point. This narrative account, taken from field notes, concentrates on Adeyemi's primary role as a middleman, and is an expanded account of cases 24 to 32 in Table 11.

> Alhaji Adebola* was a loyal client to Adeyemi. When the authenticity of Adebola's houseplot purchase was questioned by Yinka*, the daughter of the seller, Adeyemi helped Adebola successfully defend his rights to the land. He did so by arranging for Adebola to make a second payment to the daughter in return for which she gave Adebola a court-validated conveyance.
>
> After Adebola's death, his son, Mustapha*, perpetuated the tie with his father's patron. Mustapha was educated by his father and became a clerk in the treasury of the Mushin Town Council, where he loyally responded to Adeyemi's requests on behalf of other clients. At one point, Adeyemi was asked to intervene with the Town Council to lower the property taxes of Yinka, the daughter who earlier challenged the authenticity of Mustapha's father's land title, and which Mustapha and his siblings had inherited. Adeyemi did not intervene since his council contact in this request would have been Mustapha.
>
> Mustapha Adebola felt that the treasury clerkship at the Mushin Town Council was a stressful job. There were constant pressures to 'fix' things like property tax assessments, and as a consequence, there was a high rate of dismissals from his office. Therefore, Mustapha wanted to transfer to another post. Yet requests such as his were difficult to process internally without assistance from a superior which, because of his youth, Mustapha could not yet claim. Instead Mustapha turned to Adeyemi, who contacted a landlord's association colleague who was serving on the town council committee of management, and whose suggestions to the personnel manager did not go unheeded. Within a few weeks time, Mustapha was transferred to another office.

Meantime, Adeyemi's interaction with Mustapha was noticed by the council's sanitary inspector, who was in charge of Adeyemi's neighbourhood. Building code violations were monitored by the sanitary inspector. He wished to enlist the help of Adeyemi in order to increase his effectiveness in dealing with violators and levying fines in his neighbourhood. In return for assistance in finding and citing violators who were not Adeyemi's clients, the Inspector was prepared to be lenient with those who were his clients. In this way, the sanitary inspector became another link in Adeyemi's chain between neighbourhood residents and the bureaucracy.

Mrs Cole* was one of the sanitary inspector's problems. She had become Adeyemi's client a few years earlier when her mother – also Adeyemi's client – died. Mrs Cole wanted to bury her mother in the compound of the house her mother built, and which Mrs Cole and her brother jointly inherited. For health reasons, home burial was reserved as the privilege of notables; only a chief could authorise it. Adeyemi successfully petitioned the chief of his division to allow Mrs Cole's mother to be buried in her house compound, and then he supervised the digging of the grave himself. In return, Adeyemi asked Mrs Cole to join the neighbourhood landlords' association to become its secretary.

Mrs Cole was more interested in business than in being a clerk. After inheriting her mother's house she and her brother built a row of stalls at the edge of their property and rented them to traders and artisans. The stalls, however, violated planning ordinances. The violations fell within the jurisdiction of the sanitary inspector. Adeyemi arranged for Mrs Cole and her brother to pay the sanitary inspector an annual gratuity in exchange for which he did not report the violations. One year, because of the distractions growing out of a dispute with her brother's wife – which Adeyemi later settled – neither Mrs Cole nor her brother offered the pre-arranged gratuity to the sanitary inspector. They were summoned to appear in court. If convicted, the fine would exceed their ability to pay. Adeyemi responded to Mrs Cole's plea for help by agreeing to ask the presiding judge of the customary court – whom he met through party activities and who subsequently became an in-law – to adjourn the case.

Before Adeyemi reached the customary court judge, he learned that Mrs Cole had also asked his neighbourhood rival to intervene in the case. Angered by what he saw as a threat to his dominance in patronage matters, Adeyemi confronted Mrs Cole with her 'duplicity' and announced he had 'washed his hands' of her; if she desired help from him in the future, she must deal with him exclusively. Adeyemi then suggested to the sanitary inspector that he allow any other interventions on Mrs Cole's behalf to go unnoticed, and to let her case run its full course in the court.

The transactions in this brief series of cases vividly illustrate the way in which one transaction was a link in a chain of many transactions; one involvement inevitably led to another. Through Adeyemi, the most humble residents of his neighbourhood could be brought into contact with three of the highest officials of Mushin: its Native Court judge, the chairman of its town council, and one of its paramount chiefs. Thanks to his visibility in official circles, this same series of transactions provided Adeyemi with a way to expand his connections (to include the sanitary inspector) and this, in turn, gave him the ability to exercise additional power among his neighbours. The close relationships between Adeyemi and the sanitary inspector, as it developed, meant that Adeyemi could strongly influence decisions as to whether or not residents could build (illegal) stalls for trading or other business purposes.

Another aspect of these relationships – and one that increased their closeness – was that there was frequent contact among the parties. Clients were expected to, and did, visit their benefactors frequently, even when they had no problems to solve. Adeyemi, for example, was visited by Mrs Cole, Yinka, and the sanitary inspector at least once a week and sometimes more often. Still another aspect of residential relationships was that each client usually lived with his or her family members who consequently became known to leaders, and vice versa, and involved with them. This was the case with Mustapha, Yinka, and Mrs Cole. Each of these aspects accounted for the relative ease with which client networks in neighbour-hoods could be mobilised when a need arose.

Client relationships were not institutionalised in Mushin as they were in many other places in Africa, such as northern Nigeria or Rwanda. In Mushin they were instrumental and highly self-interested. Indeed, clients were always looking for many sources of support, and it was incumbent upon leaders to 'sell' themselves or, in some way, to make themselves invaluable in their clients' lives. Leaders used several tactics in order to intensify their relationships with clients whom they valued. Frequent exchanges created strong bonds and potentially instilled a greater sense of solidarity between the parties involved. An advantage for the middleman was that, by giving much in many ways, he could build a strong sense of indebtedness on the part of clients and instill strong obligations to repay. The more beholden a client was, the greater the use he was to a leader.

Adeyemi was involved with many clients for long periods of time. This was another way of intensifying his ties with them. His relationship with the late Alhaji Adebola and his son, Mustapha, spanned two generations and had begun at least fifteen years earlier. The same was true of the two-generation relationship with Mrs Cole and her deceased mother, which had begun about ten years earlier. Both relationships had developed in such a way that they later included several members of a family and not single members. Furthermore, these relationships included many transactions of quite different content.

The multiplexity of the transactions was, then, another of the binding qualities of these client relationships. Adeyemi had assisted Mrs Cole with three quite unrelated problems: a ritual matter, a bureaucratic intervention, and a domestic quarrel. The same was true in the Adebola family, where he addressed both land and employment problems. Finally, he assisted Yinka and her siblings in many types of land disputes; in fact, cases 52 and 57 involved Yinka.

Adeyemi was known for his ability to deal with the whole individual. He had a strong sense of human nature and of human response to stress. Consequently he devoted all or part of twenty days to healing and therapeutic services. Problems ranged from a simple headache to severe mental illness. Adeyemi's ability to blend his social and psychological approaches in meeting client needs was epitomised in his treatment of a client who believed that her physical illness (diabetes) was associated with ill-feeling directed at her by a co-tenant (see cases 41, 44, 45, and 47).[19] Adeyemi administered several medicines to his diabetic client – prepared by yet another healer fifty miles away – and he climaxed the treatment with the sacrifice of a goat. Throughout the process, Adeyemi spread information about his client's problems and his ministrations to her throughout the neighbourhood. His goal was to create pressure on the co-tenant so that she would restore harmony in her house and indirectly help to restore his client's feelings of well-being. Using a combination of approaches, Adeyemi thus saw to the psychic and physical well-being of his client as conscientiously as he saw to her material and social needs. Indeed, Adeyemi consciously cultivated a reputation for dealing with a broad range of problems.

Adeyemi was also known for his ability to secure medicines that protected clients when they were involved in property disputes, as in case 42. Anyone who had a land case, Adeyemi explained, could be helped by one of at least ten different preparations, depending on the particulars of the dispute. Assistance to owners had far-reaching, political consequences. Each time Adeyemi helped an owner protect his property he assisted a new and permanent member of the neighbourhood to establish a legitimate presence. There were significant returns for leaders who performed these kinds of services. In Adeyemi's case, the diverse range of services he was willing to perform was a strategy which helped him to deal, in part, with the fact that he was not among the relatively wealthy or highly placed members of his community.

By contrast, some patrons and middlemen were known for their expertise, connections, or information in certain specific domains. One of the most successful neighbourhood leaders, S. A. Ojo,* used his knowledge of property problems to achieve upward mobility. Naturally, he attracted a high-status, owner clientele.

Ojo, an early Mushin settler, rose to high levels in public life. From the beginning, Ojo attracted owner clients by concentrating on the things which had the greatest value to them. Ojo familiarised himself with his locale, after he moved into his own house, and with other opportunities for purchasing houseplots in it. He recalled assisting more than twenty people to purchase plots near his own. Ojo became a hero to his owner-neighbours when he defended their and his property rights in a series of litigations which repeatedly threatened them with the loss of their houseplots and the houses they had built on them.[20] In Ojo's words, this is what happened:

We bought our houseplots from a member of the original Awori landowning family. Later, a man called Odesanya* claimed that the same Awori family sold this area to him. Court action came, and due to a legal technicality Odesanya was declared the owner of the land. We were compelled to pay his younger sister (his heir) because Odesanya died before the final court decision was made. By that time the worth of the plots had increased in value and we each were asked to pay her £100. I begged the sister's lawyer on our behalf, and the cost was finally lowered to £40 each.

The sister was made guardian of Odesanya's minor children. But she spent the money we paid her on her own children and did not use the money to care for the rightful heirs. When Odesanya's children were older, they filed a motion in court saying that they had realised no benefits from the land. They wanted the property returned to them. This time the court referred the case to the Administrator General. He ruled the children must benefit from the sale. If we each paid the children £100 immediately, the Administrator General would sign legal conveyances. Thereafter no court action would be taken against any of us. Because I was the leader of the group, the Administrator General said I must set an example and pay my own £100 at once, or he would confiscate the land and sell it to someone else. I did, and we have been left alone since that time.

The repeated demands by sellers on Ojo and his neighbours led him to master the complex land tenure system of the then colony. He learned how to deal with lawyers and court judges, so as to work effectively and knowledgeably with them. He also found sources from which his neighbours could borrow money in order to pay the extra sums that were levied against them. The loans were made by other neighbours, friends, Ojo himself, and a moneylender. In order to get the loans, especially from the moneylender, it was necessary for an intermediary who was known personally to the lender to vouch for the borrower and to apply sanctions against him if he defaulted on the payments. Ojo played this intermediary role. The reward to him, as might be expected, was a loyal following of neighbours.

Ojo's fame, however, grew even bigger following a neighbourhood drama which occurred a few years later. He described the incident as follows:

Mr Coker* bought two plots of land side by side. He developed one and left the other vacant. Mr Coker was a quiet man who kept to himself, but he came to me as a neighbour and we were friends. When he died a few years ago his only child inherited both plots, but he was too poor to develop the empty land that stood alongside his house. Another neighbour we knew to be unscrupulous decided to do his own friend a favour and 'sell' him the empty plot. I awoke one night to hear workers behind my house on Coker's land and realised it was a case of land stealing. Coker's son ran to me in great fear. Construction proceeded and intermediaries offered Coker's son money for the land. I told him to take nothing and led him to court where my testimony resulted in an injunction to cease all construction.

Ojo benefited from this incident primarily because his testimony was accepted by the court as the 'correct' version of the dispute. He would not have received as much acclaim if his testimony had been interpreted as just one version among several. There had been no written land conveyances in the original transaction. Yet Ojo's recollections that Mr Coker had been the 'rightful' purchaser, was recognised as the valid version of what had transpired. This recognition contributed greatly to establishing Ojo as an authority on land matters and it significantly enhanced his reputation as a figure who had credit in official circles.

LEADERSHIP SKILLS

In Mushin, a successful leader was made and not born. It took many skills, developed through experience, to move from helpful neighbour to successful leader. One of the skills which Mushin's leaders developed was the ability to balance the conflicting demands which clients made on their (the patrons') own goals, or the goals of their other clients, without alienating them. When Adeyemi was asked to fix the property tax of his client, Yinka, there was a conflict of interest. Clearly, he was unable to ask a favour of a man (Mustapha), whose father was once cheated by the very person who was now asking for a tax reduction. At the same time he did not wish to turn his client away. Yinka was a wealthy woman who brought many members of her family and of her Islamic prayer group to him for assistance. Adeyemi therefore quickly paid his own property tax. He then informed Yinka that it would not be in her interest for him to petition the tax assessor's office on her behalf, inasmuch as he had himself already paid that same amount.

The ability to understand and use communications channels to their own advantage was another skill which was related to the success of neighbourhood leaders. Both Ojo and Adeyemi consciously moulded public opinion by spreading information about their cases through their neighbourhoods. Adeyemi's treatment of the diabetic woman was one example. Following his usual routine, Adeyemi visited friends, shopkeepers, and prayer groups during the late afternoon and early evening hours and casually discussed the case. Later he reported to them that his treatment had been successful: the co-tenant made amends.

Clearly it was important for a leader to maintain the upper hand in his dealings with clients. A leader's reputation rested in large measure on his ability to control clients. When Mrs Cole asked his rival to solve the same problem she had asked Adeyemi to solve, Adeyemi countered by publicly complaining that she had violated an agreement between the two of them. He immediately withdrew from the case so that an evaluation could not be made of him nor could he be measured against his rival. The loss of a client lowered a patron's reputation, particularly if that loss was laid to the patron's lack of effectiveness. However, the patron who dropped a client first was seen to control the situation. Adeyemi felt secure in taking action against Mrs Cole. There had been a long, involved series of transactions between them, and he felt from experience that she would return to his fold. Meantime, the knowledge of his action against her warned other clients of the consequences of disloyalty.

As can be seen, part of the skill of a patron or a middleman was to disseminate information that was beneficial to clients. But in the process, there was the accompanying need to protect and manage one's own reputation. As in all of their endeavours, leaders were constantly required to balance clients' goals against their own. The one constant was that information from leaders had to be reliable. When the manager of a pools and lottery establishment (see case 65) asked Adeyemi to inform people of the neighbourhood that he was a fair businessman and not, as his competitors would have it, an 'unscrupulous scoundrel', Adeyemi did not take the request lightly. He explained:

You cannot lead your friends astray. When you act, you take responsibility on your shoulders, and you must be accountable for your recommendations. I do not take this responsibility lightly; I consider requests carefully.

In this case Adeyemi's investigations revealed that the pool's manager had once been jailed for fraud. Consequently he did not attempt to clear the man's reputation through his neighbourhood gossip channels. Adeyemi was reluctant to risk his own reputation, and in this instance, through his inaction, he let pass an opportunity to secure a new client.

It should be clear by this point that the reputation of leaders was linked to the status of the people with whom they dealt. This was true both of contacts and clients. Adeyemi gained prestige by making it known that he had connections to the town council, a court judge, practising lawyers, the police, and other useful people. Ojo did the same. Connections of this nature assisted both leaders to attract clients who themselves had high standing in the community. Furthermore Ojo and Adeyemi gained prestige from the fact that many of their clients were owners like themselves.

Skilful leaders made public display of their contacts whenever possible. The usual strategy was to invite important people to one's private ceremonies. One of Mushin's most successful leaders staged a lavish reception, following his daughter's marriage, in an open courtyard next to a hotel. The person who had agreed to act as master of ceremonies was the commissioner (head) of one of the Lagos State ministries. Other honoured guests and speakers came from among the community's most distinguished notables and officials. They were seated behind a long table on a raised platform at the centre of the courtyard, and introduced with high praise. Their names also were printed on a programme which was distributed to every guest present and to every visitor to the leader's home for the next few weeks.

Leaders were also assessed on the effectiveness of their services and ministrations. This placed pressure on them to perform, but the pressure was ameliorated by one feature. A leader who could in some way indicate that he had at least 'tried' to help his client was given credit for his efforts. It was, therefore, important to be visible in one's actions and, unless privacy was demanded by the circumstances of the particular case, to bring public witness to bear on one's attempts to act on behalf of others.

The style of a leader was yet another matter for public assessment. Effectiveness was related to style. The leader who had a 'sweet mouth', who was a gifted orator, was thought to be influential. So, too, was a leader of good character, who was patient, sociable, and generous, and who associated with others 'no matter their station in life'. The ideal leader, *gbajumo*, was described as a 'highly respected member of the community' who had a 'wide-ranging reputation'. The power of *gbajumo*, as Mushin residents explained, was derived from 'many contacts', 'the ability to mix with high and low people', 'the ability to do favours, distribute resources, and get things done'.[21]

CONVERTING NON-POLITICAL RESOURCES INTO POLITICAL CAPITAL

The greatest skill of neighbourhood leaders was their ability to convert non-political resources into political gains. In this respect their roles as middlemen, patrons, and dispute settlers were entrepreneurial. Adeyemi's successes as a patron and middleman who dealt in overtly non-political problems brought him a neighbourhood chieftaincy title. His reputation was such that he was eventually called to the Mushin Town Council for periodic consultations. Here he was able to influence in small ways the decisions and policies which guided the affairs of a large urban population. As for Ojo, he was elected to serve a three-year term as a town (then district) councillor. He was elected by his fellow ward residents who included the very neighbourhood owners whose land rights he had defended over the years. Ojo's election illustrated in a pointed way how a leader could mobilise his clientele for support. The owners he had defended earlier constituted a neighbourhood clique which acted as the nominating board of his ward's political party committee, and which nominated Ojo as their candidate for the post. After this, they campaigned among other neighbours and their tenants to vote for him.

Leadership positions were possible for people of widely varying economic circumstances. But upward mobility in the political system was usually – not inevitably – restricted by factors of wealth. In this respect, the careers of Adeyemi and Ojo took sharply different turns. Leaders who wished to move up in the system were expected to exhibit the qualities of a high public figure and to meet the responsibilities of such a figure. People who wished to move ahead, therefore, found it necessary to display their entrepreneurial talents in another direction – by amassing economic resources. In some instances, like that of Ojo, it was even possible to convert political gains into economic assets.

Ojo capitalised on his expertise in land matters and his reputation as a trusted defender of property rights to expand his personal economic base. He left his job with the railway and opened a private business as caretaker and rent collector for other, sometimes absent, owners. His reputation in property matters brought many owners to contract his services. At the height of his business career, Ojo managed more than fifty properties, and his income placed him at the lower end of the income scale of the nation's governmental elite.[22]

Ojo reinvested his wealth in other political ventures. He spent lavishly on gifts and hospitality, and he supported a large number of dependents. He also constructed a house in his hometown as a sign of his interest in that place. When the highest title in his hometown chieftaincy system fell vacant he used his wealth and the status gained from serving on the Mushin Town Council to secure the title. He valued his new chiefly role more than that of local councillor, and eventually withdrew from the Mushin political scene.

Whatever level neighbourhood leaders achieved, however, the one thing all of them needed was legitimacy. If information and connections were the resources that attracted people to aspiring leaders, people were the resources that aspiring leaders needed in order to attract legitimacy to their actions. Without followers there could be no leaders. At the beginning of their political careers neighbourhood leaders were not legitimated by formal institutions; neither did most of them hold offices. The free-floating quality of authority in Mushin's neighbourhoods was different from authority in formal institutions. There were no statutory sanctions at their command. Their main source of strength in carrying out leadership roles therefore came from being accepted by the people.

Acceptance was demonstrated in one way by the size of a leader's following. In the cases examined here, acceptance also was demonstrated by a leader's ability to step into offices or titles in the authority structures of the community. The town council and chieftaincy system, the subjects to which we now turn, were two ways in which authority became formally organised in Mushin and in which neighbourhood leaders were able to transform their political roles into political statuses.

CHAPTER FIVE

THE CHIEFTAINCY SYSTEM

When the Mushin District Council was created in September 1955, a host of separate settlements were brought together under a single administrative umbrella. But the task of drawing them into a unified political community with mutually defined goals and interests lay ahead. Mushin's many neighbourhood leaders faced two problems if they were to wield collective strength in this emerging polity. The first was to organise their informal political activities. The second was to give their informal activities a legitimate status and identity. The leaders of the new district, therefore, looked to tradition for organising principles and self-definition. They found them in the institution of chieftaincy.

Developing a chieftaincy system in the 1950s may seem, on the surface, to have been an anachronism. Party politics and the prospects of an independent government, with their attendant opportunities for political participation, were gaining momentum, whereas the statutory powers of chiefs were being eroded away by a government which was turning to the educated and, in its view, progressive elements, in order to run local community affairs.[1] In such a context, one may well question why Mushin leaders were eager to breathe life into what appeared to be a withering institution. The answers were cultural and pragmatic.

So far as culture was concerned, Yoruba-speaking peoples dominated the privileged stratum from which local leadership emerged. Despite the fact that the structure of chieftaincy systems varied widely throughout Yorubaland, the one element of political culture most of Mushin's leaders held in common – the one element which, despite foreign rule and the rise of an educated ruling class, remained open to ordinary citizens, be they educated or uneducated, rich or poor – was chiefship and the idea that certain political rights and opportunities in the wider community could be derived from holding a title. The models for a chieftaincy system surrounded the new District of Mushin, and thus, when its leaders were in a position to bring cultural content to political aspiration, chiefship was a logical choice.

In pragmatic terms, politicians wished to secure the support of chiefs in political campaigns. Each title-holder was the centre of a political arena consisting of kinsmen, clients, friends, and followers, and therefore each one presided over a natural and organised constituency from which politicians could seek votes and other forms of political backing. Politicians also saw personal benefits in the institution of chieftaincy. Titles gave legitimacy to political action, security of tenure, access to the centre, and, last but not least, honour and renown. Titles were not simply hollow markers of status, but resources which could be used profitably in the quest for political power and advancement. In creating a chieftaincy system the leaders of Mushin were expanding the political resources of the community not only for those whose favour they sought but also for themselves.

During the next two decades a chieftaincy system developed. It became more elaborate and clearly defined as the years passed. By 1975 it had developed a three-tiered hierarchy which was recognised and incorporated into the local government. This chapter describes the institution of chieftaincy as it took shape in Mushin: its structure, its functions, and, above all, the reasons for its growth and significance in the contemporary urban setting of Mushin.

THE BIRTH OF A CHIEFTAINCY SYSTEM

An appeal for chiefs opened the first meeting of the Mushin District Council. In his inaugural address, Chairman F. O. Okuntola recommended that the council strengthen itself by including chiefs. They would, in his words, 'perpetuate the traditional features of our society along modern lines'.[2] The chairman's recommendation was prompted by several considerations. Throughout Yoruba-speaking Nigeria a political community was organised around and represented by the institution of chiefship. Colonial administrators had recognised the importance of traditional authority figures outside Lagos Colony by incorporating them into their governing institutions and, in most cases, by designating the ọba (king) or senior chief of a community as the life president of the local district council. Next door to Mushin, there were functioning chieftaincy systems. One was the ancient chiefly hierarchy of municipal Lagos. It offered a valuable participatory outlet for Lagos' residents, and its chiefs were familiar to Mushin villagers as the Baba Isalẹ of the early colonial period. Another was a new chieftaincy system in Agege. Like Mushin, Agege was separated from the Ikeja Area Native Authority in 1955 and given its own district council. The leaders of Agege had reacted immediately to this development by naming the *Olu* of Agege as their paramount chief [3] and recommending that he preside over their new council. Ikeja also followed suit. With these examples in mind, Mushin's thirty elected councillors opened their first term by encouraging constituents to follow Yoruba custom and designate their own *ọba* and chiefs.

The seeds of chiefship were sown in Mushin before 1955. Village *Baalẹ* carried out political functions from the earliest times, and they were later joined by settler headmen and neighbourhood leaders such as the Ojos and Adeyemis of the preceding chapter. Quickening political events in the early 1950s gave these customary authorities and neighbourhood leaders greater responsibilities and more visibility. Indeed, some settlements took the first steps towards elevating the positions of these leaders by changing their titles from *Baalẹ* and headman to chieftaincy titles in the belief that the latter were more appropriate to an urban context. The names of six of these chiefs were submitted to the Mushin District Council for official recognition early in 1956. Three names were proposed by son-of-the-soil, Awori *idile*: the *Ọsọlọ* of Isolo, *Ọnitire* of Itire, and *Olu* of Ojuwoye.[4] Three other names were proposed by settler divisions: the *Olu* of Odi Olowo, *Ọdọfin* of Ejigbo, and *Elewu* of Ewu. The Ejigbo and Ewu titles were held by lineal descendants of settlement founders, although they were not Awori.[5] The Odi Olowo title was strikingly different from the others. The *Olu* of Odi Olowo, S. A. Adeleye, was one of twelve neighbourhood chiefs – all migrants – who banded together and created a chieftaincy division in the sector of Mushin known by that name. They *elected* one of their number as the senior title-holder; the remaining eleven took subordinate titles, and joined forces as an advisory council to the *Olu*. None of the twelve chiefs attained his position by virtue of inheritance. Each one was elected by fellow members of his neighbourhood landowners' association.

The reaction to the nomination of settler chiefs, as recorded in the district council minutes, was 'violent' and 'vehement'.[6] Up to this time, the *Baalẹ* were so restricted in their separate spheres of influence that their status – either as indigenous sons of the soil or as migrant settlers – was not a matter of public concern. Once they were elevated and drawn into a higher order of community-wide political activity, this status became significant. Chiefly titles, as indicated, carried with them many dividends: prestige, power to influence local policy, access to wide-ranging networks of politically and economically influential people, and the possibility of sitting in the Western Region House of Chiefs. When the Mushin District Council sought to recognise six senior chiefs, these positions immediately became valuable, and eligibility rules became a significant issue. This, then, aroused the passions of those who stood to gain or lose in the recognition process. In the settler view, establishing new chieftaincy divisions with paramount chiefs was consistent with modern urban politics, where highly valued offices could be acquired through one's achievements and efforts and not by virtue of one's ascribed status. For the sons of the soil, on the other hand, the actions of settlers were a threat to what they felt should be their exclusive domination of a suddenly attractive field of political activity.

The indigenous Awori strongly protested against the right of migrant settlers to hold senior chieftaincy titles. In terms of customary principles, the issue was fundamental. Both the Awori and the settlers agreed that senior titles should be held by landowners. They disagreed, however, over the interpretation of ownership. Led by representatives of Ojuwoye and Itire descent groups, the Awori argued that titles of senior rank should be restricted to sons of the soil – the first persons to settle in a place. According to the custom of many Yoruba communities, sons of the soil were the founders of ruling-house descent groups which, in turn, had exclusive rights to name their members as the highest office-holders in a community. In the Awori view, therefore, this son-of-the-soil principle excluded latter-day settlers who *purchased* land from holding offices which were equal to or, potentially, higher than their own.

Settlers countered the Awori on two grounds. First, they argued that by selling land outright, Awori forfeited the customary rights of sons of the soil to monopolise traditional offices of highest rank. Under the land tenure laws introduced by the British, the principle of freehold ownership conveyed legitimate and total transfer of land rights to a purchaser. Implicit in a freehold transaction, they reasoned, was a transfer of rights to political citizenship. Second, they felt responsible for bringing a new social order to Mushin and believed they were entitled to full political rights in that new order. When they arrived, settlers stated (in defending their political rights), Mushin was rural; they transformed what they saw as a backward, undeveloped area into a civilised, urban place and hence they felt entitled to share in its political life. In all of their arguments, settlers were careful not to deny the rights of Awori to hold titles of senior rank. Rather, their goal was to offer a rationale for full and equivalent rights to hold senior titles for themselves. In their view, the principle of determining eligibility to hold a high office should be expanded from an ascriptive orientation to include the principle of holding office through achievement.

The concept of seniority was fundamental to the Awori–settler debate. Most social interaction in Mushin (as in Yorubaland and beyond) carried with it a tacit evaluation of the relative seniority of each participant with respect to every other participant. The application of the seniority principle in political interaction meant that the most senior person (defined by age, sex, order of arrival, or condition of birth in, say, a ruling house descent group) had the right to exercise the greatest amount of authority. Whatever the context, a person knew how to rank himself or herself in relation to others on the basis of certain ascribed characteristics, and how to behave according to the outcome of that ranking.

Ranking was not absolute, however. An example of the flexibility that existed with regard to ranking was to be found in the problems that arose over naming streets. The first person to establish a street was considered its founder. The founder had the right to name the street, act as its senior resident, exercise certain rights and privileges in settling disputes on the street, or, as I found, recite the history of the street. The minutes of the Mushin District Council and chieftaincy meetings, and many oral histories recited to me, were filled with disputes between people claiming to be the rightful street founder. Ambiguities arose over whether the founder was the first person to buy land on the street, the first person to begin building a house, the first person to complete a house, the first owner to actually live in a completed house, and so on. In some cases, streets were divided in such a way that two claimants could each name part of them; in a few cases, streets were given two names.

There were four points of importance here. One was that the status of first settler, and its attendant seniority rights, were significant enough for individuals to wage bitter battles over that status. The second was that the rules governing status rankings were ambiguous enough to provide some degree of flexibility in the process of evaluating and assigning seniority. The third was that when a bundle of attributes (or rules) were used to determine seniority, there were possibilities for manipulating the rules, and for arguing that certain attributes had greater weight than others. The fourth was that rules could simply be *ex post facto* justifications for whatever arguments were logical, i.e. within the parameters of cultural acceptability, and hence satisfactory solutions to the parties involved in a dispute.

In Mushin, a senior authority figure was expected to play a strong role in settling disputes. Among the Yoruba peoples, conflict was usually resolved, not by the disputing parties, but by the most senior person (or senior group) present or relevant to the context where the dispute occurred. The prerogatives of seniority were such that the act of acknowledging another person's seniority over oneself potentially constituted a loss of part of one's personal sovereignty – particularly with respect to the management of conflict. 'Seniority guarantees obedience to authority', as one Yoruba scholar wrote, and it 'reinforces the concept of leadership'.[7] Hence, people who competed for political power were loathe to recognise the seniority of a rival, and they avoided contexts in which evaluations of seniority could be made. In public affairs, particularly, there was a reluctance to acknowledge the seniority of others if it tainted one's own claims to exercise the prerogatives of senior status. The fear of recognising others as senior was grounded in the reality that seniors deprive juniors of some part(s) of their personal or communal autonomy, i.e. their self-governing functions. Seniors had legitimate moral rights over juniors. Failure to comply with the orders of a senior was tantamount to severing one's ties with a group. Seniors were held in check, however, in that they were expected to fulfill certain obligations associated with fairness and to nurture people junior to them. For these reasons, the fear of allowing settlers to occupy senior statuses reached an extreme among Awori, who felt that the recognition of settlers might jeopardise their sovereignty in chieftaincy matters.

As is usually the case, rules were interpreted and rationales were presented in ways that reflected the realities of power. Mushin's new councillors had called for chiefs; and therefore the council was the logical forum for resolving their differences. The balance of power in the 1955 council reflected the demographic structure of Mushin District. Three quarters of the district's councillors were settlers: twelve of them from the disputed settler chieftaincy division of Odi Olowo, and one the newly-named *Olu* Odi Olowo himself. Needless to say, the majority of the councillors were fully aware of the fact that a strict interpretation of the son-of-the-soil principle would thereafter render settlers like themselves and their heirs ineligible to hold Mushin's senior titles. Since the balance of power was tipped in favour of settlers, the council recommended that the government recognise both settler and Awori chiefs.

While the council recommendation was pending ministerial approval, settlers took additional steps to strengthen their position. An *iwuye*, coronation ceremony, was held to install the new *Olu* of Odi Olowo on 4 March 1956 in the presence of the Muslim Seriki of Mushin, Chief Sanusi Ajalaruru.[8] The installation was an essential step in authenticating the chiefship. It was a public act, performed before witnesses who signalled their approval of the action that was being taken by virtue of their presence. Public support was one element which officials looked for in determining whether or not a chiefship was authentic.

In the meantime, a second struggle, equally bitter, arose over the attempts of councillors to centralise Mushin's chieftaincy system. Council members and other leaders asked the six *oba*, as they were now called, to select one of their number to serve as president of the council. In effect, the selection would single out one chief as senior to the others. Strong resistance came from the three Awori chiefs, none of whom was willing to see one gain supremacy over another. In an effort to give more substance to his claim of seniority, the *Olu Ojuwoye* changed his title to coincide with the district's name and called himself *Olu Mushin* of Ojuwoye.[9] He argued that a century earlier the Mushin Market, controlled by the Ojuwoye community, was a central meeting place for the area, and therefore Ojuwoye rightfully deserved the most senior position in the community. Vigorous objections were lodged by Isolo and Itire chiefs who argued that their status was equal to Ojuwoye's since all three descended from the same ancestor. The council resolved the issue by suggesting that each *oba* serve one year as president in a six-year rotation cycle. This plan also was forwarded to the Ministry of Local Government for approval.

To the surprise of Mushin's leaders, the petitions for recognition and a rotating council presidency were rejected. Word of the Awori–settler conflict and the inability of the six chiefs to top their hierarchy with one paramount authority figure reached colonial government officials. Their denial of recognition was based on this dissension and on three other objections: there had never been a traditional centralised authority in the area; the *Baalẹ* were formerly reluctant to cooperate with one another in village group councils or the Ikeja Area Native Authority and they had sent representatives to these bodies in their stead; and the chiefs did not play a strong historical role in the development of the area. In short, the absence of unity, centrality, and deep historical tradition was equated with a lack of authenticity.

Failure to gain official recognition stimulated, rather than dampened, activities of Mushin's *de facto* chiefs. The most important response was the emergence of three new chieftaincies: two settler and one Awori. One of the new settler chieftaincy divisions was Shomolu,[10] a rapidly urbanising sector of the district. Shomolu installed Lamidi Suberu as its *Jagunmolu* in 1959 in the presence of a large crowd which included F. O. Okuntola,[11] who had advanced from his post as chairman of the Mushin District Council to become, in 1957, an elected member of the Western Region House of Assembly. This chiefship was encouraged by the Shomolu and District Welfare Association, an organisation of neighbourhood leaders originally established for this purpose. The other settler chieftaincy was at Oshodi, where a chief with Lagosian, and before that Nupe ancestry, was proposed as one of Mushin's senior chiefs.[12] The new Awori chieftaincy emerged at Onigbongbo where the *Baalẹ* (the title was not elevated) claimed he should be added to the ranks of the district's senior title-holders.[13] For reasons unknown to me, two of the original claimants to senior chief status, the *Ọdọfin* of Ejigbo and *Elewu* of Ewu, dropped out of community-wide chieftaincy activities, and allowed their claims for recognition to lapse into dormancy. By about 1960 there were, then, seven chieftaincy divisions operating informally in Mushin: four Awori and three settler.

CHIEFTAINCY POLITICS IN THE PARTY ERA

Chieftaincy politics was tied closely to party politics between 1955 and 1966. Many chiefs were active party members. A few had contested successfully under the AG banner for election to Mushin District Council posts in 1955 and 1958, and three *ọba* were appointed to serve on the Mushin District Council between 1960 and 1962. This meant that chiefs were directly involved in both party and chiefly affairs, often mixing the two together.

The Action Group (AG) also used neighbourhood landowner associations, their leaders, and chiefs as grassroots units in its organisation. Party leaders attended chiefs' meetings from time to time, asking them to campaign for the AG and to raise money. On one occasion a chieftaincy division donated £50. The relationship became even more formal in 1962 when the ǫba were asked to appoint two of their divisional council members to attend the weekly meetings of the AG's Executive Committee of Mushin. Although the chiefs carried out other functions, the relationship of many of them to the AG at this time was such that they were acting as a virtual arm of the party.

In return for their assistance, party leaders and councillors who did not hold titles acted as spokesmen for the ǫba to government in an ongoing struggle to gain official recognition for them. Indeed, the chiefs were beholden to community leaders for their continued existence and support, and they became their clients. The non-titled politician leaders, on the other side, sought large blocs of voters in their election contests; naturally they were eager to serve as patrons to the chiefs and to secure access through them to the chiefs' supporters. These politician-patrons regularly urged the seven chiefs to name a senior ǫba from within their ranks. Just as regularly the choice fell on the chief of one of the three Awori divisions of Ojuwoye, Isolo, or Itire. Each time a choice was made, however, the selection was blocked by the other two. The overriding fear of each chief was that he and his descendants would be placed permanently in a subordinate status to someone else. Despite the fact that the senior chiefs began meeting together and making sacrificial offerings on behalf of unity, any move toward topping the chieftaincy hierarchy with a single, central figure was firmly resisted. The inability of the chiefs to make this choice severely hampered the politicians' case. Yet they tried again in 1963, by submitting fourteen names – two from each of the seven chieftaincy divisions – to the government for official recognition. The petition was denied; but instead of a justification for its position, the government launched an inquiry to determine why there had been a sudden expansion in the number of Mushin's senior title-holders.[14] Political events were such, however, that the inquiry was not concluded.

Finally, seven senior chiefs were officially recognised in 1965.[15] Paradoxically, the recognitions were not sponsored by AG leaders. The explanation for this unexpected twist of fate lay in political events in the Western Region that were external to Mushin but which had a strong effect on its internal affairs. In 1963, the AG split into two factions. The AG retained its hold on Mushin, but a rival Yoruba party, the Nigerian National Democratic Party (NNDP) took over the Western Region Government. Because it seized power through a political manoevre, and not through elections, NNDP had no grassroots organisation in places such as Mushin, and to compensate for it, NNDP recognised a number of chiefs throughout the region with the hope that it would gain support and build local power bases.[16] In exchange for recognition, Mushin's ọba were expected to abandon their earlier AG loyalties and cross over to the NNDP, which some of them did, although several of them secretly returned to the AG fold. The *Olu* of Odi Olowo, who was also rewarded by the NNDP with an appointment to the Mushin District Council, however, did not return to the AG.

The defections of the ọba had an explosive effect on the community. For a complex set of reasons, not the least of which was that no rewards were offered to junior title-holders or to most of the politician leaders of the community, the newly recognised ọba were scorned by their supporters and left to pursue their new party allegiance alone. The *Olu* of Odi Olowo was ostracised by his junior chiefs and political patrons. They named a regent in his place and met without him. The houses of two ọba were burned to the ground. In one case, so it was believed, a moneylender foreclosed a chief's mortgage so that he could not rebuild on the site. Eventually several ọba fled Mushin and remained away until after January 1966 when a military coup put an end to party politics in Nigeria for the next twelve years.

CHIEFTAINCY POLITICS UNDER THE MILITARY GOVERNMENT

The military takeover threatened the existence of Mushin's chieftaincy system. Soon after taking power, the new government conducted an investigation into the authenticity of the titles which were recognised during the NNDP regime. Elsewhere, many of them were revoked, including several NNDP-backed titles at Ikeja. In Mushin, the first warning came when the district's newly convened Chieftaincy Committee was dismissed.[17]

Settlers were particularly alarmed by the military government's actions. Unlike long-established chieftaincies, the title-holding rules in settler chieftaincies were not clearly worked out. Was an elected chief a chief for life, or could he be replaced? The initial inclination to the defection of the *Olu* of Odi Olowo, after ostracising him, was to replace him. As government investigations proceeded, however, settlers reversed their position. They were advised by political leaders that if investigators learned the *Olu* had been ousted because of an unpopular party affiliation, the recognition of the title could be labelled an instrumental, partisan act rather than an attempt to perpetuate a time-honoured custom. Demonstrating that a chiefship was permanent therefore was one way to demonstrate its authenticity. With this in mind, Odi Olowo leaders and junior chiefs reinstated their ọba on the condition, as they recorded in their minutes, that he 'dance to our tune'. Without the support of his fellow ward chiefs, the *Olu* had no arena in which to function. Without their support his recognition also could be revoked, and therefore the *Olu* was forced to accept their terms.

At Shomolu, another settler division, party affairs also left their mark on the chiefship. Two pretenders had attempted to secure recognition, each through a different political party. When the military came to power, both chiefs claimed to be the rightful *ọba*. *Jagunmolu* Lamidi Suberu had been publicly installed. His rival, *Olu* Karimu Apata, had been capped in a secret 3 a.m. counter-installation. In this instance, demonstrating that a chiefship was openly and publicly witnessed was the necessary proof of legitimacy, and Jagunmolu Suberu was accepted by officials as the rightful holder of the title.[18]

As a whole, Mushin's chieftaincy system had survived the divisiveness of party politics and its aftermath. The capacity of chiefs and their followers to reconcile their differences under the military was taken as proof of their authenticity, unity, and continuity – the qualities which higher authorities sought in their evaluation and final acceptance of 'traditionality' in chiefship.

Interest in the chieftaincy system intensified once it was secure. Under the military, many avenues for political participation were reduced. There were no elected or party posts, and many politically-oriented organisations were banned. The chieftaincy system offered one of the few remaining outlets for exercising legitimate leadership roles in the community. To be sure, the government appointed civic leaders to advisory boards and committees – posts which were highly valued due to their scarcity.[19] Such appointments went primarily to people with large followings whose leadership capabilities were clearly acknowledged in the community. Thus when chiefs of Odi Olowo and other divisions revitalised their activities in 1966, they were joined by prominent civic leaders who during the party era had held councillorships, court appointments, or party offices, but not chiefly titles. These participants took active roles in chieftaincy affairs with an eye to securing what they needed in order to prove their authenticity as community leaders: titles and followers.

The chieftaincy divisions expanded in response to these new circumstances. The number of junior chiefs increased, although they had never been officially recognised. Up to this point most junior titles – all those chiefs below the *ọba* – were held by elected representatives of wards in the settler divisions, or by descent group nominees in Awori divisions. Now, the *ọba* and their councils began to confer honorary (personal) titles on prominent civic figures. As in most traditional Yoruba polities, honorary titles were for life, but they were not perpetuable. Honorary titles were usually conferred from above by an *ọba* or an *ọba* and council, in contrast to established (hereditary or ward) titles which were selected from below by the descent group or ward which held that right.

The climax of this expansion process was reached when the junior chiefs also were recognised by the government at a state-sponsored *iwuye* in May 1975. The newly recognised chiefs included both ward and descent group title-holders and honorary title-holders. Settler chieftaincies installed the majority of the junior chiefs: thirty-one in Shomolu, eighteen in Odi Olowo, and eight in Oshodi. Awori divisions installed fourteen chiefs at Onigbongbo and thirteen at Itire. Eighty-four titles were officially approved, but several intervening deaths meant that only eighty-one title-holders were actually installed at the ceremony. Moreover, the installation of Mushin (Ojuwoye) and Isolo junior chiefs was delayed so that their *ọba*, both newly named, could nominate some of their own junior chiefs. In their declarations, Ojuwoye named five and Isolo four junior chiefs, all established, but no honorary title-holders. This brought the number, although still incomplete, to fifty-seven in settler and thirty-six in Awori divisions.

The kinds of people who were recognised as chiefs were, sociologically speaking, quite similar whether they were settler or Awori. All, of course, were landowners and a majority were independent entrepreneurs, such as contractors, merchants, rent and debt collectors or artisans, or had become entrepreneurs after retiring from salaried positions as clerks or civil servants. At least eight of the authorised titles went to women, some in recognition of their roles as market leaders, some as leaders of women, and some as leaders with no particular qualification that was restricted to their gender. (At least two unauthorised titles also went to women.) Of the fourteen title-holders that were known to me, half had finished primary school, half had no education; religious preferences had divided between Christianity and Islam; and, strikingly, all but one had been party activists during the civilian regime. Settlers had wide-ranging Yoruba origins including Ilesha, Ife, Ekiti, Ijebu, and Egba, although the latter two, being close to Mushin, predominated. Even an Awori settler became a chief in a settler division. Thus, while their social lives did not appear to divide Awori and settlers, their political aspirations did.

The recognitions of chiefs culminated a lengthy series of initiatives by Mushin leaders and responses by government which were designed to strengthen traditional authorities. A new chiefly body, the Lagos State Council of *Ọbas* and Chiefs, had been inaugurated by the government in 1970. The *Olu* of Mushin, Jimoh Aileru, was elected by the nineteen paramount chiefs of Ikeja Division to represent its three districts of Mushin, Ikeja, and Agege in the State Council. A year later, in 1971, the seven Mushin chiefs were asked to reconvene the Chieftaincy Committee of the Mushin Town Council. The first chairman was the *Ọnitire* of Itire,

Sunmola Layeni.[20] Within still another year, the seven ọba of Mushin were allocated annual salaries.

During this period, government officials directed each chieftaincy division to formalise, in writing, its succession and eligibility rules. The chieftaincy declarations, as they were called, were filed with the Town Council around 1975. The acceptance of the declarations constituted the government's approval of each division and its right to exist in the form, and with the rules, set down by its members.

Official recognition of both the chiefs and the rules governing their activities did not freeze the development of the chieftaincy system. Only a few days after the eighty-four junior titles were conferred, the members of one chieftaincy division met to consider additional titles it would soon propose for official recognition. The move was intended not only to appease the disgruntled leaders who had not been given titles, but also to encourage others to feel that titles were not limited. The chiefly hierarchy also became more elaborate. One ward association began to confer titles, informally, on its own neighbourhood leaders. This action thereby introduced a third-level – a tier of chiefs below the ward chiefs – into the system.[21] Finally, the receptive climate for chiefships prompted two other divisions to apply for government recognition. One was Ewu, a division which made an original claim for recognition in 1955, and the other, Shogunle.[22] Disputes over these petitions arose, and therefore they were not resolved as of 1975.

In the final analysis, the twenty-year process of securing official recognition of seven chieftaincy divisions with some 100 senior and junior title-holders rested on the fulfillment of three conditions. First, no claim to a title could be made without the support of a substantial number of followers who, themselves, acknowledged the legitimacy of the title and an individual's right to hold the title for life. For the Awori, the necessary support came from large descent groups which, for at least a century, had named headmen of the settlements in which they lived. Settler claimants were given the support of neighbours who also chose headmen and then united behind them in landowner associations. Both the Awori and the settlers had thus followed the widespread Yoruba custom of acknowledging a senior authority figure in a residential situation. The titles were a logical extension of this authority.

Second, no claim to a title could be made without the consent and support of some of the political leaders who operated in the full community, and thus above the level of the separate chieftaincy divisions. In essence, a claim of one segment (a chieftaincy division) of the community had to meet the approval of, and fit into, the overall interests of the whole community and the people who wielded power in it, or that claim would not reach the proper forums for recognition: the Mushin District Council, the party in power, the Western Region Government, and eventually the military-run Lagos

State government. It was possible for a claimant to have the support of followers, and not that of higher-level community leaders – which is what I suspect happened to the chiefs of Ejigbo and Ewu. Without support from above, these title-holders appear to have been unable to function effectively beyond their neighbourhoods.

Third, no claim to a title could be upheld without public affirmation of its legitimacy. The holding of an *iwuye* constituted this affirmation. An *iwuye* was a rite of passage which ritually transformed an individual from the status of ordinary citizen to that of privileged member of the community who thereafter enjoyed special, spiritually sanctioned rights and obligations. The ceremony ordinarily consisted of some form of ritual humiliation during which the candidate was unclothed or in some way degraded, and then some form of ritual honour during which the candidate was reclothed in chiefly regalia and ceremoniously presented to the public. The *iwuye* invested supernatural power on chiefs with the placing of the leaves of an *akoko* tree (*Newboldia laevis, Bignoniaceae*) on their heads. The tree was believed to be the dwelling place of spiritual forces and sacred to Ogun, the god of iron and warfare, who was also symbolically represented at coronation ceremonies in the form of the 'sword of justice'.

An *iwuye* established a significant precedent. It was a public act, performed before ordinary people and prominent citizens who both acted as witnesses and signalled their consent by participating in the event. Without an *iwuye*, a title was neither legitimate nor permanent, but still open to the vicissitudes of political competition. Once a title was properly conferred, it could not be taken away; a title-holder could be promoted to a higher level in the hierarchy, but he could not be deprived of the title.

Ultimately, the *iwuye* symbolised the coming together of two kinds of support: followers from wards or descent groups, below, and prominent leaders from the full community, above. The *iwuye* also symbolised permanence: it set irrevocable precedents. The *iwuye*, then, was a display of power. Once the people of Mushin publicly displayed the breadth and the continuity of that power, their chiefly representatives were eligible for recognition by the even higher forces of the state.

THE STRUCTURE AND FUNCTION OF THE CHIEFTAINCY SYSTEM

The structure of the Mushin chieftaincy system, as it appeared in 1975, was pyramidal. The political units at the lowest level were the *adugbo* (ward or quarter), in the settler case, and the *idile* (descent group) in the Awori case. The middle level consisted of seven chieftaincy divisions, each with a council of title-holding chiefs who represented either ward or *idile* and who

were presided over by an *ọba*. The top level was the Mushin Town Council
Chieftaincy Committee on which sat the seven *ọba* representing each of the
chieftaincy divisions. Unlike most Yoruba communities, this hierarchy was
not topped by a single *ọba*. Instead, Mushin's *ọba* acted in concert, although
they eventually agreed to name a rotating chairman of the Town Council
Chieftaincy Committee, and this person temporarily served as first among
peers.

The lowest level, the wards, consisted of all households located within
specific, geographic boundaries, or the *idile,* consisted of one or more
branches of kinsmen whose political rights ultimately derived from their
status as lineal descendants of the first settlers of villages that had become
incorporated into Mushin. Both of these units were potent forces in the
political system because each of them held permanent rights to name titled
chiefs as their representatives in wider community affairs. They were, in a
fundamental sense, permanent representational units with 'constituencies'.

The ward constituents who had rights to participate in selecting the titled
chief were its houseowners.[23] But not all owners participated in chieftaincy
affairs. In one ward, roughly 20 to 25 per cent of the owners – and there were
some 400 houses – were active to varying degrees in ward association
activities; most of the inactive resident owners kept abreast of ward activities through their active neighbours. This estimate represented the number
of owners who participated in a ward where leadership was relatively
strong. Some wards had weak leadership, and therefore owners were less
active in them. Theoretically, each owner served as a link between his ward
owners' association and his tenants and clients. In practice, this relationship
was not explicit, since tenants had little interest in neighbourhood politics
as such. Their interest, and the kind of activity they were engaged in, was to
secure assistance, not to assert influence or authority – a stance which is
more fully explained in the next chapter. The title-holders in strong wards,
it might be noted, sometimes attracted followers from outside the ward
because of their abilities to make contact with higher-order institutions and
authorities. For the most part chieftaincy activities at the ward level were
geographically localised in that they were the concern of men and women
who had a vested interest in their place of residence and wished to participate actively in local political affairs.

The same partial participation can be seen among kinsmen in *idile* affairs
relating to chieftaincy. The constituents of *idile* who were eligible to join in
selecting the group's title-holder were, in theory, all of the adult members.
Some members were interested in the group and its chieftaincy activities;
others were not. Often only senior members of the *idile,* or of each branch,
were the ones who took decisions, managed the estate, and involved themselves in chieftaincy matters. Nevertheless all members were eligible to
attend *idile* meetings, although they were not able to assert the same degree

of influence as elders were in steering its affairs. Other people also took roles in *idile* affairs, such as clients, neighbours, or ex-slaves who resided in the original villages. Many of these individuals were treated as kinsmen and therefore it was often difficult to differentiate between them and lineal kin until it was time to choose a title-holder. Then a dividing line was commonly drawn between lineal (mainly biological) members who were eligible to hold a title and sociological (mainly adoptive) members who were not.

Idile chiefs also sought followers who had no role in *idile* affairs but who were interested in what the title-holder could do for them in exchange for their loyalty and support. They came from anywhere in the district or metropolitan area. In fact, many *idile* members were dispersed throughout the metropolitan area. (The *idile* was not a co-resident group as was the ward.) The extent of influence or support given a chief – whether it came from kin or not – varied according to his personal strength. One Awori chief was known to have had a very large following of Awori, settlers, and Lagosians; another appeared to have little contact outside his settlement and descent group.

The influence and activity of an Awori chief and his *idile* emanated from an identifiable place: the site of the original settlement where Awori chiefs, and particularly their *ǫba*, conventionally resided. In the process of creating electoral wards in the 1950s, these old settlements became the natural core areas for official wards. They also were the sites for meetings of the chieftaincy division's *ǫba* and council or, for what were described as, town meeting-like gatherings. However, the full sphere of influence of Awori chiefs was not geographically restricted to a ward; nor did it penetrate an entire ward. A few independent landowner associations, for example, formed in or near old Awori settlements, but they did not seem to function as part of the chieftaincy division.

Thus, Awori chieftaincies were geographically focused but not geographically bounded. As such they faced recruitment problems because their target populations were free-floating and not bound together in easily accessible units. By contrast, ward-based chieftaincies were structurally designed so that their leaders could reach out to broad ranges of people, through the automatic linkages between each resident, via the landlord or landlady, to a ward chief. This was, in my view, one of the reasons for settlers' success in organising themselves and asserting the kind of influence which brought official recognition to their chiefs.

At the middle level, each chieftaincy division was organised differently. All of them had different succession rules, which are summarised in Table 12. Eligibility to hold an *oba* title in the Awori chieftaincy divisions and in settler Oshodi was dependent on membership in a ruling house descent group. Most of these descent groups had several branches, and as a result,

Table 12 Mushin Chieftaincy Divisions: succession rules and title-holders, 1975

Recognised chieftaincy division	Isolo (Awori)	Itire (Awori)	Odi Olowo (Settler)	Ojuwoye (Awori)	Onigbongbo (Awori)	Oshodi (Settler/Lagosian)	Shomolu (Settler)
Title of senior chief in division	Osolo	Onitire	Olu	Olu Mushin	Baale	Baale	Jagunmolu
Senior title holder as of 1975	D. O. Farombi	A. A. S. Layeni	S. A. Adeleye	Y. Amodu	R. A. Asabiyi	Y. Ajenifuja	L. Suberu
Principles regulating senior chiefs							
Type of chieftaincy	Ruling house[a]	Ruling house	Elective	Ruling house	Ruling house	Settler/ Ruling house	Elective
Eligible ruling houses (in order of succession)	Alagbeji Okota Adeola	Omatashe Gbonyin Odofin Odunburu	NA	Aiyeleru Odu Abore	Olaside Abigbe Iluobi	?[b]	NA
Succession principle	Rotation of eligible ruling houses	Rotation of eligible ruling houses	Election from among ward-held titles	Rotation of eligible ruling houses	Rotation of eligible ruling houses	?	Election from among ward-held titles
Eligibility principle for senior chief	Male and female members of ruling house. Chosen by majority vote	Male members of ruling house (females only if no eligible male).	Automatic promotion up ladder of ward-held titles (arranged	Male members of ruling house (females only if no eligible male).	Male members of ruling house (females only if no eligible male).	?	Majority vote of 23 kingmakers.

Principles regulating junior chiefs

	of eligible house members.	Chosen by majority vote of eligible house members.	in pre-established order).	Chosen by majority vote of eligible house members.	Chosen by majority vote of eligible house members.	?
Junior chiefs recognised as kingmakers (titles can be established or honorary)	Chief Jagun	Bashorun	Asoju	Eletu	Balogun	Oworonsoki
	Osuro	Otun Oba	Ashiwaju	Oluwo Abore	Otun Baale	Apelehin
	Omotoba	Osi Oba	Sobaloju	Otun Ekerin	Osi Baale	Okuta
	Ogbeni Ogod	Ekerin Oba	Ajiroba	Oluwo Aiyeleru	Afobaje	Serike
		Seriki	Babaguwa	Asiwaju Oba	Ekerin	Orile Bariga
		Balogun	Bada		Aro	Igbari
		Asiwaju Oba			Ajigbeda	Owode
		Aro			Iyalode	Ifelodun
		Agbadefunoba				Magoluku
						Aiyetoro
						Ibu Owo
						Temidire
						Orile George
						Orile Shomolu
						Bashua
						Bajulaiye
						Debari
						Pedro
						Daranijo
						Obanikoro
						Idi Araba
						Abule Oja
						Anthony Segi

Table 12 continued

Recognised chieftaincy division	Isolo (Awori)	Itire (Awori)	Odi Olowo (Settler)	Ojuwoye (Awori)	Onigbongbo (Awori)	Oshodi (Settler/ Lagosian)	Shomolu (Settler)
Role of kingmakers[c]	Ratify choice	Ratify choice	Ratify choice	Ratify choice. Ifa oracle also ratifies	Ratify choice	?	Elect senior chief
Other recognised junior chiefs of divisions (not kingmakers; titles can be established or honorary)	?	Iyalode Erelu Ajigbeda Alaga si Ilu	Otun Ilu Bashorun Balogun Akogun Seriki Are Aro Sarumi Abese Odofin Jagunna	? Odofin	Are Ona Kakanfo Ajiroba Erelu Bashorun Bajito Bobajiro	Otun Baale Gboganiyi of Osi Balogun Iyaloja Are Odorin Ashipa Aro	Akogun Asiwaju Bada Iyalaje Lukosi of Abule-Okuta Ashipa Majeobaje of Akoka Shomolu
Eligibility principle for junior titles	Awori & Settlers	Awori & Settlers	Settlers	Awori & Settlers	Awori & Settlers	Settlers	Settlers

[a] Ruling house means descendants of a common ancestor who are entitled, according to custom, to nominate a candidate(s) for a chieftaincy title.

[b] Succession rules had not been filed as of June 1975.

[c] Kingmakers may select the senior title holder if several candidates are nominated or if agreement cannot be reached by a ruling house.

succession was usually regulated by rotation. By contrast, as already indicated, *ọba*ships in settler divisions were elective. The original twenty-three settlements of Shomolu each owned a junior chieftaincy title, and the *Jagunmolu* was elected by a majority vote of this full group. The twelve Odi Olowo wards also owned chieftaincy titles, and the first *ọba* was elected from, and by, the twelve chiefs. Succession to the Odi Olowo *ọba*ship after the death of the first one was by promotion, according to a pre-established order of seniority, so that each of the twelve wards would eventually hold that title in turn.

The chieftaincy divisions also developed their own rules with respect to the allocation of *junior* titles. All of them had two kinds of junior titles: established and honorary. The nature of the established titles differed according to whether the division was a ruling house or an elective chieftaincy division. Established junior titles in Awori divisions belonged to an *idile* and, although they were acquired through inheritance, candidates were still subject to a selection process conducted within the title-holding descent group or descent group branch. In settler divisions established junior titles were owned by the wards and acquired through an election conducted by local landowners. In all chieftaincy divisions, honorary titles could be given either to Awori or to settlers, but one of them, Isolo, had conferred none on settlers as of 1975. In most cases the *ọba* took the lead in conferring honorary titles, although in some instances his council of advisors asserted influence in this matter.

There was another class of titles within the junior rank, known as *kingmaker* titles. Kingmakers formed small 'committees' which performed the task of either choosing from among several nominees or ratifying the selection of an *ọba*. In Awori divisions, most kingmakers were chiefs who were members of a ruling-house descent group. In settler divisions, there were two practices. In Odi Olowo, honorary title-holders, along with a few ward chiefs served as kingmakers. In Shomolu, the full body of ward chiefs served as kingmakers.

The chieftaincy division councils of junior chiefs and their *ọba* carried out a variety of functions. They were no exception to the rule that informal authority figures were deeply involved in settling disputes. But the cases taken to them tended to be community-oriented rather than personal. Market rivalries, succession disputes, and landowner association conflicts were some of these problems. When the Chief of Aiyetoro, for example, mishandled a complaint of her fellow owners, she was instructed by the *ọba* and council to apologise to her landowner association. For the most part, the activities at the division level were largely centred on perpetuating and upholding the prestige attached to traditional offices. The chiefs' meetings frequently were devoted to allocating titles and adjusting seniority rankings – a matter to which we return in Chapter 8. Membership recruitment was also a critical task, inasmuch as the influence and honour of an ǫba and his chiefs were measured by the number and stature of persons sitting on the council and the seriousness of community matters that came before them.

Outside the chieftaincy division councils, the functions of junior chiefs were wide ranging. They were known to preside over their own descent group affairs, if appropriate; over their settlements; and starting in the 1950s, over landowner associations. In all instances, the welfare of members, followers, or clients was a key responsibility. Part of this responsibility, again, involved the management of conflict; in time it became a prime aspect of a chief's role. In the past, chiefs concentrated on seeing that their settlements were populated in an orderly fashion, that they were protected, and that taxes were collected. Later, some of these functions were taken over by the government, and ward chiefs began to lobby for things like trash removal, road upkeep and paving, flood control, and other amenities. The minutes of district council meetings and reports of government investigations indicated that neighbourhood chiefs and landowner associations were the most active pressure groups in the community. If nothing else, the chiefs provided a focus around which small-scale communal action took place.

Succession rules for (junior) ward and descent group chiefs, unlike those for the ǫba, were not formalised. Selections were, in most of the cases with which I was familiar, highly competitive and often the focus of bitter rivalries. Ideally the oldest landowner in a ward or the oldest descent group member was the natural choice. But as we have seen in analogous situations, there was a bundle of attributes which could be manipulated in evaluating the suitability of candidates or their eligibility to hold office. Wealth, knowledge, prestige gained from holding offices in other organisations, influence in political circles, and oratorical or diplomatic skills were only a few of the qualities that were weighed in the search for title-holders.

When a new ward chief was to be selected, owners who were prominent in their neighbourhoods met informally as kingmakers and began to sift through the names of possible candidates. The process sometimes required months of negotiation and compromise. Selection of a chief was carried out primarily by reaching a consensus of all interested and prominent owners in a ward. When consensus could not be reached, the ǫba and his council were asked to step in and moderate between opposing factions until a suitable candidate could be agreed upon. Even at this level it was necessary to have the support of both a constituency and influential superiors, since the latter decided the outcome of disputed contests. In truth, many of the same qualities that brought titles to neighbourhood figures such as Adeyemi and Ojo – the two entrepreneurial leaders who were described in the previous chapter – brought chieftaincy titles to others. The one element which people who desired established titles could not control was that they needed the support of the ward or descent group which controlled the title in order to receive its nomination. (The element which people who desired personal titles needed was the nomination of an ọba and his council.)

The highest level in the chieftaincy system, the Mushin Town Council Chieftaincy Committee, consisted only of the ọba. It was not a policy-making body, as it would have been in a pre-colonial system. It served as the intermediary link between two authority systems: the chieftaincy system and the local government. It advised the town council in general matters, oversaw chiefly affairs, and adjudicated cases that arose in chieftaincy divisions, usually over disputed titles. These cases represented the very telling fact that, despite the regularisation of succession rules for ọba, a title was a highly desirable item and, therefore, the selection of new chiefs produced a never-ending series of claims and counter-claims as to authenticity.

Mushin's ọba performed a crucial service in the community by serving as a channel for transmitting information from the highest levels of government to the lowest levels of the public, as they did in the pre-colonial setting. This service was made possible, of course, by the pyramidal structure of the system. In Mushin, the ọba were looked to by government officials as the first link in a network through which they could communicate to junior chiefs and then to the people. As one civil servant put it: 'The people know the ọba; they don't know us.' The ọba and chiefs interpreted government policy – in one case, tax reforms – or explained official, but sometimes unsettling procedures, such as voting and census taking. In the other direction, the chiefs relayed the pulse of the public upwards in an effort to influence and inform those who made the rules by which residents were to live. The ọba also played a role in the community's ceremonial life. They appeared at important community rituals. When a new Committee of Management of the Mushin Town Council was installed in 1975, the ọba attended as a group, wearing the regalia of office and accompanied by retinues of followers. Their presence not only lent authority and dignity to civic events, such as this one, it also brought a sense of mystical sanction to them.

The civic obligations of chiefs stemmed from the belief that the ọba were guardians of public order and community well-being. According to time-honoured custom, chiefs were repositories of social wisdom and supernatural power. In the contemporary urban context, knowledge was dispersed and it no longer was monopolised by the elder members of the society. Yet for a large sector of the population, particularly the illiterate or minimally educated residents – who were, in fact, the majority of the Mushin's adult population – the chiefs were the dispensers of sacred and secular wisdom whose ritual roles were essential to the community if it was to thrive and prosper.

Many of the new chiefs came to office not knowing how to perform rituals of community renewal, and without predecessors to teach them their new duties. They therefore sought the skills they needed from traditional authorities in other places. One Mushin chief, I was told, was trained to propitiate *Ẹsu*, the trickster *orisa* (deity) generally associated with markets and market women. Others were prepared to perform or oversee rituals associated with *Orisa Oko, Egungun*, and *AgẹmỌn*. When a cholera epidemic spread throughout the city in 1971, *Ọro* devotees came forward at the behest of one *ọba* to drive away the disease and to restore the confidence of residents. Nevertheless changes were introduced, and at least one *ọba* successfully substituted Islamic ritual for the traditional *orisa*-oriented ceremonies. In other ritual matters, the *ọba* were expected to attend or send their representatives to funerals of prominent citizens. They were empowered to authorise the burial of notables in their own compounds or beneath the floor of their rooms. In the interests of city sanitation this privilege was reserved only for persons who had enjoyed high status in life, and the *ọba* were the ritual experts who decided who these special persons were.

The styles of chiefs varied. Some were charismatic and active; others were relatively passive and inactive. In keeping with tradition, the *ọba* often remained fairly secluded. Junior chiefs could be more vigorous and public in undertaking roles as dispute settlers, middlemen, and patrons; and in two cases junior chiefs conducted the latter roles on behalf of senior chiefs. Accordingly, they attracted their own large followings. Prominence was roughly equivalent to the effort a title-holder was willing to invest in performing his duties or in some way bringing honour to that office and himself. There was, however, one important aspect of title-holding in the contemporary situation which was quite unlike the traditional situation, and which affected chiefly style to some extent: a chief's role in Mushin was played contextually and not on a full-time basis. Chiefs often worked and socialised outside of their neighbourhoods or in places where it was inappropriate to observe all of the etiquette attached to chieftaincy. A title-holder was expected to know when to play his role. All things considered, chiefs tried to reap whatever benefits they could, whenever they could, from their privileged positions. But an effective style consisted of a judicious blend of two extremes: stateliness and humility. The rewards that came to chiefs in the form of deference, prestige, and honour were, as one chief explained, 'the fruits of life's labour'.

In summary, there are two points to be made about Mushin's chieftaincy system. First, the actual structure of the chieftaincy system was unique to Mushin. Second, the basic building blocks of Mushin's chiefly structure – titled chiefs and the fact that they represented title-holding constituencies of people – were universal. But, like the structures, the kinds of units which held rights to name chiefs were not the same in Mushin as they were in other places.

A comparison of Mushin's system to other Yoruba-speaking communities illustrates these points. For example, the Lagos City chieftaincy system had no middle-level chieftaincy division councils. Instead its structure consisted of an *oba* under whom were four classes of (established) title-holding chiefs, ranked according to seniority as reckoned by their length of time in office.[24] All of these title-holders formed the *oba*'s council which was, before colonial rule, the highest administrative, judicial, and legislative body of the community. A sub-group of the council, a 'committee' of kingmakers, consisted of the leaders of the four chieftaincy classes, who always came from the same four chieftaincy families, and the two most senior chiefs, whatever their class. As for the title-holding units, all titles in the four classes of Lagos chiefs were held by *idile*. But, only the *idile* in one class of chiefs (the *Idejo* class) were descendants of first settlers. The *idile* of the other three classes established their permanent rights to name title-holders by virtue of conquest or through outstanding military, spiritual, or medicinal service to a previous *oba* of the community. Many of the original chiefs, in fact, were allocated land for houses or compounds as part of their elevation to title-holding status.

Lagos was not alone in vesting title-holding rights in groups other than wards or first-settler *idile*. In Abeokuta, for instance, one of several classes of traditional title-holders, the *parakoyi*, represented and supervised the town's trading interests; in Ijebu Ode, men's age sets, *ipampa*, once held rights to name title-holders.[25] In both places, the senior title-holders were part of, or were promoted to the community's highest governing council: the *iwarefa* in the Abeokuta case and the *ilamuren* in Ijebu Ode. In neither place, however, were these groups the only title-holding bodies; wards and first-settler *idile* also held titles and were represented in community-wide governing councils, as was the case in many Yoruba-speaking communities. What the examples indicate is that there were many kinds of political interest groups which existed at the base of a chieftaincy structure, and which held rights to name title-holding representatives to higher-level governing councils.

The point is that Mushin's chieftaincy system was a natural outgrowth of several widely shared cultural values: that a traditional government should in some way be representational, that representation was achieved through a title-holder, and that representation should be arranged hierarchically. In a pre-colonial polity, the structure of government was articulated almost exclusively through a title-holding system.[26] In contemporary Mushin, the title-holding system was no longer *the* government, but an arm of government. In its totality it had become an interest group, capable of representing the political interests of some citizens who shared similar cultural values and of organising them on a community-wide scale.

THE PROBLEMS OF URBAN CHIEFS

Chieftaincy titles were held for life. They were non-retractable, as the Odi Olowo case established. On the surface, it appeared that the number of titles was small and that there was little opportunity for recruiting new members into the system on a regular basis.

Indeed, in order to avoid becoming moribund, one of the greatest challenges facing the chiefs lay in soliciting the participation and interest of a wide cross-section of the politically active public. This problem was particularly acute in the contemporary political environment, where the chieftaincy system was not a dominant institution but only one part of a large and complex political arena. There were, therefore, several mechanisms for attracting the participation of people who did not hold titles. One was simply to bring fresh talent into the system without titles. This was accomplished by including prominent people in the decision-making activities of chieftaincy councils or in chieftaincy ceremonies. While titles might be seen as a limited good, participation was not. The powers of the chiefs were elastic; they could be stretched, expanded, and shared in many ways. One divisional council was attended by councillors, market leaders, and religious group leaders who did not hold titles but who were regularly involved in its affairs. When decisions were to be reached, these people expressed their views and were as much involved in the process of reaching a consensus as were title-holders. Another mechanism was to recruit members with promises of titles. Some participants were actually called 'chief' even though they were not officially recognised. Such measures were sufficient to secure a prospect's interest and involvement for extended periods of time. One neighbourhood leader was active in chieftaincy division affairs for more than twelve years and, although he was regularly promised an honorary title, he was passed over when they were officially assigned in 1975. Although irate, the leader was mollified and kept active in his division with promises that he would be included in the next nominations which were sent to the government. The possibility of some day holding a title was a powerful recruitment device even though, in reality, officially recognised titles were in short supply.

Another problem that faced the chieftaincy system was that of discipline. Once again, the contemporary political environment severely curtailed the ability of chiefs to deal forcefully with improprieties or unacceptable actions within the system. Exile or capital punishment – pre-colonial solutions for disciplining errant chiefs – were no longer possible. Ostracism, however, was one way of expressing lack of confidence in a chief. The case of the *ọba* who joined an unpopular political party was only one instance of this kind. In another, a ward chief lost favour with his landowner council after allowing a friend to construct a house which blocked a neighbourhood street, and, then, improperly assessing taxes. For several years, this chief's council met elsewhere under the leadership of a regent. When, a few years later, the regent died, the original ward chief, who had not lost his title, regained the confidence of ward members and resumed the duties of office.

A third problem facing the chiefs was the need to justify their position as a privileged group in society. Cohen has called this the 'problem of distinctiveness'.[27] He points out that privileged groups inevitably try to prevent less-privileged groups from joining their ranks by defining themselves as special, separate, and superior. As we have seen, Awori competed with settlers for exclusive rights to dominate the informal system of authority in Mushin. To this end, Awori chieftaincy divisions used their myth of common origin, their relatively deep history in the Mushin area and their founder status to justify and support their claims of distinctiveness. Settler chieftaincies, with their relatively shallow history of residence in Mushin and their lack of a common heritage, were at a disadvantage in this exercise. Nevertheless, they were aware of the need to establish traditions that could be used to justify the special position which they had, in fact, established.

Settlers self-consciously and deliberately created an historical narrative which recounted their 'superior' deeds in bringing a modern social order to Mushin. The minutes of the Odi Olowo chieftaincy council prefaced major decision-making sessions with what I came to recognise as a formulaic recital of that chieftaincy's history. Shomolu chiefs did the same. Odi Olowo even prepared a document which was printed and circulated in the division in about 1969. Later, a revised version of the document was sent to the Mushin Town Council as one piece of evidence in support of its claims to be recognised as a legitimate traditional chieftaincy division. The history of Odi Olowo stressed the united efforts of its leaders in their attempts to bring enlightenment to the then-outlying settlements of the area. Settlers were strangers, the narrative stated, who came to the city one by one; there they joined hands in mutual understanding in order to 'do things in common'. Settlers, the document continued, were responsible for progress, self-rule, the establishment of the Mushin District Council, the elevation of chiefs, the creation of the chieftaincy system, and a number of other 'firsts', and thus, as the history concluded: 'Considering the above Catalogue of brilliant achievements Odi-Olowo . . . cannot be ignored by any well-meaning Government'.[28]

The chiefs also developed symbols of office and ritual paraphernalia as part of their effort to establish a distinguished position in the community. Shomolu division adopted white caps in emulation of the distinctive white caps (keremesi) worn by the chiefs of Lagos.[29] Another division settled on a staff of office to be used by its *ǫba* on ceremonial occasions after it debated the appropriateness of various other items such as swords and uniforms. On a more subtle level, all of the chiefs adopted the etiquette appropriate to chieftaincy, using honorifics, praise names, special greetings, and gestures in one another's presence and (so far as possible) in public situations.

Clearly, the most distinctive feature of the chieftaincy system was that its symbols, rituals, and values were identifiable as fitting into a pan-Yoruba culture. In Mushin, as in metropolitan Lagos, Yoruba-speaking peoples were numerically and governmentally dominant. Hence the use of Yoruba culture was a logical extension of that dominance. Still, in Mushin there were two politically significant kinds of Yoruba – Awori and settler. Awori were a culturally homogeneous sub-group of Yoruba-speaking people. Settlers were a heterogeneous amalgamation of many Yoruba-speaking peoples and a few representatives of neighbouring, non-Yoruba peoples who were willing to accommodate themselves to the pan-Yoruba, Mushin-oriented culture which settlers were in the process of creating. There were, therefore, two ways of using culture for political purposes. Awori claimed that only Awori, as defined by Awori origin traditions, Awori dialect, and Awori customs were eligible to take the most senior titles in the chiefly politics of Mushin. Their boundaries in this matter were exclusive and closed. For settlers, by contrast, an exclusive and closed definition of culture was not the primary criterion by which group eligibility was determined. Instead, the standards for achieving the politically privileged status of settler were material: land and housing. Settler title-holders came from all of the major Yoruba sub-groups and a few non-Yoruba groups as well.[30] Settlers used culture in a different way. The symbols, traditions, and values they espoused in chiefly contexts were a pan-Yoruba composite. For example, the chiefs of Odi Olowo, who came from many Yoruba sub-groups, adopted Ibadan-type succession rules for their chiefs, although none of them was from Ibadan. The composite settler culture served as a rather flexible 'constitution' for appropriate behaviour and appropriate utterances. Culture was an important part of the chieftaincy system, but it was not an exclusionary device. While the Awori tightened their cultural boundaries in order to minimise competition and justify their claims to superiority in political affairs on historical grounds, settlers took another tack. They enlarged their cultural boundaries so as to include wide participation. This meant that in justifying their claims of superiority, settlers were able to field the broadest range of support.

THE CONTEMPORARY MEANING OF CHIEFTAINCY

One of the major functions of the contemporary title-holding system was to identify and provide legitimacy for individuals whose political roles in the community were developed largely outside the formal institutions of the state. Titles had an important symbolic dimension in that they made explicit roles that were implicit. Chieftaincy titles signified that individuals were outstanding members of the community. In a large, mobile population where all inhabitants were not personally known to one another, titles gave their holders an advantage, for it labelled them as 'approved' authority figures.

Legitimacy in the world of politics, however, was a matter of degree. The wider the sphere of influence and the greater the number of people who assented to and who were affected by one's actions, the more legitimacy the title-holder enjoyed. In theory, a title-holder had a greater degree of political legitimacy than a non-titled (senior or elder) authority figure because, first, he had been singled out, in some way, by others as worthy of a named position, and, second, the status was permanent and not subject to re-evaluation in each context. Some titles conferred greater prestige and more sweeping powers than others. In Mushin, Islamic organisations, Christian churches, and even secret societies conferred titles on their outstanding members. But title-holders in a religious group had a restricted field of influence; the title might be known in the community, but the effective sphere of operation by its holder was relatively narrow. By contrast, a civic title-holder had currency in the whole community and a broad sphere of operation and recognition. Legitimacy was, then, more than a simple matter of compliance or non-compliance. The more followers who complied with, or assented to, one's use of power, the more sanctioned, *ergo* the more legitimate, it was.

Titles enhanced the prestige of leaders. The status that came from holding them and from having a following was used insofar as possible, as a stepping stone to even higher positions. A title in one political field could be used to attract attention in another. For these reasons, competition for titles was intense even though the holders did not, automatically, assume crucial decision-making or law-enforcing functions in the community.

Looking at titles from another perspective, we have seen that they were the basic building blocks of the chieftaincy system. The relationships between title-holders, and the hierarchy in which they were arranged, constituted the system's structure. This structure, as I have pointed out, was not frozen. Over time it changed and became increasingly complex. There was a dynamic quality within the system which, I believe, accounted for its strength and its survival.

The chieftaincy system was an independent political structure. By this I mean that the chiefs and other participants carried out duties that were exclusive to the system. The regulation of succession rules, the performance of civic rituals, and the allocation of titles were such duties.

At the same time, the chieftaincy system was not independent in all of its activities. It was subsumed into, or utilised by, other bodies for their own specific purposes. Naturally, there were mutual advantages to this process. The government was a major co-opting institution. Initially the headmen and *Baalẹ* of Mushịn's settlements were brought into the colonial administration as tax collectors; later they were used informally for communications purposes and for maintaining order in their neighbourhoods. The great advantage to chiefs was, of course, the fact that in return for their services, they had access to government. Party organisations also made use of the chieftaincy system and vice versa. During the height of Nigeria's era of party politics, the chieftaincy divisions of Mushin were drawn into party activities, particularly in the AG, to the extent that the functions and activities of one organisation merged with the other. Finally, as we shall see, three community associations drew the chieftaincy system into their organisations from time to time to gain support for such diverse things as fighting factional battles[31] and lobbying for community improvements.

Hence one of the important qualities of the chieftaincy system, *qua* system, was its ability to take on many functions. The chiefly structure could be activated for a variety of purposes: ritual, governmental, or partisan. When a particular function was latent or ceased to exist, the structure did not cease to exist. The same structure, i.e. the same set of relationships, served other ends. The chieftaincy system was, therefore, a multi-functional institution. An analogous institution was the lineage. Traditionally, the lineage was a prescribed set of kinship relationships that could be used at one time or another, for economic, ceremonial, or political purposes. Some scholars associate multi-functional structures with institutionally undifferentiated, small-scale societies, and they associate uni-functional structures with institutionally differentiated or complex, industrial societies. This typology has been challenged by others who argue that the number or variety of functions embedded within a single structure or institution need not be equated with the scale or the developmental level of the society in which they are found.[32] The contemporary chieftaincy system of Mushin provided yet another challenge to that assumption.

Above all, the Mushin chieftaincy system offered a contemporary solution to the problems of organising political participation and rewarding outstanding, politically active citizens. It was salient in the lives of many people who were otherwise unable to participate directly in the formal proceedings of government. It provided access to public bodies and public resources. And here lay an explanation for its growth. For many people, the chieftaincy system was a political interest group which spanned the informal and formal fields of politics. When the system became legally and bureaucratically incorporated into the structures of the state, it became a formal part of the governing process. Yet, simultaneously, it operated outside the government. The chieftaincy system recruited participants and regulated internal affairs on its own, informally, according to custom, and without government intervention. The process of establishing chiefs was not an attempt to recreate the past, but to use past forms for present purposes. The leaders who worked to bring this institution to life had pragmatic goals. Beneath the facade of tradition, the system served new purposes and performed new functions which were adapted to the contemporary urban setting.

CHAPTER SIX

THE CONSOLIDATION OF LEADERSHIP

Politics is the process by which people seek power. It is a two-sided endeavour involving cooperation and solidarity, on the one hand, and competition and conflict on the other. This chapter initially concentrates on the cooperative side of the political equation. The goal here is to explore patterns of cooperation, other than the chieftaincy system, which emerged among leaders when a political community began to form. As we have seen, leadership was fragmented and not organised in the early 1950s. Yet it quickly solidified to the extent that Mushin's political system resembled a political machine by the early 1960s. At this point conflict began to dominate the political picture. The chapter therefore turns from an examination of the unifying forces in Mushin's early years as a district, to an examination of the external forces which threatened to destroy the machine, and to civil disturbances which broke out in response.

These events took place between September 1955 when local government came to Mushin and January 1966 when Nigeria's first civilian regime came to an end. This was the era of party politics, when elections dominated political processes and when self-made, neighbourhood leaders rose to the top of this new suburb's political system.

COMMUNITY LEADERSHIP: THE INSTITUTIONAL ROUTE
TO THE TOP

The old maxim, 'It takes money to make money', makes good sense when it is adapted to politics, for it takes power to make power. The politics of residence was based on the fact that it took power, in the form of property, to get power, in the form of people. In turn, it took people, in the form of followers, to move up in the hierarchy of power. The more power one had, the more one was able to attract.

Neighbourhoods were a natural starting point in the quest for power and influence in the new district. As previous chapters explained, neighbourhoods were politically important because a following could be amassed from the client relationships that developed through residential proximity and because neighbourhoods were the basic units in the chieftaincy system. After Mushin came into being, neighbourhoods took on two more significant political functions. First, they were transformed into thirty electoral wards, and from each of them one representative was elected to serve a three-year term as councillor of the Mushin District Council. Second, each ward was designated as a party chapter by the AG, the political party which quickly gained ascendance in Mushin. Thus three institutions – the party, the local government, and the chiefs – were all directly linked to residence. Consequently, neighbourhood activists – who it will be recalled came primarily from the landowning stratum – had direct contact with each institution or with neighbours who were directly involved in them. In two neighbourhoods with which I was familiar, the same core group was often active in each institution, and as a result, their activities tended to merge together. This blending, it will be recalled, also occurred in the activities of the chiefs and the AG party at the division level. It did not occur – and this is a point to be stressed – at the full district level, where meetings and activities of the various institutions were separate.

The political institutions of the community were vehicles for upward mobility. Leaders who were able to move up in the organisational hierarchy of one institution, and beyond the sphere of neighbourhood affairs, were in a stronger position to wield influence than people whose activities were purely neighbourhood-based. They were better able to secure resources and connections with important officials. Thus, their ability to perform patron and middleman roles expanded commensurately. The point, of course, is that leaders who had an opportunity to master various aspects of the larger, political system could gain ascendance in the struggle for power over leaders who had less knowledge and fewer formal contacts in the full community. This was as true of leaders who were trying to enlarge their sphere of operation from the neighbourhood to the district, as it was of leaders trying to move beyond the district into Western Region affairs.

Mushin's three political institutions were particularly important during the years 1955 to 1960, when a political community was taking shape. Because there had been few ties among and between Mushin's settlements and little interaction among their authority figures,[1] there were few, if any, pre-existing mechanisms with which to connect together the various parts of the new polity when the district was created. The chieftaincy system, moreover, was in a rudimentary state. This left the district council and the party as the main organisations through which the process of building a community initially could take place.

The Mushin District Council and Action Group party are described below. The aim is to show how people used them to strengthen and expand their leadership positions and by so doing, to bring the various parts of Mushin into a solidified system of authority.

LOCAL GOVERNMENT

Election to the Mushin District Council gave councillors a number of powers. Among them were the authority to set administrative policy for the district, to oversee management of the council, to supervise the intake and expenditure of revenue, and to award contracts. The latter was vital to councillors because it gave them an opportunity to offer patronage to clients in the business world. In the other respects, one of the unofficial duties of councillors was to settle disputes, and property cases were among the most numerous. This function gave councillors a meaningful role in the management of property issues in their district. They shared this role after 1958 with the Ikeja Town Planning Authority.[2] However, they and other community leaders were also appointed to serve on the planning authority, thereby giving councillors even greater strength in addressing housing policy issues.

Councillors also benefited from their direct contact with district council (civil service) employees. It provided them with opportunities to gain inside knowledge of the bureaucracy and to exercise influence within it. Whether or not they were correct in their perceptions, many residents believed that bureaucratic agencies were not accessible to the public without the interventions of intermediaries, and this belief created a number of occasions on which councillors could perform relatively cost-free favours for clients.

The district council staff was charged with implementing the policies set by the councillors and dispensing services to the public. Initially there were thirty-seven staff members headed by a secretary-treasurer.[3] The roster of staff responsibilities was quite broad; it indicated the importance of local government in the lives of Mushin residents, and the matters in which councillors could intervene on their behalf. Services that best lent themselves to interventions included licensing, renting market stalls, collecting fines and fees, making tax assessments, providing sanitary services, or issuing permits for construction and commercial activities. Other duties included keeping public order and supervising customary courts; providing public works and services (e.g. public water supplies, slaughter slabs, roads, markets, and transportation centres); overseeing public health and welfare services (e.g. dispensaries, maternity clinics, refuse and night-soil pick up); issuing permits (e.g. liquor, vehicles, drumming, or slaughtering animals for ceremonial purposes); and overseeing a few public education facilities.

Mushin's first councillors were firmly committed to their district. The representatives elected in 1955 were, with one exception, landowning members of the district (see Table 13). In this respect, they were quite unlike council employees who during this period were rarely members of the community they served and also were subject to frequent transfers. Furthermore, all but one of the councillors – twenty-two settlers and eight Awori – were of Yoruba descent.[4] Through their council positions,

Table 13   Mushin district councillors, elected 1955

Name	Party when elected	Awori/ Settler	Landowner/ Tenant	Occu- pation	Other
1 Abass	AG	S	L		
2 Abati	AG	S	L	Teacher	AG secy
3 Abayomi	AG	S	L	Military	
4 Adebimpe	AG	S/non Y.	L	Rent/Debt collector	Ch title
5 Adegun	AG	S	L	Trader	Ch title
6 Adeleye	AG	S	L	Trader/ Herbalist	Ch title
7 Aina	AG	A	L		Head of family
8 Ajo	AG	A	L		
9 Akinsanya	AG	A	L	Farmer	
10 Akodu	IND	S	L		
11 Baiye	AG	S	L	Retired civil servant	
12 Bashorun	AG	S	T	Trader	
13 Bello	NCNC	S	L	Farmer	
14 Goloba	AG	A	L		
15 Isiba	AG	A	L	Trader	Ch title
16 John	AG	S	L	Retired court officer	
17 Koledoye	AG	S	L	Contractor	Ch title
18 Odetola	AG	S	L	Trader	Ch title[a]
19 Ogundimu	AG	S	L	Retired	
20 Ogunjobi	AG	S	L	Trader	Ch title
21 Oke	AG	S	L		
22 Okuntola	AG	S	L		
23 Olorunfunmi	AG	A	L		
24 Oluwo	AG	S	L	Trader	
25 Saka	AG	A	L		
26 Samuel	AG	S	L	Rent/Debt collector	
27 Shodipo	AG	S	L	Court officer	
28 Shodiya	AG	S	L		
29 Taiwo	AG	S	L	Rent/Debt collector	
30 Toluwaniose	AG	A	L		Son later became councillor

[a] Title awarded later.

councillors came into contact with many groups of people and they began to assume other positions in the community, entrenching themselves more deeply into its social life.

POLITICAL PARTIES

The majority of Mushin's first councillors were also members of the Action Group party. Of the first thirty councillors, twenty-eight were members of the AG, and of the latter twelve had run unopposed. Of the second group of councillors elected in 1958, twenty-six were members of the AG. During the tenure of the first two councils the Action Group also controlled the Western Region Government. The relationship between political party and local and regional government was an important one, and needs some explanation.

The structure of Nigerian government was such that a local government like Mushin was dependent upon the dominant party in a region for its support. Nigeria met independence in 1960 as a federation of three, soon four, regions. Its government was modelled on the British parliamentary system in which control of high government posts was in the hands of the party which held the most seats in legislative bodies. Each region contained a dominant ethnic group – Yoruba, Igbo, and Hausa – and three corresponding, ethnically-dominant parties, the AG, the National Convention of Nigerian Citizens (NCNC),[5] and the Northern People's Congress (NPC), respectively. At the federal level, control of the House of Representatives and Senate required a coalition of two parties. But at the regional level any single party which gained a majority of the elected seats in its House of Assembly also controlled that region's establishment. In turn, the regional establishment, through its Ministry of Local Government, oversaw the operations of all local government councils within its jurisdiction.

The regional government allocated major political and economic rewards to local governments. Although nominally a government function, this was, in practice, a party function.[6] One reward was political appointments. The dominant regional party, for instance, controlled all appointments (including heads of regional ministries) in regional and local governments. Another reward was monetary allocations. There were two sources of funds. Regional governments received budgetary allotments from the federal government according to a pre-set formula that was designed to reduce competition among them. Regional governments, in turn, exercised the authority to set the allocations made to local government councils – the bottom tier in the national administrative hierarchy. Regional officials also had access to vast sums of money handled by marketing and development boards whose members they appointed. In exchange for these prestigious posts, appointees were obliged to convert some proceeds into patronage which, then, could be funnelled by Region officials down to local districts. In this context, local councils fared better in the allocation process if the majority of their representatives belonged to the regionally dominant political party and could lobby through party channels for their operating budgets and grants, for patronage in the form of jobs, or appointments, and for the proceeds of marketing board endeavours.

From 1951, when elections were first held on a nation-wide basis,[7] to 1962 the AG held a majority of seats in the Western Region House of Assembly, and therefore it controlled the regional government. The AG was not, however, without competition. All of the major parties, and a number of minor ones, were active to some extent in each of the regions, but the West was probably the least monolithic in terms of one-party dominance. The big challenge to the AG in the Western Region was the NCNC.

Founded in Lagos, and a prime force in Nigeria's nationalist movement, the NCNC had a strong, historical basis of support in Lagos Colony.[8] Despite becoming entrenched in the Igbo-speaking sectors of the Eastern Region through its leader, Nnamdi Azikiwe, the NCNC also was able to extend its influence into many Yoruba-speaking communities where it was able to capitalise on intra-community factionalism or other splits in Yoruba solidarity. Up to 1960, municipal Lagos was one of its strongest bastions of support, and city election results see-sawed between the AG and NCNC.[9]

On two occasions prior to 1960, NCNC influence also spilled over the city's boundaries into the Mushin area. The first occasion was in 1951 when all of Lagos Colony, for purposes of electing representatives to the Regional House of Assembly, was considered part of the Western Region. At that time, the Mushin area was part of a much larger voting constituency – a constituency which was controlled by Lagos politicians and which NCNC leaders had deemed sufficiently safe for its leader, Azikiwe, to run as Regional representative. Along with four other successful NCNC candidates, Azikiwe thus represented the wider Lagos area in the AG-controlled Western House of Assembly. (By 1960 he would become Governor General, later President, of the Federation.) The AG, officially founded in 1951, had extended its operations to Lagos in May of that year, but not in time to contest effectively against NCNC in the regional elections. The AG, in fact, did not begin to build its organisation until late in 1953[10], the year in which Lagos City was severed from its suburban neighbours and removed from the Western Region. The second victory for NCNC in the Mushin area occurred in the federal election of 1959. Again, voters elsewhere in the West supported a majority of the AG candidates, but Ikeja division (including Mushin) joined Lagos City and elected NCNC candidates. The outcome defied predictions which, based on an AG sweep of Mushin District Council elections the year before, had led the AG to field a candidate whom party leader, Chief Obafemi Awolowo, had counted on taking with him to the federal House of Representatives. The reasons for the NCNC victory are discussed in greater detail below.

In many ways, both of the NCNC victories in Mushin were anomalies. In all other contests, Action Group candidates from Mushin were elected or, as was the case with district council contests, won decisive majorities in local elections.

The AG gained strength[11] in Mushin through a highly effective policy of using residence as a basic unit in its organisation. It began by deliberately cultivating neighbourhood residents who, it thought, would make good party leaders and who would stay in constant touch with voters.[12] The link between candidate and voter in Mushin District Council contests was, moreover, a personal, neighbourly link. Nominations for AG candidates were made by ward councils or by ward representatives sitting on supra-ward constituency councils. For example, in Mushin District Council elections, the wards nominated their own ward residents to run for office. Although the party's executive committee monitored nominations, it appears to have been largely a grassroots process. Campaigning was conducted in neighbourhoods by the candidate and by his fellow neighbourhood residents who served as AG organisers and who solicited support at meetings, at rallies, or from door-to-door. Candidates themselves were able to appeal for support on a neighbourly, face-to-face basis, and to claim that their neighbours' best interests were, quite logically, their own best interests.[13] AG philosophy rested on a belief that loyalty was developed through personalised political relationships. Consequently, it discouraged the participation of little-known or outside leaders in ward or district constituencies and encouraged local participation.

The AG also sought support from organisations that contained large blocs of voters. Market organisations were especially important, as reflected in the fact that they often housed branches of all competing parties. AG even went so far as to name market 'supervisors' who were there to resolve disputes, solicit votes and contributions, and help coordinate women's campaign efforts. The markets, some religious societies, labour unions (which were not strong in Mushin *per se*), and wards were the places where the party could seek support from heterogeneous, cross-sections of the population. Otherwise party solicitations tended to be directed toward small homogeneous groups or, more specifically, toward businessmen, young people, and wage earners.[14]

The AG projected an image which was well suited to Mushin residents. The party was known throughout the Lagos region as one which catered to lower class interests, to traditional rulers, and to Muslims and Christians alike. In this it differed from the NCNC whose local image, as an early nationalist movement, was linked to its leaders who, in turn, largely represented Christian, highly educated, and professional middle-class backgrounds.[15]

In its organisation the NCNC contrasted sharply with the AG. The former had no party structure on the ward level until 1963, and even then it was loose and unmethodical. Although residents recalled that NCNC leaders sometimes held meetings in their homes, they turned for the most part, to already existing groups, most of which were ethnic group organisations, for grassroots support. Candidate nominations were made by the party's central working committee, and not ward representatives as with the AG, which meant that at the lowest levels unpopular candidates or candidates who were completely out of touch with the voters were not infrequently chosen.[16]

In regional and federal elections, the link between voter and candidate, whether AG or NCNC, was usually indirect because candidates came from a large, regional pool rather than a small residential ward. At this level of the nominating process, Ikeja Division, and hence Mushin, was not in control of its own decisions. Hence, with one exception, Ikeja Division representatives to higher legislative posts were not Mushin residents but prominent Lagos-based politicians whose nominations, if not engineered by themselves, came from high level bodies and not from local party leaders. Consequently, most of Mushin's representatives in higher legislative bodies had little direct involvement in the area. Nonetheless, and this was a significant aspect of the political system in the years up to 1962, Mushin's residents did have indirect access to these representatives, particularly AG representatives, through their highest level politicians who met with them on party committees and councils.

Adeniran Ogunsanya was one non-resident representative of Mushin to the Federal House of Representatives. Ogunsanya, the successful NCNC candidate in Ikeja Division in the 1959 federal election, was prominent in government circles for many years: a Lagos City councillor for eight of them, chairman of the Ikorodu Local Council in 1959, federal parliamentarian, one-time Federal Minister of Housing and Surveys, and eventually, under the military, Attorney General for Lagos State. He was especially prominent in his party's affairs as president of the Lagos NCNC and zonal leader for the West. A central figure in the distribution of patronage and development of party policy, Ogunsanya also was in charge of nominating candidates from his zone.[17] For the federal election in which he contested, Ikeja Division had been greatly expanded beyond its administrative boundaries to include a large Ijebu area to the east, including Ikorodu, Ogunsanya's birth place, although he was resident in Lagos. Mushin voters, who made up much of that part of the division known as Ikeja South, were considerably outnumbered by voters from Ikeja North in a ratio of one to four.[18] For Ogunsanya, Ikeja Division no doubt represented a convenient constituency from which to run for office. Not only could he benefit from home town support, it also was a year in which the AG, as we shall see, was locally vulnerable.

The AG's Alhaji S. O. Gbadamosi, also from Lagos, was another non-resident representative. He was elected by Ikeja Division voters in 1956 to the Western Region House of Assembly. Active in party affairs in Lagos from the earliest days, Gbadamosi became the AG's federal treasurer and close associate of its head, Chief Awolowo. Gbadamosi brought outstanding business contacts and skills to the party. Among other things, he became one of six directors of the National Bank of Nigeria (which was linked to the party) and a prominent shareholder in the National Investment and Properties Co. Ltd, a Lagos real estate and construction firm.[19]

Mushin's exception to the rule that non-residents served as its regional and federal representatives was F. O. Okuntola, the first chairman of the Mushin District Council. Although he lived in a then remote sector of north Mushin, Okuntola was a popular local politician. He joined Gbadamosi as an Ikeja Division representative to the Western Region House of Assembly in 1956, and was re-elected to the same post in 1960. In that same year he also returned to the Mushin District Council as an appointed councillor. Soon after this time, however, Okuntola's political role diminished, for unexplained reasons, and he figured little in local affairs.

As for party activism among other residents, property ownership was a key factor. Actual membership in political parties was high among property owners but low among tenants. In my survey, which inquired into former party memberships, 14 per cent of adult residents who had reached voting age by 1964 actually claimed to belong to a party. Of all of the landowners asked, 32 per cent were members, and of the tenant population 3.5 per cent were members. This did not prevent both owners and tenants from participating in campaigns, which they did. None the less, the people who occupied the high positions in the AG in Mushin also were property-owning residents. Most of them, like other Mushin leaders, were self-employed entrepreneurs with sufficient flexibility and discretionary time to indulge in extensive political activity at peak periods.

Local AG leaders attempted to reinforce their strong position in Mushin though large-scale patronage from party sources. They attributed progress in developing the district to the party, not the district council. For instance leaders claimed the party built a district council school at Idi-Oro, started a district court, and opened a market – named in honour of AG head Obafemi Awolowo. Similarly, local party leaders claimed they were responsible for the allocation of regional resources in the forms of business loans, contracts, scholarships, and jobs. Even district rewards, such as the granting of local contracts for, say, developing or improving roads, allocating market stalls, or even fixing taxes or dispensing licences, were atrributed, in some way, to AG largesse.

The AG served as a gateway to the outside world. In fact, it was one of the few formal avenues – outside of winning a regional election – during the party era which, structurally, could advance a leader up and out of Mushin into regional or metropolitan bodies. The AG party hierarchy through which this was accomplished paralleled the administrative hierarchy of the government (see Table 14). Using the party to move up, one Mushin AG official sat on a metropolitan-wide AG board for market leaders; several Mushin AG officials served as delegates to the party's Ikeja Divisional Council; another AG leader sat on the Western Region Executive Committee of the party. The first district council chairman, F. O. Okuntola, was elected to the Western Region House of Assembly and therefore belonged to the party's Regional Conference; this, then, gave his fellow AG activists and his former council colleagues a personal link though him to Regional party and government bodies. External positions and contracts provided Mushin's leaders with expanded networks and access to a wide range of resources which they could take back to and use in Mushin. But outside posts were limited. Only a few of Mushin's party leaders held them, and consequently they became the all-important intermediaries who could provide contact between Mushin and outside political arenas. All in all, leaders with external positions occupied structurally strong positions which enabled them to consolidate and strengthen their standing within the district. In fact, many leaders who reached the top of the AG hierarchy became top leaders of Mushin.

THE PYRAMIDING OF POWER

Power became concentrated in the hands of a few leaders in a short time. One important way this came about was through multiple office-holding in the major political bodies of the community. A position in one institution often led to a post in, or contact with, another institution. When elected to the Mushin District Council, for instance, people who were not already officers in their party automatically – at least in the case of the AG – became members of the district-level AG Constituency Council, and in some cases the District Executive Committee. (The AG Constituency Council also was made up of ward representatives and interested chiefs.)[20] Good party members were given the responsibility of turning less committed councillors into loyal party activists like themselves. The double role of elected councillors in local government and party councils, as Post wrote, meant there was 'a blurring of the division between local government as part of the administrative structure and local government as part of the working of the party machine'.[21]

The AG government had, in fact, introduced elected councils into the

Table 14   Action Group party organisation compared to
Western Region Government organisation, 1955–65

Government Hierarchy	Action Group Hierarchy	Members of Party Groups
Western Region Government	Regional Conference	Regional and National Party Officers; Elected Officials; Division (or Constituency) Delegates.
		Regional Executive Council: Federal President; Chairman and Officers of Regional Conference; Regional Ministers (or shadow cabinet if out of power);
Regional Division (e.g. Ikeja Division)	Divisional Conference/ Council (e.g. Ikeja Divisional Conference)	Chairmen of Division Conferences; and Elected Regional Officials
		Elected Officials; Constituency Council Officers.
		Division Executive Council.
Local/District Council (e.g. Mushin)	Constituency Council (e.g. Mushin)	Chairman and Secretaries; Officers of Executive Council; Elected Officials; Ward Representatives (usually ward chairs)
		District Executive Committee: Officers and Constituency Delegates.
Ward (e.g. neighbourhood)	Ward Chapter	Chairman; Secretary; Rank and file members.
		Ward Exec. Committee

Adapted from: Richard Sklar, *Nigerian Political Parties*, Princeton: Princeton University Press, 1963, pp. 422–5.

Western Region, and thus it was predisposed to seeing the possibilities for involving elected councillors, party activists, and traditional rulers in the same sphere of community-oriented governance. From the beginning in Mushin the overwhelming majority of the councillors were not only office-holding representatives in the local government, but also officials in their political party. If they were not directly active in chieftaincy affairs, more-over, they were brought into direct contact with title-holders through common institutional involvements. My inquiries revealed that six of Mushin's first council members also held chieftaincy titles,[22] meaning that at least six people held offices in the three main community-wide political institutions at the same time.

The top leaders of Mushin came to politics late rather than early in their careers (see Table 15). Intensity in political activity was almost a part of the life cycle, and it grew with age. Thus the average age of Mushin's leaders in 1962 was fifty-four years, with the range of my sample extending from forty to sixty-five. Most of these same leaders were migrants who had spent some thirty-six years in metropolitan Lagos. The political successes of these people were not dependent on educational attainments. Nine had no formal schooling; seven had spent part or all of the standard six years in primary school; two had four years of secondary school (and neither of them was among the level I leaders). Most of the leaders – nineteen of twenty-one – were men. Women were not particularly prominent in Mushin affairs outside the market context. Markets were a customary point of entry into politics for women, and through their work places they collectively exerted a strong influence in political circles. In a few cases women participated actively as chiefs in neighbourhood or chieftaincy division activities, but in Mushin, unlike some other urban areas, they rarely engaged in the exten-sive client-building entrepreneurial activities that provided the jumping-off point in the political careers of many men.

The people at the top of Mushin's political hierarchy had more formal offices or memberships in political institutions and interest groups than those at the bottom. Their memberships also tended to overlap with one another more than did those of leaders at the bottom. (This is also shown in Table 15.) There are twenty-one leaders represented in this table. They do not constitute an exhaustive list of Mushin's leaders; they are a representa-tive list. These leaders are ranked according to the widest political arena in which they held a formal position or title. The four leaders of level I, therefore, had the widest spheres of influence. Each of them had formal positions in overarching political bodies outside Mushin (regional or metropolitan-area bodies). Each of them also held formal offices in Mushin institutions which served the whole community. Hence, the four level I leaders were able to function both inside and outside Mushin in official capacities. They also were active in many other groups. They served on the

Table 15 (a) Political influence and affiliations of 21 Mushin leaders

	Sphere of influence				Highest office	Political affiliations						
	N	SD	D	R		LLA	Party Member	CS	MDC	Mkt/Tr Assns	Govt. Appts	Other
Level I												
1 T. Abiola[1]	x	x	x	x	Reg. Party EC	*	*Ch	*	4 terms	*	4	2 VAs*
2 L. Sotomi	x	x	x	x	Reg. Party delegate	?	*Ch	*	5 terms	*	7	2 VAs*
3 S. J. Odunsi	x		x	x	Reg. Party delegate	*	*Ch	*	5 terms	*	9	6 Rel. socs.*
4 Femi Duro		x	x	x	Metro Mkt Assn		*	m	1 term	*	1	?
Level II												
5 Ekundare	x	x	x	H	MDC Dept. Head	m	m	H	Employee			1 Rel. soc*
6 Ojo	x	x	x	H	MTC Councillor	m	*	H	1 term			1 VA
7 Oba Lisabi	x		x		MTC Councillor	m	m	*	2 terms	m		Oba
8 Taiwo	x	x	x		District Court President	*	m	*	Court Pres.		3+	
9 Kotonu	x	x	x		MTC Councillor	m	m	*	1 term			
10 Jibowu	x	x	x		District Police Officer	m	m	*	Govt. Employee			Secy CS Div
11 I. A. Adeyemi	x	x	x		MTC CS Advisor	*	*	*			1	1 VA
12 Prince Fagbemi	x	x	x		District Mkt Assn	m	*	*		*		2 VAs*
Level III												
13 Anjorin	x	x			CSDiv Council	m	?	*				2 VAs
14 Sofe	x	x			CSDiv Council	m	m	*				
15 Oduyoye	x	x			CSDiv Council	m	?	*				
16 Musa	x	x			CSDiv Council	m	m	*				
17 Ogedengbe	x	x			Party Div Officer	m*	m	m				1 VA*
18 Soyinke	x	x			Party Div Officer	m	m*					
19 Osue	x	x			Party Div Officer	m	*					1 Rel. soc
20 A. Ajisafe	x	x			Mkt Assn	m	*			*		1 Rel. soc
21 Oroki	x	x			Mkt Assn	m	m			*		1 VA*

(b) Social attributes of 21 Mushin leaders

	Ethnic Group	Age/ 1962	Sex	Occupation	Religion	Years in Mushin/Lagos	Educa- tion
Level I							
1 T. Abiola	Ekiti	50	M	Merchant/mixed	Xian	25	0
2 L. Sotomi	Ijebu	c55	M	Merchant/mixed	?	40	0
3 S. J. Odunsi	Egba	56	M	Merchant/mixed	Xian	34	St. VI
4 Femi Duro	Yoruba	c55	F	Market trader	Muslim	?	0
Level II							
5 Ekundare	Egba/ Lagosian	45	M	Civil servant	Muslim	30	?
6 Ojo	Ijebu	55	M	Rent/debt collector	?	35	St. VI
7 Ọba Lisabi	Egba	55	M	Herbalist/ trader	Muslim/ Xian	21	0
8 Taiwo	Ife	55	M	Rent/debt collector	?	45	St. VI
9 Kotonu	Dahomey	56	M	Rent/debt collector	Xian	Life	St. VI
10 Jibowu	Ilesha	45	M	Policeman	?	Life	?
11 I. A. Adeyemi	Ijebu	58	M	Metalsmith	Xian	38	St. VI
12 Prince Fagbemi	Egba	55	M	Merchant	Muslim	23	0
Level III							
13 Anjorin	Egba	60	M	Merchant/clerk	Xian	44	St. VI
14 Sofe	Awori	60	M	Moneylender	Muslim	Life	0
15 Oduyoye	Egba	65	M	Carpenter	Xian	35	St. VI
16 Musa	Egba	c60	M	Canoe-puller	Muslim	37	0
17 Ogedengbe	Ijebu	52	M	Merchant/clerk	Xian	20+	St. VI
18 Soyinke	Lagosian	55	F	Merchant	?	Life	0
19 Osue	Egba	40	F	Trader	Muslim	Life	0
20 A. Ajisafe	Ijebu	50	M	Cap maker	Xian	20	St. VI
21 Oroki	Ijebu	50	M	Market trader	Muslim	23	0

[1] Pseudonyms.

Table 14 Key:

N = Neighbourhood
SD = Sub-district
D = District
R = Western Region or Metropolitan Lagos

LLA = Landlord/Landlady Association
CS = Chieftaincy System
MDC = Mushin District/Town Council
Mkt/Tr Assn = Market or Transport Association
Govt. Appt. = Number of appointments to government bodies

Reg = Regional
Rel = Religious
EC = Executive Committee/Council
Ch = Chairman
VA = Voluntary Association
Soc = Society
Div = Division

H = Hometown chieftaincy title
St. VI = Primary School (usually 6 years)

m = Member
* = Officer

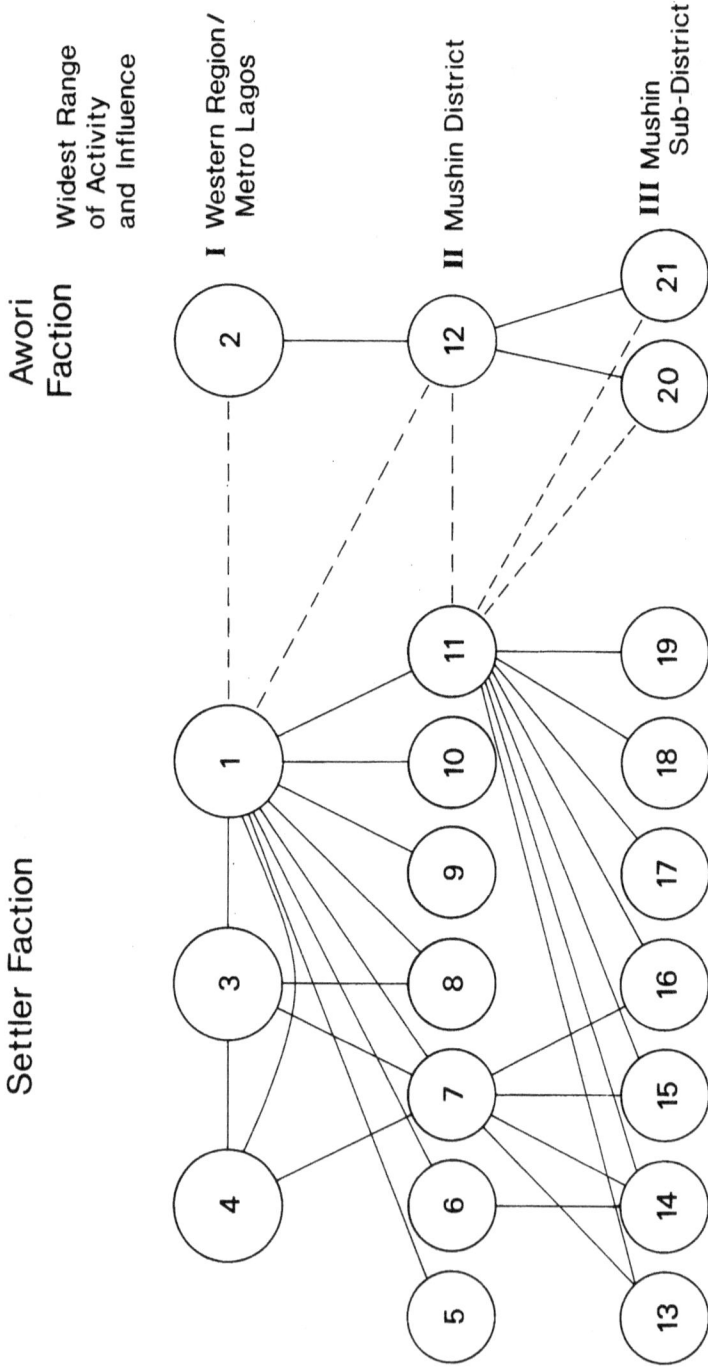

Awori Faction

Widest Range of Activity and Influence

I Western Region/ Metro Lagos

II Mushin District

III Mushin Sub-District

Settler Faction

Figure 3   Patron–client ties among 21 Mushin leaders

Lines represent patron–client ties which were either observed by the author or described in oral testimony

Mushin District Council many times, were appointed to government bodies many times, belonged to many voluntary associations, and so on. As one moves down the list, the numbers of offices and memberships declines. Consequently, the sphere of influence of lower-level leaders also narrows. Leaders of level II held their highest formal positions in institutions that functioned within the district of Mushin. Furthermore, they were clients to level I leaders. Their main access to resources and connections outside the district was through the top leaders on whom they were dependent; this was one of the main reasons they could be counted on for support. Leaders of level III held posts in institutions that functioned in (or in part of) a division of Mushin which consisted of several neighbourhoods or wards, but not in the whole district. For reasons similar to those applicable between leaders of levels I and II, the leaders of level III were dependent on those above them. All of the twenty-one leaders had thus transcended the neighbourhood sphere of political activity in some way. But having done so, their achievements in the wider political milieu were not of the same order, nor were their positions of equal rank.

The connections between leaders are schematically represented in Fig. 3. (The numbers assigned to leaders in Fig. 3 correspond to their numbers in Table 15.) Three neighbourhood leaders, who were introduced in earlier chapters, are included in this figure. They are Timothy Abiola (1), I. A. Adeyemi (11), both of whom were introduced in Chapter 3, and S. A. Ojo (6), who was introduced in Chapter 4. By 1960 these three men had risen above the neighbourhood level in political affairs and had become district-wide leaders. Abiola, moreover, became one of the district's top-level leaders with official positions as a chairman of the AG in Mushin and as a party representative to the AG's Western Region Executive Committee at Ibadan. The two other men became his clients. Years earlier Abiola had been a client to Ojo, but Abiola's high achievements in political endeavours had reversed their positions.

The relationships between Abiola and his politician clients (vertical lines) and three of his peers (horizontal lines) serve as vivid examples of the scope of influence and support that a top leader could command. It is necessary to point out again that the relationships shown in the diagram were only a representative sample and not an exhaustive compilation of all the ties among and between these leaders.

Using these ties, then, Abiola secured the support of, or communicated with, several thousand market traders and transporters. He did so through a client (12) and through alliances made with other top leaders (2, 3, 4) with whom he served in the party and the district council. He had access to the vast neighbourhood networks of the chieftaincy system through one of the district's ọba (7) and other chieftaincy title holders (3, 8, 9, 10, 11); two large Islamic societies (5, 12); a number of Christian societies (3); and several governmental bodies, such as the ITPA and the Native Courts (2, 3, 8). His clients also included an influential police officer (10), a district council department head (5), and the leader of a large and reputedly strong secret society (2). These ties demonstrate how, through direct relationships arising out of co-memberships, leaders made contact with and then used one another to gain access to large bodies of people.

The relationship between Abiola and Adeyemi (11) brings out another dimension in the leader–client chain. A top leader could gain indirect access to many lower-level leaders through a direct contact with his client, in this case Adeyemi. Adeyemi was a district leader who had a large number of clients who were leaders on a sub-district level (III) and who, themselves, had large numbers of clients. Among Adeyemi's clients there were market association leaders (12, 20, 21); ward chiefs (13, 14, 15, 16); a landlord association president (17); AG division officers (18, 19, 20); and voluntary association leaders (17, 21). Adeyemi's clients also included the large number of neighbours whose ties to him were described in some detail in Chapter 4. Again, this is a representative sample, and not Adeyemi's complete network.

Adeyemi's own sphere of influence beyond his neighbourhood was built up, for the most part, through his memberships in the AG and the chieftaincy system. In Adeyemi's view, his relationship as a client to Abiola, thanks to AG ties, brought him many clients of his own. Conversely, in Abiola's view, his relationship to Adeyemi had brought him the support of a large number of lower-level leaders who significantly augmented his own sphere of operation. Needless to say, the client ties of Abiola and Adeyemi, and the other leaders, dipped unevenly into all levels and sectors of the community. This aspect of the client system is not shown on the chart.

In time the client ties among Mushin's leaders came to form a monolithic pyramid. From bottom to top, client relationships linked ordinary residents to neighbourhood leaders, who in turn were clients to more highly placed district leaders. There were ascending clusters of patron–client ties. They invariably led to the few top leaders who represented Mushin to the outside and who brought the outside to Mushin.

The high degree of overlap among leaders created close ties among them. When leaders regularly came together to transact political business for the community, they were at the same time drawn into a multitude of transactions among themselves: compromises, trade-offs, mutual favours, and information exchanges. A web of mutual interdependencies and loyalties was created. As leaders became more involved with one another their identification with Mushin as a community increased. Their involvements also provided repeated opportunities for the exchange of ideas – ideas about how the community should be run and ideas about who should run it. As a result, the leaders developed a common political outlook to guide their actions and a rationale to justify their privileged position in the society. As we have seen, Mushin's leadership stratum successfully promulgated an ideology in which they saw themselves as the *owners* of Mushin, who by virtue of their status were entitled to positions of political privilege. This justification of their rights, together with their high level of mutual activity, provided a basis for solidarity – a quality which was essential when events brought leaders together in an effort to protect that favoured position.

THE ROLE OF THE PUBLIC IN POLITICAL PROCESSES

The ability of Mushin's leaders to entrench themselves at the top was reinforced by a lack of interest in local issues on the part of most ordinary residents. The landowning leaders of Mushin became relatively well-integrated in the political community; the tenant stratum did not. There were many reasons for the lack of tenant involvement. For one, the urban situation itself – a high level of transience and a low number of political interest groups and outlets – contributed to a low level of participation on the part of most residents. For another, the relative youth of the nation-state and the primacy of ethnic over national allegiances also discouraged political participation of minority migrant populations in alien situations. Finally, the struggle for existence in a competitive and overly-populated urban economy directed peoples' attentions away from public issues and toward public resources and ways to get them. Each of these factors – and they are given greater attention below – contributed to the ability of landowning leaders to dominate political affairs in Mushin.

The political activities of the general public were not limited to one place. There were four administrative districts in metropolitan Lagos, and political action could be oriented to any one of them. The resident who wanted a stall in a Mushin market was obliged to enter briefly into the political life of Mushin since the rights to allocate that stall were held by Mushin's local government. By contrast, the resident of Mushin who wanted a market stall in, say, municipal Lagos, directed her attention with respect to that goal to the municipal political system. All of this is to say that the political orientations of ordinary residents were not necessarily focused on any one political arena all of the time or, in the extreme, any of the time. Indeed, their public involvements were dispersed throughout the metropolitan area, and this diluted any collective strength they might have. By contrast, the energies of owners were focused. They had proprietary interests in a specific administrative district and consequently their collective position was strong.

The political attentions of ordinary residents also might be focused on their homeplaces and not on the city. Here again their position was weakened. The majority of Mushin residents did not have long-term commitments to living in the metropolitan area. They preferred to concentrate their efforts on the places where they ultimately planned to reside or where their political citizenship was unquestioned. When migrants left their homes, their kinship ties, economic rights, and political rights did not terminate. So long as they maintained close connections, their rights to be considered politically active members of their homeplaces remained intact. One way to keep home ties alive was to participate in a hometown (ethnic) voluntary association.

Ethnic group voluntary associations were important outlets for urban residents. However, the interests of these groups were largely directed away from local government issues. Although my evidence is not systematic, it appeared that only a few hometown voluntary associations joined forces as a group with the AG or political leaders in Mushin. Only two of the twenty-one leaders whose activities are discussed above were members of ethnic voluntary associations. One group had supported the AG in Mushin. The other had not; it was only concerned with hometown affairs. The two leaders who belonged to these associations also stated that they belonged to them in order to remain in touch with townsmen, so that if they went home they could more easily assert their political rights.

The fact that ethnic group associations were home-focussed meant that members' interests in political issues transcended the local Mushin situation and operated with reference to the regional and national arenas which more directly affected their home areas. In many instances ethnic associations merged with party organisations in pursuit of local, regional, or national goals, and this, of course, accounted for their reputations as being politically involved. Indeed, their very overt political involvement at higher levels resulted in their being banned after 1966 by the military, although they were allowed to continue at low levels as hometown or clan societies. In the Mushin context, it was their supra-local preoccupations which kept ethnic associations from being involved to any effective degree in local political processes. Ethnic associations of minority peoples, in truth, tried to avoid local politics as a way of avoiding direct conflict with dominant groups. Once again, this stance weakened the position of a significant segment of Mushin's public but it strengthened the hand of its landowning activists.

Ethnic associations were, however, involved at another level of local public life: competing for urban resources. Because most resources were part of the public domain, either open to public application or maintained by the government for public use, competing for them was a public, hence a political act. In terms of this resource struggle, ethnic associations played an important role in an alien context. Members worked collectively to help one another solve the problem imposed by residence in a new place. The Igbo

State Union in Lagos, for instance, was characterised as 'an ethnic employment bureau'.[23]

Surprisingly, not even a third of the residents of Mushin were members of ethnic group associations during their urban tenure.[24] Minority groups, especially Igbo peoples, were more likely than Yoruba peoples to be involved in ethnic associations. Yet the leaders of the same associations were quite dependent on help outside the group in order to help their own people. Consequently these groups sometimes collectively sought the services of prominent patrons or middlemen. The head of the Tiv Association, for one, was a client to a well-known Yoruba leader in municipal Lagos. The Yoruba leader represented the whole Tiv group to city officials and also responded to individual needs of members. As might be expected, the Yoruba leader gained local prominence because of this and other representations on behalf of large bodies of migrant residents.

In short, the power of Mushin's entrenched leaders was strengthened by virtue of the fact that the people at the bottom had diffuse political interests.[25] The leaders' clientelistic approach to catering to the public gave them a way of striking a balance between their own self-interested position in community affairs and the interests of the public in community resources. The advantage for leaders lay in the fact that they could reward with their services people who supported them and at the same time exclude these people from high places.

THE EMERGENCE OF A POLITICAL MACHINE

Mushin's political system had begun to resemble a political machine by 1960. The important elements in this process, as we have seen, included the low interest of the general public in local affairs, the high interest of a small group of leaders in them, and the national political structure which produced regional governments.[26] Urban conditions were also important. Here was a low-income, transient population intent on taking advantage of rapidly expanding economic opportunities. Yet access to such opportunities was difficult, especially for newcomers. Administrative agencies – neglected, underfinanced, and inadequately staffed – were largely unable to meet the demands of the ordinary resident. Social welfare programmes or other kinds of government assistance to the disadvantaged were also not developed. Competition for a secure place in the urban milieu was intense given the rapid growth of the population. Migration, moreover, brought a disproportionate number of young people to the city who, in moving, were deprived of the natural pool of social support that existed in their homeplaces. There was a critical need to restructure social relationships and build contacts in order to survive. A substantial response to this need lay in clientelistic relationships. All things considered, this was a natural base on which machine clientelism could be superimposed.

Mushin's political machine was like other machines that have proliferated in cities of the new nations in this century and machines of American cities of the nineteenth century.[27] It flourished at a time when it was essential to secure votes to gain access to the spoils of office. To this end the machine – as its name suggested – provided reliable, redundant control. It functioned in a diffuse, heterogeneous setting by exploiting the many close ties that already existed among leaders and their clients. Ideology was not the stuff of the political machine in Mushin; concrete reciprocity was. Like others of its kind, Mushin's party machine maintained a united front. Defectors were ostracised or harshly punished, as we shall see. Rivalries between political personalities and factional struggles were publicly subordinated to the task of gaining a place in the larger world of political rewards.

Only through solidarity was the machine able to operate. Mushin's place in the Western Region was peripheral, even though the district was one of the Region's largest.[28] The suburb had been separated from municipal Lagos and placed under the administrative supervision of the Western Region Government. Fears that it would be taken out of the Region and reunited with municipal Lagos led to its having a low standing in regional priorities. Additionally, its locally resident leaders were neither prominent in the politics of the Region, nor in metropolitan Lagos. Mushin's chiefs did not come from one of the powerful pre-colonial kingdoms of the Yoruba; they were still unrecognised and therefore they did not have the privilege even of sitting in the Western Region House of Chiefs. Councilmen and party officers lacked the kind of wealth, educational, or occupational attainments which could be used to forge close ties to the Region's elite. Indeed, the highly educated and prominent business people of the West – and there was a small but highly successful group of businessmen at independence – preferred to centre their attentions on larger regional and national arenas where appointments on marketing or development boards were made and where, because of their relative wealth, their participation was eagerly cultivated.[29] All of these factors kept Mushin's local leaders at some distance from the more prominent ruling cliques of the Region although, as indicated, they did have access to legislative representatives who represented Mushin and who were part of the ruling cliques. Inevitably their peripheral position created a problem in securing and delivering rewards to followers. Compared to other local governments, Mushin received few spoils and other items of patronage.[30] It was imperative, therefore, that its leaders join hands so that they could exert pressure on regional officials for greater attentions. But the unity which grew out of the struggle for rewards was constantly threatened.

RESPONSES TO THE CONTRACTION OF POWER

Soon after they managed to consolidate their position, the unity of Mushin's leaders was repeatedly tested by a series of major political changes which took place in the Region and in the nation. The most dramatic change came in 1962 when the AG lost control of the Western Region. This was, however, only one of four significant changes in the balance of power in Nigerian government which occurred between 1960 and 1965 and which had ramifications in Mushin. Each change eroded the official position of the machine leadership, but not its unofficial influence with the populace.

The first change occurred in 1960 when Nigeria became independent. At that time, the AG controlled the Western Region government,[31] but it was the odd party out in a three-party federal system. Party President Awolowo took steps to change the AG's image so that it could assume a more important role in national affairs. One tactic was to replace officials or councils whose performance records were tarnished. The Mushin District Council was one of these targets, and its thirty representatives, elected in 1958, were dismissed after serving only two years of their three-year terms. The performance of councillors was found to be disappointing, and they were later charged with misuse of funds,[32] although the underlying reason for their dismissal was political.

Events of 1959 presaged the council's dismissal. In that year, it will be recalled, the Ikeja constituency had failed to elect S. O. Gbadamosi, Awolowo's close associate, to a federal parliamentary post. There were several reasons behind this failure. For one, the Mushin Council had been forced to raise local taxes earlier in the year. Unfortunately the move placed Mushin residents who worked in Lagos City in the position of being doubly taxed: once through their employers to the city and once through their residence to the Western Region government. Attempts by AG officials, who made a special appearance in Mushin to convince voters that the tax would increase the level of local amenities, went unheeded by an irate public.[33] Another reason was that the area had grown rapidly in the few years preceding the election and larger numbers of minority peoples thronged to its relatively inexpensive and available housing. The NCNC routinely directed its appeal to minority groups. In this instance, NCNC leaders aroused public indignation with claims that the AG intended to disfranchise stranger elements by falsely registering AG supporters under Igbo names so that voters could deceive registration officials.[34] If elected, NCNC candidates pledged, the party would solve both problems by rejoining the area to the city and making it a part of the Federal Territory of Lagos – a move the Western Region-based AG keenly opposed.[35] A final, and perhaps more weighty reason was, it will be recalled, that Mushin voters had been vastly outnumbered when they were joined to an enlarged Ikeja constituency for purposes of the federal election. It was possible, therefore, that the election results did not represent Mushin's AG strength, since only a year later, in the Western Region House of Assembly election of 1960, Mushin voters returned AG incumbent, F. O. Okuntola, to that body.

Nevertheless, in a move no doubt designed to both reprimand and strengthen its position in Mushin, the AG government appointed a new thirteen-member committee of management in 1960 to oversee district council affairs. All of the new members were loyal to the AG. They included the newly elected Okuntola, the *Iyalode* (head) of Mushin's Awolowo Market, and, despite their lack of official recognition, the three Awori *ọba* of Itire, Isolo, and Ojuwoye. Alhaji Gbadamosi of Lagos and Ikorodu was appointed chairman.

The shift to a committee of management was significant in two respects. First, the committee was appointed, not elected. This set a precedent which was followed for the remainder of the civilian regime. It meant that subsequent electioneering in Mushin (through 1965) would focus not on local contests, but only on regional and national contests in which candidates were remote, rather than well-known neighbourhood figures. Second, the new appointees represented Mushin's large interest groups – markets, the chieftaincy system, and even several large religious bodies – and regionally-known political figures. The shift to interest group representation meant that the ward was no longer the basic representational unit in local government. Thus the shift eroded one source of residential power, even though the ward did remain as a basic unit in the AG organisation and the chieftaincy system.

The second change came in 1962 when factional struggles tore the AG in two. One group continued to be led by Chief Awolowo, to whom the top leaders in Mushin remained loyal. The splinter group was led by Chief S. L. Akintola, Premier of the Western Region. The split was fuelled partly by differences among Yoruba sub-groups and partly by differences in opinion as to the way the AG should gain power in the national arena. Awolowo believed the AG could benefit from an ideological appeal to the public that acknowledged growing inequalities in the nation. He called for economic reforms through 'Democratic Socialism'. Akintola was a pragmatist who believed federal power could be gained only if the party joined the federal coalition of Igbo-controlled NCNC and Hausa-controlled NPC and thereafter refrained from campaigning outside the Western Region. The dispute peaked when a fight broke out on the floor of the Western Region House of Assembly between supporters of the two opposing factions. It prompted federal (NCNC–NPC) officials to declare a state of emergency in the Western Region and to suspend temporarily its politicians from all active participation in government. Awolowo was jailed,[36] while Akintola was restored to his position as Premier of the Western Region, and his splinter party, the United People's Party (UPP), was put in control of the regional government. But it was control by fiat (and defections) and not by election. Following his belief that a coalition was the only way to secure federal power, Akintola entered into a federal alliance with the NCNC–NPC.

A new committee of management in Mushin came out of the party split. The dismissal of the sitting committee of management was prefaced by charges that it was guilty of maladministration, inefficiency, and political victimisation.[37] Specific complaints would later be made that this and subsequent committees allocated market stalls and locked shops to its own members, council employees, relatives, and friends[38]; allowed illegal markets to operate; allocated funds for a non-existent bridge; and, finally, failed to build a scheduled road and instead built a road to an influential resident's house in time for a private ceremony. A replacement committee of twenty-one members took office in February 1963. It pledged 'unflin-ching support' for the UPP–NCNC–NPC coalition that now brought elements of Nigeria's three regions into a single national alliance.[39] The composition of the committee of management in Mushin District also reflected the new national alignment and a newly instituted policy of deliberately appointing outsiders to it. The 1963 appointees thus included a largely unknown group of UPP and NCNC representatives, although one familiar figure, Lagos' NCNC leader, Adeniran Ogunsanya, was named chairman. AG activists were excluded, with the exception of one appointee, a settler ọba, who defected from AG to UPP in the hope that his title finally would be recognised.[40] The committee was now in the hands of people who had come to power neither through elections nor, for the most part, interest-group leadership in Mushin. It was a tactic intended to force AG officials either to defect to the UPP or otherwise exclude them from their previous sources of local and regional government rewards. This committee held office for thirteen months, until March 1964.

A third, significant shift in federal party alignments brought still another change to Mushin's local government. National developments, too complex to detail here,[41] created fear among Eastern Region (NCNC) leaders that Northern Region (NPC) leaders were attempting to dominate southern Nigeria. Their concern led to the break-up of the UPP–NCNC–NPC alliance, after several threatening events: northern politicians exerted strong influence on the newly created Mid-West Region – a southern region; a census released in February 1964, showed that the northern Nigerian population figures, believed to have been grossly inflated, were such that the north would retain its representational dominance in the Federal House of Representatives; and Akintola's exceedingly accommo-dating attitude towards the north led eastern NCNC leaders to believe the north was gaining undue influence in southern political affairs. In a desper-ate attempt to tip the balance of power to the south, the NCNC left the

UPP–NPC and formed a coalition with its old enemy the AG and a few minority opposition parties.[42] The new southern alliance was known as the United Progressive Grand Alliance (UPGA). On the other side, the UPP, now called NNDP,[43] and NPC remained together and, with a few minor southern parties, became the Nigerian National Alliance (NNA).

Once again Mushin's Committee of Management was affected by national shifts. It was, in the now familiar pattern, charged with corruption and malfeasance – the council had defaulted in making payments to district schools – and then dismissed. Subsequently, a new 26-member committee of management which represented the national NNA alliance came into being in August 1964. Four of the members had served on the preceding 1963 committee, but otherwise all entrenched local leadership was absent from its roster. The committee included several relatively affluent entre-preneurs who were not previously prominent in political affairs, and the chairman was better known in municipal Lagos than in Mushin. Public resentment against the outsider appointees was strong, and in ensuing months the house of the new chairman was burned. The committee lasted for eight months.

Meanwhile, there was social unrest throughout the country. In June 1964, a general strike was staged by 750,000 Nigerian workers protesting against wage inequities and government's lack of response to labour's problems. The disparity between earnings of a government messenger and a senior civil servant reached ratios of 1:30 and in some instances 1:40.[44] Urban areas were the most affected, and in Mushin the strike brought about a ban on all public meetings. The strike acted as a signal to the public that mass action, even violence, was an effective vehicle through which to express its dissatisfaction and desire for change.[45]

Mushin became one of the most volatile districts in the Western Region. On at least two occasions, Mushin's market women accused the committee of management of carrying out a 'vendetta' against them by demolishing stalls and impounding goods after the women – known to be largely UPGA supporters – refused to take out membership cards or to campaign on behalf of the NNDP. Additionally, more than 100 workers rioted on Christmas Eve, 1964, when the district council was late in paying their wages. In response, regional officials attempted to pour oil on troubled waters and gave Mushin a £N44,662 road improvement grant. At the same time, they contemplated dividing the district into two or more independent councils as one way of gaining control.[46] But further unrest distracted their attention away from implementing this proposal.

The fourth and most dramatic change in the Mushin District Council grew out of the federal legislative elections held at the close of 1964. Described as 'violent, erratic, contentious',[47] the election produced a local victory for the AG in Mushin but elsewhere a federal victory for the NNA coalition. Leaders of the NNDP (the Akintola-led Yoruba party) in Mushin not only failed to deliver the suburb's votes to their party, but they also failed to quell election disturbances in Mushin District. This was reason enough for regional politicians to dismiss Mushin's Committee of Management on 1 April 1965. Three months later an unprecedented 50-member committee of management was appointed. What the NNDP regime lacked in mass support, it now compensated for in mass appointments.

The 1965 committee of management reflected the increasingly desperate attempts of the NNDP to secure a foothold in Mushin. Led by a prominent Lagos barrister, G. L. Animashaun, the committee included six women and a few neighbourhood chiefs from the Shomolu area. Except for the latter chiefs, the committee members represented no local interest groups nor did they hold offices in other local organisations. Again the committee was an outsider group whose members had no significant grassroots following. A few had migrated to Mushin from northern Yoruba areas – reflecting the northern element in the NNA alliance between the NNDP and NPC. A few others were seeking personal favours in return for their committee service. Otherwise the two representational principles – ward or interest group – that once served as bases for the selection of councillors were abandoned. More than ever before, the general public and local leaders were separated from the bodies which exerted formal control over them.

The UPGA leaders of Mushin responded to their exclusion from the formal establishment by tightening their ranks in the informal political system. The chiefs, for one, drew more closely together. In Odi Olowo, a regent was named to replace the defector *Olu*; chiefs met in secret and meshed their activities with those of the party. More importantly, the chiefs of several divisions finally joined hands in the hope that they could further UPGA interests.

Mushin's resident leaders also mobilised new supporters in order to protest their exclusion from government and to campaign for locally-backed candidates in an upcoming 1965 regional election. Machine leaders obstructed the campaigning of opposition candidates and hired thugs to harass them. In the neighbourhoods, they organised reprisals against residents who defected to the NNDP, particularly if they had previously held offices in ward associations or chieftaincy divisions. Local police were largely sympathetic to UPGA and cooperated with it by deploying forces in the wrong direction, delaying responses to NNDP calls, or otherwise assisting UPGA leaders in the conduct of their campaign.

The formal advantage in electioneering was, however, in the hands of the NNDP. As the party in power, its leaders were able to place a ban on public meetings and processions in Mushin for the duration of the campaign. It used its control of the administration to campaign. But it, too, engaged in 'thuggery, rigging, obstruction, and punitive control'. NNDP officials imported 3,000 federal police into the Western Region from elsewhere in Nigeria to enforce the ban and keep public order – in its favour.[48]

Mushin reeled out of control. The climax came in October 1965, when the critical election for the Western Region House of Representatives put Akintola's splinter party to the regional voter test for the first time. When election day dawned on 11 October, polling stations opened in Mushin II, the southern and most densely populated half of Mushin district, but they did not open in Mushin I, the northern half. Thousands of voters waited for their polling places to open. When the doors remained closed many outraged voters walked to the district council offices where the electoral officer announced at noon that he had postponed voting in Mushin I.

Rioting broke out. In the ensuing mêlée police fired on the crowd, killing two men and injuring others. AG leaders, and NCNC's Ogunsanya who now represented UPGA, unsuccessfully intervened in an attempt to open the polls. Tensions were exacerbated by reports that ballot boxes and papers were found in the home of an NNDP leader while voting was in progress elsewhere. For more than ten days sporadic rioting peppered the Mushin area. District council offices were burned to the ground, and according to newspaper reports, some twenty-four houses of officials were either burned or destroyed. Schools and banks closed, market traders and shopkeepers stayed away from work, traffic was halted on main arteries and roads, and residents milled through the streets. Of the 168 persons arrested in Mushin in various incidents, ninety-five were arrested in the first three days after the election fiasco; twenty were held for breaking an emergency dusk-to-dawn curfew; and another twenty were charged with the unlawful possession of firearms. It took two days and a court order to secure a count of the Mushin II ballots. Once again Mushin gave the AG (now UPGA) an overwhelming victory, but the unrest did not stop. In search of safety, large numbers of people left Mushin, including the top AG leadership.[49]

Public appeals for peace were made by a group of leaders calling themselves the Mushin Elders Committee. Public refusals to cooperate unless the AG were restored to power were made by more alienated and militant community interests.[50] It was the latter which captured the real mood of Mushin during the next two months. Many of the suburb's residents joined dissidents throughout the Western Region in open revolt.[51] Bands of protesters attacked cars on major highways and roamed through city streets; criminal elements were drawn into the arena. Attempts by the federal government to intervene were weak and inadequate, and as a result anarchy prevailed.

Ultimately the civil disturbances in Mushin and elsewhere in the Western Region were instrumental in bringing about a military coup which toppled Nigeria's first civilian regime on 15 January 1966. The overnight coup took the lives of Chief Akintola, the Federal Prime Minister, and other national leaders. It restored calm to Mushin, and it closed the door to party politics for the next thirteen years.

EXPLANATIONS FOR SURVIVAL

Despite an era which could be described as cataclysmic, the local AG machine leaders retained their pre-eminent position in Mushin. For three years between 1962 and 1965, the NNDP and its various allies enjoyed the formal powers of making and enforcing policy in Mushin. During all of this time it failed, however, to obtain widespread support from the general public. How, then, did machine leaders manage to retain their informal power?

In the NNDP view, Mushin and its neighbouring districts were constituencies that were to be exploited rather than cultivated. Positions on the Mushin and neighbouring district councils were seen as spoils in the system of rewards. But instead of being awarded to leaders from the districts themselves, council appointments were given to outsiders. Thus the single most important characteristic of Mushin's appointed councillors after the AG/NNDP split in 1962 was that they were not resident in Mushin. According to a master plan developed in Lagos in 1963, NNDP leaders stated that 'only members that stay in Lagos . . . should be considered' for council appointments in Mushin, and, in fact, all of Ikeja. This policy was designed to encourage party supporters in Lagos and 'make them feel they are part and parcel of the Western Region'.[52]

The imposed NNDP splinter party, and the various coalitions which it formed nationally, had few if any popular foundations in Mushin. Certainly there was no constituency in the district which it wished to encourage or reward with appointments to public bodies. It was like the colonial regime of a century earlier in that there were vast structural gaps between officials and the general public. NNDP appointees on the Mushin District Council were authority figures, but their followings and their vested interests were centred outside Mushin. Before the AG/NNDP factional split, Mushin leaders had brought the disparate parts of the district into a unified political system. Their extensive client networks had bound supporters to not one but several local leaders, and their many interactions and exchanges produced loyalties and obligations that were not easily abandoned. The fact that their relationships were often reinforced by the closeness of co-residence made it easier to keep a watchful eye on the activities of party members and to enforce discipline by punishing defectors. Impersonal leadership was inimical to a society grounded in residential politics.

The top leaders of Mushin retained a viable position in the district because there was virtually no competition at the bottom of the political hierarchy. Regimes changed but urban residents still needed jobs and housing, places in schools, loans, and moral support. Disputes still had to be settled. Land purchases still had to be made and protected. The system which had grown up in response to these and other basic requirements of the public continued to exist because it was needed and because there were no viable alternatives to it. The major interest of residents – their need to compete for urban resources – and the ability of leaders to allocate and distribute some resources did not change. True enough, government-controlled resources moved outside local AG control. Yet leaders still had services to render, information to impart, alternative contacts to exploit. The diversity of roles and functions undertaken by Mushin's political specialists were weakened, but they were not rendered obsolete in the day-to-day give-and-take of urban political life. Since the AG still contested for regional and national offices, support in the form of votes was still sought and some rewards could be meted out in exchange. Clientelism was the fuel that made the system run. It was monopolised in Mushin by machine leaders who, above all, were not replaced and whose abilities to wield sufficient coercive powers kept the local balance of power in their favour.

The top leaders of Mushin were protected in several ways. First, as the previous discussion indicated, the diversified number of services and activities engaged in by leaders at all levels meant that there were alternate ways of keeping followers even when establishment rewards were in short supply. Second, redundancy in office and title-holding gave top leaders alternative sources of power and legitimacy in one institution when they were out of power in another. One of the places where some of Mushin's AG leadership took refuge, as we have seen, was in the advisory councils of the chieftaincy division where, since they already had acted as patrons to the chiefs by supporting their petitions for official recognition, they were able to continue to operate and where their interest was considered fitting and proper.

Mushin's top leaders also protected themselves with force. They stayed in place because they were able to victimise defectors and because, in so doing, they were able to mobilise assistance from the grassroots. Their ability to draw on their followers' support through extended client networks was demonstrated when the machine, an organisation of competition, became an organisation of rebellion.

Finally, Mushin's leaders stayed in place because they had no place to go. They had been excluded from the system of rewards. At the end of the partisan era, no accessible channels were open for ordinary people and their leaders to reach out to their newly appointed local authorities. No provision was made to incorporate the representatives of the public – the people who were in touch with the masses – into the new government. No opportunity was provided for residents or their leaders to develop links to the new regional ruling elite. The response to having all channels blocked was violence.

The first decade of Mushin as a political community was marked by two opposing patterns: continuity in local leadership and change in the balance of power. Leaders who rapidly rose to the top in the first five years via the formal institutions of government were slowly excluded from those institutions in the second five years, thanks to a series of shifts in national and regional governing alliances. Nevertheless, Mushin's leaders retained formal power, even as their base of operations slipped from a formal to an informal mode of organisation.

Our understanding of the patterns of political power has been enhanced by studies which reveal that there are many 'invisible' ways in which political interaction and activity can be organised. In a pioneering study, Lupton and Wilson showed that British elites controlled their society's key political and economic institutions simply through informal interactions and activities organised within a dense network of overlapping old school ties, social clubs, and intermarriages.[53] Likewise, in Mushin, power was organised in an informal pyramid of patron–client and middleman–client relationships leading from the community's least to its most influential citizens. It was through this invisible structure that local notables continued to lead the community as the formal structures began to break apart.

CHAPTER SEVEN

THE ROLE OF FACTIONS IN THE STRUGGLE FOR POWER

Military rule changed the structure of government in Nigeria. Parties were outlawed, appointed office-holders were dismissed, and legislative bodies were suspended. Decisions concerning the allocation of the nation's resources were now largely in the hands of military officers and civil servants, and thus the potential for developing power through patronage grew for military and bureaucratic officials while it diminished for civilian leaders. In spite of these revolutionary changes, the same people who came to power in Mushin as leaders of its party machine retained their positions of pre-eminence in the community's political system.

Mushin's leaders were obliged to adapt their style of operation to fit the new political order. In place of their machine solidarity, the leadership broke apart under the military. Similarly, the monolithic pyramid of clientage relationships that had centred on a few party leaders also broke into parts. The military government imposed new authority figures from above. And once again there were no links between the rulers and the ruled. This time, however, both sides made efforts to bridge the gaps. The new government appointed prominent local leaders to policy-making and advisory bodies. Local leaders responded by trying to attract the attention of officials and to acquire the few coveted appointments which were available. Finally, people lower in the system tried to align themselves with those who were successful in gaining appointments.

This process encouraged factionalism. In Mushin, factions were recruited by leaders from their client supporters to assist them in competing for offices or other kinds of rewards. The factional struggles which dominated the military period starting in 1966 were a relatively predictable development. To be sure, factions were present during the party era. However they became a prime vehicle for organising political action in Mushin, as they did in other places in the world, when the society rewarded individual strength over communal solidarity in the struggle for control and when – and this is not unrelated – competitive activity was not institutionally channelled.[1] Factionalism also was a natural outgrowth of a system in which clientelism was a dominant mode of transacting political business.[2] The extensive client networks which already permeated Mushin lent themselves to various political uses, one of which was to recruit teams of people for factional battles. Under the military regime, however, allegiances which formerly brought patrons and clients together into a united front – oriented toward a common goal – now tipped in many directions of expedience, oriented toward personal goals. From a political strategy of solidarity, the leaders of the community were now geared for conflict among themselves.

THE LOCAL RESPONSE TO MILITARY RULE

The actual involvement of the military between 1966 and 1975 at the local level was limited.[3] Decisions concerning the administration of Mushin initially were placed in the hands of civil servants until 1969, when community leaders resumed their participation in local district councils. All of this differed from the pattern of military involvement at higher levels. Federal decisions, handed down as military edicts, were taken by the Supreme Military Council which included the head of state, the heads of the navy and air force, and appointed military governors of the twelve new states which had replaced Nigeria's four regions as of May 1967.[4] Federal and state establishments continued to be run by civilians on whom the military became dependent because of their comparatively greater experience in handling the day-to-day business of government. Indeed, appointed civilian department heads and senior civil servants took a more prominent role in policy making than they had been able to take in the party period. For the most part, government attention was diverted away from local councils like Mushin, and focused on national problems, particularly on Nigeria's Civil War which broke out in July of 1967. Throughout the war – it ended in January 1970 – and beyond, the neglect of Mushin was as striking as it had been in colonial years. There was a shortage of personnel, and for the first three and a half years of military rule, Mushin was run by a sole administrator who supervised the Mushin District Council, made policy decisions, and distributed its resources. Even after committees of management began to take policy decisions, in 1969, a newspaper editorial announced the state's local government councils were 'starved' for the attentions of qualified personnel.[5] There also was a shortage of funds. The Mushin District Council spent an average of 9s. ($1.20) per inhabitant in the 1967–8 fiscal year while the Lagos City Council spent £N6.9s. ($18) per inhabitant for services and amenities. Even after the war, as oil revenues began to bolster the Nigerian economy, Mushin continued to be neglected. In 1974–5, the government's average expenditure per Mushin resident inched its way up to £₦1.5s. ($3.50) while that for the Lagos City resident continued to remain at the same, comparatively high level.[6]

For the general public, the need for informal assistance in urban matters was unchanged or, if anything, more critical, since an accelerated pace of population expansion only intensified competition for local resources. The godfathers, middlemen, and helpers, were as needed – and as responsive to their clients' needs – as they had ever been. But there was a shift in the attentions of the top layer of Mushin's patron-leaders away from their residential bases of operation. The cessation of partisan and electoral activities reduced the political importance of the neighbourhood mainly because there was no longer a need for individual voter support.

It was in the interest of the military to secure the good will and compliance of the public, despite the fact that it had the means to rule by force. Unrest and dissent, as later events in Nigeria would prove, were as threatening to a military as to a civilian regime because dissent could be used by an opposing military faction as a rationale for a counter-coup.[7] One tactic of the new regime, therefore, was to secure local acceptance by appointing to various government boards and committees prominent individuals who were known to have the support of the major interest groups in their communities and who would then act as intermediaries between government and the public. Once again there was a presumption that people would establish contact with, feel politically efficacious through, prominent middlemen representatives who could bridge the structural gaps in the political system. Looked at from the opposite perspective, middlemen-leaders needed a following in order to display their prominence. The larger the support base a leader could display, the greater was his credit with government authorities and the greater was the possibility that he could secure an appointment on a public body.

The military government's system for linking itself to the public thus called for leaders to demonstrate individual superiority. Leaders could do this in two ways. One was to hold offices in important community groups, and the other was to demonstrate that one's sphere of influence was larger or more significant than a rival's sphere of influence. Needless to say, these demands led to a continuous expansion in the scale of competition, accompanied by attempts to erode the support given to others. The strategy which evolved for conducting political rivalries in this context, as indicated, was a factional strategy. Indeed there were many factional struggles, since Mushin's top leaders were brought into constant competition with one another, vying for influence in the larger organisations of the community.

The lines of factional cleavage in Mushin were to be found in the conflicts that emerged in its formative years between settlers and Awori over rights to hold high offices and to be considered politically privileged members of the community. This conflict had been subordinated to the higher priority of solidarity during the party era. Now under the military there was no longer a common external enemy to be challenged, and the debate over local supremacy re-emerged. The debate served as a vehicle for evaluating the legitimacy or illegitimacy of political rivals and thus for undermining or strengthening their attempts to secure support in various community contexts.

Accordingly, two major factions emerged in Mushin. One was identified with Awori interests. Its most prominent supporters were the ọba and chiefs of Awori chieftaincy divisions and L. Sotomi★ who, although he was a settler, was married to an Awori woman and, among his other achievements, was a prominent merchant in a Mushin market established by an Awori ruling house and in a transport centre close to the market. The other faction was identified with settler interests, and had the support of the ọba and chiefs of settler divisions and prominent community leaders, including trade union heads. The settler faction was headed by Timothy Abiola★, among whose accomplishments was status as a merchant in a settler-dominated market and patron to Madam Femi Duro★, that market's *Iyalode* (head), and S. J. Odunsi★, also a patron to Duro's market association.[8] The prominence of the three factional leaders could be measured by their appointments to government bodies. Under the military, Abiola received five government appointments: two appointments to *ad hoc* advisory committees to the government and three appointments to serve terms (1969, 1972, and 1975) on the Mushin Town Council Committee of Management. Odunsi was appointed to serve on two *ad hoc* government advisory committees, and both he and Sotomi were named to serve three terms (1969, 1972, and 1975) on the Mushin Town Council Committee of Management. These three leaders remained at the top throughout the military period. No other Mushin figures, to the best of my knowledge, received as many government appointments. Their support fluctuated, however, and some of their clients did not offer exclusive loyalty to either one or the other faction. Depending on the context, opportunistic Awori were known to support the settler faction, and the reverse was also true.

THE POLITICAL IMPORTANCE OF MARKETS

The markets in Mushin were prime targets for factional struggles. Indeed, the top leaders in the community and lower-level leaders vied intensively for control of the markets because they contained large, organised concentrations of people. Leaders also vied for the support of transporters' groups, large religious societies, chieftaincy divisions, and even trade unions.[9]

Briefly, it is important to establish what control over an urban market represented. In human terms a market provided a large bloc of support. By 1963, Mushin's nine official markets accommodated some 24,000 traders of whom nearly 8,000 were assigned fixed stalls. Two of these – Mushin and Awolowo markets – represented more than 50 per cent of the official market space in Mushin, with 2,050 and 2,165 rentable stall spaces respectively.[10] In 1975, eighty more stalls were added to Awolowo Market. In addition to the permanent renters, there were at least 16,000 unassigned fee-paying single-day vendors, casual traders, and hawkers. The extent to which the casual trading population actually expanded the ranks of Mushin's markets is a speculative matter, although it has been estimated that, based on another market in Lagos, there were two casual traders for each trader who occupied an official stall.[11] Still this total did not reveal the full extent to which people were involved in marketing activities. There were at least eight unofficial markets. Furthermore, surrounding most markets were private houses some of which profited by renting out store space and stalls that fronted the markets. In addition, each trader within the market rarely worked alone, but with apprentices, relatives, or foster children. Aside from vendors, markets also attracted large numbers of workers: labourers such as push-cart operators or carriers, messengers, touts, and so on – all of whom made a living from the commerce attracted by the vendors.

While the majority (between two-thirds and three-quarters)[12] of the market people were women, the number of men involved was not insubstantial and neither were their roles as vendors, artisans, or performers of a diverse range of other services. Some of these men were to market personnel what neighbourhood political entrepreneurs were to their tenant clients. They arranged contacts, settled disputes, offered assistance in business dealings and advice in personal matters, or performed healing and other therapeutic services. In exchange they received gratuities, goods, or simple support in the internal political struggles for market power. By way of recognition, some of the market's political entrepreneurs were given honorary positions in market associations. As we shall see, it was in the interests of these market-based patrons and middlemen to support and to urge the traders to align with the faction which would help them (the political entrepreneurs) secure the greatest amount of influence and freedom in that market. The ultimate goal for these people was to gain the kind of base and status that would provide a point of entry into the affairs of the wider community.

Beyond their boundaries, markets had a wide sphere of influence in the community. They were, above all, the single most important source for gaining the support of non-market women. Markets acted traditionally as social and communications centres[13] and these functions continued, albeit somewhat diminished, in the contemporary urban context. A large number

of women were attuned to market affairs thanks to extensive trading networks that permeated nearly every neighbourhood and which often were
linked to distributors in market places. Additionally, a large number of
agents lived off Mushin's markets, arranging sales for out-of-town traders
who brought produce to the metropolitan area and sought out their services;
in return agents were paid a 10 per cent commission. Landlords housed
out-of-town traders in establishments next to market premises and they,
too, profited from its commerce. Agents and landlords were especially
prominent in Mushin and Awolowo because the two were feeder markets
into the city and into the rest of Mushin's markets, making them focal
points for commerce throughout the region. Awolowo Market, a daily
market, supplied nearby Kajola and Olaleye markets, while Mushin, a
four-day market (which operated at 15 per cent capacity on its three
off-days), was the primary supplier to Abule Okuta, Latilewa, Lawanson,
Oshodi, and Alade markets.[14] Thus the affairs of Awolowo and Mushin
markets were transmitted to, and received eagerly by, all other markets in
the area, and their importance as centres of influence and communications
was accordingly high.

The economic importance of markets was substantial. Much of the
community's wealth was tied up in commerce. Trade was the overwhelming
occupational choice of metropolitan Lagos women, although most traders
were outside and not inside the markets. The vast majority also relied on
market-distributed items for household food supplies, they shopped at least
three times per week, and spent an average of 42 per cent of their total
income on food.[15]

For local governments, markets provided income from fees and tolls. In
1972, Awolowo Market, the largest, yielded £N1,000 per month to the
Mushin Town Council; two years later all of Mushin's markets produced
£N30,500 in annual revenue of which only £N2,500 was expended in
market upkeep.[16] For the traders, the profit margin for market trade ranged
from pennies per day for casual hawkers to as much as £N4 per day for
large-scale traders, of whom cloth merchants were the most notoriously
properous. Altogether, the traders of a single market comparable in size to
Awolowo Market (but in the municipality) did a business of between
£N5,000 and £N25,000 per day c.1970.[17]

Markets were well-organised institutions whose personnel were highly
disciplined in their relationships with one another. A peaceful, smooth-
running market was highly valued. To these ends each market was overseen
by the local administration, and by an internally-run market association.
The Markets, Parks and Cemeteries Subcommittee, made up of appointed
councillors of the Mushin Town Council, supervised renovations, construction, site maintenance and sanitation, the arrangement of stalls and commodity sections, and the rental of stalls and shops. A paid market master

collected fees in each facility. The demands of market supervision were such that the council's market committee was one of the two busiest such groups.[18]

Each market was self-regulated by an internal market association of traders whose operating rules were based on long-established custom. All of the traders belonged to an association, such as the Awolowo Market Men and Women Association, in order to establish their right to trade in a market. The officers of an association were almost entirely responsible for maintaining order in the market. They settled disputes and they were able to enforce their decisions or to discipline dissident vendors by expelling traders from the market association, an act tantamount to being expelled from the market itself. These associations profited from compulsory entrance fees charged to traders. The fees varied with the market and the commodity, but were in the range of £N30 per annum.[19] The fees were used for social functions, gifts to the chiefs who performed rituals to benefit trade and maintain tranquillity, and administrative costs such as secretarial fees or lobbying efforts.

The head of the market, the *Iyalode*, mother of the market, was chosen by the traders. The *Iyalode* wielded a range of powers. Without her support and the market association's approval it was impossible to rent a stall or to trade casually in the market; the *Iyalode's* informal recommendation to the Mushin Town Council market committee was obligatory if a trader wished to secure space. Similarly, the *Iyalode* dealt with agents and outside commodity suppliers to the extent that, without her backing, it was virtually impossible to transact business with market traders. She assumed other duties such as settling disputes, serving as ceremonial leader of the market, and acting as the liaison from market association to the local council as well as to the *ọba* and chiefs in the division in which her market was situated.

In Awolowo Market, the *Iyalode* was assisted by a number of officers, mainly women traders, whom she appointed or whose election by other traders she recognised.[20] Under her were twenty-two leaders, known as *Iya Ẹgbẹ*, who led the vendors of each commodity which was sold in the market.[21] The *Iya Ẹgbẹ* was selected by the traders of the specific commodity she herself sold. This choice was ordinarily ratified by the *Iyalode*. Under each *Iya Ẹgbẹ* were a varying number of *Alaga* who had, along with the *Iya Ẹgbẹ*, the authority to help settle disputes among traders of the commodity they represented. There were a number of other officers who performed tasks in the market association, such as secretary or treasurer, or who held honorary titled posts, such as *Baalẹ, Balogun, Ẹkẹrin, Ashaju,* or *Sẹriki,* or who were simply designated as patrons. Some of these titled officers were men, such as the *Chief Ẹkẹrin Ọja* (market secretary). Male officers either made a living in the market through trade or they were included in the association because of their ability to link the market women to external groups or resources.

FACTIONALISM IN MARKETS

Factional struggles in Mushin's markets illustrated community leaders' abilities to compete for power under a military regime which, on one level banned 'political' activities on the part of the public, yet on another level encouraged, and even rewarded, local leadership. This seeming contradiction created a problem for activists of the community because it took competitive, politically-oriented actions to reach or to keep positions of leadership – at least the kinds of positions that the military recognised and rewarded. The response of Mushin's leaders was to seek political goals behind apolitical screens. Markets were one kind of screen.

A series of four confrontations centring on Alake Market* broke out in 1966, soon after the military came to power. The first confrontation began as a rivalry between two women for the headship of the market. It immediately escalated into a contest between community influentials who identified themselves and each other as settler or Awori faction members, and who took it upon themselves to resolve the confrontation in ways that were politically advantageous to themselves and their faction. Three subsequent confrontations had the same pattern: an internal power struggle drew the interest of external leaders who attempted to influence the outcome of the struggle in favour of one of Mushin's two main factions. As a whole, the four confrontations were related episodes in an ongoing nine-year battle for power, constituting what Gluckman called an *extended case*.[22] Each episode involved the same actors over a span of time working toward the same goal: one faction strove to retain the balance of community power in its favour while the other faction worked to shift the balance of power to its favour. Alake Market was located in the Odi Olowo settler cheiftaincy division, and it was seen as a settler stronghold. The extended case, therefore, involved a long struggle by members of the Awori faction to bring the settler market under their control and an intensive counter-struggle by settlers to prevent the Awori from succeeding.

Each episode in the struggle for power in Alake Market sheds light on a separate aspect of factional conflict. Here is the first.

Market conflict: episode one[23]
In November 1966 the right of the incumbent *Iyalode* to hold that office was challenged by a rival. The incumbent, Madam Femi Duro, had presided over Alake Market since its establishment, had served one term on the Mushin District Council Committee of Management, and had once led market women in strong support of the Action Group. The challenger was Madam S. Kumolu*, the wife of an Alake Market trader, O. O. Sunni*, who himself had been active in AG

campaigns during the party politics era. Kumolu began her campaign by
promising Alake traders that in exchange for their backing she would bring them
greater economic opportunities and useful political connections to military leaders. Feeling that she had strong backing, Kumolu announced that *Iyalode* Duro
no longer enjoyed the support of the majority of the market's traders and that she,
Kumolu, now had majority support.

The challenge was quickly brought to the attention of Odi Olowo chiefs by
Iyalode Duro. The chiefs agreed that a fight for supremacy in the market was the
proper concern of an *ọba* and his council, by virtue of custom, and not the concern
of local administrators. In response to Kumolu's challenge, the chiefs called a
series of emergency meetings, including a special session to which they invited
thirty-five well-known market figures from the whole Mushin district including
Kumolu, Duro, and their associates. At the same time they initiated inquiries into
the events in question and the people associated with them.

Within ten days of beginning their inquiries, the chiefs met privately and
concluded that the challenge represented a far wider struggle than one between
two market leaders. As they put it, 'The members of the Mushin community have
divided into two sides.' Kumolu, in their view, was part of an Awori-backed
effort, headed by L. Sotomi, to gain control of Alake Market. The most visible
backers of Kumolu were members of a clique of market people: Kumolu's
husband, Sunni, and two men from the nearby Fadi Market*, Prince Fagbemi*
and Asinde Ajisafe*, who up to this time had been loyal to settler interests.[24] The
fact that the two men had abandoned settlers and now identified with the Awori
provided the chiefs with an opportunity to arouse the indignation of their own
followers. In the chiefs' view, the bid to undermine Duro's authority was not
merely an attempt by Madam Kumolu to secure the *Iyalode* position, but also a
threat to settler control of Alake Market. The Odi Olowo chiefs thereupon turned
their attention to the larger settler-Awori issue and announced that they would
confer with Awori leader Sotomi and his followers, asking them to withdraw their
support of Kumolu.

The unexpectedly strong and immediate response of Odi Olowo chiefs was
enough to bring Kumolu's challenge to a halt for the time being. Seeing that the
Iyalode was firmly backed by settler chiefs, the Alake Market traders remained
loyal to Duro and withheld the internal support which Kumolu would have
needed in order to effectively assert her claims to leadership. Duro also had made
a show of strength inside the market by rewarding strong supporters with market
titles. Finally, Awori leaders did not respond to the settler chiefs' requests that
they meet to discuss their differences. Settlers took this as an indication that the
Awori did not wish to press their case.

Alake Market had long been a source of contention in the community. Its
predecessor, Songbo Market*, opened sometime before 1955 and at that
time it had threatened to divert trade away from an Awori Market, situated
to its north, and near the Ojuwoye settlement. The Ojuwoye community
founded its own market in the nineteenth century and thereafter it was a
landmark in the area. Privately owned and controlled by the Ojuwoye
community until 1957, when government assumed responsibility for its
care and regulation, the *Olu* (Ojuwoye) Mushin retained, in keeping with
the custom that an *ọba* was the head of markets in his territory, titular
headship of the market. He conducted sacrifices on behalf of the traders'

prosperity, settled disputes, and presided over market ceremonies. Thus when government proposed to convert the relatively small Songbo Market into Mushin's largest and most modern facility, it was in opposition to Ojuwoye leaders and to its supporters elsewhere in the community. They feared the added economic competition of a new market and they feared the political ramifications of its being in settler territory. Yet in 1960, when the expansion of Songbo into Alake Market was proposed, it was politically unrealistic to publicly oppose the new facility. As an expanding suburb, Mushin needed more markets. Moreover, the Action Group was claiming that the market was one of its finest contributions to Mushin. At that time, its detractors were forced to put party loyalties above their concern over market competition. Once the AG no longer existed officially, however, these concerns could belatedly surface.

The challenge to the *Iyalode* also resurrected the long-standing issue of settler legitimacy. The debate over settlers' rights to hold high office in Mushin, it will be recalled, dominated the early sessions of the Mushin District Council when strong objections to a settler *olu* were raised by Awori, especially Councillor Sotomi, who was an Awori spokesman. But that debate, too, was subordinated to the more pressing concern of party solidarity. In the new political climate under the military, settlers wished to protect their politically privileged position in the community. The fact that the *Iyalode* took her problem to the settler chiefs and that other market leaders accepted their chiefs' authority to intervene in the case by attending their emergency meetings was important to the settlers. It was evidence that could be used in support of settler legitimacy and in influencing public opinion to the effect that the market was a settler domain. A large constituency, such as that found in Alake Market, which could be identified as settler-controlled, could not be jeopardised. Hence, it was in the interests of settler chiefs to act immediately and decisively when a challenge was made that might tip the community's balance of power to what was, to settlers, an unfavourable, Awori, direction.

Here it is important to inject, briefly, a note about the role of rivalry in factional struggles. The conflict described in the above episode, and subsequent market conflicts, began as rivalries between individuals. Rivalries, in the Mushin view, were normal parts of social relationships. Some were inherent to certain statuses or offices – especially those offices in which the term was not permanent and succession rules did not state specific intervals at which replacements should be selected. The office of *Iyalode* was a good example. Unlike a chief, who held a title for life, the head market-woman could be replaced; but the rules for her replacement were not clear-cut. Indeed, there was ambiguity in the succession principles, and ambiguity inevitably led to conflict since there were no established methods of replacing or reaffirming the office holder in question. Other kinds of rivalries were conducted between specific individuals. Two personal enemies were 'rivals for life'. Madam Kumolu and Madam Duro were rivals for life, as well as being rivals for an office. Naturally, the two kinds of rivalry – status and personal – could and often did overlap. Most rivalries were small, private struggles. When they threatened to affect the social relationships in the wider community, they were incorporated into the public agenda, and they drew the attention of people whose interests might be jeopardised in some way. The expansion of a rivalry into the public domain, therefore, was an accretive process in human terms, and it was by virtue of accreting support or opposition that challenges like these became factional.

The *Iyalode* of Alake Market was in a strategically strong position to strengthen her base of support. She could secure backing from the traders in her own market in order to deflect Kumolu's challenge. She did so with status rewards. As market head, Duro was able to reward loyal supporters by conferring market titles on them and to punish a detractor by withdrawing a title. *Iya Ẹgbẹ* positions, as stated, were chosen by the traders themselves. But other titled posts (sometimes added onto an *Iya Ẹgbẹ*'s ordinary title), such as the *Iyalode Ọtun* or *Iyalode Osi*, the right and left hands of the *Iyalode*, respectively, were conferred by the *Iyalode*. They indicated that a certain trader had very high status in the market's leadership hierarchy and in the eyes of the *Iyalode*. As relationships changed, and fortunes waxed and waned, the ordering of titles in the hierarchy could be altered to reflect those changes. Hence, lists of the Alake Market hierarchy given to me by the *Iyalode* and in a private collection of papers each presented a different combination of titles in a different order. In one list a few names of the title-holders had changed, perhaps because there was a natural attrition rate. Otherwise, the rearrangements of the placements of title-holders in the market were made by the *Iyalode*. She was able, in this way, to tag the status of certain people in a way which could, presumably, be beneficial to her and to the running of the market.

There was room for manoeuvre in the title-giving process. By adjusting titles or rearranging the hierarchy of title-holders, the *Iyalode* could create ambiguity surrounding the relative seniority of one title-holder with respect to her place in the overall hierarchy or with respect to her relationship to another title-holder. Theoretically, several subordinates to the *Iyalode* could simultaneously claim they were in a most-favoured position – second or third in the hierarchy. On the one hand, adjustments could ameliorate tensions caused by rivalries, but on the other they might increase competition among subordinates. A major function performed by the title adjustments was to make it difficult to focus attention on any one heir-apparent to the *Iyalode*. A fixed hierarchy might engender certain expectations, while an unfixed hierarchy removed any political challenges which an heir-apparent might bring to an incumbent *Iyalode*. For instance, the husband of Madam Kumolu, according to some informants, held a title before his and his wife's challenge to *Iyalode* Duro. But *Iyalode* Duro claimed there had never been a title for him in the market hierarchy. On another occasion, the *Iyalode* gave a potential rival a low-ranking title; the low position then supported the *Iyalode*'s claim that the rival was not of sufficiently high stature to challenge her headship. At the same time that she removed this challenger (with a low-ranking title) she gave her a face-saving niche in the market hierarchy, and the recipient was not only indebted to the *Iyalode* for recognising her, but also she became less inclined to oppose her.

To her benefit, Duro also put her title-giving powers to effective political use in the wider community. Her most important move was to give honorary titles to her backers, Abiola and Odunsi, whom she named official patrons and whom she listed as titled officials in the Alake Market Association. This of course meant that they had strong support both in and from an influential interest group, and in exchange the two men befriended Duro in her own political battles. When the challenge to her authority was lodged in 1966, Abiola and Odunsi held military appointments on the 'Leader of Thought Committee' of the Western Region – a committee convened to advise the new military governor on ways to deal with problems facing local governments. Because they were the official representatives from Mushin to the new regime, the use of Abiola's and Odunsi's names by Duro was of inestimable importance in keeping market traders loyal to her. The psychological climate of the times was one in which the public was concerned to establish contacts with the new regime. Hence Duro's public links to Abiola and to Odunsi, and her use of settler chiefs to deal with her market crisis, were sufficient displays of strength to counter the activities of Kumolu and her backers.

The second episode of the lengthy battle for control of Alake Market came two years after the first confrontation.

Market conflict: episode two[25]
A second challenge to the headship of Alake Market occurred between July and October of 1968. In an oral communication to settler chiefs, traders of Alake Market complained that Madam Omo Idowu★ was to be installed as the *Iyalode Mushin*, indicating she was the head market-woman of *all* Mushin District. The installation ceremony was to be held in conjunction with the installation of a number of newly named junior chiefs in the Ojuwoye Chieftaincy Division. Members of the Alake Market Men and Women Association expressed fears that the installation of a market leader, whose title implied district-wide powers, would impinge upon their market's and their *Iyalode*'s autonomy.

The impending *iwuye* created a sense of emergency among the settler chiefs. But as they had done in the past, the chiefs took pains to investigate the complaint. They learned that Madam Idowu was an 'underling' to L. Sotomi, and therefore she was connected to the Awori faction. Madam Idowu was a neighbour to settler leader Abiola and an avowed opponent to him in settler-Awori factional struggles, as well as to Madam Duro, whose close relationship to Abiola as a client was now widely known.

The timing of the *iwuye* for Madam Idowu and the Ojuwoye junior chiefs was significant. It was to take place a few weeks before a meeting of the *ọba* of Ikeja Division (comprised of Mushin, Agege, and Ikeja Districts), at which they would select one of their number to sit for a term in the newly established Lagos State House of Obas and Chiefs. One of the leading contenders for that honour was the *Olu Mushin*. He could only win the election, however, if he secured the backing of Mushin's settler chiefs. Under normal circumstances, settlers would be likely to back the *Olu Mushin*, even if he represented an Awori chieftaincy division, in order to keep the title in Mushin and not let it fall to a chief from a rival district or to a chief with whom they had little influence. Under present circumstances, however, settlers could not offer their support to the *Olu Mushin*. Nevertheless, they sent an emissary to him to inquire into the Awori motives for naming a district-wide *Iyalode*, and to express their alarm. The emissary reported back to the settler chiefs that the *Iyalode Mushin* title should not be interpreted as a district-wide title. Rather, it was an honorary title bestowed by the Ojuwoye Chieftaincy Division, intended to apply only within the precincts of an Awori market.

The announcement that the *Iyalode Mushin* title would be restricted to the Ojuwoye Chieftaincy Division meant that the Awori attempt to establish a district-wide market hierarchy had been withdrawn. With this assurance, the settler chiefs and Alake Market leaders considered the matter resolved. The Ojuwoye *iwuye* proceeded on schedule. More importantly, settler leaders later supported the newly enthroned *Olu Mushin*, Jimoh Aileru, in his successful bid to serve a term as Ikeja Division's representative in the Lagos State House of Obas and Chiefs.[26]

A new strategy was adopted in the second attempt to gain control of the Alake Market. This time rivals did not try to replace the *Iyalode* directly, but attempted to gain control by superimposing a district-wide organisation and a district-wide *Iyalode* over Alake and other Mushin markets. Inasmuch as it was done under the aegis of the Ojuwoye Division chiefs – and was not a move that emanated from the markets themselves – it was interpreted as an Awori attempt to dominate all of the area's markets. The main fear of *Iyalode* Duro and her traders was that the establishment of a district-wide *Iyalode* title would set a precedent whereby that title-holder could claim to have seniority among all market leaders of the community. Using the principle of seniority, such a figurehead could then try to subordinate Duro and the Alake Market Association to her authority, eventually bringing in her own Awori representative to the market and, in that way, controlling it. Taking this logic to its conclusion, the Alake Market officers speculated that the position of representative would naturally fall to the Awori-backed Madam S. Kumolu.

The Ojuwoye Division chiefs, meantime, failed to calculate the full ramifications of their actions. In entering the struggle to wrest control of Alake Market from the settlers, the Ojuwoye chiefs exposed themselves to the risk of losing a battle. By publicly aiding Awori faction members who were trying to control Alake Market, the *Olu Mushin* jeopardised his ability to secure settler backing in, what would be for him, a more rewarding contest. Winning the chiefs' election, therefore, required that he back off from the market struggle. A compromise was necessary, and the *Olu Mushin* withdrew his support of Madam Idowu's plan for establishing a district-wide market association.

Beneath their indignation over the market challenge, top settler leaders were keen to accept the *Olu Mushin*'s disclaimer of his and his faction's expansionist moves. Settlers were, in truth, willing to assist the *Olu Mushin* in his election campaign to obtain a seat in the House of Qbas and Chiefs. Once he was elected, as he was, settlers would gain the ear of Mushin's only representative to that body – a representative who was in their debt. Settlers, therefore, lost no time after the election in making public capital out of the *Olu*'s obligation to them.

At this point, the *Olu Mushin* was considered sympathetic to the settler faction. Its leader, Timothy Abiola, publicised this favourable turn of events by adding *Olu* Aileru's name to his list of core members of the settler faction. The list, which contained thirteen members, had been ornately inscribed by a calligrapher on a scroll, framed and hung in Abiola's living quarters. It was called the Mushin District Community Organisation (MDCO). Those who saw it hanging on Abiola's wall could not fail to be impressed by the stature of the persons it listed and by what this implied. Here, fully displayed, was a remarkable alliance of Mushin's luminaries. It was prestigious for Abiola to be able to claim as his allies a group of dignitaries such as this one; by the same token it was an honour for each person to be included on the list. The people on the MDCO list had gained prominence in the following ways:

Past (and future) Mushin Town councillors	8
Labour Union officers (2 being national presidents)	3
Present (and future) chieftaincy title-holders	4
Religious society officers	4
Market leaders	3
Past AG party officers	12

Finally, the list contained Mushin's three and, to the best of my knowledge, only representatives then serving as appointees on Lagos State Government bodies. *Olu* Aileru, as we have seen, was a member of the House of Chiefs. Two people on the list were serving on the Lagos State Interim Advisory Committee – a twenty-member group of private citizens who, in 1967, were charged with advising government on initial phases of organising the new State of Lagos. In 1969, soon after the MDCO list was drawn up, eight of its members were named to serve on the first committee of management of the Mushin Town Council to serve under the military. All told, a third of the twenty-four-member committee of management were settler faction members; two (one-twelfth) represented Awori interests.

Abiola had formalised the settler faction on several occasions when he found it politically useful to publicise names of its core members (he called them the MDCO executive committee). It was his way of making known the importance and the extent of faction members' community activities. The first time came in October 1965 when Abiola brought together six leaders who were called the Committee of Elders of Mushin. The elders, as indicated, publicly appealed to the failing civilian government to bring an end to political strife in Western Nigeria.[27] Here again, the group included people in important leadership roles in the community:

Past and future Mushin Town Councillors	4
Labour union officers (2 being national presidents)	3
Future chieftaincy title-holders	3
Religious society leaders	3
Former AG officers	3

Five of the six members of the committee of elders were later included on the framed list that hung in Abiola's house.[28]

There were other alliances like the committee of elders, or its successor the MDCO. Abiola's rival, Sotomi, formalised his own factional alliance in 1966, calling it the Mushin District Progressive League (MDPL). This alliance was announced a few months after the elders committee was formed. A third such organisation, the Shomolu and District Welfare Organisation (SDWO), also formalised its presence on several occasions when it wished to wield influence.[29] The Shomolu group did not participate in factional struggles to control Mushin, but from time to time it appeared briefly in public view to register appeals for a separate administrative council for the Shomolu section of Mushin which, in addition to being geographically peripheral, was even more administratively neglected than was the heart of Mushin. In other respects, Shomolu was a settler-dominated area which vigorously joined other settlers in their struggles to remain politically viable against Awori opposition.

A third settler faction list was made public before government officials in August 1969. It, too, was a list of the executive committee of the MDCO. It was presented by Abiola and a fellow executive committee member – a trade-union president – when they were called to testify before a tribunal inquiring into possible ways to reorganise government councils in Lagos State. The two men testified that they spoke for the leaders and for the public of Mushin. They supported these claims by naming thirteen MDCO executive committee members who represented all of the seven chieftaincy divisions, and whose combined leadership posts included the following:

Mushin town councillors   8
Religious society leaders   4
Labour union officers (2 being national presidents)   3
Chieftaincy title-holders   3
Market leaders   3

The same five members who first appeared on the 1965 elders committee –
and on this occasion Abiola publicly confirmed that the elders were, indeed,
the forerunner of the MDCO – were on the list. Ten of the thirteen people
were included on the 1968 list that had been framed. The three new names
were leaders of Awori-dominated sub-divisions of Mushin: Itire, Isolo, and
Onigbongbo. As for its public outreach, the union president testified that
the MDCO represented 20,000 people – a figure that no doubt drew on
trade-union membership rosters. Abiola testified that 700 was a more
realistic number – a figure that probably represented his estimate of settlers
who could be called upon for support through the various networks and
organisations represented by the core leaders he had just named. Nevertheless, both men agreed that 8,000 residents had recently attended a MDCO-
sponsored fund-raising rally for soldiers who were serving in the Civil
War.[30]

The list of names served several purposes beyond the obvious one of
impressing upon government officials and visitors to the Abiola household
that a leader should be judged by the company he keeps. The seventeen
figures who were listed at one time or another as members of MDCO
included many of Mushin's most highly placed and highly honoured
settlers. Abiola benefited immeasurably by being the figure who brought
these names to public attention. It set him apart as the leader of leaders.
Collectively the range of influence of these leaders extended downward into
the large, organised bodies of Mushin residents and upward into the overarching structures of government. No better proof could be offered that,
here, in this group, were prominent figures of the community who enjoyed
the support of key interest groups and who should, indeed, serve as the
official intermediaries between government and the people.

Be that as it may, the struggle for primacy continued. For a third time,
Mushin's rivals centred their struggle on Alake market.

Market conflict: episode three[31]

Settler chiefs of Odi Olowo were summoned to a six-hour meeting in August 1972
where they were told that the headship of Alake Market was again under threat.
Now, four years after challengers had attempted to impose an umbrella organisation
over Mushin's markets, a new rival, Alhaja Toriola★, was attempting to bring Alake
and Fadi Markets under an even larger umbrella association. Toriola was the leader
of a large market in municipal Lagos. Alake Market's *Iyalode* Duro expressed the
fear that the Lagos leader would undermine her position if Alake traders decided to
join the municipal Lagos association. Already Alhaja Toriola had attracted followers
of both markets with boasts of her contacts to the *Ọba* of Lagos, the governor of

Lagos State, and even the Head of State. Moreover she promised to offer them attractive wholesale prices on some commodities, especially cloth.

The chiefs learned in their enquiries that Alhaja Toriola was invited to Fadi Market by two members of the Awori-backed Kumolu clique: Prince Fagbemi and Asinde Ajisafe. The two men had gained control of Fadi Market following the death of its *Iyalode* in 1970. Although a new *Iyalode* was selected later, she was unable to wrest control of the market from Fagbemi and Ajisafe, who used the interim period between the *Iyalode*'s death and the selection of a successor to assert their own leadership in the market. They had convinced the Fadi traders that they alone could influence government officials to build, elsewhere, a maternity clinic that was scheduled to be built on the Fadi Market site. Naturally the market women feared they would lose business if the market were demolished, or if it were moved to another, unknown, place. Fagbemi secured additional support by privately (and illegally) building a block of market stalls on the perimeter of Fadi Market and renting them out. His tenants were beholden to him; and the added business that they brought was beneficial to other vendors. For these and a host of other services the two men performed – they also engaged in trade – they were given the honorary titles of *Baba Egbe* of Fadi Market. The functions of market head were performed, *de facto*, by the *Baba Egbe* acting in concert, while the newly elected, *de jure, Iyalode* was relegated to a titular role. Now, after establishing a strong base in Fadi Market, Fagbemi and Ajisafe tried to expand their sphere of operation. They did so by inviting Alhaja Toriola to come into Fadi Market. Her role was to attract attention as a 'progressive element', from traders elsewhere in Mushin, particularly Alake Market. Eventually the two men hoped Alhaja Toriola would draw enough Alake traders into her market association and away from the Alake Market association, to wrest control from Madam Duro, and that she would then delegate responsibility for leading Alake Market to them. Subsequently, several Alake traders did begin to meet with the Alhaja and the *Baba Egbe* – meetings that alarmed some Alake Market leaders.

The matter came to a head when it was learned that a holiday had been declared at Fadi Market. The traders planned a ceremonial observance of the death of the previous *Iyalode* under the leadership of Fagbemi, Ajisafe, Toriola, and local Muslim dignitaries. The ceremony was intended to bring peace and good fortune to the market. Each trader donated £N1 to be shared among the three organisers and used for the event. Alhaja Toriola also sold cloth to each woman, at a special price, to be made into a dress for the occasion. (Wearing identical dresses known as *aso ebi*, family cloth, was a long-standing custom at ceremonies such as these.) When the chiefs of Odi Olowo learned that three of the twenty-two *Iya Egbe* from Alake Market and others of its traders had attended the ceremony, their sense of crisis was intensified.

When settler chiefs reconvened to draw up a plan of action, Abiola sent word that they should leave the matter to him. The *Olu* was displeased at this threat to his authority, but his council urged him to demur. The challenge, they reasoned, had become too big for the chiefs to handle alone. On the other side, Abiola feared the *Olu* and chiefs would take a position that might escalate the conflict. The solution to the problem seemed straight-foward to Abiola. Alhaja Toriola once served with him on an AG campaign committee, and so he approached her as a friend, playing on the sense of solidarity that had been instilled among fellow AG colleagues, and warning her that her actions in Mushin might endanger her reputation in Lagos. After all, he said, the *Iyalode* of Alake Market might go to the Mushin Town Council, where an official investigation would have to be undertaken. Unknown to Fadi and Alake Market leaders, Alhaja Toriola was experiencing a challenge to her position in the city's marketing circles. In fact, she was attempting to use the Mushin opening to demonstrate to Lagos traders that her powers stretched beyond the municipality into the whole of the metropolitan area. The warning by Abiola that the Mushin Town Council might investigate her activities and, worse, the suggestion that her challenge might be publicised in Lagos, convinced Alhaja Toriola to work out a face-saving plan of action with Abiola.[32]

Apparently, Prince Fagbemi knew nothing of the agreement. Encouraged by the support of Fadi Market traders and the inroads he and his allies had made in Alake Market, Fagbemi appeared at an *ad hoc* advisory committee meeting at the Mushin Town Council. The meeting had been called to work out a chieftaincy declaration for one of the settler divisions. As an important leader of a settler market and an active member of his ward's landowners' association, he demanded that he be allowed to participate. The chiefs and other leaders attending the meeting were enraged by his appearance and claimed that Fagbemi was an illegitimate participant. So long as Fagbemi had been loyal to them, settler chiefs had overlooked the fact that Fagbemi's brother was the actual owner of the house in which Fagbemi lived. They even overlooked his Awori sympathies. They had allowed him to participate in the neighbourhood landowner association and neighbourhood chieftaincy affairs on the strength of his brother's landowning status. After all, Fagbemi was an energetic resident who took a strong interest in local affairs. Recently, however, Fagbemi had deflected his fellow landowners' attentions away from Fadi Market when they inquired – something they felt was their prerogative – into market affairs. While he faithfully supported his landowners' association, he just as faithfully discouraged them and the neighbourhood chiefs from involving Fadi Market women in their ward activities. The owners now realised that this was another tactic by Fagbemi to strengthen his role as a middleman between the market women and local authority figures. His blatant attempt to undermine the position of still another market leader – the *Iyalode* of Alake Market – and his uninvited presence at a town council and chieftaincy meeting turned settler sentiment against him. Now his non-landowning status could be used as a reason to bar him from participating in chieftaincy deliberations. Fagbemi was sent away from the meeting.

When the chiefs and other dignitaries began to disperse at the conclusion of their chieftaincy meeting, a messenger arrived with a letter from Awori leaders demanding that the Mushin Town Council declare the settler chieftaincy divisions illegal. The letter charged the settlers with violating the custom that an *ọba* must be a son of the soil. It was a futile gesture. Not only was the *ad hoc* committee dominated by settlers, but also the town council's committee of management was dominated by settlers. Those present responded, as usual, that they were legitimate purchasers of land, and as such they did indeed have political rights to hold high chieftaincy titles. Furthermore, they replied that there would have been no chieftaincy system if there had been no settlers to establish it. With this, the Awori petition was dismissed.

Meanwhile, Alhaja Toriola saw that she was supported by a weak challenger. The Awori faction confined its backing of Fagbemi and Ajisafe to the precincts of the Mushin Town Council, but it made no outward attempt to encourage the Lagos market leader in Mushin markets. Therefore she had no choice but to withdraw. The agreement worked out earlier with Abiola was, it turned out, a welcome compromise. Under the agreement, *Iyalode* Duro was asked to join the Lagos market association as a member whose status was equal to Alhaja Toriola's. This would avoid evaluations of the two women's relative seniority with respect to one another. In return, Duro was to allow Toriola to expand her wholesale business into Alake Market but under Duro's personal supervision. As it turned out, when Madam Duro attended her first Lagos market meeting, Toriola violated the agreement that *Iyalode* Duro be treated as an equal, and she introduced her publicly as a subordinate. Madam Duro withdrew from the group. Alhaja Toriola was, in return, subsequently forced out of Mushin commerce.

Following this series of events, Madam Duro's position as *Iyalode* of Alake Market remained unchanged. But one addition to the list of market association title-holders was made. Settler faction leader Abiola was subsequently listed as President of the Alake Market Men and Women Association.

The presence of a market leader from municipal Lagos infuriated Mushin leaders. Indeed, it was perceived as a threat to the suburb's autonomy and to the pre-eminent position of its settler faction. The fundamental issue was no longer the rivalry among market leaders. It was now one of boundary-keeping. For many years the political interests of Mushin and municipal Lagos had been kept separate; the governing councils of the two places had no administrative overlap. Mushin also had had nothing to offer the city's political luminaries. By the 1970s, however, the population of Mushin and other suburbs surpassed that of the city, the state government was located in the suburb of Ikeja, and commercial and industrial enterprises were scattered throughout the metropolitan area. These were strong inducements for city leaders to expand their spheres of activity. Consider, for example, Alhaja Toriola's stature in Lagos market circles had she been able to bring Mushin's 24,000 traders into her organisation. A position on the Lagos City Council was conventionally given to Lagos's top market leader. Toriola herself had been passed over in the selection process at an earlier time because her influence was considered secondary to that of another person's.[33] Suffice it to say, the suburban portion of the metropolitan area now offered untapped resources in the struggles of Lagos's political rivals to expand their sources of support as they sought to move up in their own municipal hierarchy.

The threat to Mushin lay in the fact that Lagosian political elites were highly educated, urbane, and politically powerful in state and national arenas. For generations this advantage had placed them in favourable positions to take leading roles in governmental, educational, professional, and commercial circles of the nation. By comparison, Mushin's relatively uneducated and unconnected political leadership was at a strong disadvantage. None the less, the outlying suburb offered one of the only political arenas in which ordinary members of the public were able to rise to high places and participate in the political affairs of an urban community to which they were not necessarily born. The settler leaders of Mushin recognised this as an unusually privileged situation, and they were loathe to jeopardise it.

The threat to Mushin's boundaries prompted settler faction leader Abiola into taking a direct role in the market confrontation. The markets were in the first line of defence, so to speak. If they became linked to a municipal market association, a precedent would be set for the establishment of other alliances in other domains. Abiola was the experienced leader in political circles outside Mushin. He had learned to operate and wield the kinds of political sanctions that were effective in these circles. Therefore his knowledge of Alhaja Toriola's political vulnerability in the city was the kind of ammunition he could use in curtailing her expansionist activities in Mushin. Abiola had another advantage. His experience in politics sensitised him to the dangers associated with allowing a Mushin leader to enter into a situation in which her seniority *vis-à-vis* a Lagos leader might be questioned. To this end, Abiola drew an analogy between Lagos and Mushin. Both of its councils were autonomous and separate from one another, meaning that the two parts of the metropolitan area had equal status. Therefore, the markets of the two places also were autonomous and separate, and thus by extension they and their leaders must be given equivalent status.

The boundary threat was as real for Awori as it was for settlers. As will be recalled, the origin traditions of indigenous descent groups in Mushin linked them to the founding descent groups – now chieftaincy lines – of Lagos. Awori who resided in suburban areas and who acknowledged this original link of kinship were said to be the sons of the Lagos founder who were not favoured because they were not allocated farmland on Lagos Island. The myth gave legitimacy to Awori claims that they, too, were founding fathers. But it placed those who had not received prime land on the island in an ideologically subordinate position to those who had, and it made them vulnerable to any claims by the chiefly lines of Lagosians that they were senior to their suburban kinsmen. Any interventions by the traditional authority figures of municipal Lagos into Mushin affairs, therefore, raised the possibility that Mushin's son-of-the-soil descent groups would be subject to Lagos's claims that the latter was supreme in the political affairs of the whole metropolitan area. This explained two seemingly contradictory actions of Mushin's Awori faction leaders: first, their lack of direct support to Alhaja Toriola once the challenge to Alake Market was seen as a boundary matter, but second, their direct support of Prince Fagbemi in the form of a letter challenging the legitimacy of settlers. With the first action, Awori avoided any risk to their own position; with the second they provided Fagbemi – an Awori supporter – with a face-saving device. Despite the fact that the latter was a futile gesture, it gave the Awori an opportunity to confront their enemies yet, simultaneously, to back away from the more serious boundary-keeping problems that the market confrontation had aroused.

One of the facts of political life that became clear from this particular challenge was the importance of legitimacy, and its use by leaders, as a resource in fighting political battles. When Fagbemi cooperated with settlers, he was included in their circles with a small stretch of the principle that governed the right of political eligibility. When he did not cooperate, his legitimacy was questioned. Two kinds of legitimating rules were being played off against one another: those associated with achievement and those associated with ascription. Clearly Fagbemi had *achieved* a position of power and high standing in Fadi Market and this position was not questioned by the chieftaincy committee when it denied Fagbemi the right to participate in its deliberations. What was questioned was Fagbemi's lack of *ascriptive* qualifications – i.e. owning a house – to be included in the community's pool of 'eligible' political leaders. Put another way, when he was useful to settlers, Fagbemi's questionable qualifications could be rationalised away, and his achievements rewarded. When he created problems, the reverse was true and his qualifications to be a legitimate participant could be questioned, and his achievements made inconsequential.

On the Awori side, Fagbemi's control of one market and his desire to gain control of another were factors that confirmed his legitimacy as a community leader. When he turned to them for support, Awori leaders ignored the ascriptive, son-of-the-soil principles as they might apply to Fagbemi, and accepted him as an important personage who had achieved prominence in the community. Yet, even as they affirmed Fagbemi's legitimacy as one of their members, Awori faction leaders repudiated the legitimacy of settlers as a whole.

Legitimacy was, therefore, situationally extended or withdrawn to suit the interests of the parties concerned. As a rule, faction leaders cultivated as much support from below as possible. The one overriding consideration in accepting that support was not to jeopardise the faction's best interests in so doing. Fagbemi and Ajisafe were ostracised when their activities were out of line with a faction's interests, rewarded when they were in line. As things turned out, Prince Fagbemi and A. Ajisafe remained in control of Fadi Market despite their failure to expand into Alake Market. Their position in Fadi Market was strong, and the settler landowning chiefs in the Fadi neighbourhood eventually restored both men to membership in their landowner's association. After all, it was easier to keep an eye on neighbourhood market affairs if the principles were part of the neighbourhood in-group than if they were peripheral to it, and there was no denying the two men's achievements – like it or not – in local commerce. For their part, Fagbemi and Ajisafe also wished to benefit from inclusion in the community's still dominant faction. All things considered, the desire for support on both sides made rules governing that support quite flexible.

The two Fadi Market leaders switched factional loyalties to suit their own interests. During partisan struggles, they had been loyal clients to Abiola, and later they had been active participants in the settler-dominated neighbourhood association. One may well ask why they then broke away – for a time – from the settler faction. The answer lies in the nature of factions themselves. They are made up of individuals whose loyalties fluctuate according to their own needs and opportunities. So long as settlers were in power in Alake Market, remaining loyal to that side would require Fagbemi and Ajisafe to participate in its activities through settler channels. Given Abiola's strong support of *Iyalode* Duro's regime, and vice versa, the prospects were unlikely that the two men could obtain the kind of influence and power that they sought there.

A predictable tactic of people or groups who are at a disadvantage in political confrontations is to seek support from more powerful or more encompassing elements in the larger political system. The result is a progressive expansion in the scale of conflict. The outcome, however, is not predictable. In order to make inroads into new territory Fagbemi and Ajisafe went around their former settler patron and secured help from other, hopefully superior, forces: the Lagos market woman and Awori faction leaders. But in this instance, it was an expedient tactic which did not take into account the larger problems that would be unleased by their actions.

The final episode in the Awori–settler factional struggle expanded the scale of conflict to a greater degree than had previously been the case. This episode took place between 1974 and 1975.

Market conflict: episode four[34]

Iyalode Duro received a letter in May 1974 declaring that her headship of Alake Market was illegal and that she had been replaced by her long-standing rival Madam S. Kumolu. The written challenge claimed that Duro illegitimately held the *Iyalode* office for many years during which time Madam Kumolu had been prevented from serving as 'lady chairman', a position to which she claimed to have been elected. The letter was sent by the Mushin Town Council Market Men and Women Association. It was signed by A. Ajisafe, as chairman of the association, and by Chief Madam Omo Idowu*, as *Iyalode* of Mushin. The association declared itself to be a district-wide body, as its use of the Mushin Town Council name suggested, and it sought the participation of all of Mushin's markets. Once again the two people signing the letter represented Awori interests who repeatedly, but in differing combinations, had challenged the authority of the Alake Market *Iyalode* in order to replace her with the person of their choice.

The challenge was widely publicised. Copies were sent to government officials such as the town clerk, treasurer and committee chairmen of the town council, and the commissioner for Local Government of Lagos State; to traditional community leaders such as the *ọba* and junior chiefs; to municipal Lagos leaders, including market leaders and journalists; and finally to market leaders of Mushin. The challenge became more alarming as Madam Kumolu and her clique became increasingly active. First, Kumolu convinced a few traders to support her on the basis that she now had 'official authorisation' to head the market. Second, Kumolu in conjunction with her Fadi Market supporters, Fagbemi and Ajisafe, announced they would stage a ceremony for the well-being and prosperity of Alake and Fadi Market traders. In a surprise move, *Iyalode* Duro attended a planning meeting for the ceremony where contributions were collected from each woman present. Soon after the meeting, Duro called together her *Iya Ęgbę* and Abiola to warn them that, in her view, the ceremony was not a genuine attempt to enhance the well-being of the traders, but a test of the political climate. The ceremony, as she predicted, was never held and reasons for its cancellation were never offered.

The challenge to the *Iyalode*'s position alarmed settler chiefs. They tried unsuccessfully for one month to convene a meeting between themselves and the Mushin Market association leaders who sent the letter. The challenge also was discussed by the Markets, Parks, and Cemeteries Sub-Committee of the Town Council Committee of Management which now consisted of leaders from both of Mushin's factions.

To the surprise of settlers, a Lagos newspaper carried an announcement that a Peace Committee of the Mushin Town Council had resolved the long-standing dispute in Alake Market by effecting a compromise between two rivals. The announcement stated that hereafter Madam Duro would be known only as the *Iyalode* of the market while Madam Kumolu would be known as lady chairman of its association. The women, stated the newspaper, were now advised to forget their differences.[35] Inquiries indicated that the article was released to the press by the chairman of the Mushin Town Council's market sub-committee, a councillor known to be associated with the Awori faction, and by a prominent member of a Lagos chieftaincy lineage, also thought to support the Awori. *Iyalode* Duro questioned the right of the town council's market sub-committee to intervene in internal market affairs, and claimed that the council's mandate was strictly limited to administrative and maintenance matters. More importantly, *Iyalode* Duro and her market officers refuted the claim that Kumolu had ever been named to the post of lady chairman. In their view, the article was a blatant attempt to influence public opinion in favour of Kumolu by misrepresenting the true status of market leadership. Therefore, *Iyalode* Duro retained control of Alake Market, and its traders did nothing to recognise or implement Kumolu's claims.

The dispute lay dormant – with *Iyalode* Duro still in control of the market and its association – until March 1975. At that time, a large ceremony was held to mark the completion of eighty new stalls in Alake Market. The *ǫba* of a settler chieftaincy division, his junior chiefs, and the settler chairman of the Mushin Town Council officiated at the opening festivities. Their leading roles in the affair demonstrated that the market was still a settler-dominated facility. Yet newspaper coverage of the ceremony hinted that something was amiss in the market.[36] Certain events preceding the opening ceremony were puzzling to the settler *ǫba* and to *Iyalode* Duro. For one, the *ǫba* was shunned by leaders of Fadi Market where, despite factional animosities, he was previously received in a manner appropriate to his status. For another, Duro was treated rudely by several employees of the Mushin Town Council. The two leaders decided that the settler show of strength at the market ceremony had rankled the opposition.

A more perplexing development occurred when *Iyalode* Duro no longer received official correspondence from the Mushin Town Council. She called on settler faction leader Odunsi, patron of the Alake Market association and member of the town council's market sub-committee, to investigate. Odunsi found that as a result of a gratuity and pressure brought to bear on a council staff member by an Awori sympathiser who was a member of the committee of management, all town council correspondence intended for *Iyalode* Duro and the Alake Market association was being sent, instead, to Madam Kumolu. The Alake Market Men and Women Association leaders immediately sent a petition to the chairman of the council's markets committee stating it 'wholly and solemnly' disowned Madam

Kumolu. They insisted, moreoever, that correspondence be redirected to *Iyalode* Duro. The mimeographed petition, signed by thirty-two title-holders in the Alake Market association was distributed widely in the community.

Public exposure of the correspondence problem resolved the issue and communications were redirected to the *Iyalode*. For the time being, there were no further challenges to the market head.

The fourth episode in the struggle for control of Alake Market represented new phases in the Awori–settler factional conflict. One was the use of mass communications to influence public opinion. At the initiative of Awori, a written challenge was widely distributed and a newspaper article was published, both proclaiming the legitimacy of Awori leadership in Alake Market. Both of these steps were taken by the out-faction in its attempt to change the order of power and legitimate that change through a written challenge. The hope, of course, was that market interests would accept the new order by virtue of its being frozen into a written, hence authoritative, form. Settlers countered this challenge with similar tactics – a written, publicly distributed rebuttal. Now the public was forced to evaluate both sides of the issue with comparable, hence equally authoritative declarations. The effect of the written proclamations was to expand inordinately the range and size of the audience which would know about, or be involved in, the market struggle.

Closely related to the use of mass communications was the use of public ceremonies. They, too, set visible authoritative precedents, and they provided evidence to be used in affirming the legitimacy of those who led or participated in them. Suffice it to say that ceremonies required leadership. To be seen as the leader of a market ceremony was to affirm in full view of public witnesses one's legitimate role as an accepted leader in that domain. The settler *ọba* who took a leading role at the opening ceremony of Alake Market angered the rival faction to the extent that opponents withheld their normal courtesies because they were prevented from taking similar roles, and from setting similar precedents, at the same event. This same rationale applied to *Iyalode* Duro's earlier attempt to discredit the ceremony planned by Fagbemi and Ajisafe for Fadi and Alake Market women. If her two opponents presided over that ceremony, they could be seen as authority figures in a joint market ritual and, by extension, could assert their rights to act as authority figures in other joint market matters. Ceremonies staged by rivals clearly created a sense of crisis for those who were being challenged, and became potent weapons – like the written proclamations – for those who wished to influence public opinion.

Still another new phase in the Awori–settler struggle was its progression into the formal administrative structures of the state, i.e. to the Mushin Town Council and the Lagos State Government. Having failed to unseat *Iyalode* Duro, Awori faction members expanded their activities to the bureaucracy in the hope of expanding their base of support. Up to this point, market leaders had avoided taking their internal affairs to government officials for fear that binding precedents would be set. By expanding the conflict to the bureaucracy, civil servants became important actors in Mushin's market politics to an extent that was never before the case. The control of communications channels between the council and Alake Market, as the mail incident revealed, was a small illustration of the way a civil servant, to suit his or her own purposes, could support one leader or one group over another. Bureaucrats had thus been drawn into the local political arena and had become potential power brokers in Mushin's factional competition.

FACTIONALISM IN MUSHIN

Factions were employed to different ends. Their most obvious use at all levels in the political hierarchy, was to achieve self-interested, immediate gain. Each episode in the Alake Market headship rivalry represented an attempt by challengers to seize control quickly and instrumentally and without regard to long-term large-scale ramifications of their actions. Certainly the conventional wisdom concerning factions confirms this portrayal: teams of people entering into confrontations in order to secure material rewards or privileged places in public affairs.[37] Taken separately, each encounter in the market struggle upheld the view that self-interest was the dominant motif in factional conflict. But expansion could not be accomplished alone; an appeal to a new constituency such as a market demanded that the challenger offer better conditions or rewards than those in existence. And this is where teamwork entered the picture. Challengers needed proof of strength. Factions offered ready-made networks of potential support and ready-made identities that symbolically summed up and advertised a position or a potential set of resources. Small, self-interested rivalries automatically expanded the field of participants.

Factions were also used to maintain or to alter a community's balance of power. This was by far their most sweeping, yet their least consciously perceived, function in Mushin. This role becomes clear when we examine a series of episodes and not simply isolated confrontations. The sequence of attempts to replace the leader of Alake Market represented an ongoing threat to the political position of an entire segment of the society by another segment of the same society. Thus the headship of Alake Market was only one element in an extensive chain of support put together by settlers – the then dominant faction. But any loss weakened that chain. Each small challenge raised the larger question of supremacy. So long as the balance of power remained as it was, and so long as a faction had behind it the support of a significant portion of the public, its political importance could not be overlooked. The military government, also in need of support, had to acknowledge settler interests – they were organised, influential, vocal, and hence powerful. Winning factional battles was the settlers' way to retain government recognition of its importance in the community.

However, the way factions were used varied according to one's position in the hierarchy of power. Risk-taking marked the approach taken by lower-level leaders in their factional confrontations. People at the bottom had little to lose if they failed to win their political battles, but everything to gain. Hence the approach of people like S. Kumolu or Prince Fagbemi was risky and opportunistic. They sought help without regard to the ramifications or ultimate dangers involved. In the extended case, this lack of regard for the consequences of one's actions almost inevitably resulted in an escalation in the scale of conflict to include an outside interest or another faction, either of which might help the challengers achieve their goals.

In contrast to underlings, leaders who had the largest support bases and the widest ranges of influence employed a conservative strategy in their factional activity. The interest of those on top was to preserve the *status quo*. They worked to minimise risks, and to view confrontations in their broadest perspective. As we have seen, Mushin's top faction leaders distanced themselves from confrontations when it was possible. This gave them the freedom to claim or disclaim *ex post facto* those who won or those who lost, as the case might be. Awori, for example, stayed away from Prince Fagbemi's dealings when they threatened the community's boundaries and Awori seniority in metropolitan chiefly affairs. Yet when there was no risk involved, the Awori lent him their name in his confrontations with settlers. By far the greatest threat to people at the top occurred when conflicts escalated in scale and expanded into larger, encapsulating arenas. It was in these situations that the top leaders were in greatest jeopardy of losing their pre-eminent positions, and it was in these situations that they minimised risks by personally entering into factional battles and keeping the less experienced out of them.

It was politically important for those at the top to cultivate and secure the support of political leaders who themselves had a base of power but were lower in the hierarchy. Thus, people lower down – such as Prince Fagbemi or S. Kumolu – could call on the support of faction leaders at the top in the struggles they initiated. As self-interested as this might be, a faction leader, for obvious reasons, was eager to gain from the political victories of his clients. When the reverse was the case, leaders drew on the support of those lower down to help them in their own battles. Their support could be secured for rewards. Under the military, however, many sources of patronage had greatly diminished. One solution for faction leaders was to provide political expertise – helping the *Olu* of Mushin win a political contest, for example – or simply to allow them to amass credit against future needs. The more dramatic solution, however, was for top leaders to distribute their own form of symbolic rewards – things like honour, prestige, high status, and titles. In order to manipulate these informal rewards, leaders had to control organisations which had offices, titles, or other honour-giving mechanisms. Community welfare organisations and markets were two of the possibilities we have examined in this chapter. The chieftaincy system as we have already seen, but to which we return in the next chapter, was another.

CHAPTER EIGHT

THE INSTITUTIONALISATION
OF POWER

The goal of many of Mushin's top leaders was to perpetuate their position of power. The people who had guided the community since 1955 wished, as privileged groups do, to preserve the status quo. The military accession to power in 1966 injected a number of uncertainties into the political environment. This prompted local leaders to intensify their efforts to establish a secure and continuingly favourable place in the hierarchy of power. At the same time, the top leaders were not a monolithic body, as we have already seen. Rather they were divided into contending factions whose political goals were in conflict.

The efforts of both Awori and settlers were directed toward institutionalising legally and bureaucratically the high positions they had established for themselves. Just what it was that should be institutionalised – just what patterns of activity should be given legal recognition – was a matter of debate. There thus arose two struggles, each of them centering on a different field of political activity.

One struggle, during the years from 1966 to 1975, was to secure bureaucratic approval for an expanded chieftaincy system. Chiefly titles were permanent and not subject to the ups and downs of ordinary political life. Hence the goal of top settler leaders was to acquire titles and then to get them recognised. Awori opposition to this settler goal was diluted by their inability to unite in defence of their rights as hereditary rulers who, alone, should hold high political titles in Mushin. As a result, settlers were able to use their influence with officials to secure or retain chiefly titles, as the case may be, and to perpetuate them.

The other struggle emerged in 1975, and it centred on the Mushin Town Council. Here the tables were turned. Awori fought to increase their representation on the committee of management. Heretofore settlers had enjoyed a numerical advantage in the council by virtue of their demographic

majority in Mushin and their claim that they had established a new social
order – a contemporary urban order – and therefore they were the rightful
arbiters of that order. Awori in Mushin challenged the settler advantage in
the council by joining with a state-wide organisation whose goal was to
expand the Awori presence in official bodies. Like the settlers, they used a
new-found influence in government to increase their participation in political life.

One of the significant aspects of the two struggles was that they brought
Mushin's top leaders into a new kind of relationship with the bureaucracy.
In the 1960s recognition of chiefs came indirectly through party channels.
In the 1970s it came directly from government officials. Civil servants had
little vested interest in Mushin before 1970. After this time, they became
more interested in local affairs. Consequently, Mushin's top leaders were
obliged to deal with a new and powerful presence in an arena they had
previously dominated.

TITLE-GIVING AND TITLE-RECEIVING IN THE
MOBILISATION OF SUPPORT

When the military came to power, the regime questioned the authenticity of
the seven Mushin *oba* who were statutorily recognised in 1965 during the
closing days of the partisan era. The recognitions, it will be recalled, had
been part of a widespread, indiscriminate, and instrumental campaign on
the part of the NNDP to win favour among various segments of the
population who were resisting their takeover of the Western Region
government. Therefore the NNDP recognitions were clouded in doubt,
and an investigation was undertaken to reassess the *obas'* actual standing in
the community. In response, Mushin's chiefs were placed in a position of
proving that they were legitimate parts of the local system of authority. This
process occupied the next nine years.

The chieftaincy system was by 1966 a functional, yet informal part of
Mushin's political system. Both its Awori and settler chieftaincy divisions
were accepted by significant segments of the population. The official recognition of the seven *oba* was still in question, however, and other aspects of
the system were not sanctioned in the official, legal sense. Its junior chiefs
and its succession rules were not yet bureaucratically approved. This was
unlike most chiefly systems of the Yoruba peoples, which were precolo-
nially established. So long as Mushin's chieftaincy system, or parts of it,
were not officially accepted it was vulnerable. If it were legally and
bureaucratically recognised, this would guarantee, all things being equal,
its protection and perpetuation in the institutional framework of the
community.

Settlers took the lead in the process of re-authenticating Mushin's seven *ǫba*. They used every opportunity to influence government officials in the *ǫbas*' favour. When Timothy Abiola testified before a government tribunal which was investigating local government practices, he stressed that the chiefs were important to community well-being, and he urged that the *ǫba* be allocated small salaries, as was the practice elsewhere. Salaries were, of course, one form of bureaucratic recognition.

Settlers also took the lead in trying to secure recognition for the junior chiefs and for the succession rules of all seven of Mushin's chieftaincy divisions. To these ends, they urged the chiefs to revitalise themselves. Many chieftaincy activities had been neglected during the party struggles that tore the region apart and, in some cases, divided the chiefs' loyalties. Now it was crucial that the chiefs prove their authenticity through, among other things, their demonstrations of vitality, unity, and continuity.

An important move in the revitalisation process was taken by both settler and Awori chieftaincies when they began to confer honorary, personal chieftaincy titles on prominent citizens. Elsewhere in Yoruba societies, it will be recalled, there were two kinds of titles: established and honorary. The former generally were part of the estate of corporate groups – lineages, wards, age-sets, trading associations, and so on – which held the rights to select the title-holder. The latter were conferred on individuals in recognition of achievements, e.g. wealth or social standing, by the *ǫba* or the *ǫba* in consultation with his council. Both kinds of titles were permanent. Established titles were perpetuated, whereas honorary titles only existed for the duration of the holder's life. In 1966 honorary titles at a junior level were conferred so as to secure the active involvement in chieftaincy affairs of Mushin's top leaders who did not hold established titles but whose community standing and government contacts were such that they could help the existing chiefs in their struggle for recognition, and would want to help them, for reasons of self-interest.

Despite the renewed vigour of the chiefs, the recognition process was jeopardised by factional struggles between chieftaincy divisions. Once again settlers and Awori were locked in battle. Their various strategies aroused the same cleavages that were aroused by challenges to the headship of Alake Market. Once again, Awori sought to discredit settlers, and in response settlers sought to exploit the cleavages among Awori so as to dilute their opposition.

Factional struggles that focused on chieftaincy politics had two aspects. First, they represented individual strategies of leaders to expand and legitimate their own positions. Second, they represented collective tactics to draw boundaries around a politically privileged class – narrowly in the case of Awori, more broadly in the case of settlers – so as to enhance each group's position in the larger community. Factional conflicts centering on the chieftaincy system took place simultaneously with those in the markets. They involved many of the same people to the extent that, as we have seen, the confrontations in both fields overlapped and interwined.

Two episodes in Mushin's factional struggles which involved chieftaincy affairs are presented below. The first episode took place in conjunction with episode two – the incident in which the Awori chiefs of Ojuwoye tried to install an *Iyalode* over all of Mushin's markets – of the extended case study presented in Chapter 7. The chieftaincy-related aspects of this confrontation lasted from May 1968 to July 1969.

Chieftaincy conflict: episode one

The Ojuwoye chieftaincy division announced it would confer honorary titles on two prominent leaders who were outsiders to the Ojuwoye division. The conferral of honorary titles was set for July 1968, as part of the *iwuye* for Ojuwoye's internal junior chiefs and for the *Iyalode* of Mushin. The announcement by Ojuwoye that it would confer two personal titles angered the settler chiefs far more than the announcement that it would create a district-wide *Iyalode*. The reason for settler anger was that the titles were intended for settler faction leaders Abiola and Odunsi.

Only a few weeks before the announcement, Odi Olowo's settler chiefs also had begun to reorganise so as to breathe new life into their own division. To these ends they had sought assistance from Abiola and Odunsi. At the suggestion of these two men, the chiefs of Odi Olowo had invited their *Olu* – ostracised since his defection to the opposition NNDP party – to resume functioning as *ọba*. They had also invited representatives of Alake, Fadi, and Idi-Owo* Markets – all located in wards of Odi Olowo – to become regular participants in the Odi Olowo chieftaincy council. Abiola and Odunsi, together with three prominent leaders of the settler faction, Taiwo*, Kotonu*, and Jibowu* (see Chapter 6, Table 14, nos. 8, 9 and 10) were asked to form an *iwarefa*, executive (or kingmaker) committee of the division. The five men did not hold Odi Olowo chieftaincy titles at that time. Their prominence, nonetheless, made their participation of the *iwarefa* invaluable to the other chiefs. The scrutiny of Mushin's chieftaincy divisions by the government had prompted the chiefs to seek the formal participation of these settler leaders in their affairs so that they would have a direct interest in the re-authentication process.

When the Odi Olowo chiefs learned that Abiola and Odunsi had allied themselves with their arch-rivals, the Awori, they banned them from their meetings for what they described as a 'betrayal' of the settler cause. They also demanded that they renounce the proposed Awori titles. In a month, after tempers cooled, Abiola and Odunsi met with the settler chiefs. In a conciliatory speech, the two men announced they had refused the Awori titles. Both of them apologised to their chiefly supporters for creating what they described as a misunderstanding, and they affirmed their loyalty to the settler cause. At the same time, Abiola admonished the chiefs for allowing their own title-giving functions to lapse and become disorganised. Several chiefs had died and had not been replaced, and the proper order of the succession hierarchy was also unclear. They must rejuvenate their title-giving activities and confer more honorary titles. There was, the two stated, no better way to gain support for the settler position than to be active and to bring fresh talent into the division. As a result of the speech, Odi Olowo chiefs held a series of meetings and expanded the division's titles from twelve to nineteen, adding seven honorary titles, renaming ward titles so as to upgrade them, and establishing a new order to the line of succession. Soon, Abiola and Odunsi found their way back into the good graces of the chiefs and they retained their positions on the *iwarefa*, now led unofficially by Abiola. More importantly, they were listed among the honorary title-holders of the Odi Olowo Division. Abiola initially held the title of *Baba Salẹ*, but it was later changed.

The reconciliation of faction leaders Abiola and Odunsi with the settler chiefs was short-lived. Within a few months a dispute broke out over what some chiefs felt was the incorrect placement of two people in Odi Olowo's succession hierarchy. The dispute prompted an inquiry into selection procedures. Debate centred on where rights to name and confer titles resided and on whom the authority to exercise those rights rested. Were the rights vested in the *Olu*, the *iwarefa*, or the full council of Odi Olowo chiefs? The actual process of title-giving in recent months was veiled in obscurity. The *iwarefa* appeared to have made the recommendations inasmuch as the *Olu* had been shorn of actual power. Indeed, the *iwarefa* had just taken an oath of secrecy on both the Bible and the Koran not to leak official secrets, betray the council, or conspire against it, and a fine of one guinea was set for violations. Despite the secrecy imposed on their actions, it became known among other chiefs that Abiola and Odunsi had 'given the orders' for the title changes and for the conferral of new titles, including their own. The two men denied the charges and withdrew their names from the list of proposed honorary title-holders, 'so as not to prejudice the motive behind these activities'. The other chiefs were less concerned about the two leaders' actions than about public exposure of their influential roles in Odi Olowo chieftaincy affairs in the absence of their official status in the division. The military's investigation into the settler chiefs' authenticity, they argued, could be jeopardised if such an opportunistic use of the system came to light.

The matter was resolved with a compromise. The debate over the incorrect placement of title-holders in the succession hierarchy was dropped. In addition, the lists of Odi Olowo chiefs for the next four years either omitted the names of Abiola and Odunsi or they designated their titles as 'suspended'. The actual powers of the two were not rescinded, however, and they participated actively in the *iwarefa*, where their loyalty and their rights to take decisions were not questioned again.

This episode places in bold relief the contradiction that emerges when self-interested motivations of individual leaders conflict with the collective needs of groups in their quest for control. The attempts by Abiola and Odunsi to acquire honorary titles, first, from an Aworì chieftaincy division, and, then, from the settler chieftaincy division, reflected their strong individual desires to protect their personal political achievements by taking permanent offices. Inasmuch as there were no elective and party offices under the present regime, the kinds of official positions that conferred symbolic legitimacy on political activities were extremely limited. Appointive positions on government bodies were short-lived; patron titles in the market or elsewhere were not secure; offices in voluntary associations provided relatively limited spheres of operation. For an individual, offices in the form of titles transformed the power gained from undertaking political roles for short terms into power derived from permanent political offices. There was a second motive behind Abiola and Odunsi's attempts to secure personal titles from an Awori Division. It was an opportunistic move designed to expand their influence and base of support directly into Awori circles. The expansionist desires of the settler leaders surprised no one; but their willingness to accept personal titles from an Awori chief did. Up to this point, Abiola and Odunsi had given valuable support and direction to Mushin's chieftaincy divisions. Odunsi was, in fact, a prime mover in the 1955 attempt to secure government recognition and to bring both the Awori and the settler chiefs into the district council. Throughout the years, the two men never wavered from their roles as the chiefs' most influential patrons. In return the settler chiefs were among their strongest and most active supporters, and they in turn, being settlers, were more favourably disposed to their own kind.

The settler faction-leaders' attempts to gain *personal* rewards from the Ojuwoye chieftaincy division were, however, a violation of principle: Awori were the enemy. Honorary titles put receivers in disadvantageous positions in relation to givers, and thus there could be no *collective* advantage to settlers if their top leaders were recognised by and beholden to their rivals. While the leaders would be personally honoured by these titles, the status of all other settlers would be compromised. Still, the Ojuwoye offer – even though the titles were declined – did pave the way for an alliance between an Awori chieftaincy division and the settler faction. An alliance was different. It connoted settler equivalence with Awori, and even Awori support of settlers. An alliance, in fact, improved the position of settlers since it was another piece of evidence in support of their claims to political legitimacy. There was, then, an important distinction to be made between individual and collective advantage. So long as a relationship was established as a collective one – as an alliance – enmity was not an issue. Otherwise, as a personal transaction, it was.

One of the principal qualities of the political system, displayed in this encounter, was that leaders who were lower in the levels of community power were able to rein in those at the top.[2] In this incident the importance of settler support to Abiola and Odunsi was made absolutely clear. Without settler chiefs, settler market women, and the vast network of settler owners who were linked together through various client networks and even more tightly through a chieftaincy system whose structural underpinnings pre-dated partisan events, the top leaders did not have a base of support that was sufficiently strong and well organised to give them the human power they needed in order to stay at the top. Therefore Abiola and Odunsi were forced to respect the wishes of these vital backers and to decline the Awori titles.

Despite their mutual dependence, both lower-level and top-level leaders were in a position to exploit one another. The top leaders were a lifeline for the settler chiefs, who were at a disadvantage in community politics, since many of them did not have the expertise, experience, or close ties to the bureaucracy that the top leaders had. In exchange for their invaluable services to the chiefs, therefore, settler faction leaders were rewarded by being given the power to monitor the division's title-giving procedures. That the settler leaders used this power to confer titles on themselves was not so much a violation of principle – they had been given the authority – as it was a mistake in timing. If their actions became public knowledge before the chieftaincy division was officially recognised, they jeopardised the collective good. Therefore, the two faction leaders temporarily laid their personal aspirations aside and did not claim their titles. At the heart of the matter was the ever-present reality that the exercise of individual power, in the end, depended upon the establishment of collective legitimacy.

The titles themselves were now among the most valuable political resources existing in Mushin. This was why intense political battles were being waged over them. They were status rewards – unparalleled in their capacity to bring honour to the holder, and in their capacity to create a bond between those who gave them and those who received them. Their conferral established long-lasting debts. The chiefs and the top faction leaders of Mushin, therefore, used their title-giving authority to bring under their sway other leaders whose gratitude would be, at least for a time, unshakeable.

The conferral of titles was also used to increase the stature and power of people already active in the chieftaincy system. In theory, established titles were arranged in a fixed hierarchy of relative seniority from top to bottom. In practice, the ranking of titles in the hierarchy could be altered. The *Iyalode* of Alake Market, it will be recalled, altered title-holders' positions in the market hierarchy as one way of showing her appreciation for loyalty or her pique over disloyalty. Many criteria were used to assess a person's ranking in a titled hierarchy, e.g. wealth, age, date of selection, or influence among other chiefs or *iwarefa* members. There was no single criterion, or single rule, for assigning ranks. As we have already seen, there was a bundle of criteria and a set of rules. Hence over time, criteria and rules could be given different values or different weights in order to justify changes in status, fortunes, or other indicators of stature. Such reassessments resulted in re-ordering the hierarchy, and gave flexibility to what otherwise might appear to be a rigid system of ranking. This was an area where ambiguity and obfuscation could surround the processes by which assessments were made. In short, there was room for manoeuvre and competition in the processes of rank-ordering the established title-holders in a chieftaincy hierarchy and in providing a rationale for the changes that were made.

The *iwarefa* of Odi Olowo made several changes in the rank-ordering of its succession hierarchy for established title-holders. The rules of Odi Olowo, which were modelled on the former kingdom of Ibadan, placed the

Olu at the top of the hierarchy and ranked the remaining established (ward-selected) chiefs in a descending order of seniority. The names of the titles reflected the holder's rank. The ranks were like rungs on a ladder. When the *Olu* or any other chief died, the vacant place was filled by the chief ranked immediately below, who moved up one rung of the ladder, as did each lower-ranked chief in order. The ward that held the vacant title then elected a replacement who took the empty place at the bottom of the ladder.

From 1955 to 1975, as the fortunes of its titled chiefs fluctuated, the placement of ward chiefs in the Odi Olowo succession hierarchy fluctuated. I do not know how the *Olu* assigned titles or changed them before the *iwarefa* took over these duties in 1966. After 1966, however, the *iwarefa* altered the seniority rankings to enhance certain chiefs' statuses as is shown in the following examples:

(1) A particularly wealthy chief, who was elected to replace a deceased title holder, entered the hierarchy at the same level that was occupied by his predecessor and not at the bottom of the ladder.

(2) In several cases, the names of titles were changed to connote a higher status than the titles which were previously assigned (and which were then dropped from the division's title repertoire). This enabled one chief, who was elected to replace a deceased title-holder, to enter the hierarchy at a higher level than that of his predecessor and, again, not at the bottom of the ladder.

(3) In another case, the date of selection of a chief was changed to an earlier date, enabling the new title-holder to claim he had seniority over the others and thus to jump to a higher rung on the ladder.

As for holders of honorary titles, there also was room for manoeuvre. Holders of honorary titles, in contrast to holders of established titles, did not have places in the succession hierarchy, but remained outside the ranking system. Nevertheless in two cases, again in Odi Olowo division, honorary titles were changed to established, ranked titles (i.e. titles held by wards) when vacancies fortuitously occurred in the wards of the honorary title holders. This occurred despite the fact that the titles were 'owned' by the wards which held the jural powers to select successors but which, in these cases, were powerless to exercise those rights.

The most dramatic adjustment in the title-holding system involved faction leader Odunsi, who eventually assumed the honorary title that had been suspended. Soon after the title was finally, and officially, conferred on him in 1975, the chief of Odunsi's ward died. The deceased chief occupied the second rung of the hierarchy. Without consulting the ward or its landowners' association, the *iwarefa* moved Odunsi into the vacant position; he was not dropped to the bottom of the ladder. Odunsi's prominence was such that his fellow ward leaders would not have passed him up as ward chief even if they had been given an opportunity to elect a replacement. Yet they were presented with a *fait accompli*. As a result, Odunsi moved into the heir-apparent slot in the Odi Olowo chiefly hierarchy and, if he outlived him, would succeed to the *Olu*ship. A second transfer, of Chief Taiwo from a personal to an established ward title, also occurred after the death of a ward chief. This transfer produced a strong protest from the ward in which the vacancy occurred since, again, its landowners' association had no opportunity to make a choice and felt it had been coerced. The minutes of the chiefs' meetings indicate that the ward's protest was ineffective. Needless to say, the dependence of neighbourhood ward leaders on the more powerful civic leaders was sufficient to neutralise their objections.

The Awori chieftaincy division of Ojuwoye had, of course, employed similar strategies to the settlers by trying to bring into its camp influential people who might improve its position. But, again, the same conflict between self-interest and collective need surfaced at some cost to Awori solidarity and the Awori pursuit of common goals – particularly the goal of denying settler legitimacy. Acting on a keen desire to strengthen his own standing in Mushin, *Olu* Aileru of the Ojuwoye Chieftaincy Division attempted to confer honorary titles on the community's foremost leaders. This move indicated that his attitude had changed significantly in the decade since 1956 when he joined the *Onitire* of Itire in fiery opposition to settlers. Altered circumstances changed his position. For one thing, the Awori faction leader, Sotomi, was not appointed to advisory bodies in the first few years of the military government and he therefore enjoyed a less advantageous position than his rivals Abiola and Odunsi. For another, there were internal feuds within the Ojuwoye community. While Aileru's move to confer titles on the outsiders failed, it did not prevent him from entering into an alliance which enabled him to replace the support he had lost from other Awori with support from settlers and to win a coveted position in the House of Chiefs.

Seen from the broadest perspective, these manipulations in title-giving procedures strengthened groups as a whole. The alterations brought into the chieftaincy system prominent, influential people who had been outside it, and they elevated the status of prominent people inside it. The more important the title-giving population was in the aggregate, and the higher the positions of important people in the chiefly hierarchies, the less the system could be ignored by government officials and, therefore, the more the chiefs benefited.

All in all, title-giving and title-receiving was a two-way process. On the one hand it reflected the realities of power in a community. On the other it added to the power of a community's notables by transforming their transient political roles into permanent political statuses and thereby providing them with formal access to expanded sources of influence and resources. Government signalled its acceptance of the power of Mushin's title-holders and added to it by allocating a place for a Mushin chief in the Lagos State House of Ọbas and Chiefs in 1969. This allocation served as a re-authentication of Mushin's seven ọba and was, thus, a successful first step in the process of legally institutionalising the political activities of many of Mushin's most prominent citizens.

PUBLIC LEGITIMATION OF UNOFFICIAL AUTHORITY

The second step in the process of legalising the chieftaincy system was to secure official recognition for junior chiefs and honorary title-holders. Ojuwoye had taken the lead in this lengthy process when it staged its controversial *iwuye* for its junior tier of chiefs. In 1969, Odi Olowo scheduled its own *iwuye*. The announcement that there would be a settler installation gave rise to a second episode in the factional struggles centred on chiefship.

Chieftaincy conflict: episode two[3]
The Odi Olowo chieftaincy division scheduled an *iwuye* for eighteen junior title-holders (fourteen established and four honorary titles) on 26 December 1969 to culminate their reorganising activities and to strengthen their claims to be legally recognised. A history of Odi Olowo was printed in pamphlet form and sent to participants and government officials to inform them of the settlers' accomplishments in developing and urbanising the area and creating political order in it. Funds for the ceremony were collected, ritual regalia was prepared (including *akoko* leaves, the sign of chieftaincy), invitations were distributed to prominent members of the community and, as a final touch, Timothy Abiola was unanimously chosen to serve as master of ceremonies, the role reserved for a participant of high status. (The titles of Abiola and Odunsi were still suspended.)

Two days before the ceremony, a government order reached the Odi Olowo chiefs ordering them to stop their plans. The chiefs had been asked to call a halt to their *iwuye* after threats that the ceremony would be disrupted by violence reached the Mushin Town Council. Civil war was raging elsewhere in Nigeria, and town council officials reasoned that the well-being of the community might be endangered if an incident triggered off other local tensions.

In the meantime, believing that the threats to disrupt their ceremony had come from the Ojuwoye Chieftaincy Division, settler chiefs vowed to break their alliance with the *Olu Mushin*. Only a few months earlier, settlers had engineered and supported the *Olu*'s election to the House of Chiefs, and in return Aileru had fêted Odi Olowo chiefs at a special gathering in his compound. Now the settlers felt they had been deceived.

Three months after the cancellation of the Odi Olowo *iwuye*, the *Olu Mushin* sent word to Odi Olowo chiefs that he wished to tell them his side of the story. Again, he called the chiefs to his compound where he explained that conflict within the Ojuwoye community itself was out of his control. He, his kinsmen, and other clients had not betrayed the Odi Olowo chiefs, but other elements within the Ojuwoye Division, namely the Awori faction leader Sotomi and his followers, from whom Aileru was estranged, were responsible for the threats that went to the Mushin Town Council and which stopped the Odi Olowo installation. Settlers accepted this explanation, and Aileru again fêted them as a sign that their alliance should remain in place.

Shortly after the reconciliation, *Olu* Aileru died. For the next five years, the elders and kingmakers of the Ojuwoye Division withdrew from most of Mushin's chieftaincy activities and its factional struggles in order to pick a successor to their throne.

An *iwuye* was the legitimating element in title-holding.[4] No claim to a title could be upheld without public confirmation that it had been properly bestowed before followers and civic leaders, both of whom acted as witnesses. Attending an *iwuye* was a signal of public consent to and compliance with the conferral of authority. The holding of an installation ceremony, using proper symbols of office and proper rituals, established a precedent, since according to the customs surrounding office-holding, once a title was properly conferred it could not be taken away. A properly installed chief could be prevented from functioning through ostracism; *in extremis* an *ọba* could also be deposed, as had infrequently occurred elsewhere. Under ordinary circumstances, however, a chief could not be deprived of a title. A properly conferred chieftaincy title was held for life; a title-holder could be promoted to a higher title or higher level in the chiefly hierarchy (or even manoeuvred into a lower level) but he or she could not be deprived of the title. Without proper conferral in the form of an *iwuye*, a title was not authentic. Consequently, a person whose title was not bestowed at an *iwuye*, or whose *iwuye* was improper in some way, was open to the vicissitudes of political competition, in that the title could be contested, removed, replaced, or given to someone else.

An *iwuye* also marked the conferral of substantial rewards to the title-holder. The ritual served as a political credential, attesting to the high status and public approval of a title-holder. Once recognised a person was in a position to exploit the benefits of office. Hence an *iwuye* could be seen not only as a symbolic, precedent-setting rite, but also as a real power-conferring action.

Preventing an *iwuye* thus had strong consequences. One method of fighting political battles was to prevent or disrupt ceremonies that set political precedents or otherwise gave public consent to the exercise of authority. The situation with regard to political ceremonies in Mushin was doubly charged. This was an urban area in the process of establishing its political system and the principles which governed it. An *iwuye* did not simply validate titles, but validated the rules by which titles were conferred. In the Odi Olowo case, the *iwuye* of junior established and honorary title-holders was to be its first, and the rules that were used to designate the order of succession, ranking, and naming were being formally acted upon for the first time. After the *iwuye* was held, the rules used to bring it about could also be cited as precedents and incorporated into the communal code that governed and justified, *ex post facto*, the action taken. So long as a precedent was not set, the rules attending it also were not valid.

For Awori, the cancellation of the settler *iwuye* was a victory in their ongoing struggle to prevent settlers from taking high offices in the community and establishing their authenticity as politically privileged members of the community. Above all else, at least in this context, it prevented settlers from establishing a precedent which could be cited as evidence in support of the legitimacy of a second tier of settler authority figures.

The settler *iwuye* had been part of a campaign to signal to the government that its chiefs were accepted in the eyes of the public – a potent preface to the legalisation process. Other *iwuye* in Mushin – an earlier ceremony at Shomolu being one – were successful. Once precedents like these were set, it was difficult for government officials to deny their existence and salience in community life. Thus setting political precedents outside official circles was a show of power and as such could be used as a wedge to get inside those same circles.

While the attack against Odi Olowo's chiefs was a setback for all settlers, it was not the only way in which they could secure official recognition. What settlers lacked in historical advantage and an ability to claim son-of-the-soil status, they made up for in an ability to make contact with civil servants in high places, and in an ability to exploit Awori weaknesses.

SHIFTING ALLIANCES

The Awori were deeply divided among their chieftaincy divisions as well as within them. One source of conflict was unknowingly created more than a century earlier when leaders of the Ojuwoye community conferred an honorary title on a Lagosian. The historic incident, familiar from its mention in Chapter 2, and its twentieth-century ramifications, was as follows:

> In the mid nineteenth century, Ifadu, a representative of the powerful Lagosian *Baba Isale*, the Chief *Eletu Odibo*, was given a personal title by Ojuwoye chiefs in recognition of his services as an Ifa divination priest and as a middleman to the *Eletu Odibo*. The title bestowed on Ifadu was *Alashe Ojuwoye*.
>
> A century later in 1959, William Ladega, a descendant of Ifadu, and resident of Lagos City, claimed that the title given to his ancestor was not an honorary, but an established (hereditary) title in the Ojuwoye Chieftaincy Division. That being the case, it could be perpetuated from one generation to the next. Ladega claimed that Ifadu's ancestors were clients who had been absorbed into one of the Ojuwoye ruling house descent groups, and therefore the *Alashe* title should be subject to the customary rules governing succession to traditional office.
>
> Acting on this claim, Ladega approached the contemporary *Eletu Odibo* and arranged to be capped as the contemporary *Alashe Ojuwoye*. As part of the capping ceremony, he was presented to the *Oba* of Lagos. Once these legitimating actions were performed, Ladega began selling Ojuwoye land in Mushin that, he also claimed, was the property of the original *Alashe*, and hence the rightfully inherited property of Ifadu's descendants, i.e. Ladega and Ifadu's other living heirs.

The Ojuwoye ruling houses immediately brought suit against Ladega. In 1966, the Ikeja High Court ruled Ladega's claim to the title was unjustified. His ancestors, according to the testimony, had not been absorbed into an Ojuwoye descent group and therefore the court invalidated Ladega's claim to the title and his land sales. The decision was unsuccessfully appealed by Ladega who, first, took his case to the Mushin Town Council's Chieftaincy Committee where the Ikeja court ruling was upheld in 1974 and, then, to the Lagos State Government Ministry of Local Government and Chieftaincy Affairs.[5]

Throughout the lengthy period when Ladega's claims were under litigation, the *Onitire* of Itire supported Ladega against the Ojuwoye ruling house. At the time, the *Onitire* was chairman of the Mushin Town Council's Chieftaincy Committee – a rotating position – and this enabled him to put strong support behind Ladega's claims. The *Onitire*'s backing of a Lagosian – a Lagosian who had tried, in the Ojuwoye view, to deceive his putatively related descent group in Mushin – exacerbated an already poor relationship between the two Awori divisions. It also antagonised other Mushin chiefs who recognised no validity in Ladega's claims and therefore declared them invalid. In the aftermath, however, the *Onitire* conferred on Ladega an honorary Itire chieftaincy division title.

At this point the Itire chieftaincy division was, theoretically speaking, a liability to other Awori chiefs. Unlike the other chieftaincy divisions, Itire land overlapped into municipal Lagos, providing the *Onitire* and his followers with a natural bridge to the city's chiefly circles that could be used for their own instrumental purposes. The Itire ties to Lagos were not threatening to Mushin's leaders so long as the activities emanating from them were kept within the confines of kinship and ritual activities. When, or if, the Lagos chiefs backed Itire in support of public matters – the Ladega case being a prime example – they posed a real threat to Mushin's boundaries, and injected a disquieting element into the political affairs of this suburban district.

The reaction to the *Onitire* in support of Ladega was similar to the reaction of market leaders when the Lagos market woman intruded into Mushin market affairs. Clearly the goal of most of Mushin's chiefs was to function without interference from the more influential and firmly entrenched Lagos chiefs whose entrance into the Mushin arena would raise the spectre of dominance and the issue of relative seniority between city and suburban chiefly divisions. On this occasion, Mushin's settler and Awori chiefs joined together to oppose the *Onitire* and to declare emphatically that Ladega's claims in Mushin were illegitimate. This was their way of closing the door to relationships that might bring the chiefs of Mushin and Lagos into overlapping involvements. Other Awori, therefore, became estranged from the *Onitire* and his followers, and once again the sons of the soil were prevented from acting as a unified group.

Awori cleavages were sharpest when Mushin's chiefs elected the *Olu*

Mushin as their representative to the Lagos House of Chiefs in 1969. Settlers embraced the opportunity to back the *Olu Mushin*, since his rival in the contest was the *Onitire* of Itire. The election was complex, however, because a single representative was to be selected from the three districts of Ikeja Division. Therefore an alliance between two districts was necessary in order to win sufficient votes for any one candidate. Settlers worked behind the scenes to secure the support of the chiefs from Agege District. They promised that in exchange for Agege's votes they (the settlers) would vote for the Agege candidate in the next election to the House of Chiefs.[6]

The House of Chiefs election also brought about a significant shift in the factional alliances in Mushin. The Awori Chieftaincy Division of Isolo joined the settler (Odi Olowo and Shomolu) and Ojuwoye alliance. Itire was backed by the relatively small Awori Chieftaincy Division of Onigbongbo and the division of Oshodi (with its Lagosian origins). It was a hotly contested election with certain 'irregularities'. The *Olu Mushin* was the only chief in Ikeja division who did not receive an invitation to attend the election meeting, and only shrewd negotiations prevented the vote from taking place without his being present. I mention the incident to indicate the intensity of feeling that arose among chiefs over the event and the internal hostilities among Awori which no doubt went into creating this 'irregularity'.

These, then, were some of the internal problems which prevented Awori from effectively using the chieftaincy system as a platform from which to promote their claim of political exclusivity, or from using their *iwuye* victory over settlers to better their own position. Earlier they had lost an opportunity to force settlers into a subordinate position when they were asked – not once, but on many occasions – to cap the chiefly hierarchy with a district-wide paramount chief. The same inability to see one of their members succeed over the others was apparent in the House of Chiefs election. The Awori failure to unite and their insistence on equivalence among their own divisions, thus kept the door open for settlers to remain active and to claim equivalence with them.

BUREAUCRATIC LEGITIMATION OF UNOFFICIAL AUTHORITY

Settlers concentrated their drive to secure legal recognition for a second tier of chiefs, after the civil war ended in January 1970, on the agencies where their influence was most pronounced: the Mushin Town Council and the Lagos State Government. Their various displays of strength in the community and its major interest groups, as we saw, resulted in settler leaders being appointed to the majority of the seats in the council's committee of management. Their justification for such appointments stressed their demographic majority and urban orientation, in contrast to the Awori minority which was characterised as having a provincial outlook and poor record of community service. 'We (settlers) met this place in poor condition,' said one committee appointee. 'We . . . developed it (and made) it cosmopolitan.'

The settler advantage lay in the fact that their dominant position in the committee of management improved their opportunties to make contacts with civil servants with whom they could plead their case. The selection of committee of management members, to illustrate the point, was largely carried out by officials in the Ministry of Local Government, who based their choices on their own and the informal recommendations made by town council administrators, and the advice of community leaders with whom they came in contact. The ability to enter into this procedure helped to perpetuate in office the same core group of local leaders. Settlers were, after all, recommending settlers. As S. J. Odunsi emphasised: one had to have influence to wield it, and having it was dependent upon the prior existence of personal relationships between people who were known to one another. Informal face-to-face relationships grew out of formal contacts or, at the least, out of contacts established in formal contexts. Placing oneself in a position to make these contacts, therefore, was a significant step which subsequently allowed one to move up the ladder of community power.

Settler influence also fell on increasingly friendly ears, so much so that the second tier of Mushin's junior and honorary chiefs – eighty-four in all – was legally recognised at a government-sponsored *iwuye* in May 1975. (The *iwuye* did not occur without a final, but feeble attempt on the part of Awori, who sent a letter to the Mushin Town Council, asking it to exclude settler chieftaincy divisions from the event.) Simultaneously with the recognitions, chieftaincy declarations – the rules governing office-holding in each of the chiefly divisions – were approved by the government. This, then, was the final step in the recognition process.

Government officials had become favourably disposed toward the chiefs – settler and Awori – for several reasons. One was a new military policy which encouraged civil servants to work in their areas of origin. Consequently, civil servants were more open to local pressure groups. No doubt some of the bureaucrats desired titles as much as the rest of the population and wished to keep this avenue for achievement open. Indeed, one official who was reputedly influential in the decisions to legalise Mushin's junior established and honorary chiefs was himself the recent recipient of a chieftaincy title in a neighbouring district.

Civil servants also wished to make use of chiefs for more than their own personal gain. As one argued, chiefs were respected and influential; they were valuable as moulders of public opinion and as communication links to residents. When all was said and done, it was easier to control and use the chieftaincy system if it were co-opted into the official boundaries of government, than if it existed on the outside.

There was an even more compelling reason to accommodate Mushin's leaders in their quest for recognition of chieftaincy titles. After the military staged its 1966 coup and assumed control of Nigeria, it needed two things in order to govern efficiently: popular support and the expertise of civil servants.[7] As already stated, the pulse of the public was taken and satisfied through civilian representatives who were appointed by government to advisory panels. Many of these representatives in Mushin and throughout Western Nigeria were former AG politicians.[8]

As for the establishment, the civil service remained in place. However, under the military, the bureaucrats, especially at high levels, gained power in policy-making, decision-taking, and allocating roles. The military was limited in its ability and numbers, and the expanded role of the civil service was a natural outgrowth of these, and related, factors. The ramifications, as one might expect, were that bureaucrats interacted more with the public. They increasingly developed constituencies and clients. In turn, they were increasingly subject to scrutiny and public pressures.[9]

In Mushin, the town council officials were dependent on local leaders for goodwill and support. Malfeasance in office, for example, just as in a civilian regime, could result in dismissal, demotion, or transfer. But the problem was exaggerated under the military, since bureaucrats were taking many roles that elected representatives and appointed officials formerly took. One Mushin Town Council clerk was removed from his post following a committee of management vote of no confidence – taken because he had appropriated many committee powers to himself, particularly contract awards which were not in conformity with regulated procedures.[10] Mushin's leaders also waged bitter battles against civil servants when they failed to install public water taps. Community leaders were, then, capable of staging protests and demanding the ouster of unpopular government authorities. This made bureaucrats all the more interested in gaining approval when they could.

The desire of the military-bureaucratic regime to acquire popular support was even more pronounced in the mid-1970s when public dissatisfaction with the military reached a high pitch.[11] Indeed, the recognition of Mushin's chiefs came in May 1975, only three months before a coup which ousted the Gowon government and replaced it with another military faction.[12] The situation, it must be pointed out, was in some ways quite similar to the last-minute NNDP recognition of Mushin's seven ọba in the waning days of the civilian government in 1965.

The expansion of government interest in community affairs none the less injected a note of stability which had not yet existed in Mushin. In its first twenty years, the structure of the Mushin Town Council had changed sixteen times, seesawing between elected councils, appointed councils, and sole administratorships. There were nine policy-making councils made up of community representatives from 1955 to 1975: two elected by residents, four appointed by government at the behest of party leaders, and three appointed by state civil servants at the behest of the military. Only two councils served full three-year terms. The longevity of the others was from one month to two years with shorter periods being more the rule than the exception.[13] During the same twenty-year period, the bureaucratic arm of the council was also subject to frequent changes. Turnover was so great, in fact, that there was little administrative continuity and little incentive to provide governmental leadership and direction. Even in the early 1970s Mushin was seen as a no-man's land in the eyes of its metropolitan-area neighbours. It was attacked by the press as 'a disgrace to Nigeria' which housed the 'tough people' of the city.[14] Much of the problem could be laid to the fact that there were only 1,477 government workers trying to care for a population which exceeded that of municipal Lagos with its 6,250 municipal employees. Finally, some of these Mushin Town Council employees were not only becoming permanent fixtures, but also had a vested interest in making policy that would affect their own lives and the lives of their kinsmen, friends, and fellow townsmen. There were advantages in being a public servant and influencing the allocation of public resources in a place where one could gain favour among one's own people and, in turn, reap the benefits of that favour.

The strong interest on the part of civil servants in local affairs was briefly played out in a number of secret societies, known as secret courts. The courts replaced, to some extent, the formal outlets for widespread political participation – political parties and national ethnic unions – which had been banned by the military government. Like patrons and middlemen, the societies provided members with contacts and networks in the form of fellow members who solved one another's problems, helped them in securing urban resources, or provided avenues for fixing things with the bureaucracy. The secret of the secret courts was that they were heavily populated with civil servants. Thus, when their secret became increasingly apparent, they were dealt a crippling blow by the military, which declared them off limits to civil servants. At this point the secret courts seemed to wane.

During this time under the military, Awori took new steps to assert themselves. The creation of Lagos State in 1967 had provided a new and smaller arena in which Awori could assert leadership. Government policy also aided that process by encouraging indigenous populations to take prominent roles in their home governments. Eight years later in 1975, Awori joined hands in a state-wide voluntary association called the Awori National Welfare Association (ANWA).[15] It was important that the vehicle for unifying Awori came from outside Mushin, i.e. from the state as a whole. This meant that the organisation could transcend local cleavages and provide a neutral forum for the coming together of dissident Awori in a new, mutually reinforcing group. The ANWA bridged former cleavages by working outside the constraints of the chieftaincy system, yet it persisted in the goal of strengthening Mushin's son-of-the-soil position in community governance. The strategy of the Awori leadership at this point, in a friendly governmental environment, was to transform a category of ethnically homogeneous people – whose rivalries had heretofore undermined their political goals – into an active, focused political interest group.

Awori thus redirected their attention to the composition of the Mushin Town Council's Committee of Management. More than 2,000 people led by the ANWA, staged a demonstration at the Mushin Town Council in January 1975 demanding that more sons of the soil be included on the committee of management. The group's leaders complained publicly that the committee was inefficiently administered and that the untapped Awori talent of Mushin could rectify its problems if, of course, some of that talent were appointed to the committee.[16] Within six months – again in the waning days of the Gowon military regime – the government capitulated to the Awori demands by appointing five extra Awori representatives to the committee. The twenty-five-member group now had seven Awori and eighteen settlers.

In the final analysis, the top leaders of Mushin used power to secure official legitimacy. The settlers used the traditional symbols of authority, i.e. chieftaincy titles, and the power derived from titles in order to gain statutory recognition. Awori, in contrast, used a recently created voluntary organisation in order to assert their rights to serve on official governing bodies. The problem that leaders of both groups faced was that they were sandwiched in between the grassroots public and the overarching structures of the nation state. This meant they needed to justify and validate their political actions in society both above and below. The extensive system of unofficial authority which was established in Mushin testified to the legitimacy which had been accorded to both groups of community leaders by the public. Given this grassroots strength, the government was persuaded to confer statutory legtimacy on at least some of the local leaders and at the same time co-opt their influence. Government recognition represented self-interest. Its tactics mirrored the top leaders' tactics. Government used its own power to confer legal recognition – another kind of status reward – on influential citizens so as to obtain their compliance, support, and approval. Acquiescence in the local leaders' demands had its own set of rewards.

CHAPTER NINE

CONCLUSIONS

This book has concentrated on the development of authority in a large metropolitan suburb. The goal was to explain how ordinary people living in a new urban community found their way to elite officials and major institutions, and to show that, as part of this process, they were required to exert leadership and create their own informal system of governance. The success of these ordinary people rested on their ability to acquire and wield power, which they did largely through clientelism.

The theoretical focus of this study thus rests on the relationship between power and clientelism. My concern is to demonstrate that client politics accounts for much of the participation, as well as the amassing and use of power, that we see today in many urban polities – especially polities which have grown rapidly and have had little time to develop the kinds of structures, groupings, and other formal outlets which ordinarily channel the political needs and strivings of the masses. The weight borne by clientelism in political affairs is attested to in many ways. Clientelism helps account for much of the stability in leadership which exists despite the many changes that take place in regimes. It helps account for the paucity of overt class conflict despite extraordinary disparities between rich and poor. And it helps account for the fact that integration occurs despite the formidable barriers of ethnicity.

There are various perspectives from which to assess the role played by clientelism in political affairs. In the following discussion I stress three of them, returning again to Mushin for illustrative purposes. First, from the perspective of the individual, we see that client relationships expand social opportunities. They free individuals from the constraints of ascriptive or group ties, contributing significantly to their flexibility in acquiring support, whether for personal or political gain. Second, from the perspective of the community, client relationships organise people. They make substantial contributions to integrating diverse populations and organising power blocs.

Finally, from the perspective of the analyst, client relationships are means to greater political ends. Hence, it is imperative that we be able to distinguish between those political systems in which the ends are part of the ordinary outcomes of political interchange and those in which they are extraordinary. The latter is the case, I suggest, when the power gained from client relationships is vital to the processes of creating and institutionalising authority.

POLITICAL PROBLEMS OF URBAN SETTLERS

Mushin grew into a suburb of Lagos following the Second World War. The transformation of its quiet villages into teeming urban neighbourhoods was part of a dramatic urban population explosion which was sweeping across tropical Africa and which continued, even accelerated, into the present. Migrants from throughout Nigeria and neighbouring countries, but principally from the diverse Yoruba-speaking communities that arched behind the city for several hundred miles, crowded into metropolitan Lagos in search of new lives, new challenges, and new economic opportunities which they found in commerce, industry, bureaucracy, and a host of *ad hoc* and informal endeavours. The openness of Mushin, combined with its comparatively low-cost housing, made it a haven for workers, artisans, traders – the common people – who, together, became the backbone of its population.

Aside from the general adjustments newcomers must make in any unfamiliar environment, special problems faced the people who settled in Mushin and who adjusted to them in special ways. First, there was intense competition for urban resources, and grave difficulties in acquiring them. Mushin and its predecessor villages suffered from extreme neglect by public agencies and extreme handicaps in communicating information. So far as the general populace was concerned, taking part in local community life in ways that could be thought of as political centred on processes relating to the allocation of goods and services and on bridging the wide gaps between office holders who were the distributors of public assets and ordinary citizens who were the consumers. Kinship was not the mediating institution in these processes. One's rights in the community, with the exception of the host minority, did not devolve from status in a descent group. Indigenous descent groups were too few and unassertive in the community's urbanising years to dominate the community by absorbing new residents or by isolating and thereby disfranchising them, and migrant descent groups were either headquartered elsewhere or were too incomplete to function effectively in political ways. This left to most residents the task of establishing new relationships which would be useful in the local arena. Among them were relationships which grew out of spatial contiguity.

Second, there was intense competition for real estate – not so much because of its actual scarcity since open land was abundant and, in fact, Mushin's greatest asset, but because of the legal and political complications involved in getting and keeping it. Struggles to acquire houseplots pitted outsiders against insiders, kinsman against kinsman, one neighbour against another, creating one of the greatest sources of litigation handled by local courts. Yet out of this conflict, in the course of finding solutions for keeping and protecting their property, owners were drawn together into cooperative alliances and neighbourhood groupings. Once again relationships growing out of co-residence were meaningful.

Third, there was an urgent need to maintain order, but few formal mechanisms with which to do it. Mushin was a frontier in its early urbanis-ing years.[1] The institutional framework which usually develops alongside a gradually expanding population had neither the time nor the official encou-ragement to develop. Consequently, residents established an informal sys-tem of maintaining order. It began in their neighbourhoods where headmen and councils of resident elders organised safety patrols, supervised orderly settlement, heard disputes, and took their collective concerns to higher authorities. Eventually their activities evolved into a community-wide chieftaincy system. It was a remarkable outcome in that residents looked to the past for an idiom in which to voice contemporary political concerns. But it was a pragmatic outcome in that chieftaincy was an institution whose cultural principles were widely shared among most residents. In essence, the chieftaincy system was recreated in a new context by a constituency with diverse backgrounds in order to identify and legitimate grassroots leaders and the political functions they performed.

Leadership itself presented the fourth problem. Who were the people who would help residents acquire resources, protect property investments, form neighbourhood groups, and act as headmen, elders, and chiefs? The people who rose naturally to leadership were the owners. They controlled land and housing, Mushin's major resources, and by virtue of that control were its most powerful residents. Sheer wealth was by no means insignifi-cant in the exercise of power, although in relative terms there was little in Mushin. Moreover, successful people usually invested in real estate – one of the few forms of savings and guaranteed income open to non-elites; therefore whatever wealth some residents had, it almost automatically included property. For the relatively few affluent residents who did own real estate, there was usually no interest and thus no participation in local affairs. Owners had permanent vested interests in Mushin; tenants did not. Hence, they made up the pool from which neighbourhood and community leadership emerged.

Finally, aspiring leaders had their own adjustments to make. The way to demonstrate leadership was to create a following. The way to attract a following was to offer support – the kind of support which helped others survive in a complex and competitive society. People who made it possible for others to fulfil their needs and desires were, for obvious reasons, centres of attention. Their acceptance, particularly at the beginning of their careers, rested not so much on who they were as on what they did: acquire resources, develop skills, and then specialise in meeting peoples' needs by acting as their patrons, middlemen, and dispute settlers.

The key to success lay in mastering the art of client politics. In the course of living together in large, heterogeneous houses, owners and tenants were forced to interact together, and out of their interactions came mutually supportive social ties. Among the most valued ties for tenants and inactive owners were ones with owners who took leadership roles and were therefore able to put neighbours in contact with higher authorities. The importance of co-residence in bringing together leaders and clients cannot be understated. When Mushin became an administrative district in 1955, the community's major political institutions used residential criteria to establish basic units in their organisations: the chieftaincy system consisted of old village headmen and new neighbourhood chiefs – each representing, in some way, a geographical sector of Mushin; the Mushin Town Council consisted of elected councillors, each representing a residential ward; and the Action Group, Mushin's dominant political party, established a cell also in each residential ward. Through neighbourhood leaders – people one lived with and knew – residents were able to make connections with local institutions. Even after political parties were banned and district council members were appointed and not elected, the practice of gaining access to local governmental institutions through local leaders was firmly in place.

PARTICULAR AND UNIVERSAL ASPECTS OF CLIENTELISM

There was a long history of client politics in Mushin. It extended from the mid nineteenth century, when Lagos chiefs linked outlying villages of the Mushin area to British colonial administrators, through the mid twentieth century, when neighbourhood landowners linked their neighbours to political parties, the Mushin Town Council, state government officials, or military officers. The nature of these links changed over the years, but the ultimate goals – to bring ordinary people closer to the centres of economic and political power – did not.

Broadly-based cultural norms throughout the area also buttressed clientelism, and it appears that these and similar norms were in operation throughout the century examined in this book. Special terms – *Baba Isalẹ*, Godfather, and long-legs – were reserved for individuals who catered to clients, and special statuses – chieftaincy titles, elected and appointed offices, and informal positions of confidante or 'native advisor' – often went to leaders who were successful in attracting a large clientele. Culturally speaking, the number of client-followers was taken as a measure of a leader's strength.

Furthermore, the de-centralised structure of local government both during and after the colonial period encouraged the development of hundreds of leader-client networks. So far as the general public were concerned, interest in local affairs centred on local resources and ways to acquire them. But the difficulty in making contact with remote, inadequate, and poorly staffed agencies forced residents to develop the kinds of relationships which would help them meet the needs that public structures could not meet and bridge the gaps that officials did not bridge.

This, then, was the context which nurtured clientelism in Mushin. Each social, cultural, historical context has produced and reproduced its own particular forms of clientelism, and Mushin was no exception. The etiquette, values, and customs governing client relationships in Mushin, which I draw on in the following discussion, were quite different from those in, say, Beirut or Mexico City.[2] Those of the nineteenth and early twentieth centuries, when the Mushin area was rural, were even quite different from the relationships in post-war Mushin when it began to urbanise.

Still, there were qualities in Mushin client relationships which are universally present, and which make it possible to compare them cross-culturally. In the following pages I examine some of these qualities, concentrating on the ones which make client relationships effective in the quest for power and suggesting when and under what circumstances these ties are worth singling out for analysis. After all, client relationships are an almost universal aspect of contemporary political life, and they occur at all levels of a political system. They are never the only productive political relationships in a system, and their significance is a matter of degree. Hence their importance lies not in their presence or absence, but in the degree to which they are a formative force in public affairs.

POLITICAL ADVANTAGES OF INDIVIDUALLY-CONTRACTED TIES

One of the politically useful qualities of client relationships is that they are privately contracted alliances between two individuals. Through them people find their own sources of moral, psychological, material, and protective support, choosing who and how many partners will be, regulating the length and intensity of their relationships, and even adjusting their ties to suit changes in their own needs, objectives, and social circumstances. In modern urban settings such as Mushin, individual alliances are flexible. Indeed, Hanks concluded, following his study of political clientelism in Thailand, that the power of client relationships lay in their flexibility.[3] There are three ways in which flexibility demonstrates itself.

First, individually contracted ties allow participants to advance their own interests in ways of their own choosing. Needless to say, the parties to client relationships are free of the constraints imposed by groups.[4] They need not put collective interests ahead of individual ones, or support people they have not chosen to support. Theories of client politics are based on the proposition that self-interest is an effective mobilising force. They contrast with theories of group politics which are based on the premise that collective action is the key to exercising political power. Clearly, no political system relies on just one kind of political relationship; in virtually all systems individual and group ties exist and have different roles, however complementary or overlapping they may be. The benefit to leaders when they mobilise support through client ties, as Lande proposed, is that individually-negotiated relationships, while placing great demands on leaders to live up to obligations in which they alone are the central, responsible figures, simultaneously allow them to be their own tacticians in building bases of power.[5]

Second, individual alliances allow participants to make *new* connections. People cannot find all of the support they require within the realm of kinship or primary groups since, under most circumstances in urban societies, high levels of economic role specialisation prevent them from engaging in a sufficient number of specialities to meet all fellow members' needs. The same is true of class, occupation, etc. Hence, many relationships essential to survival in complex societies must extend beyond primary and other groupings, and in the process create new combinations of individuals who are offering support to one another.

Third, just as each relationship is a separate unit, the terms of each are separately established. The people involved are autonomous. Their loyalties are individually directed, and the criteria for them are individually established. Therefore leaders can recruit followers without being obliged to adhere to pre-established guidelines; they need not appeal to people on the basis of sharing a common ideology or common code of ethics or rules. Rather they can recruit support outside the familiar, conventional boundaries which are erected in their society, and in each instance establish fresh terms for their interaction.

The logical consequences are that the sense of obligation and distance between partners vary dramatically from one relationship to the next. Client ties are conventionally categorised as moral or instrumental, a typology I perpetuate for ease in discussion but in the full realisation that client ties range on continua from emotionally distant to close, from exploitative to highly magnanimous. The range is itself an advantage since, as will be seen below, it enhances a leader's abilities to attract a large and varied clientele.

POLITICAL ADVANTAGES OF INSTRUMENTAL AND MORAL TIES

For Weber and those who followed him, moral bonds in clientelism reveal themselves in strong sentiments and loyalties.[6] They exist when patrons and clients develop subjective feelings that they belong together or, in Cohen's view,[7] when relationships become ends in themselves and not means to realise ends. Moral bonds may represent a host of shared confidences, social interactions, advice, companionship or, as Bailey so aptly puts it, ties which have become multiplex.[8] But these are surface manifestations. Beneath the loyalties and sentiments is a deeply-embedded layer of trust, and the way in which trust is established and maintained, in the view of some scholars, is central to the analysis of clientelism.[9]

Trust is the effective dimension of client relationships – trust in people and the efficacy of their actions. Trust is an attitude of confidence, reliance, and good faith which is born of the repeated, positive experience that one's expectations will be met. Not all client ties, of course, involve the same degree or kind of trust.[10] One cannot assume that because an exchange takes place there is trust or that it is rightly placed. Trust develops. It is a personal hypothesis which, once formulated, is continually tested.

The prior condition for trust in the Mushin that I studied was accountability. Two people rarely established a client relationship without a prior introduction by a person known to each of them. Indeed, it was impolite for a person of junior status to approach an unknown senior for a favour without an introduction. The introduction was a significant part of initiating any relationship because the parties could be vouched for, traced, or otherwise held responsible, via the introducer, should either party fail to honour an agreement. Without some assurance of accountability an exchange rarely took place. This personal element in client relationships, involving as it did third parties as witnesses and guarantors, gave leaders a special advantage in exercising social control.[11]

The quality of the bond between partners to a client relationship in Mushin was revealed in terms of degree rather than of kind. It was imperative to observe certain forms of etiquette, display sincerity, and show interest in the other partner. Each of these elements carried with it observable behaviours. The more intense or exaggerated the behaviours, the more a leader or client demonstrated either a close tie or interest in establishing one.

Visiting, an essential ingredient in any relationship, involved etiquette which was highly ritualised. A client observed proper etiquette, and simultaneously sincerity of purpose, by making repeated visits to a patron and repeated requests for assistance. A petitioner who did not make return visits – clients always visited their patrons and not vice versa – was seen as not in need and by extension not sincere. A casual request had no place in the client system.

Clients, too, needed evidence of interest and sincerity on the part of benefactors so as to know they were not wasting their time and effort. The leader demonstrated genuine interest and proper etiquette through shows of hospitality: a refreshing beverage or an accommodating welcome, i.e. by diverting attention away from others or by offering a place, especially the best chair, in which to sit.

Ceremonies were also meaningful events. The more leaders and clients involved themselves in the ceremonial lives of one another, the closer the ties were likely to be. Leaders revealed the greatest degree of closeness by appearing on important occasions in their clients' lives accompanied by an entourage and making an entrance in a noticeable and dramatic manner. The presence of a prominent guest enhanced the stature of any host or hostess. It was equally important to make a monetary contribution: the larger the amount, again, the closer the tie. A very close relationship was revealed by a monetary gift that exceeded the amount a relative might donate for the same occasion.

In return, it was imperative that clients not only attend the rites of passage and ceremonies of leaders, but that they act as messengers, servants, or organisers before, during, and after them. The closeness of the bonds could thus be measured by a client's devotion to those duties and the amount of time and energy put into them. Clients were necessary parts of any public rites or appearances of leaders, since it was crucial that important people have an entourage. A following was not simply evaluated by reputation and gossip, but was visually assessed and enumerated.

Mutual protection was another sign of a strong bond. The historic *Baba Isalę*–client relationship is instructive in this regard. The *Baba Isalę*, father in the courtyard, was an authority figure who took his place among elders in a 'courtyard' where cases were heard and settled and where community decisions were taken. Clients whose *Baba Isalę* patrons were 'members' of the courtyard thus had automatic protection in any political or judicial matters which threatened or advanced their interests. In return, clients performed the unbecoming tasks public figures could not, and dared not, perform. A popular saying – as applicable in the 1970s as a century earlier – captured the essence of the obligations arising out of a strong patron–client relationship: 'An elder's hand is too large to put in the gourd.' In other words, a small inconspicuous hand was needed to remove the sediment – the unsavoury elements – that collected from time to time in its base. Each partner in his own way guarded the interests of the other, and in so doing entered into a relationship of complicity in which protective political services were the bases for bonds that residents described as 'closer than blood'.

One form of reciprocity for clients whose ties were closer than blood, Bailey would call them *core* clients,[12] was to help their leaders manage transactions with peripheral clients – those Scott described as 'easy to detach'.[13] Core clients saw to the needs of peripheral ones by serving as messengers or representatives who arranged introductions, favours, and so on. They did not replace their superiors and thereby create their own sub-clientele; core clients acted in their leaders' names and at their direction. This practice followed the custom in traditional political systems whereby important people, especially senior chiefs, were enjoined from taking direct action on behalf of followers, because it was unbefitting behaviour for people of high status to leave their lodgings and run errands or make arrangements for people of lower status. In their place, clients (or other retainers, kinsmen, or servants) acted on a leader's behalf, and with the full understanding that their actions were, albeit indirectly, the actions of their leaders. The continuation of this custom in Mushin made it possible for leaders to form many loose relationships for which they could take credit, but for which subordinates performed the legwork. The practice was congruent with the notion that patrons and clients need not be intimates.

Mushin's leaders thus maintained more clients and followers in loose, instrumental relationships than in strong moral bonds. Instrumental ties were beneficial, desirable, and necessary to both leaders and followers. They were not taken as the opposite of moral relationships, in an ethical sense, but rather as legitimate and proper relationships. Instrumental ties in Mushin were consistent with the universal definition of their being implemental, pragmatic, often single-interest relationships in which there is low emotional content. And this was their value. Both leaders and clients were more than satisfied to cultivate relationships in which both sides realised some benefit, but in which they needed to invest only a minimum amount of time and emotional energy.

Moral bonds, by contrast, placed comparatively greater obligations on both parties. But obligations were a matter of degree, inasmuch as all bonds, whether moral or instrumental, taxed the resources of leaders, placing limits on the numbers of core clients they could handle and, likewise, taxed the abilities of clients to reciprocate.[14] Each side sought to find an optimum balance in the number(s) of close or distant ties they formed. For leaders, however, it was strategically sensible to vary the spectrum with as wide a range of closeness/distance in relationships as possible since a wide following, theoretically speaking, offered the widest range of returns.

POLITICAL ADVANTAGES OF RECIPROCITY

The people in client relationships are brought together by reciprocity. Whether moral or instrumental, there is no tie if there is no exchange. The people of Mushin were well aware of the value of reciprocity and sternly warned one another that 'nothing goes for nothing'. They were equally well aware that the needs which brought them together placed them in a relationship of mutual dependence.

This is not to say that client relationships are equal. The parties to these ties are not of the same status; they do not have the same things to offer one another; and they do not realise the same benefits from their exchanges. People lower in the social hierarchy become clients in order to create personal social security systems. People higher in the hierarchy become their patrons and middlemen because they control elements which underlie security and they wish to benefit from this advantage.

The inequities in client relationships are perfectly conveyed in the historical origins of the word. The client 'has someone to lean on' – Webster's Dictionary traces the word to the Latin *clinare*, to lean; in return the client 'is at the call of his patron' – the Oxford English Dictionary prefers the Indo-European source, *cluens*, to hear.[15] Superior parties in a client relationship are superior precisely because they can be leaned on. They control a greater range of valued commodities or services than their clients do. If this were not so, there would be no demand – no leaning – on the part of clients, and no need for a relationship. Yet clients must offer something of value or patrons and middlemen would have no desire to share with them their prized commodities and services. In many cases, the resources superiors seek are the clients themselves: people who can be called on. Clients are relatively plentiful in number, and therefore the superior parties have a larger field from which to get what they value as opposed to clients who are restricted to a comparatively smaller field in order to secure what they want. (Nevertheless sanctions operate in both directions since, thanks to the fact that the ties are individually contracted, both leaders and clients have the freedom to move from one relationship to another.)

The imbalance in client relationships gives superior parties major political advantages in comparison to subordinate parties. For one thing, leaders can control the timing of their demands. People with more can wait. They can allow debts to accumulate without calling them in. For another, leaders can collect their debts in more diverse ways than clients; they can accept a wide range of services and items as repayment because immediate needs, for the most part, are neither compelling nor specific. This unevenness has led Blau to call the transactions in client relationships *social exchanges*. Social exchanges involve 'unspecified obligations' in which one thing is exchanged for another. They differ from strict economic exchanges where the amounts or kinds of things to be repaid are of equal value, pre-determined, or subject to contracts.[16] Indeed, in social exchanges one thing *must* be exchanged for another inasmuch as clients are seeking scarce commodities that, because patrons control them, clients cannot replace in kind. The pliancy in social exchanges also extends to the meaning parties attach to the things they exchange. Patrons can provide a wide range of non-political favours – from giving loans, to settling domestic disputes, to arranging apprenticeships – and ask for returns which are overtly non-political but which may be converted to politically meaningful assets. Attending a ceremony in order to repay a debt is, on one level, a simple sociable act but, on another, a swelling of a leader's entourage, advertising the fact that the person is prominent. Likewise, running an errand is not a political act in and of itself but it can indicate to observers that a leader commands the services of others. The point is that social exchanges give leaders great latitude in using reciprocity and interpreting the meanings attached to reciprocity, to advance their political aspirations.

In the same vein, superiors are in a better position to reinvest their returns in higher-order rewards than clients. Two examples make the point. In exchange for a few simple introductions, patrons may collect the votes which place them in a position to gain rewards which are far higher – salary and spoils of office – than those which have gone to the clients. Or, the repayment from one client, rather than being used for immediate, personal gain, may be directly reinvested in a second client thereby expanding a leader's following and, ultimately, the amount of indebtedness he can use in meeting his goals. The conversions made in social exchanges,[17] in these and many other ways, favour those who have high status.

One of the highest benefits is that through exchanges superior parties receive, for all intents and purposes, a mandate to lead.[18] While leaders take control in setting the timing and terms of exchanges, clients acquiesce in allowing them to do so, and in the process tacitly acknowledge the leader's superiority. A repayment in an exchange may, in fact, consist of nothing more than an acknowledgment or acceptance of leadership – a repayment which superior parties may consider sufficiently substantial in and of itself that they make no other demands.

Finally, reciprocal relationships give leaders an opportunity to protect themselves and their clients by neutralising competition, conflict, or danger. The often-repeated charges of nepotism and tribalism, with respect to the direction of exchanges in public life, convey a strong impression that nearness and beneficence in client systems follow in-group lines – that what people do for one another depends on their feelings of 'we' and 'they'. Some of the best documented cases of in-group patron–client relationships and their ability to reinforce solidarity among groups who compete for power come from West Africa,[19] and it is tempting to assume from them that parties to client relationships only take care of their own. Yet there are other cases which make such a generalisation questionable. Although their activities have not been cast in a patron–client mould, the well-known Big Men of New Guinea offer a counter to positions which take for granted the maxim that 'like feeds like'.[20] The Big Men are free-floating political entrepreneurs who, like the neighbourhood leaders of Mushin,[21] enter into exchange relationships in order to acquire followers and build bases for extending their power into ever wider political arenas. They establish the strongest ties to those who fall within the closest, 'we' domain: kinsmen and affines. Yet the latter, while having moral ties to their Big Men leaders, may give the most and receive the least, since their ties are the least breakable. Paradoxically, the people who receive the most, i.e. leaders of neighbouring groups, may well have the weakest ties to the Big Man. To them go abundant quantities of valuable resources, given in an instrumental effort to neutralise the 'they'-ness in the relationship and, temporarily at least, to convert distance into nearness for purposes of alliance in warfare or trade.[22] The protective aspects are obvious whether the exchange relationships are between autonomous polities or rival factions or ethnic groups. The practice of establishing client relationships outside one's kinship or ethnic groups in Mushin meant that the most valuable items and services not only often went to outsiders – e.g. land offered by an indigenous Awori chief to leaders of a rival faction of newcomers – but that boundaries also were crossed with the express purpose of disarming opponents and neutralising their politically competitive activities.

There are many nuances in the protective dimensions of clientelism, not the least of which is that a passive relationship can be as valuable as active support. There are two demands in exchange relationships: people are obliged to help those who help them, or at the least, not to harm those who help them.[23] 'Business', Mauss wrote, 'has always been done with foreigners.' We/they relationships – necessary strategies in human survival – are possible because, in Mauss' words, partners 'lay down their spears' so long as they can benefit by doing so.[24] The requirements of living in any society present individuals with constant, conflicting demands on their loyalties, energies, and resources. People can choose to carry out their part of a relationship by helping or by not hindering. In choosing the latter course, they are able to shield themselves (and their followers) from some of the contradictions which political struggles otherwise impose.

THE ORGANISING POWERS IN CLIENT RELATIONSHIPS

Client relationships do not exist in isolation; they form chains, or inter-dependent networks, of people who are tied together through exchanges and overlapping obligations arising from those exchanges. Patrons have clients, who in turn have clients, and so on down the line. Given these properties, client systems (made up of many interlocking dyadic ties) can be thought of as a form of social organisation. As such they perform two vital functions: organising diversity and centralising power.

ORGANISING DIVERSITY

Client systems are socially heterogeneous. The very fact that, by definition, client ties join people of unequal statuses brings this about. Client ties can also cross class lines, bringing together haves and have-nots; cross cultural lines, bringing together individuals of different ethnic groups; cross administrative lines, bringing together bureaucrats and supplicants; cross occupational lines, religious lines, caste lines, and more.[25] That people use clientelism in order to establish connections which lie outside conventional categories and groups is not at issue; the effects of these relationships is, however, not fully appreciated, for in many societies client networks, by organising diversity are among the primary effectors of political integration.[26]

Client systems do not rely on monolithic value systems in order to operate. There is a widespread assumption that when norms and values differ, fundamental contradictions arise which stand in the way of social interaction and integration.[27] Wallace characterises this view as the fear that 'a society will fall apart and its members scatter if they are not threaded like beads on a string of common motives'. This view persists – in fact it has acted as a barrier to our full appreciation of political dynamics in complex societies – despite studies which 'show conclusively' that it is not necessary to share common ideologies and orientations in order to interact and share institutions. On the contrary, separate orientations facilitate the separate life styles necessary to mastering all of the roles and tasks that a complex society requires. In Wallace's view, which I share, people are able to learn that certain behaviours yield predictable results, irrespective of their motives.[28] When fundamental needs are at stake, the tactics that bring support are quickly learned. Above all, outsiders must master the rituals of clientelism; in Mushin, these included visiting, supporting ceremonies, or swelling an entourage.

Client ties need not take precedence over ethnic group ties. They do not contradict them; rather, in Mushin they existed in addition to and as complements to them. One client, an Igbo businessman, was protected in

the house of his long-time Egba Yoruba patron and business contact during
the Nigerian Civil War, despite the two men's opposing political loyalties.
Following the war and the restoration of the Federation, the Igbo client
repaid his benefactor by setting up business opportunities for him in Igbo
circles – he was an active member of his Igbo hometown voluntary association – and by deliberately sending customers to him in a Mercedes Benz car
so that, as he put it, 'the man's importance would be publicised among his
neighbours'. Another minority group member, a Tiv who held high office
in his ethnic group association, was a loyal client to a Lagosian politician
who helped the Tiv leader and his compatriots make contact with local
bureaucrats when they needed government services. The Tiv, it so happened, were loyal to a third, rival Nigerian political party. None the less
they repaid their benefactor by swelling his entourage when he made public
appearances and by performing traditional dances under his aegis at community events. The transactions in these instances were sufficiently neutral
not to threaten the parties involved. They neither violated nor contradicted
the norms and values of the participants, as they manifested themselves at a
personal level, nor did they compromise the political loyalties which were
expected of either side in terms of their public ethnic group ties.

Overt political support is not a necessary part of client relationships. It
was repeatedly pointed out to me by outsiders who were of minority ethnic
status that it was impossible to operate in a city that was politically dominated by another ethnic group without having patrons from that group. For
obvious reasons the most effective, knowledgeable, and active patrons were
in many cases politicians who, largely owing to the fact that they came from
a different ethnic background, often had political allegiances that conflicted
with those of their clients. Neither the Tiv nor Igbo clients were asked
during partisan days to vote for or, in other ways, give support to their
patrons. The same might be said if the clients and patrons had been of
different classes, religious backgrounds, or occupations. Direct political
support was not expected. Indirect political benefits, on the other hand,
were clearly involved in each relationship. This, of course, was the value of
social exchange. The transactions in these instances were sufficiently
neutral to be unthreatening to the parties involved. They neither violated
nor contradicted the norms and values of the participants, nor did they
compromise the political loyalties which were expected of either side in
terms of their ethnic group ties. As a rule, direct political support from
clients increased with close ties, and decreased with distant ties.

One of the qualities of client relationships which accommodates cultural
and social diversity among participants is that the parties are free to arrange
their ties so that they can opt into certain kinds of exchanges and opt out of
others. So long as leaders and clients meet one another's expectations the
privacy of each relationship provides the freedom to both sides to act on

their own impulses in the wider society with respect to public political allegiances.

This is not to say that client relationships are purely voluntary or free of politically coercive elements. Clientelism can be as repressive and exploitative as class and ethnic systems,[29] particularly when a few patrons monopolise vital resources or access to them. This is why it is important to stress the integrating features of clientelism. Whether or not they are coercive or voluntary, client exchanges involve repeated personal interactions which in turn promote the interchange of opinions, ideas, and information among peoples of diverse backgrounds. Over time this gives rise to new over-arching value systems or new categories of people. Paradoxically, clientelism tolerates diversity, at the same time that it promotes and organises new solidarities.

CENTRALISING POWER

The advantages of client relationships are strongly related to the spheres of influence of the parties involved. In other words, the people with whom leaders and clients establish relationships and their positions in the community are as important to their political, economic, or social fortunes as the closeness or distance of their bonds. From a client's perspective, it is desirable to establish connections with patrons and middlemen who have wide spheres of influence, since they can offer stronger support and security, to say nothing of greater prestige, than those with narrow spheres. From a leader's perspective, it is desirable to attract eminent clients, especially clients who have clients, since they automatically expand one's power base.

It is useful to think of spheres of influence according to levels. In Mushin there were, heuristically speaking, three levels: the neighbourhood, the division consisting of several neighbourhoods, and the whole community, i.e. Mushin District. Most leaders who acted as patrons and middlemen in their neighbourhoods had other neighbours as clients. Their connections upwards tended to concentrate on a few division or community leaders, but they were otherwise undeveloped or neighbourhood leaders would have been able to function on a politically higher level. The same was true for division-level leaders, who operated in several neighbourhoods but who did not have extensive contacts beyond them. Community leaders, however, had influence throughout the entire district and even beyond Mushin into the overarching political arenas of the metropolis and the state. Leaders at the top of the hierarchy, because of their wide contacts and access to rewards could subordinate intermediate, division-level leaders to them as clients, and they in turn could call on neighbourhood-level clients below them. Clearly, the higher the leaders were in the hierarchy, the greater the number of human resources they could mobilise.

The hierarchical property in client systems is what renders leaders at the top formidable in political battles. When leaders align themselves with established groups and institutions they bring with them the ability to influence or communicate with vast networks of people. This was the case in Mushin when its local leaders were able, through client networks reaching into every neighbourhood, to turn Mushin's political system of the early 1960s into a machine. Their power was dramatically and tragically reaffirmed when they mobilised support through those same networks to protest, in violent and repeated outbursts, against an imposed regime which had deprived them of access to it and its resources. Finally, the strength of local leaders was recognised by a new military government in 1966 which included them in advisory councils despite the break-up of their monolithic client pyramid into several factions.

By being on top, leaders increase, in geometric proportion, their power and influence. As many scholars have pointed out, and as Mushin confirms, client relationships are layered into pyramids or clusters of interlocking and overlapping networks.[30] Power resides in the aggregations. Patron–client hierarchies, to be sure, are not as neatly layered in reality as they appear in a model. There are many points to which they can be directed, and many arrangements leading to those points. A patron in one hierarchy may be a client in another. Furthermore the processes by which hierarchical client networks form are in constant flux. The irregularities would, in truth, be impossible to capture in any model. Be that as it may, leaders at the top have a vast range of interconnected support and influence at their command, in contrast to those at the bottom. And it is this hierarchisation in client systems that is a politically centralising force.

THE PERPETUATION OF POWER

In many nations there is a crisis of authority. It is less apparent at the top where elite office-holders run the affairs of state and at the bottom in remote villages and towns which have managed to maintain continuity between past and present systems of authority. The crisis is more apparent at the middle levels in new and quickly expanding communities where there is both a lack of official authorities – as seen by incomplete centralisation and communications – and a lack of continuity in the personnel who hold official positions. Herein lies, of course, a contradiction, for there is no lack of people willing to fill middle level authority positions.

A recurring theme of this study has been that official inattention gives rise to unofficial action. The unofficial solution to the lack of official authority which emerged in Mushin was a proliferation of a free-enterprise type of leadership.[31] There were few ready-made constituencies for political aspirants in the relatively new community of Mushin: few large kin groups or compounds teeming with political supporters, and few if any guilds or cult groups, where membership was often established at birth, as could be found in old communities with relatively stable populations. In the new and transient population of metropolitan Lagos, residents who wished to assume leadership positions had to generate their own constituencies, establish their own bases of support and legitimacy, and then give public airing to their prowess in these endeavours. Free enterprise leadership was dependent for its success on clientelism – the one institution which allowed political hopefuls to acquire the acceptance and the followings they needed in order to exercise power.

A drawback of free-enterprise leadership is its insecurity and vulnerability. The Big Man is vulnerable even though he may preside over an alliance of many polities, whereas the chief is safe. Thus, upwardly mobile leaders of Mushin worked to convert their leadership roles into permanent offices.

An office does two things. It improves leaders' access to public resources, thereby increasing their ability to reward and acquire more followers. By the same token, if it is permanent, it reduces the pressure on leaders to perform, especially if they have no desire to continue moving up in the political system. Hence an office can be a means to higher ends or an end in itself. Whatever the case, an office provides leaders with security and the public with a certain degree of continuity in political affairs. For the people of Mushin that office often consisted of a chieftaincy title.

One of the seeming anomalies in African authority systems in post-war years has been the survival of chiefly offices. Both colonial and independent governments restricted the powers chiefs held in pre-colonial days and imposed on them new duties which appeared to conflict with the old. Early studies in Central Africa, focusing on the durability of chiefs and headmen, led scholars to conclude that traditional authorities who stood in the middle ground, performing the linking roles between various segments of their societies, were doomed because they were trapped between the conflicting demands of their followers and those of higher government authorities.[32] How, for instance, could a chief punish the people he was supposed to protect? To some extent, the measure of chiefs' strength was evaluated on the basis of whether or not they were functioning in old ways. And these evaluations were reinforced by similar views echoing across the continent. One scholar proposed that traditional and bureaucratic systems of authority in East Africa could not coexist because they demanded separate role performances and separate attitudes that were fundamentally opposed.[33] Another suggested that West African chiefs were vulnerable and ineffective because economic and political changes restricted their access to resources on which they traditionally relied for maintaining power.[34] The picture that emerged was bleak, and the expectation that chiefship would disappear was realised in one instance when copperbelt workers abandoned traditional headmen and turned to labour union leaders who were, they decided, better able to represent their concerns to the new institutions on which workers depended for survival.[35]

Surprisingly, however, chiefship survived in places where the greatest decline might have been expected – growing urban centres where social change and cultural diversity rendered continuities with the past least probable. One of the most extensive studies of chiefship, or headship as it was called, traced the ups and downs of this vital institution in Freetown for nearly two centuries. During this time official recognition of the headmen, who led and acted as patrons to a diverse array of settler groups, was extended and then withdrawn on a number of occasions.[36] Official status had little effect on the functioning of the headmen, for with or without it these grassroots leaders were highly valued by both administrators and ordinary citizens for their critical services as administrators, adjudicators, spokesmen, distributors of resources, and protectors of the needy. The prestige attached to these posts was sufficient to attract a variety of talented people including civil servants, merchants, and religious leaders. In the absence of other integrative mechanisms, headship filled major gaps in Freetown, attracting talented people who performed vital political functions. Freetown was not alone in its support of chiefs; they continued to perform significant political roles in such cities as Accra, Kampala, Kumasi, Monrovia, and Ouagadougou, and in some cases actually to increase in their strength.[37]

Traditional title-holding represented one of the few ways non-elite members of the public could still exercise authority, however truncated that might be; it was a key factor in upholding the general system of social control; it was a valuable outlet for members of the general public who wished to participate in local affairs. In West Africa, titles also represented highly valued status symbols – a mark of honour – which even the elites were proud to exhibit.

Chiefship survived not because chiefs clung to tradition but because they adapted to the present. Chiefly figures learned to operate in both bureaucratic and communal arenas. In truth, there was some question as to whether or not they had ever been daunted by the separate demands that each of these two sectors placed upon them. From the first days of colonial rule, chiefs successfully acted as political middlemen, presenting the demands of the public to government and, conversely, translating the orders of government to the public. They continued in the same vein after independence. All in all, chiefs learned not to be squeezed by being in the middle, but rather to exploit precisely those leadership opportunities which existed in the middle.

Chiefship, however, was not a beginning point for common people who wished to take active roles in local political circles. Instead it represented one of the end points in the lengthy process of developing and legitimating authority. And it is for this reason that I have stressed the relationship between clientelism and the exercise of power.

Clientelism is a means to political ends rather than an end in itself. As such, it is more productively analysed as a political process – a method for producing political results – than as a type of political system or stage in political development.[38] Client processes merit attention when they are instrumental in propelling people into positions of authority or modifying the structure of authority. They are significant when political aspirants use client relationships to demonstrate leadership, move from disadvantaged to relatively advantaged positions in the political system, and then institutionalise those positions.

When the privileged holders of state power consent to recognise informal authority and thus give it formal status, they do so largely for self-interested purposes: to co-opt that power into their own ranks or to aggrandise their own positions. Yet this act requires that those at the top extend power and privilege to others. In the course of human events, the extension of power has not been freely made, but comes as a result of the recognition by ruling elites that to keep power they must retain – through real or illusory means – the compliance of the people they govern. In focusing on the dynamics of legal, bureaucratic recognition, we are able to see more clearly the ways in which formal political systems intersect with informal systems. At the same time, we isolate those processes – in this case clientelism – which, at critical moments in history, bring together elites and masses, rulers and ruled.

EPILOGUE

It is appropriate that this book end with mid 1975, just as the political community of Mushin seemed, sociologically speaking, to have reached a rather satisfying state of 'completion'. In that year, eighty-three junior chiefs were recognised, a new committee of management was sworn in, and the old guard of community leaders stood firm. But stasis is not the story of Mushin. On 29 July, 1975, a *coup d'état* brought a third military government to power in Nigeria. In some ways the takeover was reminiscent of the closing days of Nigeria's first civilian regime in 1965 when seven Mushin *ọba* were recognised by the government only a few weeks before it was overthrown by the military. The reasons behind the recognitions at these critical points in Nigeria's history were, I believe, the same. As the two governments waned in popularity, each grasped an opportunity to gain support of the masses by recognising leaders they believed were close to the public pulse.

Regime changes are the harbingers of local government reform. And 1975 was no exception. Soon after Brigadier Murtala Mohammed took control, and after his assassination seven months later, when Lieutenant General Olusegun Obasanjo took over, local government reforms were instituted. The first change was to disband the committee of management and place a sole administrator (civil servant) in charge of the district.

In 1976, Mushin District and the political community which flourished within its boundaries, no longer existed. Once again, as had happened many times before, the large territories surrounding Lagos City were divided into smaller and more administratively manageable units. It was not an unexpected move. Mushin's population was pushing toward two million, and thus the district which had been in place between 1955 and 1975 – the critical years of this study – was divided into two districts: Mushin East and Mushin West. The effect of the division was to separate the Shomolu area from the rest of Mushin. It was a separation for which Shomolu leaders had long campaigned. In the same year, local government elections were held in preparation for Nigeria's return to civilian rule. In Mushin West, twenty-three councillors were selected by residents to run local affairs; only seven represented the old guard. In Mushin East (Shomolu), nine Councillors were elected; only two appeared to come from earlier leadership circles. A new generation of leaders was beginning to replace the old.

The longevity of Mushin East and West was brief. Civilian rule returned to Nigeria on 1 October 1979, and before a year had passed far more sweeping changes than those of 1976 were instituted. The old Mushin was again divided, this time into six local government councils: Mushin (Central), Odi-Olowo/Ojuwoye/Onigbongbo, Itire/Ikate, Oshodi/Isolo, Shomolu, and Kosofe. In the eyes of the new government, these divisions were designed to bring the government closer to the people, generate more grassroots activity, and involve people in community development projects. The divisions (which unofficially took effect in 1980 but which were not official until 1982) were controversial, and charges abounded that they were not made for better government but for firmer control at the top. At least 90 per cent of the population of Lagos State now lived in metropolitan Lagos. The city proper housed many of the nation's most talented and high-ranking peoples. The Lagos City government, together with the local governments of suburban areas, were powerful tails collectively capable of wagging the state dog. Therefore, dividing metropolitan Lagos and Lagos City into smaller local government councils was an effective divide-and-rule approach to solidifying and centralising control in state-level agencies. The governor now took charge of appointing chairmen and members of the local government councils, and appointments were given primarily to loyal supporters.

As for the chiefs, the seven Mushin chieftaincy divisions survived the local government changes, but not without some changes of their own. All traditional rulers in Lagos State were grouped into fourteen chieftaincy committees in 1982. Three committees consisted solely of the seven former ọba of Mushin: Mushin, Itire, Odi Olowo; Shomolu and Onigbongbo; and Oshodi and Isolo. If for no other purpose than this, the failure of Mushin's chiefs to name a single paramount ruler during the era of Mushin District had its eventual reward, since the fields of competition were substantially narrowed with this new arrangement.

The dividing and re-dividing of the Mushin area is, I suspect, a process which will continue for many years to come. A military coup in January 1984, toppling the civilian regime of President Shehu Shagari, bought with it the inevitable desire to review local government practices. By May 1984 officials announced they would re-study and then change local government since, in their view, the proliferation of councils earlier in the decade had reduced their effectiveness.

Administrative boundaries are but one element in a political system. Whether Mushin is a single polity, as it was between 1955 and 1976, or many polities, the quest for power in each one of them will not abate. As I stated at the beginning, the patterns and processes by which power is organised and distributed are continually reshaped. This study concentrates on one pattern. Given the ever-changing political map of the Mushin area, this means the study of its politics has only begun.

METHODS OF RESEARCH

Research was conducted between September 1971 and October 1972 and again from May through July 1975. During both periods I lived in Mushin, the first time in a separate flat with my family and the second as a guest in the house of a Mushin leader. Each residence was located in a different neighbourhood, thus giving me an opportunity to observe and compare the social interactions of neighbours from two perspectives. I learned to know people and areas of Mushin outside these neighbourhoods through visits, attendance at meetings and ceremonies, and through many introductions. For the most part, research consisted of the usual participant observations augmented by intensive interviews, a census of one neighbourhood, and several surveys.

INTERVIEWS

Interviews during both periods were devoted to a wide variety of topics and, depending on the expertise of the informants and their willingness to elaborate on the questions asked, were conducted for varying periods of time. Some interviews were only of an hour's duration while others took from ten to twenty hours and even more, and were conducted over several weeks or months. I used two main strategies in interviewing.

The first kind of interview was *systematic*. Here I simply asked the same questions of many informants until patterns emerged. Once I could begin to predict the answers, or range of probable answers, to my questions I felt sufficiently secure to move on to new topics. Usually I prepared a set of questions or cues on, say, note cards that I then used to prompt my memory and to make sure that every point or question was discussed.

The topic for one set of systematic interviews was kinship. During the course of 1972, I interviewed fifty men and women from one to three hours about their descent groups. Although the discussions were, in part, free-ranging, I also asked each person the same set of questions. In this way I secured a rough quantitative measure of the activities, the ways of calculating membership and inheritance, and the rights, duties, and functions of descent groups.

Another set of systematic interviews focused on the topic of property ownership. In this case, I interviewed 100 landlords and landladies, excluding the 150 who were questioned as part of the house-to-house census and the random survey. Whenever owners were interviewed, I secured the same information on the ways they acquired property and on how they perceived their roles as owners.

The second kind of interview was *open-ended*. These interviews often took the form of relatively focused but informal conversations. This method probably was the most productive for obtaining information about political processes. Hence, the greater part of my time was spent in repeatedly visiting knowledgeable informants, most of whom were not only generous with their time, but also candid, instructive, and patient.

During each interview, whatever the type, and usually at the beginning, I inquired into the social background of the informant even if the interview was aimed primarily at historical, current, or other aspects of the political system and not necessarily germane to the individual concerned. I was not able to interview all of Mushin's notables. However when I secured information about someone I was unable to interview personally, I attempted to double-check the validity of that data.

THE CENSUS

During the first few months of 1972, I took a house-to-house census in one Mushin neighbourhood – an area that was roughly three city blocks wide by about eight blocks long. There had been no census in metropolitan Lagos since 1963, and the data from it were, in any case, in question. Hence there was no way of establishing how one part of Mushin might resemble or differ from the rest of Mushin, from other metropolitan-area suburbs, or from Lagos City. With the help of an assistant – a government clerk who was the son of a neighbourhood landowner – and with the backing of the neighbourhood landowners' association, I made a census of 155 houses and their nearly 7,000 inhabitants. The area was selected in order to include several types of housing – from older, single-storey structures to a few buildings with large flats – and as socially heterogeneous a population as possible. The census was designed to obtain data on household composition, age, sex, occupation (or schooling), and ethnic identification of all residents.

One of the unexpected benefits of the census was that it served to explain my presence in the area. This introduction, as it were, facilitated subsequent contacts with residents, something which otherwise would have been difficult, given the large and socially differentiated population of Mushin.

THE RANDOM SURVEY

I used the census as a basis for selecting respondents to be interviewed in a random survey conducted from July to September 1972. Three assistants – two students at the University of Lagos and the same clerk who lived in the neighbourhood and assisted me with the census – administered the survey questionnaire after they and I had each administered a pilot questionnaire to respondents in one another's presence. Thereafter I met daily with the three assistants to go over each completed questionnaire and to clarify ambiguities or other problems in the answers.

The survey was administered to 276 men and 84 women of Yoruba or Igbo-speaking backgrounds. Although it was a random sample, the selection was initially stratified so as to include proportional representation of the following age groups: 20–29, 30–39, 40–49 and 50+ years. Questions were designed to elicit the following information:

(a) Languages spoken and, if possible, proficiency level.
(b) Residential data: place of origin of informant and informant's mother and father; year of arrival in Lagos and sources of assistance; length of residence in current neighbourhood and house.
(c) Education and occupation profile; occupations of mother and father.
(d) Marital history; relationship to in-laws.
(e) Number, age, schooling or occupation, and place of residence of children.
(f) Number of foster children; relationship to respondent.
(g) Religious preferences.
(h) Residential commitment to Lagos; sources of social support in Lagos.
(i) Relationship and commitment to hometown.
(j) Kinship data: descent group memberships and activities.
(k) Voluntary association activities.
(l) Neighbourhood social involvements.

VOLUNTARY ASSOCIATION SURVEY

In addition to the data obtained in the above survey, I took a separate non-random survey inquiring into the voluntary association activities of 125 adult residents of Mushin. The survey was administered early in 1972 by myself and two assistants, one a student at the University of Lagos and the other a secondary school graduate residing in the area. The questionnaire elicited information concerning past and present memberships in all types of associations: political parties, sports clubs, social organisations (e.g. dancing, debating, literary, youth, veterans, or alumni clubs), work-related associations (e.g. trade unions, market organisations, or cooperatives), religious groups (beyond attendance at worship services), and ethnic associations (based on shared language, clan, family, town, or district). The following information about the associations themselves also was elicited: place of meetings, activities, dues, benefits, formal ties to other societies, and so on.

ORAL HISTORIES

During both research periods, I collected many oral histories on various aspects of the development of Mushin and on people's personal lives. The respondents were not randomly selected, but represented people who were available and to whom I had introductions.

First in 1972, I collected career and migration histories from seventy-five men and women. Each history took at least one hour, and usually two. They began with a routine elicitation of the informant's social background: age, sex, ethnic group, educational level, religious preference, and residential status (landowner or tenant). Respondents were then asked to reconstruct, chronologically, their educational experiences and occupational training, their changes of residence, including all moves from one community to another, and their work experiences.

Second, during both research periods I obtained the life histories of three Mushin leaders, each of which took up to thirty hours.

Third, again during both periods, I collected accounts of various aspects of past and present political events from two dozen leaders, including chiefs, ex-party officers, a court judge, and officials of the Mushin Town Council and Ministry of Local Government.

Fourth, in 1972, I collected twenty oral histories primarily from neighbourhood elders (who were not reckoned among the community's notables), recounting the physical development of Mushin. Most of these accounts were from settlers who had come to the area after the Second World War, but a few were from members of old Awori families. Many of the settler recollections included accounts of the ways in which they had acquired land and houses and the disputes and other problems involved in making these acquisitions.

OTHER SYSTEMATIC DATA

Accompanied by an assistant, I took a neighbourhood census of street vendors, businesses, churches, and private schools during January and February 1972.

At my request, an informant who moved to Mushin in January 1972, kept a diary of his daily activities, contacts he made in order to establish himself, and all assistance he received both in settling in and in meeting new people.

Finally, in mid 1972, I collected a series of dispute settlement studies, summarised in Chapter 4.

DOCUMENTS: PRIMARY SOURCES

Thanks to the generosity of three residents who were active in public affairs, and who have asked to remain anonymous, I was given access to private papers and files which were invaluable in reconstructing the development of Mushin's political institutions from 1955 to 1975. One former official made available his collection of documents from the early years of the Mushin Town Council, 1955–6. All of the files and documents in the council itself were destroyed when it was burned in post-election disturbances of 1965. Another leader made available papers from government committees and tribunals of inquiry from the years 1966 to 1974.

The files of the Odi Olowo Chieftaincy Division from the years 1960 to 1975, and selected chieftaincy files in the Mushin Town Council, for the years 1973 to 1975, were also made available.

The importance of newspapers and published court cases in a study such as this, particularly in orienting one toward productive lines of inquiry and toward prominent issues, cannot be overemphasised. The *Daily Times* Library was especially useful, and I appreciate the access its editors gave me to their old files.

Printed documents and archival papers, which were essential to this study, are listed in the bibliography.

NOTES

1. INTRODUCTION

1 Elite refers to high ranking members of society. A ruling elite thus refers to high ranking members of society who wield power in public affairs. For discussions of Africa's elite see Miller, 1974, pp. 521–42; Markovitz, 1977, pp. 199–229.

2 Nigeria, 'A Survey of Graduate Employment Prospects, 1973/74 to 1975/76', *Manpower Studies* no. 16, National Manpower Board, Lagos, Federal Ministry of Economic Development and Reconstruction, 1974.

3 For a discussion of the convergence of economic and political power in the hands of high government officials in Nigeria see Lloyd, 1974, p. 71ff.

4 Kinshasa figures are from Abate, 1978, p. 27. Metropolitan Lagos figures are from Nigeria, *Population Census of Lagos, 1950*, Lagos, Federal Office of Statistics, 1950; Nigeria, *Population Census of the Western Region of Nigeria, 1952*, Lagos, Government Statistician, 1953–4; Nigeria, *Population Census, Lagos and Western Region*, Lagos, Federal Office of Statistics, 1963; *Business Times* 11 January 1977, p. 1; *West Africa* no. 3107, 24 January 1977, p. 139.

5 Scott, 1972, p. 102.

6 See Peil, 1976, pp. 144–7; Ross, 1975, pp. 87ff; Gutkind, 1967, pp. 186–214, 380–405.

7 Kasfir, 1976; Sandbrook, 1982.

8 Weingrod, 1967, pp. 121–34.

9 Some of the best examples are: Bond, 1976; Hopkins, 1972; Owusu, 1970; Parkin, 1969; Ross, 1973; Schildkrout, 1978; Vincent, 1971.

10 A. Cohen, 1969 and 1974b.

11 Two of the classic studies are Mintz and Wolf, 1950, pp. 341–68; Foster, 1961, pp. 1173–92.

12 Here the classic studies are Bailey, 1969; Barth, 1966; and Boissevain, 1974.

13 See Scott, 1972, for a discussion of this shift. Examples of the application of the client paradigm in Africa, Latin America, the Mediterranean, and Southeast Asia are found in Schmidt, *et al.* 1977; Strickon and Greenfield, 1972; Gellner and Waterbury, 1977.

14 Medard, 1982, p. 170–1.

15 Peace, 1979.

16 For an example see Sandbrook, 1972, pp. 104–19.

17 Hanna and Hanna, 1971, p. 170.

18 Barrows, 1974, pp. 284–5.

19 Cohen, 1981, p. 35; LaFontaine, 1970, pp. 236–7; Mercier, 1959, p. 72; and Schildkrout, 1975, pp. 170–1.

20 Lemarchand, 1972, p. 70.

21 Mboya, 1969, p. 91.

22 Sandbrook, 1982, pp. 197–8.

23 Lloyd, 1974, pp. 132–3.

24 Hanna and Hanna, 1971, pp. 199–201.

25 The definitions on which I have relied are found in Kaufman, 1974, p. 285; Paine, 1971, pp. 8–21; Scott, 1972, pp. 92–5.

26 For example see Scott, 1972, pp. 95–6.

27 Mauss, 1954.

28 See Fallers, 1965, p. 246; Lemarchand and Legg, 1972, pp. 156–9; and Zolberg, 1966, p. 141.

29 Medard, 1982, p. 185.

30 Gellner, 1977, p. 4.

31 Scott, 1969, pp. 1142–3. See also Landé, 1973; Gilbert and Gugler, 1982, pp. 138.

32 A similar emphasis on the need for help from patrons was expressed by people in the city of Ibadan (ninety miles from Lagos) and Agege (also in metropolitan Lagos). See Lloyd, 1974, pp. 156, 160, 164–7, 197 and 200.

33 Nigeria, *Third National Development Plan, 1975–80*, Vol. 1, Lagos, Central Planning Office, Federal Ministry of Economic Development, 1975, p. 1–5.

34 See note 4 above.

35 Adesina, 1975, p. 131; Fapohunda, 1978, pp. 5, 12, 51–3; and Nigeria, *Second and Final Report of the Wages and Salaries Review Commission, 1970–71*, pp. 22, 84.

36 Fapohunda, 1978, p. 41; Nigeria, *Third National Development Plan, 1975–80*, p. 1–2.

37 Fapohunda, 1978, p. 58.

38 Up to 1972 the exchange rate was £N1 = £1.17 = \$2.80. The Naira was then introduced and ₦2 = £N1.

39 Income figures of occupational groups come from Fapohunda, 1978, pp. 51–7. The national *per capita* income is from *West Africa*, no. 3107, 24 January 1977, p. 148. The breakdown of occupational groups is from Nigeria, *Population Census*, 1963; this was the last time such figures were collected. I have combined the census figures from Lagos City and Ikeja Division (Mushin, Ikeja and Agege) in order to secure a rough estimate of the metropolitan area occupational breakdown.

40 Nigeria, *Population Census*, 1963.

41 Mabogunje, 1968, pp. 296, 305; Nigeria, *Population Census*, 1963. My own 1972 survey of 360 adults confirmed this same occupational distribution in Mushin.

42 Mabogunje, 1968, pp. 300–7; Fapohunda, 1978, p. 67.

43 Akinola and Alao, 1975, p. 120.

44 Lagos City Council, 'Draft Estimates, 1975–6', Lagos, mimeograph, 1975, pp. 56–132; Mushin Town Council, 'Draft Estimates, 1975–6', Mushin, mimeograph, 1975, pp. 5–26.

2. THE MAKING OF MUSHIN

1 For accounts of Lagos Colony history, the reader is referred to Aderibigbe, 1975, pp. 1–26; Baker, 1974; Burns, 1963; Cole, 1975; Kopytoff, 1965; Losi, 1967; CSO 26/29939, Vol. I, R. L. V. Wilkes, 'Intelligence report on the Ikeja District of Lagos Colony', 1934; CO 657/50, E. J. Gibbons, 'A Preliminary Report on the Administrative Reorganisation of the Colony Districts of Nigeria', Sessional Paper No. 9, Lagos, Government Printer, 1939.

2 Various versions of the origin myth can be found in Aderibigbe, 1975, pp. 1–5; Baker, 1974, p. 17; Cole, 1975, pp. 11–15, 25–6; and Folami, 1982, pp. 3–6.

3 A title, not a name.

4 Awori territory stretched some forty miles to the north of Lagos Island. See Pius O. Sada, *The Metropolitan Region of Lagos, Nigeria: A Study of the Political Factor in Urban Geography*, Unpublished PhD thesis, Bloomington, Indiana University, 1968, p. 32.

5 Cole, 1975, p. 25.

6 CO 147/24, Folio 486, 'Hennessey to Colonial Office', 30 December 1872; and CSO 26/29939, Wilkes, p. 8.

7 Ojo, 1966, p. 96.

8 See Map 3 for locations of markets located in Lagos Colony. See also CO 700/Lagos/1, 'Sketch of Lagos and the Adjacent Country, 1865'; and G3/A2/0, No. 191, 20 October 1884, 'Notices of the villages between Ebute Metta and Otta'. I am indebted to Dr Babatunde Agiri for bringing the latter source to my attention.

9 *Alase* (*ala* = one who has; *ase* = sifter).

10 Cole, 1975, p. 21.

11 CO 657/50, Gibbons, p. 7.

12 Another tradition states than an extension of the same, or a different wall, stands near the present site of Onigbongbo. Still another states that the builder was Barikisu, a wealthy woman who left gold wherever she went and who, so it was said, built a wall from Dahomey to Warri. For the latter, see CSO 26/29939, Wilkes, p. 9.

13 Both Awori and Lagosian are ethnic identities. An ethnic identity is a communal label which grows out of common bonds of kinship (real or fictive) or territory (usually place of origin). An ethnic identity is a frame of reference used to classify people according to various common, often stereotypic, characteristics to the extent that the identity is used to define status in a community with respect to relative privileges and privations. In this respect, ethnicity is a form of political identity. An ethnic identity is not necessarily exclusive. Individuals potentially have more than one ethnic identity (e.g. Lagosians of Awori descent) which they may use, depending on the context and the rewards or drawbacks in so doing. For detailed discussions of ethnic identity in urban Africa see A. Cohen, 1969 and 1974a; and Shildkrout, 1978.

14 Elias, 1951, pp. 176, 201; Forde, 1951, p. 65; G. O. Gbadamosi, 'Patterns and Developments in Lagos Religious History', in Aderibigbe, 1975, pp. 175–6; and CSO 26/29939, Wilkes, p. 6.

15 CSO 26/29939, Wilkes, *passim*. See also Cole, 1975, pp. 24–9.

16 It was first known as the Settlement of Lagos.

17 CO 700/Lagos/1, 'Sketch of Lagos'; and W. M. N. Geary (Sir), 'The Development of Lagos in 50 Years – From Head Town of "Slave Coast" to be "The Liverpool of West Africa" ', *West Africa*, 16 August–4 October 1924.

18 The colony territory and its annexation are described in Burns, 1963, pp. 131–3. See also G3/A2/0, No. 191, 'Notices of the villages'.

19 The Colony of Lagos was an anomaly in that direct rule was employed, whereas in the rest of Nigeria (annexed later) indirect rule was the governing principle.

20 CO 151/9, 1871, p. 228.

21 Nicholson, 1969, pp. 36–8.

22 CSc 505/12, N. J. Brooke *et al.*, 'Report of the Native Courts (Colony) Commission of Inquiry', Lagos: Government Printer, 1952, p. 5.

23 Burns, 1919, p. 80.

24 Burns, 1919, pp. 138–9; and Cole, 1975, p. 53.

25 Burns, 1919, p. 217; and Cole, 1975, p. 65.

26 Talbot, 1926, p. 124.

27 CSO 26/29939, Wilkes, pp. 6–7, 47–75; and G3 A2/0, No. 191, 'Notices of the villages'.

28 Despite this clarification, there have been ongoing debates and small adjustments to the boundaries. See Adejuyigbe, 1969, pp. 480–4.

29 Nicholson, 1969, p. 57, 65; CO 147/24, Folio 619, 19 April 1872.

30 Burns, 1963, p. 233.
31 Nicholson, 1969, p. 54.
32 L. C. Gwam, *An Inventory of the Administrative Records Assembled from the Colony Province*, Ibadan, Nigerian National Archives, 1961, p. 19. Gwam's inventory is prefaced by an informative essay. See also Co 151/2A, 1863, p. 27.
33 CSc 505/12, Brooke, p. 4.
34 The Supreme Court was presided over by a Chief Justice and four Puisne Judges who oversaw the colony, its police and district officers, and commissioners who also had power in civil cases. See Burns, 1919, pp. 81–2. Other useful information concerning the court system of administration is found in CSc 505/12, Brooke, pp. 22–3; and CO 657/50, Gibbons, *passim*.
35 CSc 505/12, Brooke, p. 10; CO 657/50, Gibbons, p. 6; and Com. Col. IKEDIV 3 C.P. 497, 'Night Patrols', 1941.
36 CSO 26/29939, Wilkes, p. 39.
37 CSO 26/29939, Wilkes, p. 14; and CO 657/20, 'Annual Report on the Colony for the Year 1927', Sessional Paper No. 33 of 1928, Lagos, Government Printer, 1928, p. 2. See also CO 657/50, Gibbons, p. 11.
38 CO 657/20, 'Annual Report, 1927', p. 2.
39 CSO 26/29939, Wilkes, p. 1–2; CO 657/38, 'Annual Report on the Colony for the Year 1934', Lagos, Government Printer, 1935, p. 3; CO 657/40, 'Annual Report on the Colony, 1935', Lagos, Government Printer, 1936, p. 4.
40 CSc 505/12, Brooke, pp. 4, 8–9, 18; CO 657/50, Gibbons, p. 13; and CO 657/41, 'Annual report of the Colony, 1936', Kaduna, Government Printer, 1937, p. 2.
41 MSS Afr.t.15, W. Fowler, 'A Report on the Lands of the Colony Districts', (mimeo), ca. 1947, Colonial Records Project, Rhodes House Library, Oxford, p. 31.
42 The political structure of settlements is reconstructed from CSO 26/29939, Wilkes, pp. 18ff, and interviews conducted in 1972 and 1975.
43 CSO 26/29939, Wilkes, p. 6.
44 Cole, 1975, p. 24.
45 Burns, 1963, p. 317.
46 Losi, 1967, p. 82.
47 Nicholson, 1969, p. 67; and Cole, 1975, pp. 80–1.
48 Ifadu Alashe died in June 1907. Aganran became *Baalę* of Ojuwoye in February 1905, succeeding one Aileru who died in May 1904. See Lagos Colony, *Central Native Council Minute Book*, 1901–13, p. 158; Mushin Town Council Chieftaincy File, 1975, p. 329; and G3 A2/0, No. 191, 'Notices of the Villages'.
49 CO 147/24, Folio 438, 19 April 1872, 'Inquest on the body of Agunson a man said to be murdered'. Records do not indicate the whereabouts of other constables stationed outside Lagos city.
50 The *Baba Isalę* village ties are recorded in the following: Cole, 1975, pp. 24–5, 173; MSS Afr.t.15, Fowler, 'A Report', p. 29; Mushin Town Council, Files of the Chieftaincy Committee, 1974, pp. 272, 301, 330; CSO 26/29939, Wilkes; and interviews with Itire family members, September 1972.
51 Nigeria, *Census of Nigeria, 1931*, Vol.III, London: Crown Agents for the Colonies, 1932, p. 19.
52 CSc 505/12, Brooke, p. 12; CO 657/45, 'Annual Report on the Administration of the Colony for the Year 1937', Lagos, Government Printer, 1938, pp. 7–8.
53 Cole, 1975, pp. 29, 173.
54 CO 657/40, 'Annual Report, 1935', p. 4.
55 Crime problems were an ongoing preoccupation. See various Annual Reports: CO 657/30, 1931, p. 6; CO 657/36, 1933, p. 4; CO 657/38, 1934, pp. 2, 4; and

administrative reports: CSO 26/29979, R. L. V. Wilkes and W. G. Wormal, 'Intelligence Report on the Central Awori Group in the Ikeja and Badagri District of the Colony', 1934, p. 2; and CSO 26/29939, Wilkes, p. 7.

56 CSO 26/29939, Wilkes, p. 37.
57 CSO 26/29939, Wilkes, p. 16.
58 Cole, 1975, p. 274 n. 65.
59 Mushin Town Council, Chieftaincy Files, 1974, pp. 270–2, 278–80, 284–7, 329–31, 341.
60 CSO 26/29939, Wilkes, p. 24.
61 CO 657/22, 'Annual Report on the Colony for the Year 1928', Sessional Paper No. 20 of 1929, Lagos, Government Printer, 1929, pp. 3–16; and CO 657/54, 'Annual Report for the Northern, Western, Eastern Provinces and the Colony, 1940', Lagos, Government Printer, 1941, p. 33. The tax rate in muncipal Lagos was 1 per cent on incomes of £30 or more, an inequity which caused an outcry among outlying area residents. The inequity continued into the 1940s when Ikeja tax was 2 per cent and that of Lagos City 1.25 per cent on incomes up to £200.
62 CO 657/24, 'Annual Report on the Colony for the Year 1929', Lagos, Government Printer, n.d., p. 5; and CO 657/27, 'Annual Report on the Colony for the Year 1930', Lagos, Government Printer, n.d., p. 6.
63 CSO 26/29939, Wilkes, p. 22; and CO 657/45, 'Annual Report, 1937', p. 8.
64 CO 657/45, pp. 8–9; CO 657/55, 'Annual Reports for the Northern, Western, Eastern Provinces and the Colony, 1942', typescript, p. 3.
65 CO 657/22, 'Annual Report on the Colony for the Year 1928', Sessional Paper No. 20 of 1929, Lagos, Government Printer, 1929, p. 20; and CSc 505/12, Brooke, p. 48.
66 CO 657/40, 'Annual Report, 1935', p. 3.
67 CO 657/38, 'Annual Report, 1934', p. 2.
68 CSO 26/29939, Wilkes, p. 39; CO 657/50, Gibbons, p. 10.
69 CO 657/38, 'Annual Report, 1934', p. 4.
70 Com.Col. IKEDIV 3, CP 497, 'Night Patrols', 1941.
71 CO 657/47, 'Colony: Annual Report for the Year 1939', p. 89.
72 CO 657/54, 'Annual Reports, 1940', p. 32.
73 CO 657/66, 'Annual Reports for the Northern, Western, Eastern Provinces and the Colony, 1946', Sessional Paper No. 28 of 1947, Lagos, Government Printer, 1947, pp. 36–7.
74 Com.Col. IKEDIV 6 79 Vol. XV, '1947 Annual Report'; and Com.Col. IKEDIV 6. 79 Vol. XXII, '1954 Annual Report, Ikeja Division'.
75 CSc 505/12, Brooke, p. 9.
76 CO 657/56, 'Annual Reports for the Northern, Western, Eastern Provinces and the Colony, 1944', Sessional Paper No. 25 of 1945, Lagos, Government Printer, 1945, p. 37; CSc 505/12, Brooke, p. 19.
77 Com.Col. IKEDIV 6 79 Vol. XV, '1947 Annual Report, Ikeja Division'; Com.Col. IKEDIV 6 79 Vol. XVI, '1948, Annual Report, Ikeja Division'; and CO 657/66, 'Annual Report, 1948', p. 36.
78 Mushin Town Council, Chieftaincy Files, 1974, p. 302.
79 The election was an indirect, three-level process in which two representatives were chosen to serve from the district in the regional legislature. The primary level of the ladder consisted of public gatherings of taxpayers in specially demarcated wards who elected representatives to an Intermediate Electoral College. This second intermediate body elected representatives to a Final Electoral College, and this body elected two persons to serve in the regional legislature. See Lloyd, 1952, pp. 82–3.

80 The election also aroused unrest in the Mushin area. Com.Col. IKEDIV 6 224/c, 7 March 1952, 'Mushin Social Club'.
81 These fears were kept alive by Lagos State movement pressure groups which lobbied for a separate administrative unit soon after the city and Colony District were separated and which eventually was successful when Lagos State was created in 1967. See Baker, 1974, pp. 246–8, 261.
82 Com.Col. IKEDIV 3 C.P. 497, 'Night Patrols', 1941; IKEDIV 6 224/S.5, 'Ikeja District People's Party', 1953; IKEDIV 6 224/S.13, 'United People's Party', 1954; IKEDIV 6 224 S.4 'Mushin Improvement Association', 1953; and interviews with Mushin leaders, 1972 and 1975.
83 Mushin then became one of three districts in Ikeja Division: Mushin, Agege and Ikeja Districts. Earlier in 1948, the Ikorodu and Ijede areas of Ikeja Division had been removed and placed under a separate administrator at Ikorodu.
84 CO 657/45, 'Annual Report, 1937', p. 8.
85 One of the only Awori areas that enjoyed early urban expansion directly was Ojuwoye village.
86 In a few instances settler identity was given to residents who leased houseplots, and even a few long-term tenants if they intended to remain permanently and wished to exercise the rights and duties of local citizenship. A leader in Oshodi told me that long-term tenants were sometimes considered settlers in Oshodi, probably because leases and long-term tenancies were more the norm in this particular area than outright freehold ownership was.

3. LAND AND HOUSING AS SOURCES OF POWER

 1 Coker, 1966, p. 321.
 2 The centrality of land issues is discussed in three works which are focused primarily on municipal Lagos. They are: Cole, 1975, pp. 89–97; Baker, 1974, pp. 94–103; and Marris, 1961.
 3 MSS Afr.t.15, Fowler, p. 15.
 4 CSc 505/12, Brooke, p. 6.
 5 Cole, 1975, p. 90.
 6 CO 657/90, 'Annual Report on the Land Department of the Western Region of Nigeria for the Year 1952–3', Nigeria, Government Printer, 1954, pp. 6–7.
 7 Simpson, 1961, p. 145. Some of these cases are found in Nigeria, *Selected Judgments of the Federal Supreme Court of Nigeria, 1959*, Vol. IV, compiled by The Hon. Mr Justice M. J. Abbott, Lagos, Federal Government Printer, 1960; and Nigeria, *Law Reports of the High Court of the Federal Territory of Lagos, 1960*, Federal Director of Printing, 1963.
 8 *Daily Times*, 8 August 1972, p. 24.
 9 Squatting was not widespread. The open, private land market appeared to have minimised this type of land appropriation.
10 MSS Afr.t.15, Fowler, pp. 30–1; Olawoye, *Proof of Title to Land in Nigeria*, LLM Thesis, University of Lagos, 1968, pp. 254–5.
11 An excellent case study of this type of problem in nearby Ibadan is presented by Aronson, 1978, pp. 253–69.
12 Early allocations and reallocations of the same parcels of land are discussed in CSO 26/29939, Wilkes, p. 28.
13 MSS Afr.t.15, Fowler, p. 31–2.
14 See Coker, 1966; Elias, 1951; James, 1965, pp. 3–23; James and Kasunmu, 1966; Lloyd, 1962; Olawoye, *Proof of Title*; S. R. Simpson, *A Report on the*

Registration of Title to Land in the Federal Territory of Lagos, Lagos: Federal Government Printer, 1957; and MSS Afr.t.15, Fowler.

15 Two scholars have written that, among northern Yoruba peoples, descent was traced unilineally, through males. See Lloyd, 1959, pp. 235–51; and Schwab, 1955, pp. 352–74. Lloyd has written that among southern Yoruba peoples descent is cognatic, through males and females. See Lloyd, 1966, pp. 484–500. These views contrast with those of other scholars who have tended to argue that kinship reckoning in most Yoruba-speaking areas is, at base, cognatic (or bilateral), and quite flexible in the permutations that descent group member-ships take. For these views see Eades, 1980, pp. 45–56; Peel, 1983, pp. 50–4; and Fadipe, 1970, pp. 134–5.

16 MSS Afr.t.15, Fowler, p. 5.

17 Cole, 1975, p. 90; Elias, 1951, p. 9; and CSO 26/29939, Wilkes, *passim*.

18 Simpson, *A Report on the Registration of Title to Land*, pp. 13–14.

19 Coker, 1966, pp. 15–16; CSc 505/12, Brooke, p. 24; and MSS Afr.t.15, Fowler, pp. 12–15.

20 MSS Afr.t.15, Fowler, p. 13.

21 MSS Afr.t.15, Fowler, p. 6, 12.

22 Elias, 1951, p. 222.

23 MSS Afr.t.15, Fowler, p. 31.

24 Simpson, *A Report on the Registration of Title to Land*, p. 6.

25 James, 1965, p. 19.

26 Akinlawon L. Mabogunje, *Lagos: A Study in Urban Geography*, Unpublished PhD Thesis, University of London, 1961, p. 147.

27 Pseudonyms are indicated by asterisks.

28 The cost of Abiola's houseplot in 1946 was roughly equivalent to what a labourer would have earned annually in the early 1940s. See Nigeria, *Report of the Cost of Living Committee*, Lagos, 1942.

29 Baker, 1974, pp. 40–1.

30 The death of a freehold owner was an occasion for illegitimate claims on ownership rights to arise against heirs by competitors who hoped that con-veyances had been lost or that descendants were not informed of all aspects of the original sale agreement.

31 Fapohunda, 1978, p. 55.

32 The 1964 estimates of house-building costs come from Koenigsberger *et al.*, 1964, p. 134.

33 Owners occupied 59 per cent of the houses in my 1972 census. The other houses were income-producing investments of which owners sometimes held two or more.

34 Some multi-storey buildings had up to 150 residents. Builders of these large blocks, as they were called, found in the 1970s that three to six high-cost rental flats in a building were more lucrative and easier to manage than what up to that time was a tendency to build blocks with separate rented rooms. Flats could be leased under annual or biannual contracts to employers or relatively high-income renters who made lump-sum payments in advance.

35 Government financing tended to favour high-income sectors of the population or government workers. See Barnes, 1982, p. 8.

36 The rates in the first half of the century ranged from 30 to 60 per cent per annum. See MSS Afr.t.15, Fowler, p. 36. Two landowners told me in 1972 that their neighbourhood moneylender charged a monthly rate of as much as 6 shillings on each £N1 borrowed. One moneylender with whom I was familiar acquired several properties through foreclosure.

37 A study of 126 owners in metropolitan Lagos and seven other West African cities showed that 55 per cent of all houseowners earned less than £500 per annum (c. 1971–2), when the average worker's wage in 1971 in Lagos was £N287. See Fapohunda, 1978, p. 55; and Peil, 1981.

38 Members of the national elite did invest in some Mushin property but they rarely lived in it. It is important, however, that elite status was not the *sine qua non* for property ownership. Since land was privately controlled, purchase was dependent on one's ability to pay and not on one's influence with government.

39 See Fapohunda, 1978, pp. 66–7; Sada and Adefolalu, 1975, p. 91.

40 The cognatic principles, as applied in the Mushin area, made it possible for individuals to trace inheritance rights simultaneously through several descent lines, e.g. mother's father, mother's mother, father's father, or father's mother, and hence to exercise simultaneously the rights and duties pertaining to property use in several descent groups.

41 My survey of 163 Yoruba tenants and owners of both sexes showed that 75 per cent of the owners held or attended descent group activities and meetings in the metropolitan area whereas only 32 per cent of the tenants did so.

42 The marriages of landladies tended to be serial. Moreover female owners often lived separately from their husbands.

43 In the few instances when tenants had more than one wife they solved space problems by sometimes lodging them in separate rooms in separate buildings.

44 Membership in religious groups and societies, like attendance at places of worship, was evenly divided between Islam and Christianity among Yoruba-speaking residents.

45 Nigeria, *Third National Development Plan*, p. 308.

46 Mushin Town Council, 'Draft Estimates, 1975–6', p. 1.

47 Okpala, 1979, p. 26.

48 Lagos State, *Third National Development Plan 1975–80: Lagos State Programme*, Lagos, 1975 (mimeograph), p. 2.

49 This figure is based on tax assessment figures taken from the Mushin Town Council, 'Draft Estimates, 1976–6', and population estimates. See also *West Africa*, 24 January 1977, no. 3107, p. 39.

50 cf. Peace, 1979, pp. 51–2.

51 Babalola, 1966, pp. 244–9.

4. THE RESIDENTIAL BASIS OF LEADERSHIP

1 Bailey, 1969, p. 36.

2 Peel, 1983, pp. 33–6.

3 See Chapter 3, Tables 3 and 4 for occupational and educational diversity. A high degree of heterogeneity in urban houses throughout West Africa is reported by Peil, 1981, pp. 114–21.

4 86 per cent of the owners in my Mushin neighbourhood census were of Yoruba descent; this compared to 72 per cent of the metropolitan area population – owners and non-owners – which was Yoruba. The percentage of Yoruba owners elsewhere in the metropolitan area was lower. For example, in the suburb of Ajegunle, 60.5 per cent of the owners in a random survey were Yoruba (Margaret Peil, Personal Communication). A 1960 study in municipal Lagos, to give yet another example, showed that Ghanaians owned 30 per cent of the houses in Obalende (eastern Lagos Island) and Igbo owned 23 per cent of the houses in Surulere (on the mainland). See Mabogunje, *Lagos*, pp. 143–5; and Nigeria,

Population Census, 1963.

5 My survey of the language abilities was taken among Yoruba and Igbo adult residents only.

6 See Map 4, p. 80.

7 Two Mushin neighbourhoods in which this study was conducted had population densities of roughly 320 persons per acre.

8 The majority of adult Yoruba women (72 per cent) were trading by the time they were 30 years old, according to my census. Contrary to the popular view, however, only a small fraction of them traded in markets.

9 The majority of the men (55 per cent) worked on Lagos Island or in the industrial areas of Ikeja, Apapa, and Ijora.

10 A few prayer groups or small congregations worshipped inside houses and, therefore, they were not counted.

11 Religious groups were among the first organisations newcomers joined after their arrival. People usually waited several years before joining other kinds of voluntary associations. See Barnes, 1975, p. 83.

12 For discussions of the role of land and landowners with respect to political resources elsewhere in metropolitan Lagos – Lagos City and Agege, respectively – see Baker, 1974, pp. 74–114; and Peace, 1979, pp. 35–9.

13 Discussions of these political roles which have guided my thinking are found in Bailey, 1969, p. 167; and Boissevain, 1974, pp. 147–8.

14 Eighty per cent of the people in my survey indicated that it was necessary to have the help of patrons and middlemen. Yoruba peoples were more likely to establish client relationships with people who were not kinsmen or fellow townsmen than Igbo peoples were.

15 *Sunday Times*, 26 March 1972, p. 9.

16 See Chapter 3.

17 The interviews involved kinship, real estate, and occupation and migration histories.

18 Bailey, 1969, pp. 63–6.

19 The diabetic client was not of Yoruba descent; the co-tenant was.

20 One of Ojo's clients in this series of land problems was Timothy Abiola. See Chapter 3.

21 cf. Lloyd, 1974, p. 51; Peace, 1979, p. 37ff. Peace uses the term *bǫrǫkinni* (*bǫǫkini*) to describe the 'Big Men' of Agege – a term which is roughly synonymous with *gbajumǫ*.

22 A conservative estimate of Ojo's income was £N2,750 per annum. The salary range for senior civil servants, business executives, and professional people in Lagos c. 1970 was between £N2,000 and £N4,000. See Baker, 1974, pp. 40–1; and Fapohunda, 1978, p. 55.

5. THE CHIEFTAINCY SYSTEM

1 cf. Peel, 1983, p. 199.

2 Mushin District Council, Minutes and Notes, 1955–6, Private File.

3 The *Olu* Agege was J. I. Ogunyi. See also Mushin Town Council, Chieftaincy File, 1974, p. 296.

4 The titles of *ǫǫni, ǫba,* or *olu* ordinarily connote kingship. *Ǫnitire*, for example, was an elision of *ǫǫni* and Itire. The official titles of Mushin's chiefs differed from their informal titles. In address and reference, residents ordinarily used the title *ǫba*. For official purposes, however, the *olu, ǫǫni,* and *Baalę* titles were used.

5 The Ejigbo chief came from a settlement which was founded by northern Yoruba believed to have fled to Mushin c. 1835 from the Ede area near Ibadan. The Ewu chief came from a settlement founded by Shabe Yoruba who came from Dahomey c. 1850. See CSO 26/29939, Wilkes, pp. 51, 63–4.

6 The following debate is reconstructed from: Mushin District Council, Minutes and Notes, 1955–6; Chief J. O. Tade, 'Short Biography of the City of Odi-Olowo', Ebute-Metta, Lagos, Ogunrotimi Printing Press, n.d.; and oral testimony.

7 Fadipe, 1970, p. 128. See also Aronson, 1978, pp. 93–4; and Bascom, 1942, pp. 37–46.

8 Mushin Town Council, Chieftaincy File, 15 August 1973, 'The Origin History of *Olu* of Odi Olowo, Mushin'.

9 The title appears to have been changed c. November 1955, by the *Olu* elect, Jimoh Aileru. See Mushin Town Council, Minutes and Notes, 1955–6. There were objections to the name change, but they were resisted.

10 There was little Awori presence in Shomolu. Large portions of this area originally were owned by the Oloto family, one of the Idejo landowning chieftaincy descent groups, of Lagos. The backgrounds of Shomolu settlers were quite heterogeneous, although many of the earliest inhabitants were thought to have come to the area via Lagos. However, no interest in Lagos or Lagos chiefs was displayed when the area was visited in 1934 by a British district officer. See CSO 26/29939, Wilkes, pp. 56–8.

11 Mushin Town Council, Chieftaincy File, 1974, p. 298.

12 Large portions of Oshodi were originally owned by Isolo. See CSO 26/29939, Wilkes, p. 53.

13 Onigbongbo was believed to have been closely related to Ojuwoye. CSO 26/29939, Wilkes, p. 59.

14 Mushin Town Council, Chieftaincy File, 1974, p. 332.

15 The seven were: Isolo, Itire, Odi Olowo, Ojuwoye, Onigbongbo, Oshodi, and Shomolu. See Nigeria, *Western Region Legal Notices*, Nos. 250 and 308 of 1965.

16 See Chapter 6 for further discussion of the impact of partisan politics in Mushin.

17 See Nigeria, *Western Nigeria Legal Notices*, No. 151 and Edict No. 3, 1966.

18 Mushin Town Council, Chieftaincy File, 1974, pp. 296–302, 332–4, 337–8.

19 See Chapter 7 where the process of securing government appointments is discussed.

20 The Onitire was succeeded in 1975 by the *Olu* of Odi Olowo.

21 There were ten titles, two of which were conferred on prominent neighbourhood women leaders.

22 These claims were made in 1973. In resubmitting its request for approval, Ewu claimed to be an Awori settlement, although in 1934 its leaders told a district officer their ancestors were from the Shabe Yoruba kingdom of Dahomey. (See note 5 above.) Ewu also claimed that it owned the land on which the Shogunle settlement developed; therefore it asked that the Shogunle chief be considered junior to the chief of Ewu. Mushin Town Council, Chieftaincy File no. 5, Vol. 5, 1973–4.

23 I found two instances in which the original freehold purchaser died. In both of them the heirs selected the eldest to represent them collectively at landowner meetings.

24 Cole, 1975, pp. 16–17.

25 Lloyd, 1962, pp. 146–8, 233–5.

26 For one of the clearest examples see Peel, 1983, pp. 36ff.

27 A. Cohen, 1974b, p. 69.

28 Tade, n.d.

29 The Lagos chiefs protested this use of their emblem of office, but the Shomolu chiefs continued to wear the caps.

30 There were three non-Yoruba chiefs to my knowledge. They were of Fon, Egun, and Igbira descent.

31 It has been pointed out that Lagos City chiefs willingly aligned themselves with factions as one way of insuring their survival. See Cole, 1975, p. 164.

32 A thorough discussion of this point is presented by A. Cohen, 1974b, pp. 49–54.

6. THE CONSOLIDATION OF LEADERSHIP

1 See Chapter 2.

2 The Ikeja Town Planning Authority grew out of the Ikeja Planning Authority which was established in 1948. The ITPA was succeeded in 1972 by the Lagos State Development and Property Corporation, a statewide planning body.

3 The staff expanded to 1477 after twenty years in operation, and a town clerk became the chief administrative officer.

4 The non-Yoruba councillor did, however, speak the language and he had assimilated to Yoruba culture.

5 The NCNC was first known as the National Council of Nigeria and the Cameroons. The name was changed in 1961.

6 The importance of regions in the system of rewards is discussed in more detail by Post and Vickers, 1973, pp. 53–5; and Rimmer, 1978, pp. 147–8.

7 Elections were held previous to this time as early as the 1920s in Municipal Lagos and Calabar. See Baker, 1974, pp. 148 and 330 n.2.

8 Post, 1966, pp. 406–7.

9 NCNC candidates won a majority of the Lagos Town Council seats in 1950, 1951 and 1959; AG candidates won a majority in 1953, 1957, 1962 and 1965. See Baker, 1974, p. 156.

10 Post, 1963, p. 118.

11 The AG was a strong force in the Mushin area by 1954; an AG ward chairman, for instance, was selected and was active in the Odi Olowo sector in that year. See Com.Col. IKEDIV 6 224/S.5.

12 Post, 1963, p. 119.

13 The same was true in municipal Lagos where the AG, using a strategy probably emulated by Mushin, turned each ward into a party chapter and thus overcame an earlier entrenched NCNC. See Baker, 1974, pp. 142–3, 161–2.

14 cf. Baker, 1974, pp. 151, 234–43.

15 Mackintosh, 1966, pp. 430–7; Baker, 1974, p. 139.

16 See Post and Vickers, 1973, pp. 23–4; Baker, 1974, pp. 126, 135–8, 336 n.44.

17 Post, 1963, p. 265; Post and Vickers, 1973, pp. 169, 195; and Baker, 1974, p. 136.

18 Post, 1963, map p. 157; and Nigeria, Western Region, 'Report on the Holding of the 1956 Parliamentary Election to the Western House of Assembly, Nigeria', Western Region, Government Printer, 1959, p. 13.

19 Post, 1963, pp. 60–3, 265; Baker, 1974, p. 335.

20 Sklar, 1963, p. 423.

21 Post, 1963, p. 129.

22 Eventually one-third of the first elected council would hold chieftaincy titles in Mushin.

23 Baker, 1974, p. 83.

24 A 1959 study indicated that 31 per cent of the mostly male heads of households in two municipal Lagos neighbourhoods were active in ethnic associations. Nearly the same number, 30 per cent of Mushin adults indicated in 1972 that they had at one time or another participated in them. See Marris, 1961, p. 157; Barnes, 1975, p. 78–80; and Peace, 1979b, p. 22.

25 The minutes and proceedings of the Mushin District Council and of other local government panels indicated that there were few organised attempts to influence decisions or policies. The exception was neighbourhood associations which did make formal appeals on behalf of community interests from time to time. But these associations represented the landowning stratum and not the tenant population.

26 See Zolberg, 1966, p. 123, who points out that political machines were common in West Africa even though the societies were incompletely integrated.

27 I am guided in this discussion of machine politics by Scott, 1969, pp. 1143ff.

28 *Daily Sketch*, 30 October 1964.

29 Hanna and Hanna, 1971, pp. 164–5.

30 See Sada, *The Metropolitan Region of Lagos*, p. 83.

31 In 1960 the AG held 80 of 124 seats in the Western Region House of Assembly. See Post and Vickers, 1973, p. 67.

32 J. S. O. Ogunnaike (Ch.) and Femi Ayantuga, *Proceedings of the Tribunal of Inquiry into the Reorganisation of Local Government Councils in the Lagos State*, 1970, p. 49.

33 *Daily Express*, 24 February 1959.

34 *West African Pilot*, 29 June 1959.

35 Post, 1963, pp. 361–2.

36 Awolowo was convicted of treason, on charges that he plotted to overthrow the government, and sentenced to ten years in prison. He was released in 1966 after the military came to power.

37 *Daily Express*, 20 December 1962.

38 Seventeen stall assignments were made to committee members and fourteen to council employees. See Chief A. Ilori (Chmn.) *et al.*, *Report of the Tribunal of Inquiry into the Administration and Financial Management of Ajeromi, Ikeja, Mushin, and Agege District Councils*, V.I. and II, Lagos, 1970, pp. 132, 163–4, 230–1.

39 *Daily Times*, 24 June 1963.

40 See Chapter 5, p. 105.

41 The situation is described in Post and Vickers, 1973, pp. 87–103.

42 Despite considerable enmity against NCNC in Mushin in earlier years, its meetings and other activities were not obstructed as were those of the NNDP (see n. 43 below).

43 In March, 1964, the UPP merged with several small southern minority parties and became the Nigerian National Democratic Party (NNDP).

44 Ostheimer, 1973, p. 55. See also Peace, 1979a, p. 142.

45 cf. R. Cohen, 1974, p. 168.

46 *Daily Sketch*, 28 May 1965; *Daily Express*, 19 May 1965; *Sunday Express*, 9 May 1965.

47 Post and Vickers, 1973, p. 161.

48 Post and Vickers, 1973, p. 222.

49 *Express*, 12 October 1965; *Pilot*, 12 October 1965; *Telegraph*, 13 October 1965; *Daily Times*, 12, 13, 14, 22 October 1965. See also Post and Vickers, 1973, pp. 231–2.

50 *Daily Times*, 22 October 1965; *Sunday Express*, 24 October 1965.

51 Public reaction to what the authors describe as 'harsh and blatant' tactics of the
NNDP is discussed by Post and Vickers, 1973, p. 232.
52 Baker, 1974, pp. 130–1.
53 Lupton and Wilson, 1959, pp. 30–51.

7. THE ROLE OF FACTIONS IN THE STRUGGLE FOR POWER

1 Swartz, 1968, p. 278.
2 Bailey points out that transactional relationships are necessary in order to
mobilise factions. See Bailey, 1969, p. 52.
3 Municipal Lagos was an exception because it was the federal capital and therefore the military was closely involved in its administration.
4 In April 1976 the twelve states were replaced by nineteen states.
5 *Daily Times*, 25 January 1973.
6 Mushin Town Council, 'Draft Estimates', p. 2; Lagos City Council, 'Draft
Estimates, 1975–6', Lagos, mimeograph, 1975, p. vii; Ishola Oluwa and S. I.
Talabi, *Report of the Tribunal of Inquiry into the Reorganisation of Local
Government Councils in the Lagos State* (dissenting report), Lagos, 1970, p. 67.
7 The January 1966 military coup was followed by another in July 1966. The
second military regime remained in power until July 1975 when a third military
coup took place. The leader of the latter rout, Brigadier Murtala Mohamed, was
assassinated seven months later in an abortive coup which, none the less, put a
fourth military leader, General Olusegun Obasanjo, into the office of head of
state.
8 See Chapter 6, Table 14 and Fig. 4, where the four people named were listed as
top leaders of Mushin: T. Abiola no. 1, L. Sotomi no. 2, S. J. Odunsi no. 3, and
Madam Femi Duro no. 4.
9 A study of metropolitan Lagos listed the following as the major interest groups as
of about 1968: ethnic associations, market associations, trade unions, religious
groups, transporters' associations, and teachers' groups. See Williams and
Walsh, 1968, p. 27.
10 Sada and McNulty, 1970, p. 23.
11 See Sada and McNulty, 1974, p. 153, n. 3.
12 This estimate is based on findings for municipal Lagos markets. See Baker,
1974, p. 223.
13 Sudarkasa, 1973, pp. 63–4.
14 Sada and McNulty, 1970, pp. 12–13.
15 Peil, 1973, p. 13; and Sada and McNulty, 1974, p. 162.
16 Mushin Town Council, 'Draft Estimates', pp. 3, 9; *Daily Express*, 21 September
1972.
17 See Baker, 1974, p. 227.
18 The other important committee, Highways and Plans, reflected the significance
of transport centres in Mushin.
19 Sada and McNulty, 1974, p. 163.
20 The ranking of officers in markets differs from place to place. See, for example,
Sudarkasa, 1973, pp. 57–63; Baker, 1974, pp. 229–31; and Sada and McNulty,
1974, p. 152.
21 The *Iya Egbe* of Awolowo Market represented the following commodities:
bananas, beans, china, cloth, cooked foodstuffs, cooked rice, fowl, gari, gold,
ground pepper, kola nuts, medicines and herbs, packaged and canned provisions, pounded yam, rice, singlets, stock fish, tomatoes, and yam. Hair plaiters

(dressers) also had their own *Iya Ẹgbẹ*.

22 Gluckman, 1961, pp. 5–17.
23 Compiled from oral testimony and from private chieftaincy files.
24 See Chapter 6, Fig. 4, and Table 14, where Prince Fagbemi no. 12 and A. Ajisafe no. 20 are listed.
25 Compiled from oral testimony and from private chieftaincy files.
26 Further complications arising from this installation and the election of a representative to the House of Chiefs are discussed in chapter 8.
27 See Chapter 6, p. 152, n. 50.
28 The announcement of the elders committee was one of the first public signals that leaders had divided into factions. Two days after the elders committee membership was announced, Abiola's rival, Sotomi – perhaps unsatisfied with not being included as an Elder – made his own public appeal concerning the disorder in Mushin.
29 See Chapter 6, p. 103.
30 Ogunnaike and Ayantuga, *Proceedings*, p. 44.
31 Compiled from oral testimony and author's observations.
32 A member of the Mushin Town Council's markets committee accompanied Abiola to his meeting with Alhaja Toriola.
33 See Baker, 1974, pp. 239–41.
34 Compiled from oral testimony, author's observations, and newspaper accounts.
35 *Nigerian Tribune*, 16 July 1974.
36 *West African Pilot*, 7 March 1975.
37 Bailey, 1969, pp. 51–5; Boissevain, 1974, p. 192; Nicholas, 1977, p. 71; and Silverman, 1977, pp. 89–93.

8. THE INSTITUTIONALISATION OF POWER

1 Compiled from oral testimony and private chieftaincy files.
2 The ostracism of the *Olu* of Odi Olowo was a similar display of this ability.
3 Compiled from oral testimony and private chieftaincy files.
4 *Iwuye* is *iwọ oye*, 'enter the title'; or *wu oye*, 'celebrate the title'. I am indebted to J. D. Y. Peel for suggesting the first translation and to Abraham, 1958, p. 673, for the second.
5 Mushin Town Council, Chieftaincy File, 1975, pp. 286–7. The case had not been officially resolved as of 1983. However, an unofficial view was that the Alashe family, which still had a residence in Ojuwoye, did own an established title (i.e. the title first held by Ifadu Alashe in the nineteenth century had been converted from a personal to an established title) and that it could rightfully confer it on a family member of its choice. I was unofficially informed that Ladega, however, was not chosen as the title-holder, but that another member of the family was. The question of landownership was not resolved.
6 This agreement was honoured in 1974 when the second Ikeja Division representative – this time from Agege – was selected to replace the (late) *Olu Mushin*.
7 A study of the relationship between the military government, the bureaucracy, and the public, based on extensive interviews with military, political, and government officials, is found in Bienen, 1978, pp. 187–251.
8 Bienen, 1978, pp. 218–19.
9 The relationship between bureaucrats and military regimes in tropical Africa is discussed by Kasfir, 1976, p. 234. For a discussion of the post-civil war

flowering of Nigeria's civil service as a political arena, see *West Africa*, 18 January 1985, p. 143.

10 *Nigerian Tribune*, 2 July 1973; *West African Pilot*, 31 July 1973; *Daily Express*, 1 August 1973.

11 The military government which came to power in 1966 under General Yakubu Gowon originally set a target date for returning to civilian rule in three years. It was set aside, however, after Civil War erupted in July 1967. The war ended in 1970. Ten months later General Gowon declared it would be six years before war damage could be sufficiently rectified to restore civilian rule. In October 1974 the head of state shocked the country when he announced that the six-year target date would not be met. The popularity of the regime plummeted, unrest broke out, and in July 1975 a third *coup d'etat* brought another military faction to power. It vowed to return the government to civilian hands by 1 October 1979 and in fact did so. See Kirk-Greene and Rimmer, 1981, pp. 3–23.

12 See Chapter 7, p. 158, n. 7.

13 These changes are discussed in Barnes, 1977, pp. 30–1.

14 *Sunday Post*, 9 August 1970; *Nigerian Tribune*, 9 August 1971; and *West African Pilot*, 12 July 1971.

15 An Awori Welfare Association was in operation in 1970. It represented the interest of Awori living in Ikeja Division at a government hearing into local government practices. See Ogunnaike, *Proceedings*, p. 29.

16 *Daily Sketch*, 27 January 1975; and *New Nigerian*, 28 January 1975.

9. CONCLUSIONS

1 For a full treatment of Mushin as an urban frontier see Barnes, 1986.

2 Examples of the unique cultural elements that surround patron–client relationships in each context are found in Cornelius, 1977, pp. 340ff; Johnson, 1977, pp. 209ff.

3 Hanks, 1975, p. 199.

4 I am indebted to Landé whose cogent comparisons of the political advantages in group- versus individually-based political systems are responsible for many of the ideas in this section. See Landé, 1965, pp. 141–8; and 1977, pp. xiii–xxxvii.

5 Landé, 1977, p. xvi.

6 Weber, 1947, pp. 136–9; and Fallers, 1955, p. 300.

7 Cohen, 1969, pp. 36–7.

8 Bailey, 1969, p. 49.

9 Eisenstadt and Roniger, 1984, p. 29.

10 John L. Aguilar divides trust into two types: *rational trust*, a non-intimate kind of trust based on 'assessments of acceptable or unacceptable levels of risk', and *psychological trust*, based on subjective evaluations of the safety or danger involved in sharing confidences, secrets, or plans. See Aguilar, 1984, p. 3.

11 Kaufman, 1974, p. 285.

12 Bailey, 1969, p. 45.

13 Scott, 1972, p. 99.

14 Bailey, 1969, p. 46; and Scott, 1972, p. 99.

15 *Webster's Third New International Dictionary*, Springfield, Mass., Merriam–Webster, Inc., 1981; and *The Shorter Oxford English Dictionary*, Oxford, Clarendon, 1973.

16 Blau, 1964, pp. 91–4.

17 For a discussion of conversions in client exchanges, see Boissevain, 1974, pp. 158–63.

18 Landé, 1977, p. xxviii.
19 Cohen, 1969 and 1981.
20 Sahlins, 1963, pp. 285–303; and Strathern, 1971, pp. 214–29.
21 Peace applies the concept of 'Big Man' to relatively wealthy, influential leaders of Agege, another suburban community in metropolitan Lagos. See Peace, 1979b, pp. 28ff.
22 There are two things to consider here: close ties do not necessarily correlate with the significance or the amount of material reciprocity in a relationship; however, poor material rewards may be offset by indirect benefits, particularly protection.
23 Gouldner, 1960, p. 171.
24 Mauss, 1954, pp. 79–80.
25 See, for example, Jackson, 1978, pp. 347–8; and Whitaker, 1970, pp. 374–5.
26 Landé has suggested that our appreciation of the integrative qualities of clientelism stem from network analysis which 'casts light on the basis of cohesion in societies' where strong governments or organised groups are absent. See Landé, 1977, p. xxxiv. My own feeling is that network is not as powerful a concept as *client network* or *client system* since network is frequently reserved for relationships between equals, and it is the asymmetry of clientelism – both in status of participants and in things exchanged – that gives individually-contracted (dyadic) ties relative durability and cohesiveness.
27 Hanna and Hanna suggest that in tropical African cities, integration is the result of actions of 'key townsmen' who operate in several cultural systems at once and therefore mediate between them. See Hanna and Hanna, 1971, p. 201.
28 Wallace, 1961, pp. 29–41.
29 Lemarchand, 1981, pp. 9–10.
30 Landé, 1965, p. 146; Lemarchand, 1972, p. 76; and Scott, 1972, p. 96–7. Still another way of organising client relationships is the chain-to-centre structure, as described by Eisenstadt and Roniger, 1984, p. 222.
31 Lewis, 1974, p. 16.
32 Gluckman, 1949, pp. 93–4.
33 Fallers, 1955, pp. 301–2.
34 Busia, 1951, 209ff.
35 Epstein, 1958.
36 Harrell-Bond, Howard, and Skinner, 1978.
37 The survival of urban chiefs was particularly apparent in West African towns where fewer controls were placed on indigenous authorities than in Southern and Central African towns. For examples see: Acquah, 1958; Fraenkel, 1964; Gutkind, 1966, pp. 249–65; Schildkrout, 1970, pp. 251–69; Skinner, 1974; Southall and Gutkind, 1957. For an entire collection of studies devoted to the survival of chiefs see Crowder and Ikime, 1970.
38 A helpful discussion of the various approaches to using the concept of clientelism is presented by Lemarchand, 1981, pp. 11–16.

BIBLIOGRAPHY

I PRINTED SOURCES

Abate, Yohannis, 'Urbanism and Urbanization', *Issue*, 8(4), 1978, pp. 23–9.

Abraham, R. C., *Dictionary of Modern Yoruba*, London: University of London Press, 1958.

Acquah, I., *Accra Survey*, London: University of London Press, 1958.

Adejuyigbe, O., 'Evolution of the Boundaries of Lagos', *Nigeria Magazine*, No. 101, July–September, 1969, pp. 480–84.

Aderibigbe, A. B., 'Early History of Lagos to about 1850', in *Lagos: The Development of an African City*, A. B. Aderibigbe (ed.), Nigeria: Longman, 1975, pp. 1–26.

Adesina, Segun, 'The Development of Western Education', in *Lagos: The Development of an African City*, A. B. Aderibigbe (ed.), Nigeria: Longman, 1975, pp. 124–43.

Aguilar, John L., 'Trust and Exchange: Expressive and Instrumental Dimensions of Reciprocity in a Peasant Community', *Ethos*, 12(1), 1984, pp. 3–29.

Akinola, R. A. and N. O. Alao, 'Some Geographical Aspects of Industries in Greater Lagos', in *Lagos: The Development of an African City*, A. B. Aderibigbe (ed.), Nigeria: Longman, 1975, pp. 108–23.

Aronson, Dan R., 'Capitalism and Culture in Ibadan Urban Development', *Urban Anthropology*, 7(3), 1978, pp. 253–69.

The City is Our Farm: Seven Migrant Ijebu Yoruba Families, Cambridge, Mass.: Schenkman, 1978.

Babalola, S. A., *The Content and Form of Yoruba Ijala*, Oxford: Clarendon, 1966.

Bailey, F. G., *Strategems and Spoils: A Social Anthropology of Politics*, New York: Schocken Books, 1969.

Baker, Pauline H., *Urbanization and Political Change: The Politics of Lagos 1917–1967*, Berkeley and Los Angeles: University of California Press, 1974.

Barnes, Sandra T., 'Voluntary Associations in a Metropolis: The Case of Lagos, Nigeria', *African Studies Review*, 18, 1975, pp. 75–87.

'Political Transition in Urban Africa', *The Annals of the American Academy of Political and Social Science*, 432 (July), 1977, pp. 26–41.

'Public and Private Housing in Urban West Africa: The Social Implications', in *Housing the Urban Poor in Africa*, M. K. C. Morrison and P. C. W. Gutkind (eds.), Syracuse: Maxwell School of Citizenship and Public Affairs, Foreign and Comparative Studies Program/African Series, No. 37, 1982, pp. 5–32.

'The Urban Frontier in West Africa: Mushin, Nigeria', in *The African Frontier: The Reproduction of Traditional African Societies*, Igor Kopytoff (ed.), Bloomington: Indiana University Press, 1986.

Barrows, Walter, L., 'Comparative Grassroots Politics in Africa', *World Politics*, 26(2), 1974, pp. 283–297.

Barth, Fredrik, 'Models of Social Organization', *Occasional Paper No. 23*, London: Royal Anthropological Institute, 1966.

Bascom, W. R., 'The Principle of Seniority in the Social Structure of the Yoruba', *American Anthropologist*, 44(1), 1942, pp. 37–46.

Bienen, Henry, *Armies and Parties in Africa*, New York: Africana Publishing Co., 1978.

Blau, Peter M., *Exchange and Power in Social Life*, New York: John Wiley, 1964.

Boissevain, Jeremy, *Friends of Friends: Networks, Manipulators and Coalitions*,

Oxford: Basil Blackwell, 1974.

Bond, George C., *The Politics of Change in a Zambian Community*, Chicago: University of Chicago Press, 1976.

Burns, A. C. (Sir), *The Nigeria Handbook*, Lagos: Government Printer, 1919 (2nd edition).

History of Nigeria, London: George Allen and Unwin, 1963 (6th edition).

Busia, K. A., *The Position of the Chief in the Modern Political System of Ashanti*, London: Oxford University Press (for International African Institute), 1951.

Cohen, Abner, *Custom and Politics in Urban Africa: A Study of Hausa Migrants in Yoruba Towns*, Berkeley and Los Angeles: University of California Press, 1969.

'Introduction: The Lesson of Ethnicity', in *Urban Ethnicity*, A. Cohen (ed.), Association of Social Anthropologists, Monograph No. 12, London: Tavistock, 1974a, pp. ix–xxiv.

Two-Dimensional Man: An Essay on the Anthropology of Power and Symbolism in Complex Society, London: Routledge & Kegan Paul, 1974b.

The Politics of Elite Culture: Explorations in the Dramaturgy of Power in a Modern African Society, Berkeley and Los Angeles: University of California Press, 1981.

Cohen, Robin, *Labour and Politics in Nigeria 1945–71*, London: Heinemann, 1974.

Coker, G. B. A., *Family Property among the Yorubas*, London: Sweet and Maxwell, 1966 (2nd edition).

Cole, Patrick, *Modern and Traditional Elites in the Politics of Lagos*, Cambridge: Cambridge University Press, 1975.

Cornelius, Wayne A., 'Leaders, Followers, and Official Patrons in Urban Mexico', in *Friends, Followers, and Factions*, Steffen W. Schmidt *et al* (eds.), Berkeley and Los Angeles: University of California Press, 1977, pp. 337–53.

Crowder, M. and O. Ikime (eds.), *West African Chiefs: Their Changing Status under Colonial Rule and Independence*, New York: Africana, 1970.

Eades, J. S., *The Yoruba Today*, Cambridge: Cambridge University Press, 1980.

Eisenstadt, S. N. and L. Roniger, *Patrons, Clients and Friends: Interpersonal Relations and the Structure of Trust in Society*, Cambridge: Cambridge University Press, 1984.

Elias, T. O., *Nigerian Land Law and Custom*, London: Routledge & Kegan Paul, 1951.

Epstein, A. L., *Politics in an Urban African Community*, Manchester: Manchester University Press (for Rhodes-Livingstone Institute), 1958.

Fadipe, N. A., *The Sociology of the Yoruba*, Ibadan: Ibadan University Press, 1970.

Fallers, Lloyd A., 'The Predicament of the Modern African Chief: An Instance from Uganda', *American Anthropologist*, 57(2), Part 1, 1955, pp. 290–305.

Bantu Bureaucracy, Chicago: University of Chicago Press, 1965 (first pub. 1956).

Fapohunda, Olanrewaju J., *et al*, *Lagos: Urban Development and Employment*, Geneva: International Labour Office, 1978.

Folami, Takiu, *A History of Lagos, Nigeria*, Smithtown, N.Y.: Exposition Press, 1982.

Forde, Daryll, *The Yoruba-Speaking Peoples of South-Western Nigeria*, London: International African Institute, 1951.

Foster, George M., 'The Dyadic Contract: A Model for the Social Structure of a Mexican Peasant Village', *American Anthropologist*, 63(6), 1961, pp. 1173–92.

Fraenkel, M., *Tribe and Class in Monrovia*, London: Oxford University Press (for International African Institute), 1964.

Gbadamosi, G. O., 'Patterns and Developments in Lagos Religious History', in

Lagos: The Development of an African City, A. B. Aderibigbe (ed.), Nigeria: Longman, 1975, pp. 173–96.

Geary, W. M. N. (Sir), 'The Development of Lagos in 50 Years – From Head Town of "Slave Coast" to be "The Liverpool of West Africa" ', *West Africa*, 16 August–4 October 1924.

Gellner, Ernest, 'Patrons and Clients', in *Patrons and Clients in Mediterranean Societies*, E. Gellner and J. Waterbury (eds.), London: Duckworth, 1977, pp. 1–6.

    and John Waterbury (eds.), *Patrons and Clients in Mediterranean Societies*, London: Duckworth, 1977.

Gilbert, Alan and Josef Gugler, *Cities, Poverty, and Development: Urbanization in the Third World*, Oxford: Oxford University Press, 1982.

Gluckman, Max, 'The Village Headman in British Central Africa: Introduction', *Africa*, 19(2), 1949, pp. 89–94.

    'Ethnographic Data in British Social Anthropology', *The Sociological Review*, N.S. V.9(1), 1961, pp. 5–17.

Gouldner, Alvin, 'The Norm of Reciprocity: A Preliminary Statement', *American Sociological Review* 25(2), 1960, pp. 161–78.

Gutkind, P. C. W., 'African Urban Chiefs: Agents of Stability or Change in African Urban Life?' *Anthropologica*, 8(2), 1966, 249–65.

    'The Energy of Despair: Social Organization of the Unemployed in Two African Cities: Lagos and Nairobi', *Civilisations*, 17(3 and 4), 1967, pp. 186–214 and 380–405.

Hanks, Lucien M., 'The Thai Social Order as Entourage and Circle', in *Change and Persistence in Thai Society*, G. W. Skinner and A. T. Kirsch (eds.), Ithaca, N.Y.: Cornell University Press, 1975, pp. 197–218.

Hanna, William J. and Judith L. Hanna, *Urban Dynamics in Black Africa*, Chicago and New York: Aldine–Atherton, 1971.

Harrell-Bond, B. E., A. M. Howard, and D. E. Skinner, *Community Leadership and the Transformation of Freetown (1801–1976)*, The Hague: Mouton, 1978.

Hopkins, Nicholas S., *Popular Government in an African Town*, Chicago: University of Chicago Press, 1972.

Jackson, Karl D., 'Urbanization and the Rise of Patron–Client Relations: The Changing Quality of Interpersonal Communications in the Neighborhoods of Bandung and the Villages of West Java', in *Political Power and Communications in Indonesia*, K. D. Jackson and L. W. Pye (eds.), Berkeley and Los Angeles: University of California Press, 1978, pp. 343–92.

James, Rudolph W., 'The Changing Role of Land in Southern Nigeria', *Odu*, 1(2), 1965, pp. 3–23.

    and A. B. Kasunmu, *Alienation of Family Property in Southern Nigeria*, Ibadan: University of Ibadan Press, 1966.

Johnson, Michael, 'Political Bosses and Their Gangs: Zu'ama and Qabadayat in the Sunni Muslim Quarters of Beirut', in *Patrons and Clients*, E. Gellner and J. Waterbury (eds.), London: Duckworth, 1977, pp. 207–224.

Kasfir, Nelson, *The Shrinking Political Arena*, Berkeley and Los Angeles: University of California Press, 1976.

Kaufman, Robert R., 'The Patron–Client Concept and Macro-Politics: Prospects and Problems', *Comparative Studies in Society and History*, 16(3), 1974, pp. 284–308.

Kirk-Greene, A. and D. Rimmer, *Nigeria Since 1970: A Political and Economic Outline*, London: Hodder and Stoughton, 1981.

Koenigsberger, Otto, *et al*, *Metropolitan Lagos*, New York: UN Programme of Technical Assistance, 1964.

Kopytoff, Jean Herskovits, *A Preface to Modern Nigeria: The 'Sierra Leoneans' in Yoruba, 1830–1890*, Madison: University of Wisconsin Press, 1965.

LaFontaine, J. S., *City Politics: A Study of Leopoldville, 1962–63*, Cambridge: Cambridge University Press, 1970.

Landé, Carl H., *Leaders, Factions, and Parties: The Structure of Philippine Politics*, Southeast Asia Studies, Monograph Series No. 6, New Haven: Yale University, 1965.

'Networks and Groups in Southeast Asia: Some Observations on the Group Theory of Politics', *American Political Science Review*, 67(1), 1973, pp. 103–27.

'Introduction: The Dyadic Basis of Clientelism', in *Friends, Followers, and Factions*, Steffen W. Schmidt *et al* (eds.), Berkeley and Los Angeles: University of California Press, 1977, pp. xiii–xxxvii.

Lemarchand, René, 'Political Clientelism and Ethnicity in Tropical Africa: Competing Solidarities in Nation Building', *American Political Science Review*, 66(1), 1972, pp. 68–90.

'Comparative Political Clientelism: Structure, Process and Optic', in *Political Clientelism, Patronage and Development*, S. N. Eisenstadt and R. Lemarchand (eds.), Beverley Hills: Sage, 1981, pp. 7–32.

and Keith Legg, 'Political Clientelism and Development: A Preliminary Analysis', *Comparative Politics*, 4(2), 1972, pp. 149–78.

Lewis, Herbert S., 'Leaders and Followers: Some Anthropological Perspectives', Addison–Wesley Module in Anthropology No. 50, 1974.

Lloyd, P. C., 'Some Comments on the Elections in Nigeria', *Journal of African Administration*, 4(July), 1952, pp. 82–92.

'The Yoruba Lineage', *Africa*, 25(3), 1959, pp. 235–51.

Yoruba Land Law, London: Oxford University Press for Nigerian Institute of Social and Economic Research, 1962.

'Agnatic and Cognatic Descent among the Yoruba', *Man*, N.S.1(4), 1966, pp. 484–500.

Power and Independence: Urban Africans' Perceptions of Social Inequality, London: Routledge & Kegan Paul, 1974.

Losi, John B., *History of Lagos*, Lagos: African Education Press, 1967 (first pub. 1914).

Lupton, T. and C. S. Wilson, 'The Social Background and Connections of "Top Decision-Makers" ', *Manchester School of Economics and Social Studies*, 27(1), 1959, pp. 30–51.

Mabogunje, Akin L., *Urbanization in Nigeria*, London: University of London Press, 1968.

Mackintosh, John P. *et al*, (eds.), *Nigerian Government and Politics*, Evanston: Northwestern University Press, 1966.

Markowitz, Irving L., *Power and Class in Africa*, Englewood Cliffs, N.J.: Prentice–Hall, 1977.

Marris, Peter, *Family and Social Change in an African City*, London: Routledge & Kegan Paul, 1961.

Mauss, Marcel, *The Gift*, Trans. I. Cunnison, London: Cohen and West, 1954.

Mboya, Tom J., 'The Impact of Modern Institutions on the East African', in *Tradition and Transition in East Africa*, P. H. Gulliver (ed.), Berkeley and Los Angeles: University of California Press, 1969, pp. 89–103.

Medard, Jean-Francois, 'The Underdeveloped State in Tropical Africa: Political Clientelism or Neo-Patrimonialism?' in *Private Patronage and Public Power: Political Clientelism in the Modern State*, Christopher Clapham (ed.), New York: St. Martin's, 1982, pp. 162–92.

Mercier, Paul, 'Le vie politique dans les centres urbains du Senegal: Étude d'une periode de transition', *Cahiers Internationaux de Sociologie*, 26, 1959, pp. 55–84.

Miller, Robert A., 'Elite Formation in Africa: Class, Culture, and Coherence', *Journal of Modern African Studies*, 12(4), 1974, pp. 521–42.

Mintz, Sidney W. and Eric R. Wolf, 'An Analysis of Ritual Co-Parenthood (Compadrazgo)', *Southwestern Journal of Anthropology*, 6(4), 1950, pp. 341–68.

Montagu, Algernon (comp.), *Ordinances of the Settlement of Lagos; Royal Charters; Acts of Parliament; Orders of Council; Treaties of the Government of Lagos with the Native Chiefs, etc. etc., 1862–1870*, London: Eyre and Spottiswoode, 1874.

Nicholas, Ralph W., 'Factions: A Comparative Analysis', in *Friends, Followers, and Factions*, Steffen W. Schmidt *et al* (eds.), Berkeley and Los Angeles: University of California Press, 1977, pp. 55–73 (first pub. 1965).

Nicholson, I. F., *The Administration of Nigeria, 1900–1960*, Oxford: Clarendon Press, 1969.

Ojo, G. J. Afolabi, *Yoruba Culture*, London: University of London Press, 1966.

Okpala, D. C. I., 'Accessibility Distribution Aspects of Public Urban Land Management: A Nigerian Case', *African Urban Studies*, N.S.5 (fall), 1979, pp. 25–44.

Ostheimer, John M., *Nigerian Politics*, New York: Harper and Row, 1973.

Owusu, Maxwell, *Uses and Abuses of Political Power: A Case Study of Continuity and Change in the Politics of Ghana*, Chicago: University of Chicago Press, 1970.

Paine, Robert, 'A Theory of Patronage and Brokerage', in *Patrons and Brokers in the East Arctic*, Robert Paine (ed.), Newfoundland Social and Economic Papers No. 2, Institute of Social and Economic Research, Memorial University of Newfoundland, 1971, pp. 8–21.

Parkin, David, *Neighbours and Nationals in an African City Ward*, Berkeley and Los Angeles: University of California Press, 1969.

Peace, Adrian, *Choice, Class and Conflict: A Study of Southern Nigerian Factory Workers*, Atlantic Highlands, N.J.: Humanities Press, 1979a.

'Prestige, Power, and Legitimacy in a Modern Nigerian Town', *Canadian Journal of African Studies*, 13(1–2), 1979b, pp. 25–51.

Peel, J. D. Y., *Ijeshas and Nigerians: The Incorporation of a Yoruba Kingdom 1890s–1970s*, Cambridge: Cambridge University Press, 1983.

Peil, Margaret, 'The Cost of Living in Lagos', *Lagos Notes and Records*, IV, 1973, pp. 12–16.

Nigerian Politics: The People's View, London: Cassell, 1976.

Cities and Suburbs: Urban Life in West Africa, New York and London: Africana, 1981.

Post, K. W. J., *The Nigerian Federal Election of 1959*, London: Oxford University Press, 1963.

'The National Council of Nigeria and the Cameroons', in *Nigerian Government and Politics: Prelude to the Revolution*, J. P. Mackintosh *et al.*, (eds.), Evanston: Northwestern University Press, 1966, pp. 405–26.

and Michael Vickers, *Structure and Conflict in Nigeria 1960–66*, Madison: University of Wisconsin Press, 1973.

Rimmer, Douglas, 'Elements of the Political Economy', in *Soldiers and Oil: The Political Transformation of Nigeria*, K. Panter-Brick (ed.), London: Frank Cass, 1978, pp. 141–65.

Ross, Marc H., *The Political Integration of Urban Squatters*, Evanston: Northwestern University Press, 1973.

Grass Roots in an African City: Political Behaviour in Nairobi, Cambridge, Mass.: The MIT Press, 1975.

Sada, P. O. and A. A. Adefolalu, 'Urbanisation and Problems of Urban Development', in *Lagos: The Development of an African City*, A. B. Aderibigbe (ed.), Nigeria: Longman, 1975, pp. 79–107.

and M. L. McNulty, 'Market Structure in Metropolitan Lagos', paper presented at the 15th Annual Conference of the Nigerian Geographical Association, Ile-Ife: University of Ife, December 18–23, 1970.

'Traditional Markets in Lagos: A Study of the Changing Administrative Processes and Marketing Transactions', *Quarterly Journal of Administration*, Jan., 1974, pp. 149–65.

Sahlins, Marshall D., 'Poor Man, Rich Man, Big-Man, Chief: Political Types in Melanesia and Polynesia', *Comparative Studies in Society and History*, 5(3), 1963, pp. 285–303.

Sandbrook, Richard, 'Patrons, Clients, and Factions: New Dimensions of Conflict Analysis in Africa', *Canadian Journal of Political Science*, 5(1), 1972, pp. 104–19.

The Politics of Basic Needs: Urban Aspects of Assaulting Poverty in Africa, Toronto: University of Toronto Press, 1982.

Schildkrout, Enid, 'Strangers and Local Government in Kumasi', *The Journal of Modern African Studies*, 8(2), 1970, pp. 251–69.

'Economics and Kinship in Multi-Ethnic Dwellings', in *Changing Social Structure in Ghana*, J. Goody (ed.), London: Oxford University Press (for International African Institute), 1975, pp. 167–79.

People of the Zongo: The Transformation of Ethnic Identities in Ghana, Cambridge: Cambridge University Press, 1978.

Schmidt, Steffen W., *et al* (eds.), *Friends, Followers, and Factions: A Reader in Political Clientelism*, Berkeley and Los Angeles: University of California Press, 1977.

Schwab, William B., 'Kinship and Lineage among the Yoruba', *Africa*, 25(4), 1955, pp. 352–74.

Scott, James C., 'Corruption, Machine Politics, and Political Change', *American Political Science Review*, 63(4), 1969, pp. 1142–58.

'Patron–Client Politics and Political Change in Southeast Asia', *American Political Science Review*, 66(1), 1972, pp. 91–113.

Silverman, Marilyn, 'Village Council and Factionalism: Definitional and Contextual Issues', in *A House Divided? Anthropological Studies of Factionalism*, M. Silverman and R. F. Salisbury (eds.), Social and Economic Papers No. 9, Institute of Social and Economic Research, Memorial University of Newfoundland, 1977, pp. 66–98.

Simpson, S. R., 'Towards a Definition of "Absolute Ownership" II', *Journal of African Law*, 5, 1961, pp. 145–50.

Skinner, E. P., *African Urban Life: The Transformation of Ougadougou*, Princeton: Princeton University Press, 1974.

Sklar, Richard L., *Nigerian Political Parties: Power in an Emergent Nation*, Princeton: Princeton University Press, 1963.

Southall, A. W. and P. C. W. Gutkind, *Townsmen in the Making: Kampala and Its Suburbs*, East African Studies No. 9, Kampala: East African Institute of Social Research, 1957.

Strathern, Andrew, *The Rope of Moka*, Cambridge: Cambridge University Press, 1971.

Strickon, Arnold and Sidney M. Greenfield (eds.), *Structure and Process in Latin America: Patronage, Clientage and Power Systems*, Albuquerque: University of New Mexico Press, 1972.

Sudarkasa, Niara, *Where Women Work: A Study of Yoruba Women in the Marketplace and in the Home*, Anthropological Papers, Museum of Anthropology, No. 53, Ann Arbor: University of Michigan, 1973.

Swartz, Marc J. 'Rules, Resources, and Groups in Political Contests', in *Local-Level Politics*, M. J. Swartz (ed.), Chicago: Aldine, 1968, pp. 271–79.

Tade, Chief J. O., 'Short Biography of the City of Odi-Olowo', Lagos, Ebute-Metta: Ogunrotimi Printing Press, nd.

Talbot, P. Amaury, *The Peoples of Southern Nigeria*, 4 vols., London: Oxford University Press, 1926.

Vincent, Joan, *African Elite: The Big Men of a Small Town*, New York: Columbia University Press, 1971.

Wallace, A. F. C., *Culture and Personality*, New York: Random House, 1961.

Weber, Max, *The Theory of Social and Economic Organization*, New York: The Free Press, 1947.

Weingrod, Alex, 'Political Sociology, Social Anthropology and the Study of New Nations', *British Journal of Sociology*, 18, 1967, pp. 121–34.

Whitaker, C. S. Jr., *The Politics of Tradition, Continuity, and Change in Northern Nigeria, 1946–1966*, Princeton: Princeton University Press, 1970.

Williams, B. A. and A. H. Walsh, *Urban Government for Metropolitan Lagos*, New York: Praeger, 1968.

Zolberg, Aristide R., *Creating Political Order: The Party-State of West Africa*, Chicago: Rand McNally, 1966.

II MANUSCRIPT SOURCES

(A) GOVERNMENT ARCHIVES

Nigerian National Archives, Ibadan
1 CSO Series: Files in the Chief Secretary to the Government's Office. Intelligence Reports.
2 Com.Col. Series: Papers in the Commissioner of the Colony's Office. Ikeja Division 1932–1956.
3 Gwam, L. C., *An Inventory of the Administrative Records Assembled from the Colony Province*, 1961.

Public Records Office, London
1 CO 147: Lagos Correspondence, 1861–1898.
2 CO 150: Lagos, Government Gazettes, 1881–1886.
3 CO 151: Lagos, Blue Books, 1862–1905; 1906–1913.
4 CO 592: Southern Nigeria, Council Papers and Annual Reports, 1906–7.
5 CO 657: Nigeria, Administrative Reports, 1925–52.
6 CO 700: Lagos, Maps, 1865–1905.
7 M.P.G. 403: Lagos, Map, 1865.

(B) OTHER ARCHIVES

Church Missionary Society, Birmingham University Library
1 G3/A2: Yoruba Mission, Correspondence, 1880–92.

Rhodes House Library, Oxford
1 MSS.Afr: Colonial Records Project. Administrative and Intelligence Reports.

British Museum Library
1 CSc Series, Nigeria, Miscellaneous Papers, 1940–52.

(C) OTHER GOVERNMENT PUBLICATIONS AND REPORTS

1 Lagos
Lagos City Council, 'Draft Estimates, 1975–76', Lagos: mimeograph, 1975.
Lagos Colony, *Central Native Council*, Minutes of Meetings, 1901–1913.

2 Lagos State
Ilori, Chief A. (ch) *et al, Report of the Tribunal of Inquiry into the Administration and Financial Management of Ajeromi, Ikeja, Mushin, and Agege District Councils*, V.I and II, Lagos, 1970.
Ogunnaike, Chief J. S. O. (ch) and Dr Femi Ayantuga, *Proceedings of the Tribunal of Inquiry into the Reorganisation of Local Government Councils in the Lagos State*, Lagos, 1970.
Oluwa, Ishola and S. I. Talabi, *Report of the Tribunal of Inquiry into the Reorganisation of Local Government Councils in the Lagos State* (dissenting report), Lagos, 1970.
Third national Development Plan 1975–80: Lagos State Programme, Lagos: mimeograph, 1975.

3 Mushin
Mushin Town Council, *Chieftaincy File*, 1973–75, and *Chieftaincy Committee File*, 1972–75.
Mushin Town Council, 'Draft Estimates, 1975–76', Mushin: mimeograph, 1975.

4 Nigeria
Census of Nigeria, 1931, V.III, London: Crown Agents for the Colonies, 1932.
Law Reports of the High Court of the Federal Territory of Lagos, 1960, Federal Director of Printing, 1963.
Population Census, Lagos, V.I and II and *Western Region*, V. I, II and III, Lagos: Federal Office of Statistics, 1963.
Population Census of Lagos, 1950, Lagos: Federal Office of Statistics, 1950.
Population Census of the Western Region of Nigeria, 1952, Lagos: Government Statistician, 1953–54.
Report of the Cost of Living Committee, Lagos, 1942.
Second and Final Report of the Wages and Salaries Review Commission, Lagos: Federal Ministry of Information, 1971.
Selected Judgments of the Federal Supreme Court of Nigeria, 1959, V. IV, The Hon. Mr. Justice M. J. Abbott (comp.), Lagos: Federal Government Printer, 1960.
Simpson, S. Rowton, *A Report on the Registration of Title to Land in the Federal Territory of Lagos*, Lagos: Federal Government Printer, 1957.
A Survey of Graduate Employment Prospects, 1973/74 to 1975/76, Manpower Studies No. 16, National Manpower Board, Lagos: Federal Ministry of Economic Development and Reconstruction, 1974.
Third National Development Plan, 1975–80, V. I. Lagos: Central Planning Office, Federal Ministry of Economic Development, 1975.

5 Western Region
Report on the Holding of the 1956 Parliamentary Election to the Western House of

Assembly, Western Region of Nigeria: Government Printer, 1957.
Western Region Legal Notices, 1965.
Western Nigeria Legal Notices, 1966.

III THESES

Mabogunje, Akinlawon Ladipo, *Lagos: A Study in Urban Geography*, PhD Thesis, University of London, 1961.
Olawoye, Clifford Odunayo, *Proof of Title to Land in Nigeria*, LLM Thesis, University of Lagos, 1968.
Sada, Pius O., *The Metropolitan Region of Lagos, Nigeria: A Study of the Political Factor in Urban Geography*, PhD Thesis, Indiana University, 1968.

IV NEWSPAPERS AND JOURNALS

Business Times	*Daily Times*	*Nigerian Tribune*	*Sunday Post*
Dail Express	*Express*	*Pilot*	*Telegraph*
Daily Sketch	*New Nigerian*	*Sunday Express*	*West Africa*
			West African Pilot

INDEX

Abate, Y. 227n
Abeokuta 21, 119
Abiola, T.* 56–9, 61, 63, 138–9, 141–2, 159, 167–78, 185–8, 191–2, 233n, 235n, 239n, 240n
Abraham, R. C. 240n
Abule Ijesha 35
Abule Okuta Market 161
accountability 51, 207
Accra 25, 218
Acquah, I. 242n
Action Group (AG) 141–2, 147–50, 163, 198, 237n, 238n
 and chiefs 103–5, 124, 127
 in markets 132
 in Mushin 128–9, 132, 134–5, 144, 148, 152–4, 165
 officers 169–70, 172
 structure 130–6
 in wards 104, 127, 132
Adaranijo 42
Adebola, Alhaji* 88, 90
Adebola, Mustapha* 82–3, 88–90, 93
Adefolalu, A. A. 234n
Adejuyigbe, O. 229n
Adeleye, S. A. 112, 129, see also Olu Odi Olowo
Aderibigbe, A. B. 228n, 229n
Adesina, S. 228n
Adeyemi, J. A.* 57–8, 61, 63, 79–91, 93–5, 99, 116, 138–9, 141–2
adjudication see dispute settlement
administration
 agencies 5
 British model 25–6
 budget 15
 early colonial period 15, 29–31
 late colonial period 36–43
 Mushin 97–9, 128–30, 157, 204, 220
 reorganisation 18, 41–2, 198–9
 see also boundaries; colonial period; government and neglect
Ado 20
adugbo see ward
Africa
 Central 217–18, 242n
 East 3, 7, 29, 217
 South 29, 242n
 West 212, 217–18, 233n, 238n, 242n
age sets 185
Agege 21, 36, 68–99, 228n, 235n, 242n
 chiefs 99, 107, 168, 196, 240n
 Planters Union 32
Agiri, B. 229n
agriculture 13, 32–3, 40–1
 produce 20, 30, 31, 40
Aguilar, J. L. 241n
Aileru, J. 107, 168–9, 191–3, 230n, 236n
 see also Olu Mushin/Olu Ojuwoye
Aiyetoro 115
Ajalaruru, Chief S. (Seriki of Mushin) 102
Ajegunle 11, 14, 234n
Ajenifuja, Y. (Baale Oshodi) 112
Ajisafe, A.* 138–9, 164, 172–3, 176–7, 179, 240n
Akessan 35
Akinogun 34
Akinola, R. A. 228n
Akintola, S. L. 148–9, 151–2
Akoka 42
Alade Market 161
Alagbado 21, 34

Alake Market* 163–9, 171–80, 185–6, 189
Alao, N. O. 228n
Alase 21, 229n
Alashe, Ifadu 35, 38, 194, 230n, 240n
 see also Ladega, W.
alliances
 chieftaincy divisions 188, 191–2
 districts 196
 governmental 155
 individual 205–6
 leaders 141, 170
 parties 149–50, 153, 155
 political groups 175
 polities 212, 217
allocation, as political process 10, 88, 130–1, 156, 191, 199
amenities, urban 4, 14, 39, 48, 116, 128, 147, 157
Amodu, Y. 112
 see also Olu Mushin/Olu Ojuwoye
Animashuan, G. L. 151
Apata 42
Apata, Karimu 106
Apelehin 42
appointments 236n
 advisory groups 156, 159, 167, 191, 198
 governing bodies 130, 156, 158–9, 169, 187, 198, 205, 221
 Mushin councils 148–51, 153, 196–7, 199–200, 204, 216
apprenticeships 56–7, 66, 85, 160, 211
arbitration see dispute settlement
architecture see house plan
Aronson, D. R. 232n, 236n
Asabiyi, R. A. (Baale Onigbongbo) 112
asho ebi (family cloth) 172
associations
 community 124, 182
 hometown/ethnic 144–5, 199–200, 214, 238n, 239n, 241n
 market 160, 162, 173–4, 178, 239n
 religious 66, 71, 78, 159, 234n, 235n, 239n
 revolving credit 58
 teachers' 239n
 trade 185
 transport 159, 239n
 voluntary 66, 71, 78, 138, 141–2, 187
 see also parties; trade unions
authority
 creation of 201–2, 216–19
 customary 25, 29, 31–6, 97–125
 figures 82, 86, 93, 127, 156, 175, 179, 194, 208
 of owners 76
 pre-colonial 18
 structures 15
 systems 31, 42
 types 96
 unofficial 43–6, 200
 see also government
autonomy
 communal 174–5
 personal 101, 206
 village 18, 22–3, 31–2, 70
Awolowo Market 160–2, 239n
Awolowo, Obafemi 131, 134, 147–8, 238n
Awori
 chiefs 99–100, 102–4, 106–9, 111–15, 122, 148, 184–7, 191, 212
 councillors 129
 culture 23
 faction 140, 158–81, 183–96
 founders 19–20, 175

identity 22, 33, 44–5, 52, 122, 229n
land tenure 51
landowners 92, 100
market 164
Mushin population 44, 121
representation in local government 184, 197, 199–200
settlements 32–5, 171, 236n
territory 228n, 232n
Yoruba-speaking group 14–15, 22
Awori-Ajeromi District Council 11
Awori National Welfare Association (ANWA) 199–200
Awori Welfare Association (AWA) 241n
Ayantuga, F. 238n, 240n
Ayobo 21
Azikiwe, Nnamdi 131

Baale 22, 42, 44, 82, 103, 112–14, 236n
customary authority 29, 31–9
factional involvements 32, 41, 99, 124
owners 68, 76
settlers 45
see also chiefs; headmen
Baba Isale (father in the courtyard/quarter) 31–9, 43, 46, 98,
    187, 194, 205, 208, 230n
rights and duties 22
system 19, 21–3, 35, 43
Babalola, S. A. 234n
Badagri 231n
Bailey, F. G. 70, 207, 209, 227n, 234n, 235n, 239n, 240n,
    241n
Bajulaiye village 42
Baker, P. H. 228n, 232n, 233n, 235n, 237n, 238n, 239n, 240n
Bariba 28
Bariga 33, 41
Barrows, W. L. 6, 227n
Barth, F. 227n
Bascom, W. R. 236n
Bashua village 33, 35, 42
Benin 20, 26, 28
Bight of 19
Bini people 23, 33
King of 19
Bienen, H. 240n
Big Men 212, 217, 235n, 242n
Bini see Benin
Blau, P. M. 211, 242n
Boissevain, J. 227n, 235n, 240n, 242n
Bond, G. C. 227n
borokinni 235n
    see also Big Men
boundaries 181, 195, 206, 212
administrative 29, 45–6, 220–2, 229n
class 185
ethnic 122
maintenance of 174–5
political 15, 222
Brazilians in Lagos 26
Bright 42
British conquest 19, 21
British subjects 36
    see also citizenship
British rule see colonial administration
broker see middleman
Brooke, N. J. et al 229n, 230n, 231n, 232n, 233n
bureaucracy
informal influence in 7, 86, 89, 128, 180, 189, 214, 218
job opportunities in 202
jurisdiction 51
legal powers 16
role in institutionalising customary authority 124, 183–5,
    196–200, 219
    see also administration; government; institutionalisation
    process
bureaucratic services 30, 83–4, 86, 89, 90

burial practices 89, 118
    see also ceremonies
Burns, Sir A. C. 27, 229n, 230n
Busia, K. A. 242n
business 15, 89–90, 96, 132, 134, 146, 235n
clients 128
neighbourhood 72–5, 94
small 13
strategies 56–7
businessmen, case studies 56–8, 213–14
businesswomen 12
    see also trade; markets

campaigns, party 10, 95, 98, 104, 132, 134, 150–1
career patterns 56–8, 70, 79–82
census, population 27, 40–1, 76, 117, 149, 227n, 238n
centralisation
government 23, 38, 102–4, 205, 221
incomplete 10, 31, 216
Central Native Council 34
ceremonies 94, 149, 179, 195, 208, 211, 213
chieftaincy 38, 117–18, 120, 122, 186, 192–4, 196–7
civic 117, 123, 193
deities 118
funeral 84, 118
healing 84, 91
housewarming 68
market 162, 164–5, 167–8, 172, 177–9
    see also descent group; iwuye
chiefs, African 217–9, 242n
chiefs, Lagos see Lagos chiefs
chiefs, Mushin 138, 142, 159, 184–98
as clients 104, 154
as patrons/middlemen 37, 188
duties 34
elected 99, 105, 112–15
etiquette 122, 209
functions 32, 185–9
installation 38, 186 see also iwuye
market involvements 167–9, 172–3, 177–8
meetings 151
powers 97
problems 120–2
skills 116, 118
styles 118
symbols 121–2, 192–3, 200, 237n
women 137
    see also under individual titles; chieftaincy divisions
chieftaincy
affairs 38, 83, 137, 151, 163, 167, 181, 188, 193
declarations 107
families 43
military era 105–9
party era 103–5
politics of 37, 103–9, 186–9
succession rules 83, 99–100, 108, 110–17, 122–3, 184–7,
    189–90, 193, 194, 197
chieftaincy councils 38, 105, 107, 176, 221
    see also Lagos State Council (House) of Obas and Chiefs;
    Western Region House of Chiefs
chieftaincy rituals see ceremonies
chieftaincy system 16, 97–125, 127, 148, 182, 200
creation of 203–4
culture of 122, 203
divisions 159, 167, 178, 188, 191–4, 197, 221, 236n
functions 115–18, 122–5
government recognition of 105, 108, 183–5, 189, 192,
    196–8, 200, 220
hometown 96
networks 141
structure 15, 109–15, 118–19, 123–4
children 65, 72, 75–6, 82, 92
Christianity 73, 107, 123, 132–3, 141, 234n
citizenship 25, 33, 36, 44, 69, 100, 144, 232n

civil servants
  as chiefs 107, 218
  colonial 29
  district council 128
  earnings 150, 235*n*
  influence with 194
  role in community 180, 184
  salaries 235*n*
  secret courts 199
  sole administrators 220
  under military 156–7, 197–9, 241*n*
Civil War *see* wars
class 2–6, 206, 213–15
  see stratification
clerks 2, 13–14, 107
client
  defined 210
  followers 16, 70, 76, 85, 95–6, 98, 205
  network 9, 15–16, 79–93, 153, 154, 157, 188, 205, 213,
    242*n*
  paradigm 6–11, 227*n*
  politics 204
  types 209
client relationships 36, 43, 70, 82–95, 104, 127, 137, 140,
    142–6, 156, 202, 205–15, 235*n*
  instrumental 206–12
  moral 206—12
  organising powers 213–16
  see also patron—client relationships
client system 6, 9–10, 19, 43, 78–94, 140–2, 242*n*
  case studies 82–94
  etiquette 205, 207–8
  institutionalised 90
  powers 201, 213–19
  scale 43
  structure 215–16
  types 10, 59
client systems compared 5–7, 205
  Africa 6, 227*n*
  Kumasi 7
  Latin America 5–6, 227*n*
  Mediterranean 6, 205, 227*n*
  Mexico City 205
  Northern Nigeria 90
  Rwanda 90
  Sierra Leone 7
  Southeast Asia 6, 227*n*
  Thailand 206
clientelism
  concept 7, 8, 11
  historic role, 18, 46
cliques 5, 95, 146, 164, 177
cloth 19, 21, 172
Cohen, A. 4–5, 121, 207, 227*n*, 229*n*, 237*n*, 241*n*, 242*n*
Cohen, R. 238*n*
Coker, G. B. A. 232*n*, 233*n*
Cole, P. 228*n*, 229*n*, 230*n*, 232*n*, 233*n*, 236*n*, 237*n*
Cole, Mrs* 82, 84, 89–90, 93–4
colonial period 2, 157, 205, 228
  administration 18–19, 23–31, 36–43, 45, 52, 98, 103, 124,
    153, 204, 217–18
  expansion 26
  history 15, 18–19, 23–46
Colony and Protectorate of Southern Nigeria 26
Colony of Lagos *see* Lagos, Colony of
commerce *see* trade
Committee of Elders of Mushin 170
communication 72, 160
  channels 34, 39, 45, 93–4, 117, 124, 161, 180, 197, 202,
    216
  mass 179
  problems 10, 48, 212
community
  creation 47

development 221
  involvement 11, 66–9, 77, 158, 165, 188, 202
  lack of 45
  leadership in 106, 108, 145, 157–9, 163, 183, 191, 198,
    203–4
  political 46, 69–70, 97–9, 126–8, 142–3, 155, 220–1
  pressure group 116, 124, 152, 182
  relationships 61, 66–7
  status 94–5, 109, 123, 130, 165
conflict *see* dispute settlement; factions; protest
constitution 42
construction
  financing 55–61, 233*n*
  growth of 40
  house 31, 44, 47, 49, 55–6, 62, 67, 121
  industry 68
  permits 128
Cornelius, W. A. 241*n*
cost of living 13
councillors *see* Mushin District (Town) Councillors
coup d'état 158, 198, 220–1, 239*n*, 241*n*
  see also military coups
court
  cases 38, 92
  circuits 30
  commissioners 30
  financing costs 50
  government 39, 41, 83–5, 89, 92, 128, 134, 142, 203
  informal 32, 41
  rulings 55
  secret 123, 142, 199; *see also* secret societies
  see also native courts; Supreme court
crime 32, 39–40, 230*n*
Crowder, M. 242*n*
culture 23, 122, 213, 237*n*, 241*n*, 242*n*
  plural 26
  shared 119–20, 204–5
customary law *see* legal system

Dahomey (Republic of Benin) 23, 26, 33, 229*n*, 236*n*
Dakar 7
deities 35, 109, 118, 194
dependents 65, 96
descent group 51–5, 69, 202
  Awori 23, 45
  ceremonies 64
  estate 51
  founding 32–5
  landowning 48–50, 52, 99; *see also* son-of-the-soil
  meetings 63–4, 110
  membership 22, 51
  political role 109–11
  rights and obligations 61
  ruling house 100, 107, 111–17, 119, 159, 178, 194–5,
    233*n*, 234*n*
  structure 61–4, 233*n*
  village 31
  see also kinship
direct rule 25, 29, 38, 229*n*
dispute settlement 30, 32, 39, 41, 64, 77–8, 115–18, 208, 211
  adjudication 32, 86–7, 117
  arbitration 32
  mediation 86–7
dispute settler
  Baba Isale as 34
  chiefs and headmen as 164–5, 203, 218
  councillors as 128
  elders as 204
  market leaders as 132, 160, 162
  owners as 70
  role 22, 85–8 *passim*, 101
disputes 62, 82–7, 89, 91–3, 154
  co-tenant 75
  land 30, 48–55, 91–3

owner-tenant 75
succession 20, 32
District Officer 37–41, 44, 230n, 236n
Districts of Lagos area 25, 27, 131, 143, 153
    Agege 232n
    Central (Colony) 45, 52–3, 232n
    Eastern 23, 29
    Ikeja 36–45, 232n
    Lagos 29, 30, 32, 35–6, 45
    Mushin 45, 102, 107, 111, 127, 140, 151–3, 164, 167, 168,
        215, 220–1, 232n
    Northern 23, 26, 29, 45
    Vicinity 23
    Western 23, 29
dogs 40
Duro, Madam Femi* 138–9, 159, 163–4, 166–8, 171–4,
    177–9, 239n

Eades, J. S. 233n
ebi see descent group
economy, urban 20, 37, 67–9, 143, 145, 158
Ede (Yoruba) 28, 236n
Edo 14, 71
    see also Benin
education
    as resource 74
    higher 37
    levels 44, 60, 77, 117, 234n
    of leaders 56, 57, 97, 107, 133–7, 139, 146
    of women 71
    schools 31, 39, 41, 134, 154
    teachers 239n
Efik 14, 71
Egba (Yoruba) 14, 28, 64, 107, 214
Egbado (Yoruba) 19, 28
Egun 237n
Eisenstadt, S. N. 241n, 242n
Ejigbo 35, 109, 236n
Ekiti (Yoruba) 28, 107
elders 36, 85, 123, 208
    colonial reliance on 38
    control of knowledge 117
    councils 18, 22, 31, 42, 203
    Mushin 170–1, 193, 204n
    owners as 64
    village 29, 32
elections 131–7, 147–52, 237n
    banned 187
    chiefly 105, 169, 196, 205, 240n
    local council 95, 199, 204, 221
elections by year
    1951: 42, 131, 231n, 232n
    1955: 129
    1958: 130, 147
    1959: 131, 133
    1962: 131
    1964: 150
    1965: 152
elite 201, 219
    British 155
    defined 227n
    educated 42, 51
    Lagosian 174
    national 11, 13, 60–1, 79, 96, 221, 234n
    power of non-elite 203, 218
    regional 146, 155
    residence 14
    ruling 2–4, 6, 16, 96, 216
employment 3, 13, 66, 68, 90
    informal 3, 13
    patterns 6, 13–14
    self- 13, 55, 60, 68, 134
    wage 13, 55, 60, 68
    see also income

English language 71–2
entourage 208, 211, 213–14
entrepreneurs, political 70, 95–6, 116, 137, 160, 212
Epstein, A. L. 242n
e se gigun see long legs
estate agents 48, 68, 96, 107
ethnic group 8, 130, 133, 139, 144–5, 199, 206, 212, 213–14,
    238n, 239n
ethnicity 2, 5–7, 11, 71, 143, 200–1, 215, 229n
Europeans 2, 19, 29, 38
Ewu 35, 108–9, 236n
extended case method 163, 181, 186
Eyisha family 32–3

factions 5, 16, 156–82, 185–6, 192–3
    in Action Group 104, 148
Fadi Market* 164, 171–3, 176–9, 186
Fadipe, N. A. 233n, 236n
Fagbemi, Prince* 138–9, 164, 172–3, 175–7, 179, 181, 240n
Fallers, L. A. 227n, 241n, 242n
families compared 65–6
family see descent group
family property, concept of 51–2, 54
Fapohunda, O. J. 228n, 233n, 234n, 235n
Farombi, D. O. (Osolo Isolo) 112
farms 20
Federal Group Councils 42
Federal House of Representatives 130, 132–3, 147, 149
Federal Territory of Lagos 42
Folami, T. 228n
Fon 237n
Forde, D. 229n
fortifications 21
Foster, G. M. 227n
fosterage 65, 160
Fowler, W. 230n, 232n, 233n
Fraenkel, M. 242n
freehold, concept of 52–4, 61, 64, 100, 232n, 233n, 236n
Freetown 25, 218

Gbadamosi, G. O. 229n
Gbadamosi, S. O. 134, 147–8
gbajumo 235n
    see also Big Men
Geary, Sir W. M. N. 229n
Gellner, E. 10, 227n, 228n
George village 26, 42
Gibbons, E. J. 228n, 229n, 230n, 231n
Gilbert, A. 228n
Glover, Sir John H. 25, 30, 34
Gluckman, M. 163, 240n, 242n
godfather (patron) 11, 78, 158, 205
Gold Coast Colony 25, 28
    see also Ghana
Gouldner, A. 242n
government
    bodies 7, 142
    revenue (tax) 15, 37, 43, 128, 161
    self 42–3, 201, 217
    state 157; see also Lagos State
    structure 130–1, 136, 147–53, 156
government, civilian 4, 126, 148, 152, 154, 156, 158, 170,
    198, 200–1
government, federal 11, 130, 147–9, 152, 155
government, local 39, 135–7, 148, 161, 205, 238n, 241n
    change 220–2
    issues 143–4
    Mushin 126–30, 157–9
government, military 241n
    changes 156, 184, 220
    civil service under 197–200, 240n
    factionalism under 156–9
    local level effect 157, 239n
    public contact 158, 181, 200, 216, 220

regimes in Africa 4
Supreme Military Council 157
Gowon, General Yakubu 198, 200, 241n
Greenfield, S. M. 227n
Gugler, J. 228n
Guinea Coast 3
Gutkind, P. C. W. 227n, 242n
Gwam, L. C. 230n

Hanks, L. M. 206, 241n
Hanna, W. J. and J. L. 227n, 238n, 242n
Harrell-Bond, B. E. 242n
Hausa 5, 7, 14, 26, 32, 148
headmen 30, 36, 44, 124, 203–4
    stipendiary 30
    village 18, 35, 38
    see also Baale; chiefs
healers 86–7
healing 84, 91, 93, 160
history
    Lagos 19–23
    Mushin 18–46, 64, 68, 70, 103
    uses of 16
hometown
    houses 63, 96
    ties 13, 63–4, 72–3, 134, 143–5, 199, 214, 235n
    titles 64
Hopkins, N. S. 227n
hospitality 65, 76, 96, 208
house
    building 47, 49, 55–9, 62, 233n; see also construction
    heterogeneity 71, 204
    -mates 72
    management 76, 85
    owning 47–69, 175; see also landowners
    plan 58–9
    spatial arrangements 65
    styles 56–9
houseowners
    see landowners; landlords; landladies
houseplots 44, 47–8, 51, 55–8, 85, 91–2, 203, 232n, 233n
housing 15, 47–69, 74, 147, 154, 202, 234n
    conditions 14
    economics of 55–61, 67
    government built 67
    policy 128
    private 67–8
    reservations 13
    shortages 67–8, 76
    source of power 47–69
    source of revenue 15
Howard, A. M. 242n

Ibadan (Yoruba) 28, 122
Ibadan, town of 42, 141, 189, 228n, 232n, 236n
Ibibio 14
identity markers 5–6, 22, 33, 44–5, 51, 180, 229n, 232n
    see also Awori; descent group; settler
Idi-Iroko 33
idile see descent group
Idimu 32
Idi-Oro 31, 134
Idi Owo Market* 186
Idoma 71
Idowu, Chief Madam Omo* 177
Ifadu see Alashe
Ife (Yoruba) 107
Igbira 14, 28, 237n
Igbo 14, 71, 130–1, 145, 147–8, 213–14, 234n, 235n
    language 72
Igbo State Union 144–5
Igbobi 21, 35
Ijaw 14, 71
Ijebu (Yoruba) 14, 19, 21, 28, 64, 79, 107, 133

Ijebu Ode 82–5, 119
Ijede 232n
Ijesha (Yoruba) 28, 107
Ijora 235n
Ikate 221
Ikeja 11, 13, 36, 40–2, 99, 105, 107, 135, 147, 153, 174,
    195–6, 228n, 231n, 235n
    District 11, 36, 39–40, 42, 48, 168
    District Council 43
    Division 107, 131, 133–6, 168, 196, 228n, 232n, 240n,
    241n
Ikeja Area Native Authority 98, 103
Ikeja Town Planning Authority (ITPA) 41, 128, 142, 237n
Ikime, O. 242n
Ikorodu 133, 148, 232n
illness see healers; healing
Ilori, A. 238n
Ilorin (Yoruba) 28
Ilupeju 13
income 13, 61, 68, 95–6, 161, 228n, 231n, 233n, 234n, 235n
    average 13
    levels 13, 40, 55–9, 75, 145–6, 150
    sources 58, 69
incorporation processes 33, 44–5
Independence 3, 97, 130, 146–7, 218
    movement 42, 131–2
indirect rule 38–9, 229n
industrial areas 43, 67
industrial workers 13
industry 3, 11, 15, 174, 202
information 4, 39, 48, 70, 77, 93–4, 96, 154
    see communication
inheritance 53, 61–2, 67, 85, 89, 92, 99, 194, 234n
institutionalisation
    concept 16
    of power 1, 183–200, 216–19
institutions
    government 3–4, 78
    political 2
    urban 3, 18
instrumental relationships 6–7, 90
    see also client ties
integration 2, 201–2, 215, 218, 238n, 242n
    clientelistic 43
    political 2, 42, 45, 213
    residence 14, 70–6
    social 2, 8
investments 47, 54, 56–7, 61, 66, 68, 203, 233n
Irenpa 20
Iro 20
Isale Eko (old Lagos) 20
Isheri village 20
Islam 73, 84, 93, 102, 107, 118, 123, 132, 141, 234n
Isoko 14
Isolo 20–1, 32–5, 38, 42, 102, 104, 107, 112–15, 148, 171,
    196, 221, 236n
Isolo Village Group Council 42
Itele (Etele) 35
Itire 20–1, 32, 35, 42, 100, 102, 104, 107, 112–14, 148, 171,
    191, 195–6, 221, 230n, 235n, 236n
Itsekiri 71
ivory 19, 21
iwarefa see kingmakers
iwuye (installation ceremony) 22, 102, 106–7, 109, 167–8,
    186, 192–4, 196, 240n
iyalode (market head) see markets

Jackson, K. D. 242n
Jagunmolu Shomolu 103, 106, 112–15
James, R. W. 232n, 233n
Jibowu* 138–9, 186
Johnson, M. 241n
judicial system 30, 36, 38, 77
    functions 32

judiciary *see* dispute settlement

Kajola Market 161
Kalabari 71
Kampala 218
Kasfir, N. 227n, 241n
Kasunmu, A. B. 232n
Kaufman, R. R. 227n, 241n
Keta 28
Ketu (Yoruba) 28
king *see oba*
kingmakers 35, 114–16, 119, 186–7, 189, 190, 193
Kinshasa 3, 7, 227n
kinship *see* descent group; marriage
Kirk-Greene, A. 241n
Koenigsberger, O. *et al* 233n
kola 20, 21
Kopytoff, J. H. 228n
Kosofe 221
Kosoko, *Oba* 35
Kotonu* 138–9, 186
Kumasi, 7, 218
Kumolu, Madam S.* 163–4, 166–8, 177–9, 181

labour 13
  see also union
Ladega, W. 38, 194–5, 240n
  see also Alashe, Ifadu
Lafontaine, J. S. 227n
Lagos chiefs 19–23, 25, 29, 34–7, 53, 98, 119, 121, 175, 178, 194–5, 204, 236n, 237n
  see also Baba Isale
Lagos City (Municipality) 131, 145
as capital 11, 26, 42, 239n
  economy 11, 13
  importance 11, 13
land 232n, 235n
leaders 174–5, 177
  mainland 20
  map 12, 24
  political separation from Mushin 174, 195
  size 11
  tax 231n
  trade 11
  see also Districts of Lagos area
Lagos City Council 11, 133, 157–8, 174–5, 228n, 237n
Lagos City State (pre-colonial) 11, 18–23, 45, 53
  origins 20
  political system 19–20
Lagos Colony 11, 15, 18–19, 42, 45, 47–8, 52, 56, 98, 229n, 230n
  administration 23–31, 36–9, 45
  expansion 26
  map 24
  Settlement of 229n
  territory 23–5
Lagos Federal Territory 42, 147
Lagos Island 18, 20, 22–3, 25–6, 29–30, 175, 228n, 235n
Lagos markets 20, 160, 171–5, 177
  see also markets
Lagos metropolitan area 10–11, 221, 227n
  administrative districts 143; *see also* Districts of Lagos area
  economy 68, 174
  interest groups 239n
  leaders in 140, 146, 175, 215
  map 12
  party in 135
  Yoruba peoples in 71, 122, 234n
Lagos State 13–14, 94, 133, 172, 199–200, 215, 221, 232n
  government 11, 108–9, 169, 179, 196
Lagos State Council (House) of Obas and Chiefs 107, 168–9, 170, 174, 191–2, 196, 204, 240n
Lagos State Interim Advisory Committee 169

Lagos State Ministry of Local Government and Chieftaincy Affairs 11–13, 103, 130, 177, 195, 197
land
  buyers 48–51, 54–7
  competition 47–50, 128
  disputes 30, 47–69, 84–5, 90, 203, 232n, 235n
  gifts 21–2, 33, 35, 49–50, 52, 212
  power from 47–69
  scarcity 50, 63, 203
  sellers 48–52, 54–5
  speculation 49
  theft 48, 92
  transactions 30, 49–52, 54, 56–8
  see also property; landowners
Landé, C. H. 206, 228n, 241n, 242n
land tenure system 23, 48, 50–5, 92, 100
  conveyancing 53, 55
  documents 48, 50, 54
  registration 48, 54
  see also legal system
landladies 60, 67, 111, 234n
  compared to tenants 60
  compared to landlords 60, 67
landowner associations
  as interest groups 116, 238n
  as neighbourhood organisations 79, 83, 110–11, 142
  as sources of contacts 88–9
  conflicts within 115
  councils of 42, 203
  involvement with chiefs 99, 108, 116, 121
  involvement with parties 104
landowner-tenant comparisons 60–1, 64–7, 69, 234n
landowner-tenant relationships 58, 61, 70, 76, 83, 204
landowners 47–96 *passim*
  absentee 33, 233n
  as chiefs 20, 100, 115–16
  as leaders 127, 129, 134, 143–4, 203–4
  as patrons to strangers 161
  biographies of 56–8
  incomes of 234n
  meaning of 100, 143
  status of 47, 61, 67–9, 176
  see also houseowners; son-of-the-soil; settlers
language 71–2, 235n
Latilewa Market 161
Lawanson Market 161
law enforcement 30–1, 37–40, 51, 123–4, 128, 152, 203
  see also police
Layeni, Sunmola (*Onitire* of Itire) 108, 112
leaders 43–6, 137–43
  career patterns 137, 204
  community 104–5, 109, 159
  local 38, 43, 132, 183, 197, 200, 203
  migrant 39
  neighbourhood 76–95, 99, 104, 126
leadership 70–96, 126–55
  consolidation of 126–55
  roles 78–93; *see also* dispute settler; middlemen; patrons
  skills 16, 70, 87, 93–6, 204
  style 95
legal system 50–4, 77, 86–7, 124
  British 51–3
  customary 38, 51–4, 62, 125
  institutions of 37
  Nigerian 51, 53
  rights 61
  services 30
Legg, K. 227n
legitimacy
  evaluations of 159, 165, 173–7, 191
  need for 96, 121, 175, 217
  official 108, 196–200
  sources of 106, 109, 123, 154, 175, 179, 187
  through titles 98, 108, 123, 184–5, 187, 192–4, 219

unofficial 16, 97
leisure 72
Lemarchand, R. 7, 227n, 242n
Lewis, H. S. 242n
lineage see descent group
lingua franca 71–2
linking mechanisms 5–6, 8–9, 110–11, 156, 163, 204–5, 217
Lisabi, Oba* 138–9
Lloyd, P. C. 227n, 228n, 231n, 232n, 233n, 235n, 236n
local government see government
long legs (connections) 11, 78, 205
Losi, J. B. 228n, 230n
Lupton, T. 155, 239n

Mabogunje, A. L. 228n, 233n, 234n
Macaulay, H. 35
Machiavelli 1
machine politics 16, 126, 136, 145–9, 151, 153–4, 156, 216, 238n
Mackintosh, J. P. et al 237n
manufacturing 3
marketing system 20–1
markets 79, 134–5, 137, 141–2, 188, 195, 239n
    conflict 83, 115, 163–82
    deity 118
    factions 163–80
    leaders 107, 162–9, 169–71
    political importance 137, 159–63
    titles 162, 166–8, 172, 174, 189, 239n
    see also individual listings; Mushin markets; trade
    fees 162
    organisation 160–3
    stalls 128, 143, 149, 160, 162, 238n
Markowitz, I. L. 227n
marriage 57, 65, 82, 86–7, 94, 234n
Marris, P. 232n, 238n
Marx 1–2
Mauss, M. 9, 212, 227n, 242n
Mboya, T. 7, 227n
McNulty, M. L. 239n
Medard, J. F. 227n, 228n
merchants 2, 19–20, 68, 76, 107, 159, 161, 218
Mercier, P. 227n
middle class 2
middlemen
    chiefs as 22, 68, 118
    groups as 199
    in markets 160, 173
    owners as 70
    role in clientelism 8–9
    roles 78–95
    settlers as 43
    village use of 39
migrants
    absorption 45
    backgrounds 15, 28
    leaders 39, 100
    types 44
    villages of 37
    see also home ties; settlers
military 16, 105–9, 133, 156–7, 183, 239n
    see also government
military-bureaucratic coalition 156–7, 198
military coups 105, 152
    see also coup d'état
Miller, R. A. 227n
minorities 44, 143–5, 147, 197, 202, 214
Mintz, S. W. 227n
mobility 11, 88, 91, 95, 127, 135, 217
Mohammed, Brigadier Murtala 220, 239n
moneylenders 59, 92, 105, 233n
Monrovia 218
moral ties 10, 75, 209–10, 212
Muroko 21, 26

Mushin chiefs see separate titles; chieftaincy divisions
Mushin Committee of Management
    appointments and dismissals 149–51, 169–70, 196–7, 220
    inaugural 117
    representation on 183, 200
    under military 157, 159
Mushin councillors 128–30, 169–71
    functions 128
    selection 151, 204
Mushin District Community Organisation (MDCO) 169–71
Mushin District (later Town) Council 127–30, 136, 150, 157
    creation 43, 46, 97–8, 121
    elections 103, 127, 131–2, 135
    influence in 83–4, 88, 95
    revenue 15, 67
Mushin District Progressive League (MDPL) 170
Mushin Elders Committee 152
Mushin history 15–16, 18–46
Mushin map 12, 24, 28
Mushin markets 20–1, 35, 102, 159–80, 186
    see also individual markets
Mushin villages 15, 18
    see also individual villages
Mushin Town Council Chieftaincy Committee 38, 105, 107, 110, 117, 195
Mushin Town Council Market Men and Women Association 177

Nairobi 7
National Convention of Nigerian Citizens (NCNC) 130–4, 147–9, 152, 237n, 238n
nationalist movement see independence movement
Native Advisory Board 34
Native Authority 41, 44
    courts 30, 41, 44–5
    school 41
    treasury 39
    see also Village Group Councils
neglect 14, 18–19, 29–31, 40, 43, 45, 145, 157–8, 199, 202
neighbourhood
    as political unit 42, 70, 78, 109–10, 141, 158, 203, 215
    business 72–4, 127, 132
    clients 70, 110–11
    leadership 68, 78–96, 97, 99, 103, 137, 148, 160
    networks 141, 161, 204
    power 76–8
    status 76
    support 49, 56, 73–6, 95, 108, 110, 142
neighbourhood residence patterns
    heterogeneity 71
    housing 58, 71
    interaction 70–6, 92
    layout 72, 80–1
networks
    client 5, 153–4, 188, 216
    concept 242n
    elite 155
    information 48
    neighbourhood 141
    social 66–7
Nicholas, R. W. 240n
Nicholson, I. F. 229n, 230n
Nigeria, Colony and Protectorate of 26
Nigeria, Federation of 13, 130, 214
Nigerian National Alliance (NNA) 150–1
Nigerian National Democratic Party (NNDP) 104–5, 150–3, 184, 186, 198, 238n, 239n
Northern Peoples Congress (NPC) 130, 148–51
Nupe (Tapa) 14, 23, 26, 28, 32, 35, 71, 103

oba (king) 97–125 passim
    as market head 164
    Lagos 23, 29, 34–5, 171
    on District Council 98, 103, 110

political activities of 104–6, 149
pre-colonial 19
see also chiefs; chieftaincy
Obalende 234n
Obasanjo, Lt. Gen. Olusegun 220, 239n
occupational patterns 13–14, 40–1, 55–8, 96
occupations 60
  construction related 68
  of Mushin councillors 129
  of Mushin leaders 139
  training for 66
Odesanya* 92
Odi Olowo 42, 98–125 *passim*, 163–4, 171–2, 186–96 *passim*,
  221, 236n, 237n
  early urban settlement of 44
  military fortifications at 21
Odofin Ejigbo 99, 103
Odunsi, S. J.* 138–9, 159, 167, 178, 186–7, 190–2, 197,
  239n
Office holding 3, 78, 135–42, 154, 158, 165–6, 182, 187–8,
  216–17
Ogba 21, 26
Ogudu 20–1
Ogunnaike, J. S. O. 238n, 240n, 241n
Ogunsanya, Adeniran 133, 149, 152
Ogunyi, J. I. (*Olu* Agege) 235n
Oja 33
Ojo, G. J. A. 20, 229n
Ojo, S. A.* 91–6, 99, 116, 138–9, 141, 235n
Ojuwoye 99–122 *passim*, 164–81 *passim*, 186–96 *passim*, 221,
  236n
  Awori village 20, 32–5, 232n
  chiefs 38, 148, 230n, 240n
  village group 42
  see Olu Mushin/Ojuwoye
Okpala, D. C. I. 234n
Okuntola, F. O. 98, 103, 129, 134, 148
Olaleye Market 161
Olawoye, C. O. 232n
Olowo, Taiwo 34–5
Olu Mushin (formerly *Olu* Ojuwoye) 99, 102, 107, 112–14,
  164, 168–9, 172, 181, 192–3, 194–6, 240n
Olu Odi Olowo 99, 102, 105–6, 112–14, 151, 186–7, 190–1,
  236n, 240n
Olu Shomolu 106
Oluwa, I. 239n
omo ibile (indigenous landowners) *see* son-of-the-soil
Òndo (Yoruba) 14
Onigbongbo Village Group Council 41
Onitire Itire 99, 107, 112–14, 191, 195–6, 236n
origin traditions 20, 35, 121–2, 175, 228n, 236n
orisa see deities
Oshodi 33, 103, 107, 111–14, 196, 221, 232n, 236n
  chief 103
  settlement 35
Osolo Isolo 99, 112–14
Óstheimer, J. M. 238n
Otta 20–1, 34
owners *see* landowners
ownership, concept of 52–3
Oworonshoki 33, 42
Owusu, M. 227n
Oyo (Yoruba) 14, 28

Paine, R. 227n
palm produce 19–21, 40
Parkin, D. 227n
participation, political
  in government affairs 4, 157, 184
  of migrants 44, 143–4, 203
  through chieftaincy 110, 120, 124, 218
  through parties 97, 132
  under military 106, 199
party politics 130–42, 147–55

activists 107, 156
affiliations of councillors 129
  as Mushin institution 15–16, 127
  era of 126, 237n
  ethnic group involvement in 144
  see also individual parties
patron–client relationships 5–6, 18–19, 21, 23, 76–7, 142,
  155, 211, 241n
  see also client relationships; client system; clientelism
patronage
  leaders' use of 76–7, 85, 88
  through local council 128, 146
  through party 130–1, 133–4
  under military 156, 181
patrons 11, 210
  chiefs as 118
  colonial 18, 43
  leaders as 78–85, 88–95, 188
  market based 160, 167, 178
  need for 158, 228n
  owners as 70
  pre-colonial 15, 22
  see also client relationships; client system; godfathers;
    middlemen
Peace, A. 227n, 234n, 235n, 238n, 242n
Pedro 33, 42
Peel, J. D. Y. 233n, 234n, 235n, 236n, 240n
Peil, M. 227n, 234n, 239n
petroleum 11, 159
pidgin *see lingua franca*
police 14, 30, 35, 38–40, 84, 94, 142, 151–2, 230n
political
  competition 16–17, 146
  organisation 18, 37, 70, 145, 153, 156
  patterns 4–7, 222
  principles 1, 97, 100, 110, 176, 188
  processes 4–5, 17, 95–6, 126, 143–6, 219
  relationships 5, 7, 9–10, 70, 100–1, 205–12
  skills 1, 33, 95–6; *see also* leadership skills
political community 15
political economy 2–3, 5
political institutions 16
  see bureaucracy; chieftaincy; party
political interest groups
  chieftaincy system as 119, 124
  ethnic group as 200
  market as 167
  in metropolitan Lagos 239n
  representation in government 148–9, 151, 158
political participation 10, 15
  see also participation
political resources 1
politics
  defined 126
  grassroots 4, 104
  informal 4–5, 16, 97, 124, 151, 155, 216–17, 219
  residential 70–96, 108, 127, 132, 153, 158, 203
population 14, 202
  density 62, 72, 235n
  foreign 14, 52
  growth 3, 26–7, 31, 50, 52, 145, 147, 158, 174, 201–2, 220
  heterogeneity 14, 26, 36–40, 44, 47, 71, 146
  size 11, 13, 25–6, 30, 38, 42, 143, 149, 199
Post, K. W. J. 135–6, 237n, 238n, 239n
poverty 3, 10, 55, 64, 75, 85
power 1, 215–19
  concentration 135–42
  contraction 147–53
  display 94, 109
  in material base 16, 47–69, 76, 88, 203
  in neighbourhood 76–96
  in people 7, 78
  in property 47–70, 76, 134
  in social relationships 69

institutionalisation of 16, 183–200, 216–19
patterns of 1–4, 6, 155, 191, 222
processes for organising 16–17, 215–16, 222
struggle for 156–82
property (land and houses) 47–69, 70, 126, 194, 203, 234n,
    235n
  acquisition 20, 44, 233n
  benefits 47, 61–7, 134
  economics of 55–61, 92
  management of 62
  protection 84, 91–3, 96, 203
  specialists in 82, 85, 90–3
  use rights 33
  see also land; housing
Protectorate
  Northern Nigeria 26
  Southern Nigeria 26
protest 105, 150–4, 216
  disruptions 8, 193
  riots 152
  violence 126, 150–1, 154–5
public opinion 37, 39, 79, 85, 93, 117, 178–9, 197

quarter see ward

railway 30
real estate see housing; land; property
reciprocity 210–12
  see also client system
refuge 21, 26
regional government see Western Region Government
religion
  as interest group 148, 159, 169–71
  Awori 23
  identity based on 6
  in neighbourhoods 73
  leaders 120, 123, 139, 169–71, 218
  parties and 132
  see Christianity; deities; Islam
rent 69, 233n
  collection 71, 75, 83, 96, 107; see also estate agents
  cost to tenants 67
  income 56–8, 61, 62
renters see tenants
reputation 77, 82, 85–7, 91, 93–6, 172, 208
research methods 223–6
residence patterns 13–14, 44, 61, 64, 132, 143–4, 203–4,
    232n, 233n
  heterogeneous 14, 234n
  homogeneous 14
  permanent 44–5, 67, 69, 74, 91; see also settlers
  temporary 44, 77, 143, 145
  see also neighbourhood; residence, politics of
residence, politics of 70–96
resource
  allocation 134–5, 154; see also allocation, as political
    process
  competition 8, 10, 11, 143–4
  control 2, 10, 47, 67, 154
  distribution 2, 10, 95
  lack 14
  management 30
  political importance 70, 95–6
resources, types
  clients 210
  connections 9, 77, 96, 127
  expertise 9
  information 9, 77, 96
  office-holding 78
  people 82, 96, 216
  property 47–70
  public 143, 145, 156, 158, 217
  urban 4, 11, 74, 154, 199, 202
  see also titles; power

Rimmer, D. 237n, 241n
riots see protest
ritual see ceremonies
Roniger, L. 241n, 242n
Ross, M. H. 227n
rural period 18–19, 22–3, 40, 50, 100, 205

Sada, P. O. 228n, 234n, 238n, 239n
Sahlins, M. D. 242n
sanctuary see refuge
Sandbrook, R. 227n
sanitary inspector 83, 89–90
scarcity, environment of 4, 10, 48, 177, 211
Schildkrout, E. 227n, 229n, 242n
Schmidt, S. W. et al 227n
Schofield, I. F. W. 38–9
schools 30
  see education
Schwab, W. B. 233n
Scott, J. C. 10, 209, 227n, 238n, 241n, 242n
secret societies 123, 199
seniority
  in choosing leaders 33
  of market leaders 173, 175
  principle of 100–2, 168, 189
  in title-holding 32, 100, 115, 116, 189–90
  of wives 86
settler
  case studies 56–8
  chiefs 33, 99–122 passim
  councillors 129
  faction 140, 158–81 passim, 182–200 passim
  leaders 19, 43–6, 99–100, 102
  see also migrants
Shabe (Yoruba) 21, 28, 236n
Shagari, Shehu 221
Shogunle 108, 236n
Shomolu 26, 33, 35, 41, 83, 103, 106–7, 112–15, 121, 151,
    170, 194, 196, 220–1, 236n, 237n
Shomolu and District Welfare Association (SDWO) 103,
    170
Shongbo 21
Sierra Leone, people of 7, 26, 28
Silverman, M. 240n
Simpson, S. R. 232n, 233n
Skinner, D. E. 242n
Skinner, E. P. 242n
Sklar, R. 136, 237n
slaves 20, 26, 32, 35
  freed 26, 52, 111
  raids 21
  trade 19, 21, 25
Sole Administrator 157, 199, 220
Songbo Market* 164–5
son-of-the-soil (indigène) 30, 194–5, 200
  chiefs 98–122 passim, 163–81 passim
  citizenship rights 69
  villages 32–4, 37, 44
  see origin traditions
Sotomi, L.* 138, 159, 164–5, 167, 170, 191–2, 239n, 240n
Southall, A. W. 242n
squatters 48, 55, 232n
strangers 32–3, 53, 79, 121, 147, 153, 212
Strathern, A. 242n
stratification 68–9, 95, 132–3, 201
  patterns 1–7, 13, 14, 47, 61
  residential 13–14, 76
  see class; seniority
street naming 101
Strickon, A. 227n
strikes 150
Suberu, Lamidi (Jagunmolu Shomolu) 103, 106, 112
Sudarkasa, N. 239n
Sunni, O. O.* 163–4

Supreme Court 29–30, 38, 50, 230n
Supreme Military Council 157
  see also government; military
Surulere 234n
Swartz, M. J. 239n

Tade, J. O. 236n, 237n
Taiwo* 138–9, 186, 191
Talabi, S. I. 239n
Talbot, P. A. 27, 229n
Tapa *see* Nupe
tax 37, 40, 117, 121, 128, 135, 147, 231n, 234n
  collection 37–40, 116, 124
  property 15, 67, 83, 88, 93
  revenue from 37, 40
tenants 71–96 *passim*, 234n
  customary 32, 35, 44
  long-term 232n
  men and women compared 60
  political interests of 110, 129, 134, 143–5, 203–4
  rural 33
  urban 47, 55–61, 64
  see also landowner-tenant comparison; landowner–tenant
    relationship
Tinubu, Ali 21
Tinubu, Madam Efunroye 21
titles
  conferral of 108–9, 123, 184–98, 240n
  meaning 235–6n
  Mushin 112–14
  political use of 184–92
  rewards 35, 182, 189
  rights to 119–20, 183
  resources 98, 117, 189
  rewards 35, 123, 182, 189
  symbols of authority 200, 218
  see also chiefs; chieftaincy system; markets
Tiv 14, 145, 214
Toriola, Alhaja* 171–5, 240n
town planning 41, 48
trade 18, 26, 30–1, 40–1, 56–7, 68, 72–5, 84, 202, 212, 235n
  legitimate 19
  networks 161
  routes 22, 30
  street 13, 56, 72–3
  see also markets; merchants; slave trade
traders 13–14, 50, 55, 89, 141, 152, 160, 174, 178
trading camps 21
transporters 13, 57, 76, 138, 141, 159, 239n
Treaty of Cession 23, 25, 34
trust 96, 207
  defined 207
  relationships 75, 79
  types 241n

unemployment 3, 13, 85
unification, process of 18–19, 25–6, 38–45, 126, 146
unions (trade) 6, 132, 159, 169–71, 218, 239n
United Native Authority School 41
United People's Party (UPP) 149–50, 238n
United Progressive Grand Alliance (UPGA) 150–52
urbanisation
  African 3
  Ikeja District 40, 43
  Lagos 22
  Mushin 18, 50, 202–3, 205
  Odi Olowo 192
  Shomolu 103
urban culture 79
urban experience 65–7, 143
urban property *see* housing; land; property

Urhobo 14, 71
usufructuary rights 52

Vicente 26
Vickers, M. 237n, 238n, 239n
village 19–23, 25–6, 30–46, 97, 110–11, 204, 211, 230n
  clients 22, 32, 36–8, 204
  groups 23
  migrant 33
  Mushin 15, 18–21, 28, 31, 38–43, 70, 202
  rivals 37–9, 44
  types 32–4
Village Group Councils 39–45, 103
Vincent, J. 227n
violence *see* protest
visiting 64, 72–3, 90, 93, 208, 213
voluntary associations *see* associations

wage earners 6, 13, 132, 150
Wallace, A. F. C. 213, 242n
walls 229n *see also* fortifications
Walsh, A. H. 239n
ward (quarter)
  as voting unit 127
  chieftaincy affairs within 106–11, 115–17, 119, 121, 185,
    190
  party affairs within 132, 133, 136, 141–2, 204
Warri 229n
wars 3
  Civil 107, 171, 192, 196, 214, 241n
  internal 21, 26
  World War I 29
  World War II 40–1, 45, 202
Waterbury, J. 227n
Weber, M. 1, 10, 207, 241n
Weingrod, A. 227n
West African Settlements 25
Western Region 43, 146, 148, 153, 167
  Government 108, 130, 136, 147–9
  House of Assembly 103, 134, 148
  House of Chiefs 99
  parties 135, 136–7, 141, 184
  politics 104, 127, 131, 146–7, 150, 152, 170, 184, 198
Whitaker, C. S. 242n
Wilkes, R. L. V. 228n, 229n, 230n, 231n, 232n, 233n, 236n,
  238n
Williams, B. A. 239n
Wilson, C. S. 155, 239n
Wolf, E. R. 227n
women
  in politics 132, 137, 150
  language patterns 71–2
  title holders 107, 137, 236n
  work patterns 13, 40–1
  see also chiefs; landladies; landowners; markets; trade
work places 72–3
Wormal, W. G. 231n

Yinka* 88, 90, 93
Yoruba
  cities 5, 70
  defined 14
  language 14, 71–2
  pan-Yoruba 122
  territory 26
  see also individual sub-groups

Zaire 3
Zolberg, A. A. 227n, 238n

For Product Safety Concerns and Information please contact our EU
representative GPSR@taylorandfrancis.com
Taylor & Francis Verlag GmbH, Kaufingerstraße 24, 80331 München, Germany